D0174967

THEORIES OF CAREER DEVELOPMENT

Third Edition

Samuel H. Osipow

The Ohio State University

Prentice-Hall, Inc., Englewood Cliffs, New Jersey 07632

Library of Congress Cataloging in Publication Data

Osipow, Samuel H.
    Theories of career development.

    (Century psychology series)
    Includes bibliographies and index.
    1. Vocational guidance.   I. Title.   II. Series:
Century psychology series (Englewood Cliffs, N.J.)
HF5381.09 1983   158.7   82-13214
ISBN **0-13-913640-1**

IN THE CENTURY PSYCHOLOGY SERIES

Printed in the United States of America

10 9 8 7 6 5 4 3 2 1

Editorial/production supervision: Maureen Connelly
Cover design: Zimmerman/Foyster Design
Manufacturing buyers: Edmund W. Leone and Ron Chapman

ISBN 0-13-913640-1

Prentice-Hall International, Inc., *London*
Prentice-Hall of Australia Pty. Limited, *Sydney*
Prentice-Hall Canada Inc., *Toronto*
Prentice-Hall of India Private Limited, *New Delhi*
Prentice-Hall of Japan, Inc., *Tokyo*
Prentice-Hall of Southeast Asia Pte. Ltd., *Singapore*
Whitehall Books Limited, *Wellington, New Zealand*

To Sondra, Randall, Jay, Reva, and David

CONTENTS

PART THREE: DEVELOPMENTAL THEORIES

PART FOUR: SOCIAL SYSTEMS AND CAREER DECISIONS

PART FIVE: AN OVERVIEW

PREFACE

Since the earliest memories of human beings, we have been required to earn our daily bread. The meaning and variety of the work in which we have engaged over the centuries and across various cultures have differed, depending upon the particular context. However, the generally distasteful attitude held toward work has not changed. To be poor meant to work long and hard simply to stay alive. To be wealthy meant to have someone do your work for you. Only relatively recently have social scientists clearly recognized that more is accomplished by one's daily work than the maintenance of bodily needs. Considerable psychological gratification is derived from work in Western cultures despite our chronic complaints.

As one attempts to define work it becomes increasingly clear that definitions confined to economic and societal factors alone do not include the wide variety of behaviors involved. Work is partly an attitude in the mind of a person toward the activity in which he or she is engaged at the moment. One person's work is another's play. It is clear that working holds an important place both in society and in the psychological lives of individuals.

Our civilization has evolved to the point that, in Western society at least, we possess an element of choice concerning the activity with which we will occupy ourselves. Though the variety of work from which we may choose varies from broad to narrow, one of the most highly prized freedoms in our culture is the right to decide what kind of work we will do, for whom, and when. Although we do not always exercise this freedom, the potential of choice is highly valued.

It is not surprising in a society in which many people have the opportunity to choose their careers and in which the broad significance of work is recognized, that attempts to understand the decision-making processes involved in career development should be made. Early attempts to understand career decisions were largely unsystematized and empirical, but more recently theorists have become concerned with the problem and have turned their attention to questions of career development.

The purposes of this book are several. First, an attempt will be made to fill the need that exists for an examination and evaluation of current theoretical and empirical findings relevant to the vocational decision-making process. It is important to realize that theories of career development are not theories in the traditional sense. They do not conform to all the particular requirements of theories following the physical science model. We would be wise to keep in mind that the physical science model may not be suitable to the study of behavior. Nevertheless, current theories of career development are not full-blown but rather are theory "fragments" which attempt to integrate and systematize a portion of human behavior with respect to a specific human problem. The current theories of career choice are the prototypes of future theories and serve much the same functions that theories in the more sophisticated sciences do. This book, then, describes and assesses the major theories of career choice and related research.

Juxtaposing one theory with another leads to a second function. A comparison of the similarities and differences of the theories becomes possible, allowing judgments to be made as to relative strengths and weaknesses of the theories. A further purpose of this book is to attempt to synthesize some general theoretical statements which might integrate the more useful and effective constructs of the various theoretical positions, as well as to identify the ingredients common to most of the theories. Finally, this book has been written with an eye toward the needs of the practicing counselor. The procedures involved in vocational counseling currently vary from the extreme of no more than the interpretation of a standard battery of interest and ability measures on one side to the extreme of extended psychotherapy on the other. Little guidance exists to help the counselor sort and select appropriate procedures. It seems likely that a sufficient theoretical basis relevant to the conduct of vocational counseling exists to be of use to the counselor. What appears to be lacking is the means of translating the theory into explicit terms useful to counselors. Thus, the fourth purpose of this book is to consider the theories with respect to their implications for career counseling.

We hope to describe and clarify the various theoretical conceptions about career development that have been proposed, assess them with respect to their adequacy as theories, examine and evaluate research relevant to them, synthesize and integrate the variety of approaches that currently exist, and examine their potential utility for counseling.

The need for the first revision of this book became abundantly clear within four or five years of publication. The late 1960s and early 1970s witnessed an explosion of interest and research in the psychology of career development. Since 1973, when the second edition appeared, the rate of growth in publications dealing with career development has, amazingly, accelerated from even that high level. Thus, the task of revision yet another time to produce the third edition was formidable and even intimidating. However, a number of new emphases in career development theory have appeared, demanding that another edition be produced. In doing so, some selection had to be made about what should be removed from the earlier editions to avoid developing an encyclopedia rather than a textbook. Readers interested in earlier work in career development should consult one of the first two editions should something in their area of interest have been deleted from this present effort.

A number of people helped to shape my ideas about these theories and the way that I have organized and expressed these ideas in this book.

The generally stimulating atmosphere provided by colleagues on the staff of the Division of Counseling at the Pennsylvania State University between 1961 and 1967 and by my colleagues here at the Ohio State University since that time are in no small way responsible for the execution of this book. It should also be noted that the first edition of the work was facilitated by the opportunity for reading in reflection provided by five months spent as a Visiting Research Associate at the Center for Research in Careers of the Harvard Graduate School of Education in 1965.

Following are the names of people who provided significant advice and comment on one or more of the three editions of the book: Donald H. Ford, James A. Gold, Ann Roe, John Holland, Donald E. Super, Edward J. Polder, W. Bruce Walsh, Donna McKinley, John Valley, John Hartung, Keith Taylor, Ann Simon, and Gladys Hosansky.

Susan Katz, the Prentice-Hall Education editor, mobilized my lagging efforts toward completion of the third edition. She recruited several fine colleagues to review my efforts. These professionals provided helpful, courteous criticism of the revision: Jerry M. Greiner, Charles C. Healy, Robert C. Reardon, Charles W. Ryan, and Kenneth W. Wegner.

Three people whose secretarial efforts toward the books' production in the three editions deserve acknowledgment: Nancy Andrews, Myrtle Ely Moon, and Sally Wilcox.

Finally, I would like especially to thank my wife, Sondra, who contributed to all three editions of this book in numerous ways. My sons Randall and Jay also helped with various aspects of the process, particularly in the earlier editions.

S.H.O.
Columbus, Ohio

INTRODUCTION

SCIENCE AND COUNSELING

Goals of Science

It is generally agreed that the goals of science include the understanding, prediction, and control of some kind of natural phenomena. In the natural sciences theoretical advances have led to increased physical and biological control of the world around us. This increased control, in turn, has immensely altered our environment. People are healthier, live longer and more comfortably; machines do more and more of the routine work that must be done; communications are improving at a phenomenal rate, even though they are already unbelievably rapid, all as a consequence of our scientific establishment. The science of psychology has developed the theoretical structure, empirical base, and technological knowledge which permit it to predict and control human behavior with increasing efficiency and effectiveness. A reader of B. F. Skinner (1953) cannot help but be impressed with the many examples from daily life illustrating the techniques through which simple and even complex behaviors can be manipulated.

While there is undoubtedly a great deal about human behavior that is not clearly understood, the development of psychology as a science seems to be following the development of older sciences (Sarton, 1952) in that applications and technology follow closely on the heels of each empirical or theoretical advance. As a consequence, many of the most widely accepted principles concerning human behavior have already been applied to a variety of human endeavors. For example, it was very quickly discovered that research in human visual perception has implications for the design of complex control equipment operated by human beings. In another context, we see that data derived from the operant conditioning studies of pigeons led to the development of principles which have influenced and vitalized the development of programmed instruction and assorted mechanical teaching devices. The detailed study of the arrangement of working conditions for human beings leading to the specialty of industrial psychology is built upon principles of learning and personality theories which have a bedrock of empirical observation and experimental data. Psychotherapy rests on a similar body of theory and data, though the arrangement of that body and the emphasis given to aspects of it are different from industrial psychology since applications in psychotherapy are sought with respect to the diagnosis and treatment of disordered behavior. Much of the educational practice of Western society is based on psychological theory and research in the area of learning and human development. A lengthy catalog of applied psychology could be compiled to illustrate the diverse uses of our knowledge about human behavior.

Of course, the applications of the basic study of human behavior made in the fields of counseling, clinical, industrial, and other psychological specialties are clearly incomplete. Consumers of psychological data, including psychologists themselves, are often quick to point out gaps in basic and applied knowledge and inconsistencies in expert opinion. Criticisms notwithstanding, many demands are made on psychologists by the public, suggesting that many of the applications of the study of human behavior are very useful indeed.

A Definition of Theory

Theory in social and behavioral science has its roots in the more mature physical sciences. The theoretical structures which have served physical scientists stand as the models that have guided the shape that psychological theories have taken. Hence, it is important that the groundwork be laid for an accurate understanding of the role and character of theory in general before we undertake a discussion and evaluation of theories of career development.

Role of theory. As is to be expected when treating highly abstract topics, some disagreement exists among theoreticians as to the proper role of theory (Allport, 1955; Marx, 1951). Despite the differences of opinion, several common elements basic to theory construction stand out. Traditionally, theory has served as a generalized statement designed to facilitate broad conceptualization about natural events. Theories relate what would otherwise be a number of disparate empirical observations. Ideally, one theory should serve as a basis for conceptualization about all events; in practice, many theories exist, separated in a number of scientific disciplines and further subdivided into theories to deal with events within the disciplines.

It should be pointed out that although theory begins with the observation of events, it becomes more complex as it brings together diverse happenings and permits, by deduction, predictions to be made about other events involved in the framework under observation. Thus, theories lead to "deduced theorems" which, in turn, can be translated into research whose predictive value partly allows the appraisal of the validity of the theory (Allport, 1955). In this sense theory serves as a tool of the scientist. Also important in comparing theories is the recognition that theories should differ in the predictions made within the same framework; if they in fact do not, then one theory exists where two were originally thought to be. Ultimately, it is the empirical and not the logical or philosophical difference between theories that is important (Marx, 1951).

Not to be ignored is the part that theories play in understanding events. At their best, theories produce "new understandings" about the universe; a good theory clarifies events and leads to further predictions about related events. It must be recognized that explanation in science refers to an increasing detail in describing events, yet a detail that grows in generality as it increases in specificity. According to Marx (1951) two types of explanation exist in science. *Reductive explanation* describes the functional role of phenomena at a level of description more fundamental than observation of the phenomena themselves would permit. Explaining human behavior in terms of physiological processes is an example of reductionistic explanation. *Constructive explanation*, on the other hand, consists of the description of phenomena in terms of constructs or hypotheses. The intervening variables used to account for an apparent relationship between two sets of events are examples of constructive explanation. In the end both types of explanation come down to description at some level. It is in the adequacy and generality of the description that theories may differ.

Evaluating theories. It becomes possible to assess theory in terms of the degree to which it fulfills the roles just discussed (Allport, 1955). Do the data, as they exist, support the predictions that grow from the theory? While it is true that theories are not "proven or disproven" on the basis of experimentation, the adequacy of a theory is inferred from the degree to which tests of the predictions yield expected results. How general is the theory? Judgments about the adequacy of a theory should, at least in part, consider the range of the phenomena the theory is capable of integrating and explaining. How well does the theory explain the phenomena it deals with? Does it lead to new understandings of events? How operational is the theory? How available are the constructs of the theory to immediate experimental work? How explicit are the referents of the theory? Does the theory possess logical consistency? Obviously, an illogical theory is not useful. The degree to which the theory can parsimoniously deal with events is important. A good theory should cover the widest possible range of phenomena with a minimum of postulates.

Psychology and Theory

It becomes apparent from the preceding discussion that all theory is imperfect, a fact that is sometimes overlooked by zealous psychologists seeking to "prove" theories. It should properly be assumed that theories will eventually die and be replaced by newer theories that deal with observed events in a more general and useful way than their predecessors. The misapplication of theory and the excessive interest that some psychologists show in theory construction have led other psychologists to view theorizing as undesirable and premature. Still other psychologists have complained that the physical science model applied to behavior theory is inappropriate and has created unnecessary difficulties in psychological conceptualization and research.

Despite these views, it seems likely that some of the problems stemming from psychological theory are not exclusively the result of the theories themselves. Many of the difficulties in generating applications for human endeavor based on psychological theory lie with the consumers as well as the producers of theory. For example, many educators have been disappointed in the lack of utility of learning theory for educational practice, despite the relatively long history of learning theory in the brief span of formal psychological theory. Until recently, however, many of the attempts to apply learning theory to educational practices were uninspired. There are signs now, however, in the use of programmed instruction, concept formation, language development, and the like, that new ideas based on psychological theory are taking hold in the field of educational methods. Furthermore, these new ideas use psychological data and theory boldly, thus offering the potential to improve educational methods more significantly than any idea since the invention of the printing press.

Applying Theory to Human Problems

Applied psychologists have often said that theory is useful if one is required to do no more than solve abstract hypothetical problems, but if one is faced with warm-blooded people in trouble or in need of assistance in decision-making, theory must be left at the interview door and the applied psychologist must assume an eclectic position, even if it means working intuitively. Such an argument is countered by theoretically minded practitioners, who answer that to work blindly is to invite error and waste. Perhaps the most reasonable answer to claims both for and against the usefulness of theoretical formulations underlying counseling is analogous to the discussion by Rodgers (1964) on differences between academic and professional training for psychotherapists. Rodgers suggests that, depending upon the goals one has and the assumptions one makes about the problems with which psychologists deal, either kind of training might appear to be good or bad.

Thus, he points out, when faced with the question of what sort of treatment is appropriate for a schizophrenic, the academician's answer is to begin a research project to study the question; possibly, with luck, in x number of years a recommendation based on the results of the research might be forthcoming. The professional, on the other hand, must develop the best possible plan of action, regardless of limitations, on the basis of the data available at present. Each psychologist seriously criticizes the approach of the other; the professional attacks the academician for being heartless and indifferent to human misery as well as unrealistic, while the academician criticizes the professional for being slipshod and misleading in methods used and sacrificing scientific integrity by jumping to premature conclusions. Actually, both are sincerely acting within the framework of their own job roles. It is the professional's job to do as good as possible, with the tools available, for people in immediate difficulties, all the while recognizing that even one's best efforts are imperfect. Similarly, it is the academician's job to investigate thoroughly every question posed and to be wary of drawing premature conclusions. Indeed, if either party did otherwise it would be an act violating professional obligations.

Returning to the question of theoretical utility in counseling with the academic versus professional training controversy in mind, it is not unreasonable to suggest that current theoretical formulations in vocational psychology are imperfect, largely unvalidated, and suggestive of minimal though varying practical applications, yet at the same time hold potential for the future sophistication of career counseling. Counselors must deal with the here and now, which might frequently force them to work outside a theoretical context. To do so and meet with some degree of success is both necessary and remarkable, but not ideal.

The Role of Theory in Vocational Psychology

What is the proper role of theory in vocational psychology? Practitioners of counseling have often been disappointed in the lack of relevance of psychological theory, both basic and "applied," to their general practice. Theoretical applications to practice have often been attempts to apply fragments of behavior theory to counseling problems, but as a result of their fragmentation they have limited their viability by damming themselves from the flow of the mainstream of behavior theory. Other attempts at building theories directly applicable to counseling interviews have suffered from a narrowness of purpose or have generally been too sterile, as a result of their sweeping style, to produce valid techniques for vocational counseling. The pendulum has swung back and forth between the slogan of "round pegs in round holes" and existential conceptions of man's role in the world of work.

The solution of many counselors to this problem of theoretical weakness has been to work without systematic theory. The consequences of counseling without a theory are frequently overlooked. Eclectic counselors work intuitively and often feel they have accomplished some worthwhile purpose if they have listened sympathetically to someone's difficulties. Surely, professional training should result in something more than skill in sympathetic listening. Furthermore, counselors without theoretical orientations must of necessity find it difficult to integrate the many disjointed research findings into some meaningfully organized body of knowledge.

Implicit and Explicit Theories

Close examination of interview procedures is likely to reveal that every counselor has ideas about cases and conducts interviews on the basis of those ideas. Counselors must have some notions about how human behavior works because they cannot proceed without them. What may vary, however, is the degree to which counselors make their ideas explicit and systematic, or implicit and probably less systematic.

The counselor who possesses implicit notions about a client's behavior may be unable to describe those notions clearly to an observer because the ideas have never been explicitly verbalized. Such a counselor is probably hard pressed to explain counseling in an orderly fashion, indicating for what purpose actions were taken, not because there is no basis for the behavior but because there was no one occasion to formally describe the antecedents of the counseling procedures. When asked about a case, it is likely that the counselor responds in terms of fragments of underlying ideas and rarely, if ever, is required to set out all the pieces of a "theory" and interpret them to someone else in an orderly and systematic fashion. As part of the justification for the rejection of any system, the counselor may explain that no system is entirely correct, so the selection of certain aspects of many theories is to be preferred. However, in making this type of judgment a counselor runs the risk of confounding system-based technique with system-based conceptualization. That is, while counseling procedures derived from a particular theoretical system may apply to other systems, the effectiveness of the procedures is likely to depend upon the manner and timing of their introduction. Since the application of the procedures is likely to be specified in a well-developed counseling theory, the use of such procedures may make little sense out of context. The counselor who follows an explicit theory of behavior is guided in hypotheses-making about the client behavior and possesses a common conceptual thread which connects otherwise disparate professional experiences.

Thus, one type of criticism directed at the prematurity of vocational development theory (Crites, 1965) seems to miss the point of theory. Theory correctly precedes or accompanies empirical knowledge and orients a body of knowledge while it is in its development. How counselors use theory and the essential ingredients of a theory are correctly subject to various interpretations (Hewer, 1963; McCabe, 1958), but a strong case can be made for the usefulness of theory even in the primitive stages of the development of a discipline.

Considering the differences between the highly systematic counselor and the unstructured counselor, it would appear that the major issue is not whether or not a counselor uses theory, but rather to what degree the use of theory is explicit and systematic. Unfortunately, the issue of explicit versus implicit theory in relation to behavioral concerns is premature. At the very least, theory stimulates research and gives direction to activity, and at its best it may integrate highly diffuse data into some meaningful whole. Others, arguing that no single current theory is adequate for vocational counselors, are probably correct but have no real substantive basis for their position since no one has in fact compared the theories in a direct and orderly fashion.

Results of Failure to Apply Theory to Counseling

As a result of the difficulty of organizing research findings, combined with the distaste of counselors for such tasks and their lack of time, counseling is left with many notions about career development that have gone more or less unchallenged. Some of the ideas are holdovers from folklore pertaining to vocational choice; for example, the idea that for every person there is a job more suitable than any other job. Once probable reason for the persistence of many of these ideas, which sometimes sound plausible but which imply many unverified hypotheses, is that often no systematic study or research has been made on these questions.

Among the concepts about career counseling that go more or less un-challenged is the notion that occupational information—in other words, pamphlets, films, visits to factories and offices, and speakers representing various career fields—facilitates occupational choice by better informing youth about the "facts" pertaining to careers. However, many questions can be raised about the role of occupational information in vocational counseling. How does this information ac-complish the task of facilitating career choice? Under what conditions does it do so? Does occupational information provide useful data for all students at all times in the early stages of their career decision-making? Are there circumstances in which occupational information obscures rather than enlightens students about careers?

Some of the few pertinent research findings raise questions about the effects of certain practices in occupational information, suggesting that the process is not as simple as it appears to be (Osipow, 1962; Rauner, 1962; Samler, 1961; Remenyi and Fraser, 1977). Other questions about factors in career choice may be raised. Do people think in terms of careers and entry jobs, or school subjects and college majors, or the attractiveness of various industries, when they choose their "occupa-tions"? Under what circumstances do people select careers because of the security they offer versus their promise for growth? What are the characteristics of those who choose careers because of the security they offer as opposed to the ambitious risk-takers? Are some people activity oriented and others outcome oriented and if so, why, and how do we identify the different types? Once identified, do we counsel them differently? Is appropriateness of vocational choice a useful outcome criterion of counseling (Gonyea, 1962)? How effective are counselors in this regard (Gonyea, 1963)? Do counselor recommendations about educational-vocational plans really result in greater academic success for students when the recommenda-tions are followed (Marks, Ashby, and Zeigler, 1965)?

How does adolescent physical development influence vocational interest (Hulslander, 1958)? Does early physical maturation affect the career process? The question of interests is especially difficult to cope with without a theoretical frame-work. For example, a counselor may be faced with (1) a student who says he or she has no interests, (2) a student who says he or she possesses various interests but cannot decide which to follow, or (3) a student who complains of an inability to implement interests into a behavior pattern that translates them into successful performance. Faced with such problems, the counselor must ask a number of questions about the nature of interests. What are interests? When the first student complains of having no interests, what does that mean? Doesn't everybody have interests? Or does the student really mean that the connection between interests and the various career patterns is hard to find?

What does the undecided student mean when complaining of an inability to commit to a career pattern? When do people decide on careers? Just what is meant by a career decision? When should certain decisions be made? Is indecisiveness a general behavior pattern or is it restricted to career choices? Does indecision refer to a strong distaste for a realistic second choice? Some research by Holland and Nichols (1964), Ashby, Wall, and Osipow (1966), and Osipow, Ashby, and Wall (1966) sheds light on indecision as a factor in career decisions (Osipow, Carney, Winer, Yanico, and Koschier, 1976; Osipow, Barak, and Carney, 1976; Lunneborg, 1976; Holland and Holland, 1977). What about the student who cannot perform adequately in his or her field of interest? Is the problem a matter of aptitude or commitment? What the counselor decides to do when faced with such situations depends upon the conception held about interests, in other words, what they are, how they are acquired, what factors determine career patterns in the normal course of events, and what circumstances can prevent a pattern from crystallizing as it should. Questions such as these, viewed in a cohesive theoretical framework, may be systematically studied. Furthermore, the results of research obtained in such a context are more likely to be integrated into counseling practice than results of research that do not stem from theory.

The Effect of Theory on Counseling

What the counselor decides to do when confronted with career-choice questions depends upon an estimate of the source of the problem and the precise nature of its behavioral correlates. The remedy applied to the situation will be chosen in terms of what is needed to correct the situation. Thus, if the counselor decides that career choice is a process of matching oneself, wherever possible, against jobs or positions in terms of interests and aptitudes, opportunities for the client to explore a variety of positions will be arranged. Typically this will be done by using a sequence of several techniques. First, procedures designed to enable the client to clarify the personal details will be introduced. Reflection, clarification, interest and aptitude tests, and questions such as "Who are you?" are all procedures which contribute to the clarification of self. Self-clarification, however, not being a sufficient condition for career choice by itself, the counselor also turns attention to the clarification of various career patterns either specifically in terms of positions or more generally in terms of abstract career titles. Procedures such as reading occupational literature, visiting plants, offices, and professional establishments, and hearing discussions and lectures on careers by their practitioners are designed to implement this goal.

Following these two clarification procedures, the final step is the matching of the self with the career through interview procedures and the subsequent initial decision of career direction in terms of education, or job, or both. Let us suppose, however, that our counselor decides that career development is not appropriately conceptualized in terms of a matching of interests and aptitudes with occupations. Suppose our counselor theorizes that career development is an elaboration and extension of the self. Counseling efforts will thus probably be directed toward creating an interview environment which is conducive to self-exploration and self-expression, and the counselor is likely to conclude that the introduction of tests, inventories, and occupational information will inhibit the process of self-discovery and expression. The task, seen thus, is very different from that of our first counselor and is likely to be a longer process with a less explicit outcome.

A third counselor might assess the client's inability to make independent vocational decisions and conclude that the client is an obsessive-compulsive personality and that the inability to make a vocational decision can best be remedied through psychotherapy designed to identify and remove the sources of the obsessive-compulsive behavior. Although some research (for example, Strupp, 1958) has suggested that successful clinical psychologists employ procedures more like one another than unsuccessful ones, the possibility that even successful psychologists employ different procedures with different kinds of cases must not be ignored. Strupp's conclusion can lead to error as to where one focuses observations. Differences may be maximized or minimized, depending upon one's vantage point. The point is that counselors with different theoretical persuasions will think differently about their cases and are very likely to have different expectations and procedures as a result.

CAREER DEVELOPMENT THEORY

Any attempt to categorize models of behavioral phenomena of any kind runs the risk of oversimplification. Nevertheless, some classification of the assorted explanatory motifs is a prerequisite for intelligible discussion about them. Obviously, a variety of labels can be used to identify the models, and the models can be categorized in many different ways. Thus, some arbitrariness is involved in the particular manner in which these models are described here. For our purposes, five distinct approaches to thinking about career counseling appear to fall into place.

Trait-factor theories.   The oldest theoretical approach has been known by a variety of names, most commonly by the name of the trait-factor approach. This system assumes that a straightforward matching of an individual's abilities and interests with the world's vocational opportunities can be accomplished and once accomplished, solves the problems of vocational choice for that individual. Some of the original trait-factor theorists who influenced thinking about vocational psychology are Parsons (1909), Hull (1928), and Kitson (1925). Within this model several special approaches have developed over the years. The vocational testing movement has grown from the trait-factor point of view. Thus, interest inventories such as the Strong-Campbell Interest Inventory and the Kuder Occupational Interest Survey, and aptitude tests such as the Differential Aptitude Tests and the Guilford-Zimmerman Aptitude Survey are based on the trait-factor stream of thought. Currently, the trait-factor model has been absorbed into many other approaches to career counseling, though few practitioners of vocational counseling today are pure trait-factor adherents. A paper by Hewer (1963) illustrates the procedures implemented by a counselor with a trait-factor orientation. The development of the trait-factor approach has been summarized by Williamson (1965) and Crites (1978).

Sociology and career choice.   A second set of approaches might best represent a sociological model of career development. Other descriptive names for the position have been the reality or accident theory of vocational choice. This approach has as its central point the notion that societal circumstances beyond the control of the individual contribute significantly to career choices and that the principal task confronting a person is the development of techniques to cope effectively with the environment. Factors influencing level of aspiration assume importance (e.g., Sewell and Hauser, 1975; Sweet, 1973). This approach is illustrated in the writings of Caplow (1954), Hollingshead (1949), and Miller and Form (1951). (See also Harmony, 1964, for a case study illustrating the sociological approach to conceptualizing career choice.)

Developmental/Self-concept theory.   A third approach actually weaves two models into one and can be called either the developmental or the self-concept theory. This position grows out of the early work of Buehler (1933), and more recently, the work of Super (1957), Samler (1953), Ginzberg and his associates (1951), Dudley and Tiedeman (1977), and Knefelkamp and Slepitza (1978) on the one hand and Carl Rogers and client-centered counselors on the other (1951). The approach holds as its central theses that (1) individuals develop more clearly defined self-concepts as they grow older, although these vary to conform with the changes in one's view of reality as correlated with aging; (2) people develop images of the occupational world which they compare with their self-image in trying to make career decisions; and (3) the adequacy of the eventual career decision is based on the similarity between an individual's self-concept and the vocational concept of the career eventually chosen.

Vocational choice and personality theories.   A fourth category might be called the personality approach to the study of career development. Here the ideas range from elaborate lists of needs inherent in the process of vocational choice (Hoppock, 1957) and the detailed personality types for career areas described by Holland (1959) to the assorted empirical studies of Small (1953), Schaffer (1953), Roe (1957), and many others on the particular personality factors involved in career choice and career satisfaction. There are also the many research projects on the personality characteristics of people in different vocations, the life styles of various professionals, psychopathology associated with professional activity, and the specific needs of workers in particular industries or jobs. The general hypothesis underlying these studies is that workers select their jobs because they see potential for the satisfaction of their needs. A corollary hypothesis is that exposure to a job gradually modifies the personality characteristics of the worker, so that, for example, accountants eventually become like one another if indeed they were not similar in personality to begin with.

Behavioral approaches. Recently we have seen the development of approaches reflecting interest in observing individual environmental interaction in a behavioral mode. A good example of the new behavioral applications to the career development theory is the social learning approach to career decision-making, best represented by Mitchell, Jones, and Krumboltz (1979) and by Thoresen and Ewart (1978).

Although it can be argued that other arrangements of the approaches to conceptualizations about career choice might be made, even the splinter points of view, such as the psychoanalytic, may be fit into the general scheme described above. The reader must avoid concluding that these types of models are independent of one another. They are closely intertwined and in many instances draw heavily upon one another both in terms of actual practice and in empirical research. For example, in the self-concept or developmental approach, part of the image of self-concept is based on tests which reflect the trait-factor approaches; also, Roe's personality theory of career choice includes many developmental factors.

PLAN

The discussion of the theories is carried out in four general sections. First, a statement is made of the general nature and scope of the theory and its basic thesis. Next, the results of research stimulated by the theory or relevant to it are discussed and evaluated. Then the implications of the theory for the specific conduct of career counseling are considered. Finally, the theory is evaluated and the expectations for future development are discussed.

Each theory is evaluated with respect to the criteria pertinent to a good theory which were discussed earlier. The theories are considered in the light of their comprehensiveness, their logical consistency, the degree to which they increase our understanding of the events under consideration, how operational they are, and the degree to which predictions derived from them are borne out. In addition, the applications growing from each theory are discussed and evaluated, along with new proposals about the roles these theories may play in practical affairs not originally suggested by their authors.

It is evident that the research and observational data on which a certain portion of the theories are evaluated are subject to limitations imposed by the problem of criterion definition. No attempt has been made here to resolve the many difficulties involved in clearly stating desirable behavioral outcomes of counseling, even though the problem has a certain relevance to the application of the theory. Some of the research that is considered is based on counseling procedures generated by theories which should lead to specific predictable case outcomes. Since criterion problems concerning case outcome deserve detailed attention in themselves, however, no extensive discussion seems appropriate here. It should be sufficient to state that without adequate criteria, outcome studies are entirely without meaning.

Important distinctions must be made concerning the differences among vocational selection, preference, and attainment. These differences are particularly well illustrated by Vroom (1964), who points out that vocational preference is the answer a counselor receives from a student to the question, "What career would you like to follow?" Vocational preference differs from vocational selection, since selection is a behavioral entity (broader than verbal) reflecting individual action and acceptance of consequent outcome. Finally, there is vocational attainment, which is reflected in the actual position the individual holds. It is obvious that while vocational preference, selection, and attainment may be identical within a given person, they need not be. Preference carries with it the concept of what would be done assuming all things are possible; selection includes the results of the compromises the individual makes in the face of perceived limitations; and attainment reflects the ability of the individual to implement the selection.

SUMMARY

Work holds an important place in human behavior, and consequently the varieties of work and the ways men choose their work in Western culture have attracted the interest of behavioral scientists. In this introduction, an attempt was made to illustrate the role that theory in general plays in the development of science and technology and, in particular, in the development of approaches to vocational psychology. As a corollary to the role theory plays in vocational psychology, the implications of counseling without an explicit theoretical base were discussed.

The direct comparison between current theoretical modes of thought in vocational psychology is a primary purpose of this book. Other goals include an attempt to catalog the assorted techniques suggested by the major theories of vocational choice and an attempt to generate a synthesis of current research and theory in vocational psychology that will be of use to the practicing counselor in daily interactions with the public.

The existing theories of career development were assigned to one of five categories: the trait-factor theories, the sociological theories, the self-concept or developmental theories, the personality-in-career theories, and the behaviorally oriented social learning approaches. Furthermore, several criteria were described against which each of the theories discussed in the book will be evaluated. Each theory will be assessed in terms of its comprehensiveness with respect to career development, the degree to which it explicitly states propositions concerning the process of career decision-making, and its internal consistency.

REFERENCES

Allport, F. *Theories of perception and the concept of structure.* New York: Wiley, 1955.
Ashby, J. D., Wall, H. W., and Osipow, S. H. Vocational certainty and indecision in college freshmen. *Personnel and Guidance Journal,* 1966, *44,* 1037–1041.
Buehler, C. *Der menschliche lebenslauf als psychologisches problem.* Leipzig: Hirzel, 1933.

Caplow, T. *The sociology of work.* Minneapolis: University of Minnesota Press, 1954.

Crites, J. O. Review of D. V. Tiedeman and R. P. O'Hara, "Career development: choice and adjustment." *Contemporary Psychology,* 1965, *10,* 80–81.

Crites, J. O. Career counseling: A review of major approaches. In Whiteley, J. and Resnikoff, A., Editors, *Career counseling.* Monterey, Cal.: Brooks-Cole, 1978.

Dudley, G. A., and Tiedeman, D. V. *Career development: exploration and commitment.* Muncie, Ind.: Accelerated Development Co., 1977.

Ginzberg, E., Ginsburg, S. W., Axelrad, S., and Herma, J. L. *Occupational choice: an approach to a general theory.* New York: Colombia University Press, 1951.

Gonyea, G. G. Appropriateness of vocational choice as a criterion of counseling outcome. *Journal of Counseling Psychology,* 1962, *9,* 213–219.

Gonyea, G. G. Appropriateness of vocational choices of counseled and uncounseled college students. *Journal of Counseling Psychology,* 1963, *10,* 269–275.

Harmony, M. A vocational biography. *Vocational Guidance Quarterly,* 1964, *13,* 37–40.

Hewer, V. What do theories of vocational choice mean to a counselor? *Journal of Counseling Psychology,* 1963, *10,* 118–125.

Holland, J. L. A theory of vocational choice. *Journal of Counseling Psychology,* 1959, *6,* 35–45.

Holland, J. L., and Nichols, R. C. The development and validation of an indecision scale: the natural history of a problem in basic research. *Journal of Counseling Psychology,* 1964, *11,* 27–34.

Holland, J. L., and Holland, J. E. Vocational indecision: more evidence and speculation. *Journal of Counseling Psychology,* 1977, *24,* 404–414.

Hollingshead, A. B. *Elmtown's youth.* New York: Wiley, 1949.

Hoppock, R. *Occupational information.* New York: McGraw-Hill, 1957.

Hull, C. L. *Aptitude testing.* Yonkers-on-Hudson, N.Y.. World, 1928.

Hulslander, S. C. Aspects of physical growth and evolution of occupational interest. *Personnel and Guidance Journal,* 1958, *36,* 610–615.

Kitson, H. D. *The Psychology of Vocational Adjustment.* Philadelphia: Lippincott, 1925.

Knefelkamp, L. L., and Slepitza, R. A cognitive-developmental model of career development: an adaptation of the Perry Scheme. In Whiteley, J. and Resnikoff, A., Editors, *Career counseling.* Monterey, Cal.: Brooks-Cole, 1978.

Lofquist, L., and Dawis, R. *A theory of work adjustment.* Englewood Cliffs, N.J.: Prentice-Hall, 1969.

Lunneborg, P. W. Vocational indecision in college graduates. *Journal of Counseling Psychology,* 1976, *23,* 402–404.

McCabe, G. E. When is a good theory practical? *Personnel and Guidance Journal,* 1958, *37,* 47–52.

Marks, E., Ashby, J. D., and Ziegler, M. L. Recommended curricular changes and scholastic performance. *Journal of Counseling Psychology,* 1965, *12,* 17–22.

Marx, M. H. The general nature of theory construction. In Marx, M. H., Editor, *Psychological theory.* New York: Macmillan, 1951.

Miller, D. C., and Form, W. H. *Industrial sociology.* New York: Harper & Row,1951.

Mitchell, A. M., Jones, G. B., and Krumboltz, J. D., Editors. *Social learning and career decision making.* Cranston, R.I.: Carroll Press, 1979.

Osipow, S. H. Perceptions of occupations as a function of titles and descriptions. *Journal of Counseling Psychology,* 1962, *9,* 106–109.

Osipow, S. H., Ashby, J. D., and Wall, H. W. Personality types and vocational choice: a test of Holland's theory. *Personnel and Guidance Journal,* 1966, *45,* 37–42.

Osipow, S. H., Carney, C. G., and Barak, A. A scale of educational-vocational undecidedness: A typological approach. *Journal of Vocational Behavior,* 1976, *9,* 233–243.

Osipow, S. H., Carney, C. G., Winer, J., Yanico, B., and Koschier, M. *The career decision scale.* Columbus, Oh.: Marathon Consulting and Press, 1976 (3rd rev.).

Parsons, F. *Choosing a vocation.* Boston: Houghton Mifflin, 1909.

Rauner, T. M. Occupational information and occupational choice. *Personnel and Guidance Journal,* 1962, *41,* 311–317.

Remenyi, A. G., and Fraser, B. J. Effects of occupational information on occupational perceptions. *Journal of Vocational Behavior,* 1977, *10,* 53–68.

Rodgers, D. A. In favor of separation of academic and professional training. *American Psychologist,* 1964, *19,* 675–680.

Rogers, C. R. *Client-centered therapy.* Boston: Houghton Mifflin, 1951.

Roe, A. Early determinants of vocational choice. *Journal of Counseling Psychology,* 1957, *4,* 212–217.

Samler, J. Toward a theoretical base for vocational counseling. *Personnel and Guidance Journal,* 1953, *32,* 34–35.

Samler, J. Psycho-social aspects of work: a critique of occupational information. *Personnel and Guidance Journal,* 1961, *39,* 458–465.

Sarton, G. *A history of science.* Cambridge: Harvard, 1952.

Schaffer, R. H. Job satisfaction as related to need satisfication in work. *Psychological Monographs,* 1953, *67,* No. 14 (Whole No. 364).

Sewell, W. H., and Hauser, R. M. *Education, occupation, and earnings.* New York: Academic Press, 1975.

Skinner, B. F. *Science and human behavior.* New York: Macmillan, 1953.

Small, L. Personality determinants of vocational choice. *Psychological Monographs,* 1953, *67,* No. 1 (Whole No. 351).

Strupp, H. H. The performance of psychiatrists and psychologists in a therapeutic interview. *Journal of Clinical Psychology,* 1958, *14,* 219–226.

Super, D. E. *The psychology of careers.* New York: Harper & Row, 1957.

Sweet, J. A. *Women in the labor force.* New York: Seminar Press, 1973.

Thoresen, C., and Ewart, C. Behavioral self control and career development. In Whiteley, J. and Resnikoff, A., Editors, *Career counseling.* Monterey, Cal.: Brooks-Cole, 1978.

Vroom, V. *Work and motivation.* New York: Wiley, 1964.

Williamson, E. G. *Vocational counseling: some historical, philosophical, and theoretical perspectives.* New York: McGraw-Hill, 1965.

CHAPTER ONE
ROE'S PERSONALITY
THEORY OF
CAREER CHOICE

Anne Roe, trained as a clinical psychologist, became involved in the field of career development through her research on the personality traits of artists. Her studies of the personality factors related to artistic creativity led her to conduct a major series of investigations into the characteristics of eminent scientists.

The formal series of theoretical statements followed (Roe, 1957; Roe and Siegelman, 1964) years of research which heavily influenced the development of Roe's point of view about vocational choice. The theory grew out of a series of investigations into the developmental backgrounds and personalities of research scientists in various specialties and is summarized in several monographs (Roe, 1951a; 1951b; 1953). From her findings Roe concluded that major personality differences exist between physical-biological and social scientists, primarily in the type of interactions they have with people and things. A second conclusion she drew was that the personality differences that exist among various kinds of scientists are in some part the result of influences of child-rearing practices.

THE THEORY

The theory proposes that every individual inherits a tendency to expend energies in some particular way. This innate predisposition toward a manner of expending psychic energy, combined with various childhood experiences, molds the general style an individual develops to satisfy needs. The resulting style has specific and major implications for career behavior. It is the relationship between the genetic factors and early childhood experiences on the one hand and vocational behavior on the other that Roe's theory attempts to make explicit.

15

Roe's theory, recently revised (Roe and Siegelman, 1964), has three important components. Two major personality theories are used in deriving the propositions of the theory. The influence of Gardner Murphy (1947) is implicit in the use of the concept of canalization of psychic energy and in the basic assumption that experiences of early childhood are likely to be related to vocational choice. A second major personality theme which is significantly related to Roe's theory of vocational choice is "need" theory, specifically Maslow's (1954). The third major component in Roe's formulations, the notion of genetic influences on vocational decisions as well as in the development of need hierarchies, is explicitly woven into her discussion.

The theory itself seems to have two levels. The first level is in the form of general statements that in themselves are very difficult to test empirically. This portion of the theory states that each individual's genetic background underlies abilities and interests, which in turn are related to vocational choice. Further, each individual expends psychic energy in a manner not entirely under personal control, and this involuntary expenditure of energy, which is presumably genetically determined, is influential in the development of the individual's abilities. Combined with the expenditure of psychic energy is the development of need primacies based partly on early frustrations and satisfactions and partly on genetic factors such as those outlined by personality theorists, particularly Maslow (1954). Maslow, it should be pointed out, assumes that the needs of humans may be arranged in a hierarchy, with lower-order needs such as food, drink, and oxygen ranked as greater than higher-order needs such as love, affection, knowledge, and self-actualization. A prerequisite for the expression of a need is the satisfaction of the needs which are more basic in the needs hierarchy. Thus, love would not emerge as a strong need in a starving person.

Genetic factors and need hierarchies combine to influence the selection of a vocation, as a part of their effect on the total life pattern. The degree of motivation toward the attainment of a vocational goal is a product of the arrangement and intensity of the individual's particular need structure. The degree to which an individual is motivated along a particular vocational line may be inferred from his/her accomplishments. In other words, given "equal" endowments genetically, differences in occupational achievement between two individuals may be inferred to be the result of motivational differences which, theoretically, are likely to be the outcome of different kinds of childhood experiences. There is the suggestion that some interaction between genetic and environmental factors occurs, but the theory fails to attempt to cope with the details of the nature of that interaction.

The second level of the theory pertains to the manner in which the development of patterns and the strengths of the basic needs are affected by childhood experiences. The interactions that Roe describes in this portion of her theory are more explicit and are more open to empirical validation than the general statements concerning psychic energy and genetic structure of personality. Three specific propositions emerge: (1) Needs that are routinely satisfied do not become unconscious motivators. (2) Higher-order needs, in the sense of Maslow's self-actualization need, will disappear entirely if they are only rarely satisfied. Lower-order needs, in the Maslovian sense, will become dominant motivators if they are only rarely satisfied; in the event they become dominant motivators, they will block the appearance of higher-order needs. (3) Needs that are satisfied after unusual delay will become unconscious motivators under certain conditions. The influencing conditions are the strength of the need, the amount of delay between the arousal of the need and its satisfaction, and the value that the satisfaction of the need has in the individual's immediate environment.

Thus, it is the second portion of the theory that contains the features that make it distinctive from personality theory in general and from other theories of vocational choice. Reflection upon the circumstances under which needs might be satisfied or frustrated in early childhood brings one directly to those principal agents of childhood gratification and frustration, the parents. Consequently, Roe proposes that child-rearing practices relate directly to both the kinds of needs satisfied and the delay involved in their gratification.

Modes of Child Rearing

Several specific child-rearing techniques have been described, all of which have to do with the manner in which the parents interact with the child. One type of parent exerts attention very directly on the child, either by overprotecting or making excessive demands. A second type of parent tends to avoid the child, either neglecting physical requirements or, more significantly, rejecting the child emotionally. A third parental style is one of acceptance, either of a casual, unconcerned nature or of a loving nature. Roe specifies how these parental styles affect the satisfaction of the child's needs. The overprotective parent will fully and quickly satisfy the child's physiological needs but will be less prompt to gratify the child's demands for love and esteem and, where the child's demands are met, will reward behavior that is socially desirable. Furthermore, the overprotective parent teaches the child to place a great deal of emphasis on the speed with which needs are gratified. Thus, the child is fully and quickly gratified at the lower-need levels; but higher-order needs, such as love, esteem, and a sense of belonging, are connected to dependency on others and to conformity. On the other hand, while overdemanding parents share many practices with overprotective parents, the two groups differ in several important aspects. Like the overprotective parent, the overdemanding parents promptly and more than adequately satisfy the child's physical needs. Also like the overprotective parent, they impose conditions on the love offered the child. This love is offered in return for conformity and achievement. The child's needs for information and understanding are also accepted and gratified, but only under specific circumstances where they contribute to the achievement of the child as the parent sees such achievement.

The rejecting kinds of parents have some explicit effects on the needs of their children. Those parents who, within certain limits, ignore the physical well-being of their children probably do not injure their children as much as parents who withhold love and esteem under all conditions. Roe, unclear on the differential effects of these two kinds of rejecting parents with respect to the resulting needs hierarchies of the children, points out that unless the rejected children see others treated in a different way, they will suffer from a stunted, but not necessarily distorted, development.

Finally, the accepting parents of both the loving and casual types offer satisfactory gratification of their children's needs at most levels. The two types of parent will gratify their children's needs in somewhat different ways and to slightly different degrees. Still, the personality that results from accepting parental techniques is able to seek the gratification of needs at all levels.

Early Experiences, Needs, and Adult Behavior

What is the relationship between these various practices, the resulting needs hierarchies, eventual adult behavior patterns in general, and vocational selection in particular? The scheme is basically organized in terms of the degree to which an individual is oriented toward or not toward persons. Thus, according to Roe's (1957) occupational classification, people in service occupations are primarily oriented toward persons and probably come from homes which generated a loving, overprotecting environment, while scientists tend not to be oriented toward persons and come from a cold home atmosphere where rejection and avoidance of the child predominated. The home atmosphere influences the *type* of vocational activities, while such items as the genetic structure and the involuntary pattern of expenditure of psychic energy influence the occupational *level* the worker achieves. Such factors as the intensity of needs, influenced by the early environment, may raise the occupational level because of an increase in motivation, but such an increase can only be within the limits set by the genetic factors influencing intelligence, combined with the socioeconomic background of the individual.

Roe (1957) has organized the world of work into eight fields (service; business; organization; technology; outdoor; science; general cultural; and arts and entertainment) and six levels (professional and managerial I; professional and managerial II; semi-professional; small business skilled, semi-skilled, and unskilled). These eight fields were originally viewed as psychologically related to each other on a continuum in such a way that those fields most resembling each other regarding psychological environment generated were adjacent. Therefore, a person working in an organization field would experience a psychological environment very similar to that experienced by a person in a technological field which was adjacent on the one side or by a person in a business field on the other side. Furthermore, the system was designed as a cylinder with the horizontal plane representing the fields in a circular manner so that one could enter the system at any point; it was continuous in nature. Therefore, the first field, service, was also next to the eighth field, arts and entertainment, as far as psychological similarity is concerned. The vertical plane represents the levels, with the highest levels being at the top and the lowest levels at the bottom.

Roe and Klos (1969) modified Roe's original conception of the occupational classification system from a cylindrical to a conical shape. This change was made to indicate that, regardless of field, low-level jobs are more similar to one another psychologically than high-level jobs are to one another. The cone places the high-level position at the wide top, which reflects a very substantial differentiation psychologically for workers in different fields operating at high levels. At the bottom the column narrows reflecting the idea that lower level work differs more as a function of the context in which it occurs than as a function of its inherent characteristics. In other words, a sweeper in a lab does not have a psychological experience very distinct from that of a cleaner in an artist's studio, while the scientist and the artist actually inhabit very different psychological environments.

Roe, Hubbard, Hutchinson, and Bateman (1966) and Roe and Hutchinson (1969) attempted to validate the psychological aspects of classification systems in terms of the occupational changes made over a period of years. Osipow (1966), with a similar purpose, examined the consistency of an individual's occupational preference according to occupational field. The results of these studies provide some support for Roe's notion that adjacent occupational fields are more closely related psychologically than distant fields. Meir's (1970) attempt to examine the spatial structure of Roe's original classification system led her to conclude that the structure of the classification system was adequate for the higher occupational levels but not, however, for the lower levels—an observation consistent with Roe and Klos's (1969) revision of the structure from a cylinder to a cone. In another study, Meir (1973), using the smallest space analysis method, concluded that the psychological assumptions of continuity that Roe makes about the system are basically sound.

Another significant modification of the occupational classification scheme of Roe made by Roe and Klos (1969) lies in the arrangement of the eight occupational fields along two axes. One axis reflects an orientation to purposeful communication versus resourceful utilization while the other axis is concerned with an orientation to interpersonal phenomena as opposed to an orientation to natural phenomena. Thus, it is possible to "plot" the location of an occupational field in this differentiated psychological space in relation to the basic wheel depicting Roe's theory.

Summary

The theory attends to every important aspect of vocational selection. The development of needs influences the general vocational context, that is, toward others or not toward others. The factors in the early environment that influence the development of needs are clearly specified. The manner in which a normal individual develops is indicated, as are several ways that normal development may become misdirected. Motivation is largely the result of the intensity of needs, which is a function of the degree of deprivation of an individual combined with his genetic structure. Finally, the level of vocational activity (complexity and responsibility) is largely the product of the genetic differences between people, which result in differences in intelligence and in the ways people attempt to manipulate various aspects of their environment. Conceivably, then, careful appraisal of an individual's childhood and the child's perception of parents' attitudes plus an accurate assessment of the child's aptitudes should lead one to predict with accuracy the general occupational class to be pursued. Or, after the fact, people in different occupations on the same level should report childhood environments that differ, according to the system described by Roe.

RESEARCH

There are two kinds of research relevant to the evaluation of Roe's theory. The first type is represented by investigations conducted by Roe herself, prior to her formal statement of the theory. The results of these studies guided her thinking about personality factors important to career choice. The other kind of research relevant to Roe's theory was conducted after the model was formally stated. Such research was primarily conducted by other investigators to evaluate Roe's theory by devising studies which predicted certain classes of vocational events based on the propositions of the theory and then assessing the degree to which the predictions correlated with those events.

Preliminary Studies

The research conducted by Roe prior to the development of her theory does not subject her position to rigorous test, since much of it is descriptive and, in any event, the theory was not developed fully enough to test. Nevertheless, it is relevant to consider the design of her studies and the generalizations she drew from the results, since the research she conducted during the period prior to the publication of her theory had a significant influence on the direction and shape of the theory. The research was primarily a series of investigations into personality characteristics, background factors, aptitude, and intellectual abilities as they related to vocational choice. The results are reported in a series of papers, but the main findings are summarized in several monographs on the characteristics of men who have outstanding reputations in the physical, biological, and behavioral sciences.

Roe's studies had two general themes. The first studies consisted of the assessment of the results of several group projective and ability tests administered to biologists, physicists, and chemists. From these studies, she was able to report differences and similarities in responses to the Rorschach Inkblot Test, in some cases the Thematic Apperception Test (TAT), and on certain ability tests (Roe, 1949a; 1950; 1951c; 1951d; 1952a; 1952b; 1949b; 1951a; 1951b; 1953) for scientists in different fields. The second step in her research program was her investigation of the characteristics and backgrounds of eminent scientists. Her procedures in these studies were at first to select men judged to be outstanding in their field by their peers and then to enlist their cooperation in her schedule of interviews and tests. Detailed interviews were conducted in which topics such as family background, early experiences, psychosocial development, religious experiences and beliefs, and work experiences were discussed thoroughly. In addition, tests of verbal-spatial-mathematical abilities were administered, as well as two personality measures, the TAT and the Rorschach Inkblot Test. Comparisons between scientists in different fields were then made with respect to the data collected.

Of major significance to the development of her theory were the generalizations she drew from the interviews. By and large she concluded that these groups of eminent scientists had childhood experiences which differentiated them from one another. For example, an unusual number of the eminent biologists she studied came from families broken either by divorce or the death of one parent. None of the social scientists came from a home permanently broken by parental conflict, though several were broken by a parent's death. The biological scientists reported more than the usual amount of difficulty in psycho-sexual development. Both the physical and biological scientists seemed somewhat distant in their relations with their parents and siblings, in contrast to the behavioral scientists (psychologists and anthropologists), who reported more interaction, though not necessarily positive, with their families. The parents of the social scientists were more overprotective and overcontrolling than those of the physical and biological scientists. The anthropologists, in particular, were often openly rebellious and hostile in their interactions with their parents.

Age at first commitment to their eventual vocation varied considerably for the different scientific groups. The physical and biological scientists tended to make their decisions earliest, the anthropologists and psychologists later. Of course, there was a wide range in age at the time of choice and considerable overlap among the groups. Nevertheless, the general trend for psychologists was to decide in college or later, while a few anthropologists decided in high school, and a larger number of physical and biological scientists decided in high school. (The parallel with Holland's theoretical predictions about the clarity and time of emergence of choice for different types of students is remarkable, as shall be seen in a later chapter.)

Also of interest is the finding that a prolonged illness leading to personal isolation during childhood seemed to play a significant role in development, especially among the theoretical physicists. Finally, as would be expected from a group of eminent professionals, all men scored very high on all the abilities measures, with the social scientists having the highest mean score on the verbal test, the physical scientists scoring highest on the spatial and mathematical tests (the mathematical test was not appropriately difficult for the physical scientists), and the social scientists scoring lowest on the mathematical test. All the eminent scientists impressed Roe with their unusual dedication to their work and the role their professional activities played in providing gratification for them. It would not be improper to infer that their dedication to their profession was closely related to their unusual vocational achievements, although, as Roe points out, such an inference is weakened by the lack of similar data on "less eminent" scientists to serve as a comparison group.

Roe's findings led her to conclude that there are distinctions in the personality characteristics of men in different vocations, that men in different vocations report qualitatively different childhood experiences, and that the major distinction between vocational orientations is in the dimension of interest toward persons or not toward persons. These conclusions played a significant role in fashioning the theory of vocational choice she later formulated.

Evaluation. The validity of Roe's studies of eminent scientists is dependent on the accuracy of the retrospective report of the scientists about their parents' attitudes and behaviors toward them, the early influences on their preferences and interests, feelings about themselves and other people, and also on Roe's interpretations of the interview material that revealed the scientists' recollections. Of course, some of Roe's conclusions were based on judgments she made about the scientists on the basis of Rorschach and TAT protocols. However, numerous problems exist in research based on projective tests, since the validity of the interpretations based on these tests has been questioned as well as the reliability of responses to projective items. Furthermore, tests such as the Rorschach are primarily oriented toward the diagnosis of psychopathology and have questionable utility in work with normal populations. Results based on Rorschach tests are likely to emphasize personality disorders rather than normal personality patterns.

Some question may be raised concerning the wider usefulness of generalizations based on studies of outstanding figures. Roe's eminent scientists were clearly unusual people. It is also unfortunate that Roe did not attempt to integrate her research program explicitly into the existing stream of research in child development. Despite these limitations, the studies were imaginative and very useful as pilot work in the study of the interaction between childhood experiences, personality development, and vocational choice.

Other Research

The first studies specifically designed to test Roe's theory were conducted by Grigg (1959). He chose to investigate differences in childhood recollections about parental treatment among women studying mathematics and science as compared with women studying nursing. He predicted that the mathematics-science majors would recall a "colder, less attentive" parental attitude than would the nursing students. Grigg compared the answers to a 15-item questionnaire about recollections of parental reactions during childhood, feelings of acceptance as a child, and father's and mother's reactions to the responsibilities of parenthood of 24 women graduate nursing students and 20 women graduate students in chemistry, physics, and mathematics. In addition, he inquired into their general interests during childhood. The results indicated that no differences existed between the two groups in the child-parent interaction recollections or parental role acceptance. Grigg did find, however, that the women in the mathematics-science fields had been more interested as children in things and gadgets than the nursing students had been and that nursing students had been more interested in companionship. Grigg concluded that his results failed to support Roe's theory, since Roe's model predicts that differences in childhood experiences with parents along the cold-warm, accepting-rejecting dimensions should be related to such divergent careers as science and nursing.

Hagen (1960) assessed Roe's theory by means of a longitudinal approach. Basing his study on a large sample (245) of Harvard sophomores first contacted between 1938 and 1942, he used family history data that pertained to vocational, social, personal, and medical information. Parents, and at times other individuals, provided retrospective information about the subjects' childhood personality and parental child-rearing practices. Data were obtained too concerning the subjects' current practices in rearing their own children. These subjects were also required to respond to open-ended questionnaires concerning their attitudes toward and adjustment to their work.

The subjects' childhood experiences based on the family history data were then rated independently according to Roe's categories of child-rearing practices by two judges. The judges agreed in their assignment of practices to categories in 70 percent of the sample. The 30 percent of Ss whose parents' child-rearing practices were not consistently evaluated was not used in the research. Then each subject's occupation was assigned to a category within Roe's vocational classification scheme and several predictions were made. It was predicted that the people in service occupations would be found to have come from a protecting childhood climate, people in business contact or general cultural occupations from a demanding climate, people in outdoor occupations from a rejecting climate, and people in technological fields from a casual climate. The results indicated that when childhood climate was paired with current occupation, only one of the child-rearing categories was significantly related to current vocation. Half the people from a casual atmosphere were in appropriate occupations, which proved to be significant beyond the .01 level of probability, but the sample was very small, and in view of the lack of predictive success for the other categories, Hagen concluded that Roe's theory was not supported by the data.

Assessing Roe's theory on the agreement between childhood parental practices and the productions of orientations toward persons or not toward persons, Hagen still failed to find results corroborating Roe's theory. Of 112 subjects classed in the demanding or overprotective categories, 69 were in vocations oriented toward persons and 43 in careers not oriented toward persons. Of the 42 Ss from rejecting, neglecting, or casual environments, only 16 were in occupations not oriented toward persons (which is where the theory predicted they should be), while 26 were in fields where orientation toward persons was predominant. These distributions failed to be significant, leading to the conclusion that the data fail to support Roe's model in even the broadest way. Hagen points out that the possible inadequacy and inaccuracy of the background data might have contributed to his failure to find support for Roe's theory. Nevertheless, some theoretical limitations seem likely, most significantly the fact that a variety of orientations is possible within a career, so that a scientist may not be oriented toward persons and work in a laboratory, or may be oriented toward persons and teach or administer research projects.

Kinnane and Pable (1962) devised a study primarily concerned with the investigation of another model of career development (Super, 1957, which is discussed elsewhere), but several of the hypotheses they tested related very closely to Roe's theory. Kinnane and Pable were interested in identifying the relationship between family background and work-value orientations of adolescents. Their sample of 121 eleventh-grade boys responded to a biographical inventory devised by Super and Overstreet (1956), designed to assess variables in family background such as cultural stimulation, family cohesiveness, social mobility, and adolescent independence. To provide added data Kinnane and Pable developed a scale measuring materialistic atmosphere in the home. They also used the Work Values Inventory (WVI) and another instrument devised by Super and Overstreet (1960). The latter two instruments rounded out the information necessary to assess home-family influences on the one hand and resulting work-value orientations on the other. The hypothesis of particular relevance to Roe's theory is their prediction that an orientation toward persons develops in a home atmosphere of warmth. A warm home is characterized by parental concern for children, with some possibility of parental overprotection or overcontrol.

Upon examining the correlation between work values and family background, they found a significant correlation between family cohesiveness and an orientation toward working conditions and associations. Such a finding is consistent with Roe's position, though it does not rule out other theories. A finding that was unexpected and which is difficult to explain is that a materialistic orientation was correlated with family cohesiveness to an even greater extent than orientation to people. The study possesses one major shortcoming, as the authors point out. A stronger test of the hypotheses would result from a comparison between work values and biographical factors if the measures of each were more independent of one another. When such measures are as closely connected to each other as in Kinnane and Pable's study, there is some risk that the subjects' perceptions of one factor may influence their response to the other in a spurious manner.

Another approach to the evaluation of Roe's theory was devised by Utton (1962), who proposed the hypothesis that individuals in people-oriented occupations would report more "altruistic love" toward humanity than people in occupations that are essentially nonperson-oriented. He further predicted that the subjects in person-oriented occupations would recall warmer early childhood experiences than subjects in nonperson-oriented careers. His subjects were 33 female social workers and 25 female occupational therapists representing the person-oriented occupations, and 41 female dieticians and 28 female laboratory technicians representing the nonperson-oriented occupations.

To test the first hypothesis he administered the Allport Inventory of Values (AIV), which he found differentiated the two groups significantly on the Social Scale, confirming the hypothesis that the person-oriented subjects were more altruistic in their concern for others than the nonperson-oriented subjects. His second hypothesis was assessed by devising and administering a Childhood Experience Rating Scale (CERS) primarily measuring the warmth recalled from childhood experience. He found that the CERS scores of women who had scored above the mean for women in general on the Social Scale of the Allport Inventory of Beliefs (AIB) were no different from the CERS scores of women who had scored below the mean on the Social Scale. Furthermore, he found that the CERS scores were the same for subjects in both person- and nonperson-oriented careers. Utton did, however, find that when the SVIB scores of subjects with B or higher scores in their field were examined and their CERS backgrounds compared, some differences were evident, but not always differences that were consistent with his predictions. Social workers and occupational therapists with B or higher on the appropriate SVIB scale did have higher CERS scores than social workers and occupational therapists with less than B SVIB scores for their occupations. However, occupational therapists and dieticians were similar to each other in their recollections of their childhood experiences, whereas social workers and laboratory technicians resembled one another closely. Thus, the findings are not consistently related to Roe's theory and consequently generate questions about the adequacy of the suggestion of the theory that a warm-cold dimension in childhood exerts an influence on the later choice of a vocation.

Switzer, Grigg, Miller, and Young (1962) designed a study attempting to correct some of the deficiencies that Grigg's (1959) earlier study possessed with respect to the adequacy of his instrument to measure childhood experiences. Switzer and his associates predicted that ministerial students, representing a person-oriented career, would perceive their parents as more demanding and less rejecting of them in childhood than would chemistry majors, representing a nonperson-oriented field. They studied 40 graduate students in theology, 40 undergraduate students in theology (called ministerial), and 40 undergraduate chemistry majors, all of whom represented themselves as certain of their vocational choice. A questionnaire designed to measure the demanding and rejecting aspects of the attitudes they recalled their parents having held toward them during their childhood was administered to the subjects.

The findings did not reflect any consistent relationship between occupational selection and parental attitude. In fact, some of their results were the reverse of theoretical expectations. For example, Switzer and his associates found that the ministerial and theological students reported more rejecting experiences than the chemistry majors did, and again the ministerial and theological students scored lower on the overdemanding scales than the chemists. Each of these findings is the opposite of what Roe's theory predicts. As with other research, however, the adequacy of the inventory measuring parental reactions and the memory of the respondents might be questioned. It could be, for instance, that the ministerial and theological students, being more socially perceptive than chemists, might have accumulated richer childhood recollections subject to more rigorous standards of parent-child interaction than the chemists.

Reasoning that jobs do not always possess the same characteristics even though they have the same titles, Levine (1963) controlled the social interaction within an occupation by having subjects from ten occupational groups which covered a wide range of social interaction possibilities. He predicted that people with a strong "human orientation" will be found in occupations where a high degree of social interaction is necessary. He also predicted that people who see their jobs as requiring considerable social interaction will rate themselves higher on scales measuring the possession of social manipulation skills than people in low social interaction jobs. To test these hypotheses, he developed a scale to assess the social requirements of jobs, a brief questionnaire (ten items) to measure the Ss' tendency toward human or nonhuman approaches to problem solving, and another brief questionnaire (three items) on which the Ss rated themselves with respect to their possession of manipulative skills.

His findings indicated some support for the first hypothesis, that people with a high degree of human orientation are likely to be found in occupations demanding social interaction. Thus, he found that salesmen were significantly different from all his other groups in the degree of human orientation indicated by their higher scores, while accountants were significantly lower in human orientation than social workers, draftsmen, laboratory technicians, and electrical engineers. The second hypothesis was not supported. Although questions can be raised about the adequacy of the execution of the study—for example, the reliability of a ten-item, human-nonhuman, problem-solving orientation questionnaire and a three-item questionnaire on rating of manipulative skills—Levine's results support Roe's broad conception of the dichotomous work orientation of toward persons/not toward persons. However, the results shed no light on how or even if background factors influence the development of social or nonsocial preferences classified in terms of Roe's taxonomical system. Jones (1965) also observed that his subjects expressed their occupational preferences fundamentally in terms of occupations oriented toward or away from people.

Green and Parker (1965) designed a study using adolescents as a sample to overcome the problems which previous investigators encountered concerning the retrospective reconstruction of childhood experiences. Seventh grade boys and girls, living with their parents, were given Roe and Siegelman's Parent-Child Relations Questionnaire, modified for use with seventh graders. The responses to this inventory provided data about the current home atmosphere of the children, which were then related to the person or nonperson orientation of their occupational preferences. The results suggest that for boys the perception of either parent as warm and supporting results in person-oriented occupational choices, while for girls cold parental relationships result in nonperson career choices. Curiously, boys from a cold environment do not make nonperson-oriented career choices, nor do girls from a warm environment make person-oriented career plans. Nevertheless, these findings offer more support for Roe's theory than most other studies and point to the importance of gaining current data about parental treatment of children in such studies. It would be interesting to follow these subjects as years go by, to see, first, how constant their perceptions of parental treatment are, and second, how these perceptions continue to be related to the orientation of their career decisions.

Crites (1962) tested the hypothesis that a continuum of the importance of interpersonal relations exists for occupations. He required 100 students to rank eight occupational fields with respect to the degree that the fields required interpersonal relations with people as the main work activity of the job. The resulting empirical scale did not correlate significantly with the theoretical scale derived from Roe's model. Crites concluded that Roe's theoretical scale was not as valid as the empirically derived scale that he developed, at least so far as the ordering of judgments about job orientation toward persons or not toward persons is concerned. Although the differences between the two orders is slight, errors in Roe's theory in the degree of importance that person orientation has for a career field might be partially responsible for the failure of research to validate Roe's position.

Another study with important implications for Roe's theory was an attempt to construct a Family Relations Inventory (FRI) which might test the theory more effectively. Brunkan and Crites (1964), critical of the efforts that have been made by other investigators to test Roe's theory by using background information questionnaires of uncertain reliability and doubtful validity, have worked systematically to develop a more effective instrument with which to assess family background factors that might be related to vocational choice. However, in Brunkan's (1965) attempt to apply the instrument to test Roe's theory once again, no systematic connection between early environment and orientation of occupational choice was found. Brunkan administered the FRI to 298 college undergraduate male students enrolled in psychology courses. Scores on the FRI were related to the category of the occupational choice in Roe's system and from this he predicted that the occupational choices would reflect the warmth or coldness of the family environment. None of these predictions was supported. Thus, even with a more carefully developed instrument to assess family environment, the data fail to support Roe's theory.

Appleton and Hansen (1969) administered the Roe-Siegelman (1964) parent-child questionnaire, the Kuder CH Social Service Scale, and 40 items restated from the Edwards Personal Preference Schedule reflecting the nurturance, succorance, and dominance scales to 173 high school males and females in order to examine the relation between occupational plans and Roe's theory. The findings of this research did not reflect any significant relationship between reports about parent-child relations and vocational orientation. Appleton and Hansen speculate that these negative results can, at least in part, be attributed to deficiencies in the questionnaires, but the results add further to the questions about the validity of the theory. In another study, Byers, Forrest, and Zaccaria (1968) predicted that clergymen differ from a "men-in-general" group in the way they recall early parental relations. Some of the predicted differences were observed; for example, the clergymen recalled more father-avoidance on the Family Relations Inventory than the normative group, but in general, the statistical relationships are weak and do not provide strong theoretical support.

Some positive support for the theory has been produced by Medvene (1969; 1970). In one study, Medvene (1969) found significant relations between perceived home atmosphere and vocational choice for 461 male graduate students in psychology. In another study (Medvene, 1970), he found that person-oriented students more frequently came from homes where there was acceptance of and emotional concentration on the child than nonperson-oriented students. He further found that students in different specialties within psychology describe their family backgrounds in different terms. In previous research concerning Roe's theory few "within occupational" distinctions have been made, though there are data (De Coster and Rhode, 1972) indicating substantial intraoccupational differences in accountants' personality traits as a function of specialty and age. The failure to consider such differences could account for lack of support for Roe's theory, since the mixture of various personality types in one field might cancel the opportunity to observe the effects of personality on career.

Medvene and Shueman (1978) found that engineering students are likely to have dominant parents who avoided them rather than parents who accepted or concentrated on them, while sales and technical service students were more likely to have dominant parents who accepted them. Overall, Medvene, and Shueman found some support for Roe's theory that dominant parents who avoid their children produce offspring who have a nonperson orientation.

Kriger (1972) applied a modified version of Roe's theory to the study of career versus homemaker orientation in women. Kriger reasoned that for women the most critical career decisions reside in career versus homemaking commitments. Thus, Kriger predicted that women in female-dominated occupations will report parents' attitudes toward them as overprotective, while women in male-dominated occupations will report recollections of more casual and accepting parental attitudes. To test these predictions, Kriger studied the responses of three groups of 22 women each on the Parent Attitude Research Instrument (PARI) and their need achievement scores as determined by the Edwards Personal Preference Schedule. The three groups of women represented homemakers, women in female-dominated occupations, and women in male-dominated occupations. Kriger observed that women in male-dominated occupations were highest in achievement need, followed by women in female-dominated occupations and then homemakers. She also found relationships between parental practices and career orientation; the field and level of a woman's occupation seemed to be a function of her achievement orientation, which, in turn, was apparently related to her perception of the treatment she received from her parents. Kriger concluded that instead of developing an orientation toward or not toward people, parental treatment affects females in a way that orients them toward homemaking or toward a career, in that a controlling atmosphere leads to a homemaking orientation while casual treatment leads toward a career.

Over the years since she first published her theory, Roe has recognized the limitations that a general series of statements about parent-child interactions have in predicting adult behavior. She and a collaborator (Roe and Siegelman, 1964) report an attempt to identify the role that needs play in the development of interests and to clarify the nature of childhood experiences that influence the kinds of interests adults acquire. In the design of the study, Roe and Siegelman made explicit statements about certain antecedent conditions (childhood experiences) which should lead to particular sets of subsequent events (adult interests). Three factors emerged from a factor analysis of childhood experiences to be included as part of the antecedent conditions: loving-rejecting (LR), casual-demanding (CD), and overattention (O).

The study conducted by Roe and Siegelman attempted to tie the three antecedent factors and relevant group scores to a series of subsequent events (adult activities). These events were assessed by the administration of several inventories and questionnaires to a sample of 24 male and 25 female engineers, 22 male and 23 female social workers, and 142 Harvard University seniors representing a wide variety of academic concentrations. The questionnaires included information about the subject's general interests, occupational interests (assessed by the career chosen or followed, depending on status as a student or professional, and by scores on the California Occupational Interest Inventory), and several measures of personality and orientation toward or not toward persons. The personality measure that was finally used in the study represented factor A (Cyclothymia-Schizothymia) of the Cattell 16 PF Test.

The general hypotheses that Roe and Siegelman investigated were related to the effect that early personal experiences have on adult interest patterns. They hypothesized that the degree of adult person orientation is a function of the extent and satisfaction of early personal relations. Using Roe and Siegelman's experimental terms, the hypothesis was that factors LR and O, closeness to parents, and early social activity would correlate positively with the subsequent measures of person orientation. Roe and Siegelman also predicted that there would be some Ss who would be person-oriented as adults, although they had experienced early rejection. Finally, it was predicted that early nondemanding but adequately nurturant (casual) personal relations would not be found to have affected the degree of adult person orientation.

Roe and Siegelman's findings generally support the major hypotheses, although the results point up some surprising events. They found that factor O, taken separately for each parent, and factor LR for the mother correlate positively with subsequent measures of person orientation. More significantly, they found that memories about early social experience seemed to be the most important of the group scores in relationship with later person orientation. Thus, the combination of LR plus O and early social experiences is the most effective set of antecedent conditions for producing later person orientation. As predicted, the factor CD (casual-demanding) was found to be unrelated to the degree of adult person orientation.

Roe and Siegelman first concluded that the amount of early social experience seems to be related to the amount of later person orientation; secondly, the hypothesis that particular kinds of early parent-child interactions will affect vocational choice in a certain way was found to be too specific to be valid, since parental interaction with their children is not constant, and one parent will often behave in a manner that will offset the impact which the behavior of the other parent has on the child. Finally, they concluded that factors such as the labor market, an individual's socioeconomic background, education and abilities, and chance are likely to be very important to the choice of a specific vocation.

Such conclusions are not inconsistent with the observation that while person-nonperson orientations are influenced by early childhood experiences, such orientations seem remotely related to occupational choice. However, Roe and Siegelman's conclusions leave the status of Roe's theory in disarray, since the suggestion that vocational selection is largely a function of chance factors discourages further attempts to systematize the role that personal developmental factors play in vocational selection.

Four recent attempts to devise interest inventories based on Roe's theory have been made which offer promise for the continued vitality of some of Roe's ideas. The first of these is the Hall Occupational Orientation Inventory, which is based on the development of psychological needs in occupational terms (Hall, 1968). The results of one study based on this inventory are encouraging (Hall, Shappell, and Tarrier, 1971). A second new instrument has been developed by Meir (described in Meir and Barak, 1974), which requires respondents to indicate their preferences for occupational titles by field and level according to the Roe classification. The result is a simply derived set of data describing the degree to which a student's interests are focused by level and field, thus indicating to the counselor the nature of the counseling task required by the individual. A companion instrument based on occupationally oriented course titles without the levels component is also available. Finally, Lunneborg (1977) has published an instrument called the Vocational Interest Inventory, based on the Roe classification scheme. In one study, Lunneborg and Lunneborg (1978) found that the four interest factors in Roe's and Holland's frameworks were also to be observed in the Vocational Interest Inventory. The Vocational Interest Inventory, thus, seems to have potential as yet another measurement method based on Roe's occupational classification system. A fourth instrument is the California Occupational Preference System Interest Inventory by Knapp, Knapp, and Buttafuoco (1978). While it is too soon to fully assess the validity of any of these instruments, they appear to demonstrate that there is substantial interest in the Roe system of classification and some interest in her theory, that attempts to measure constructs associated with the theory are warranted, and that it is feasible to develop such instruments. If the history of other theories is repeated, it is not unreasonable to expect to see a resurgence of interest in studying Roe-related notions. That is, one can clearly observe that when a theory is constructed with easily used instruments to measure its constructs, research is stimulated which brings further clarity either by supporting or failing to support the implications of the theory.

Evaluation.   Several general shortcomings in the research methodology are apparent. The data upon which judgments were made about the nature of early parental behaviors toward children were essentially unreliable. To base what is the crux of the research design on retrospective data, reported through interviews or, worse, through short, unvalidated questionnaires, is highly risky. Furthermore, the samples studied were either very small or included occupational groupings of such a specific nature as to make generalization almost impossible. Many of the studies used students as the sample and, without making it explicit, were really using occupational preferences and selection rather than occupational attainment as the criterion against which early experiences were compared.

Finally, none of the investigations adequately attempted to handle the problem of parental inconsistencies in child-rearing patterns and their effect on subsequent personality development and vocational choice. To fail to do so is to ignore the confounding effects that differences between parents in child-rearing attitudes have on personality development, as well as the effects of changes in these attitudes as the children grow older. These two factors alone are important variables for study within a theoretical context stressing childhood and parental practices. Despite these shortcomings, the evidence is very strong against the likelihood that Roe's theory as originally proposed is an adequate representation of the crucial features of vocational development.

STATUS

The Implications for Counseling

Roe makes no explicit recommendations in either her original theoretical statement or her later revised statement that are relevant to counseling. Despite her failure to do so, however, it is possible to infer certain implications. Her first theoretical statement has more potential impact for counseling, since it carries with it a strong statement that vocational choice is closely related to personality characteristics developed during early childhood. Her revised statement of theory has fewer implications for counseling practice, since the relationship between personality factors, their manner of development, and vocational choice seems less clear as a result of the research. Roe and Siegelman's conclusion that chance plays a greater role in career choice than suggested in the earlier theoretical statement reduces the contribution counseling may make to career development.

Considering the early formulation alone, it can be seen that if the needs structure of an individual is related to vocational choice in the sense that a vocation is selected with an eye toward the satisfaction of needs, then counseling is logically aimed at helping the individual effectively understand needs, identify occupations in which needs can best be satisfied, and, if necessary, overcome circumstances which might have thwarted the development of a needs structure. This last feature deserves elaboration. For individuals whose background has caused their needs hierarchies to halt at a relatively low level, counseling might resemble psychotherapy aimed at reliving and learning to understand childhood patterns of gratification. Thus, if an individual was the child of overdemanding parents and found that the resulting needs structure developed in a way that led to efforts to seek approval from other significant people, counseling might be directed to help in understanding the stunting of needs, developing higher-order needs, and acquiring the techniques to satisfy such needs.

Translating Roe's theory into counseling procedures for a typical vocational choice problem results in a series of activities oriented toward identifying a student's psychological needs structure and then matching the resulting hierarchy of needs with those offered by various occupations. Thus, a counselor would assess client needs through interview procedures or some relevant inventory, then assess the student's family background to determine whether or not the individual has had a reasonably normal family background in terms of needs development. If the interviews reveal that the student was at an appropriate point in needs development, two choices would be open to the counselor. One would be to try to help the student evaluate the potential of various fields for the satisfaction of current needs, the other to try to help the student further evolve a needs hierarchy through interview procedures. These procedures would probably emphasize the client's perceptions of parental attitudes toward the kinds of gratifications they provided and the conditions they imposed for gratification. Thus, the student might become aware of background forces that stunted or misguided the developing needs system and correct it accordingly. Unfortunately, however, the theory fails to explicate the interview procedures with which to accomplish such a task.

What procedures would the revised theory suggest for counseling? As a result of Roe and Siegelman's conclusion that economic and chance factors are important, the revised position would logically place more emphasis on occupational information designed to help the student make the most expeditious use of his/her abilities. Needs would not be ignored, however, but would be considered more in terms of satisfaction within an acceptable socioeconomic framework. Since Roe and Siegelman concluded that person-nonperson orientation is not directly related to vocational choice, less emphasis would be placed on that aspect of needs. In neither the original nor revised formulation, however, is counseling practice accorded much concern.

Evaluation

Several general observations may be made about the overall tone of Roe's theory. The model possesses a very strong psychoanalytic tone, which is modified somewhat by the introduction of Maslow's hierarchy of needs. The theory has stimulated some research activity. The results of most of the research, however, have not supported the specifics of Roe's model. What remains after attempts at empirical validation is a general statement that individuals are either person- or nonperson-oriented in their interests and that their orientation influences the choice of their vocation. Roe and Siegelman's study, however, generates some doubt about even this mild conclusion.

Roe's propositions concerning the effects of parent-child interactions on the development of needs hierarchies—which in turn influence, among other behaviors, vocational choices—possess several ambiguities which contribute to the inability of investigators to validate the theory empirically. Assume, for example, that the parental acceptance of children's behavior represents a normal and desirable interaction between children and their parents. If all parent-child interactions were normal and Roe's theory correct, we would eventually have only restricted classes of vocational choice. Do most scientists come from families that deemphasize interpersonal relations? Such is the implication of Roe's theory. Roe and Siegelman (1964) found, however, that male engineers seemed to be following their natural inclinations rather than choosing engineering as a reaction to parental treatment.

Another difficulty arising from Roe's propositions about the impact of parent-child interactions on vocational choice lies in the impurity of parental behavior styles. Parents do not uniformly reject or overprotect or love their children. What are the effects of such mixtures on children's needs? What are the effects of differences between the parents themselves on the child's developing needs hierarchy? One parent might be loving and the other overdemanding. Although in the revised theory (Roe and Siegelman, 1964) some serious attempts were made to resolve this dilemma, the results are not entirely satisfactory. Finally, parental attitudes themselves are not likely to be constant across the various stages of childhood development. How old are children when parental behaviors begin to lose their impact on the development of needs? The age must be young or still another parent-child variable confounds the predictions of the theory.

How does the theory stand in terms of fulfilling the requirements of a desirable theory? Certainly, the model is comprehensive. It includes in its scope not only vocational decision-making but general personality development as well. In fact, the later version of the model is described in terms that make it seem more like a fragment of a personality theory than a theory of vocational choice. The theory rates well on the feature of explicitness. Roe carefully states propositions and the behavioral implications of each proposition. Furthermore, the propositions are logical and suggest new ways of interpreting and predicting vocational behavior. She traces in detail the features of normal personality development which lead to appropriate vocational selection. She suggests clearly the circumstances under which personality development will become misdirected and result in inappropriate vocational choice.

Is the theory operational? The numerous attempts to test the theory make it appear to be operational, but the ambiguous results of the research suggest that the theory may not be as open to testing as it might appear. Probably the inability of investigators to put the theory to a rigorous test is mainly the result of the ambiguities in Roe's theory as discussed above, and to some extent the result of the difficulty of adequately assessing parent-child interactions many years after they have occurred. Are children's perceptions of parental attitudes toward them enough to influence personality development to the extent Roe suggests? If so, then the accuracy of recollections may be unimportant since the perceptual recall might be the main factor influencing a person's style of life. Such a question is not easily resolved even through the use of longitudinal studies.

The theory has little to say about procedures useful in vocational counseling. If one were to judge the adequacy of the theory only on those procedures the theory explicitly recommended, the model would be inadequate, since no procedures are suggested. Inferences about techniques that can be drawn from the general nature of the theory suggest few procedures different from other, less systematic approaches to counseling. The theory presents no goals for counseling, no recommendations with respect to useful or suitable counseling techniques or procedures, and no descriptions of desirable behaviors or sequences of behavior. Some inferences might be made concerning the origin of deviant vocational patterns, but no remedial measures are recommended. Consequently, there is nothing built into the theory that would lead to evaluation studies. As for likely goals, the theory only suggests that counseling should help an individual to identify basic needs, to remove blocks retarding the development of the needs hierarchy, and to develop techniques to satisfy needs. No procedures to accomplish these ends are recommended.

Unless it is possible to develop the premise that parental treatment influences some stream of intervening variables (such as cognitive style), it is difficult to see how the theory can prove viable. The theory has few applied implications in its current state and little empirical support. Consequently, without a major revision it is not likely to have a growing impact on vocational counseling.

REFERENCES

Appleton, G. M., and Hansen, J. C. Parent-child relations, need-nurturance, and vocational orientation. *Personnel and Guidance Journal*, 1969, *47*, 794–799.

Brunkan, R. J. Perceived parental attitudes and parental identification in relation to field of vocational choice. *Journal of Counseling Psychology*, 1965, *12*, 39–47.

Brunkan, R. J., and Crites, J. O. An inventory to measure the parental attitude variable in Roe's theory of vocational choice. *Journal of Counseling Psychology*, 1964, *11*, 3–11.

Byers, A. P., Forrest, G. G., and Zaccaria, J. S. Recalled early parent-child relations, adult needs, and occupational choice. *Journal of Counseling Psychology*, 1968, *15*, 324–328.

Crites, J. O. An interpersonal relations scale for occupational groups. *Journal of Applied Psychology*, 1962, *46*, 87–90.

De Coster, D. T., and Rhode, J. G. Analysis of certified public accounting subgroup and accounting student personality traits using the California Personality Inventory. *Journal of Vocational Behavior*, 1972, *2*, 155–162.

Green, L. B., and Parker, H. J. Parental influence upon adolescents' occupational choice: a test of an aspect of Roe's theory. *Journal of Counseling Psychology*, 1965, *12*, 379–383.

Grigg, A. E. Childhood experience and parental attitudes: a test of Roe's hypothesis. *Journal of Counseling Psychology*, 1959, *6*, 153–156.

Hagen, D. Careers and family atmosphere: a test of Roe's theory. *Journal of Counseling Psychology*, 1960, *7*, 251–256.

Hall, L. G. *Hall occupational orientation inventory*. Chicago: Follett, 1968.

Hall, L. G., Shappell, D. L., and Tarrier, R. B. An application of Roe's vocational choice model: inventory, counseling goals and strategies. *The School Counselor*, 1971, *19*, 43–48.

Jones, K. J. Occupational preference and social orientation. *Personnel and Guidance Journal*, 1965, *43*, 574–579.

Kinnane, J. F., and Pable, M. W. Family background and work value orientation. *Journal of Counseling Psychology*, 1962, *9*, 320–325.

Knapp, R. R., Knapp, L., and Buttafuoco, P. M. Interest changes and the classification of occupations. *Measurement and Evaluation in Guidance*, 1978, *12*, 119–129.

Kriger, S. F. Need achievement and perceived parental child-rearing attitudes of career women and homemakers. *Journal of Vocational Behavior*, 1972, *2*, 419–433.

Levine, S. Occupation and personality: relationship between the social factors of the job and human orientation. *Personnel and Guidance Journal*, 1963, *41*, 602–605.

Lunneborg, P. W. *Manual for the vocational interest inventory*. Seattle: Univ. of Washington Assessment Center, 1977.

Lunneborg, C. W., and Lunneborg, P. W. Construct validity of four basic interest factors. *Journal of Vocational Behavior*, 1978, *12*, 165–171.

Maslow, A. H. *Motivation and personality*. New York: Harper & Row, 1954.

Medvene, A. M. Occupational choice of graduate students in psychology as a function of early parent-child interactions. *Journal of Counseling Psychology*, 1969, *16*, 385–389.

Medvene, A. M. Person-oriented and non-person-oriented occupations in psychology. *Journal of Counseling Psychology*, 1970, *17*, 243–246.

Medvene, A. M., and Shueman, S. A. Perceived parental attitudes and choice of vocational specialty area among male engineering students. *Journal of Vocational Behavior*, 1978, *12*, 208–216.

Meir, E. I. Empirical test of Roe's structure of occupations and an alternative structure. *Journal of Counseling Psychology*, 1970, *17*, 41–48.

Meir, E. I. The structure of occupations by interests—a smallest space analysis. *Journal of Vocational Behavior*, 1973, *3*, 21–31.

Meir, E. I., and Barak, A. A simple instrument for measuring vocational interests based on Roe's classification of occupations. *Journal of Vocational Behavior*, 1974, *4*, 33–42.

Murphy, G. *Personality: A bio-social approach to origins and structure*. New York: Harper & Row, 1947.

Osipow, S. H. Consistency of occupational choice and Roe's classification of occupations. *Vocational Guidance Quarterly*, 1966, *14*, 285–286.

Roe, A. Analysis of group Rorschachs of biologists. *Journal of Projective Techniques*, 1949, *13*, 25–43. (a)

Roe, A. Psychological examination of eminent biologists. *Journal of Consulting Psychology*, 1949, *13*, 225–246. (b)

Roe, A. Analysis of group Rorschachs of physical scientists. *Journal of Projective Techniques*, 1950, *14*, 385–398.

Roe, A. A psychological study of eminent biologists. *Psychological Monographs*, 1951, *65*, No. 14 (Whole No. 331). (a)

Roe, A. A psychological study of eminent physical scientists. *Genetic Psychology Monograph*, 1951, *43*, 121–239. (b)

Roe, A. A study of imagery in research scientists. *Journal of Personality*, 1951, *19*, 459–470. (c)

Roe, A. Psychological tests of research scientists. *Journal of Consulting Psychology*, 1951, *15*, 492–495. (d)

Roe, A. Analysis of group Rorschachs of psychologists and anthropologists. *Journal of Projective Techniques*, 1952, *16*, 212–224. (a)

Roe, A. Group Rorschachs of university faculties. *Journal of Consulting Psychology*, 1952, *16*, 18–22. (b)

Roe, A. A psychological study of eminent psychologists and anthropologists and a comparison with biological and physical scientists. *Psychological Monographs*, 1953, *67*, No. 2 (Whole No. 352).

Roe, A. *The psychology of occupations*. New York: Wiley, 1956.

Roe, A. Early determinants of vocational choice. *Journal of Counseling Psychology*, 1957, *4*, 212–217.

Roe, A., Hubbard, W. D., Hutchinson, T., and Bateman, R. Studies of occupational history. Part I: Job changes and the classification of occupations. *Journal of Counseling Psychology*, 1966, *13*, 387–393.

Roe, A. and Hutchinson, T. Groups of the Roe system. *Journal of Counseling Psychology*, 1969, *16*, 390–395.

Roe, A. and Klos, D. Occupational classification. The *Counseling Psychologist*, 1969, *1*, 84–92.

Roe, A. and Siegelman, M. The origin of interests. *The APGA inquiry series*, No. 1, Washington, D. C.: American Personnel and Guidance Association, 1964.

Super, D. E., and Overstreet, P. I. *The vocational maturity of ninth grade boys*. New York: Bureau of Publications, Teachers College, Columbia University, 1960.

Switzer, D. K., Grigg, A. E., Miller, J. B., and Young, R. K. Early experiences and occupational choice: a test of Roe's hypothesis. *Journal of Counseling Psychology*, 1962, *9*, 45–48.

Utton, A. C. Recalled parent-child relations as determinants of vocational choice. *Journal of Counseling Psychology*, 1962, *9*, 49–53.

CHAPTER TWO
PSYCHOANALYTIC
CONCEPTIONS OF
CAREER CHOICE

According to Erik Erikson (1950), Freud once stated that the most significant indication of a psychologically normal being was the ability "to love and to work" effectively. Elaboration upon the first half of the statement, love, is not relevant here. The second aspect, however, illustrates the implicit role that work has in the psychoanalytic conception of personality and psychopathology. Basic in the system of psychoanalysis is the mechanism of sublimation. It provides an acceptable way for an individual to release parts of his or her psychic energies that would be unacceptable in society if expressed directly. Work is ideally suited to provide outlets for sublimated wishes and impulses. Considering the general role that work plays in psychoanalytic theory and the general pervasiveness of psychoanalytic concepts in psychology as a whole, it is not surprising that some attempts have been made to conceptualize the process of vocational development within the framework of psychoanalysis.

GENERAL PSYCHOANALYTIC
THEORY AND CAREER
CHOICE

Several analytic writers have indicated that they are concerned, at least indirectly, with matters of vocational choice. Perhaps Brill, of all the analysts, devoted the most attention to career choice. He elaborated upon the notion that vocational selection is one realm of behavior in which society permits an individual to combine the pleasure and reality principles (1949). The pleasure principle drives an individual to behave in a manner that is immediately gratifying ignoring the future consequences of actions, while the reality principle focuses attention on eventual and long-term gratifications at the expense of immediate ones. In choosing a vocation an individual presumably is able to compromise between the two principles. Ideally, a person gets some immediate satisfaction as a consequence of the choice, while at the same time laying the foundation for future success. For example, the selection of law as a career goal provides the law student with some prestige, status, and vicarious satisfaction in addition to the potential stability of eventual entry into the profession.

Brill further elaborated on the theme that sublimation is intimately bound up in vocational choice. He proposed that the particular vocation an individual chooses is not the result of an accidental arrangement of events. Rather, personality and impulses lead one to choose a career in which basic life impulses may be satisfied through sublimation. According to Brill, unconscious motives underlie all behavior, including vocational selection. Brill documents his position by reporting several cases in which he personally observed the role that occupation plays in the gratification of impulses. To illustrate the role of psychopathological tendencies in career selection, Brill suggests that sadistic impulses may be satisfied in such diverse activities as those of butchers, surgeons, and murderers. Jones (1923) describes a patient who successfully transformed his childhood fascination with the process of urination and with bodies of water in general into a successful career as an engineer constructing bridges and canals. Zilboorg (1934) discusses a patient whose father, a successful toilet fixtures businessman, was extremely concerned with his son's bowel functions.

Among Brill's ideas about vocational choice is the interesting notion that vacations represent "neurotic fads" for which well-adjusted individuals have neither need nor desire. According to Brill, the well-adjusted person works because work is enjoyable and because it includes activities which allow participation in otherwise tabooed behaviors. In support of this assumption, Brill points out that those who retire lose interest in life and die earlier than those who do not retire. (Of course, other explanations of this difference in longevity can be made. For example, early retirees may do so because of physical illnesses or less vigor, which may cause earlier death; then, too, the loss of identity as a worker could be a factor producing apathy, rather than an inability to satisfy unacceptable impulses.)

Brill concluded that physical and mental abilities alone play only a partial role in the kind of career a man chooses, since sublimation is the key ingredient. Accordingly, vocational counseling based on abilities and interests is likely to be of little value, although Brill conceded that such counseling might be of temporary value for certain individuals whose personality organization is insufficient to permit them to sublimate their impulses effectively. In general, however, vocational counseling is ineffective, according to Brill, and the few attempts he made to advise patients about vocational matters invariably had undesirable outcomes. He concluded that psychoanalytic techniques would not, in passing, facilitate the selection of a satisfactory vocational choice. That is, when basic problems of psychopathology are resolved, issues in daily life—the selection of a mate or a vocation, for example—will proceed smoothly and without the need for outside consultation.

While not taking as extreme a position as Brill, other psychoanalytic writers have illustrated how psychopathology, viewed in psychoanalytic terms, may account for vocational problems. By the case method, Bell (1960) illustrates the manner in which irrational vocational choices may persist in the service of ego integrity. Forer (1953), in depicting the role that personality variables play in vocational selection, chose to stress the importance unconscious motivation has in the selection of a career in relation to libidinal needs. Drasgow (1957) reported the results of a survey involving the reasons people had for selecting the vocation they chose. His results indicated that nearly every person in his very large sample expressed more than one reason for their choice. Such findings, he concludes, suggest that Freud's principle of overdetermination operates in vocational choice in that no one factor alone influences a career decision; it is the interaction of many factors.

Writing from the point of view that the pleasure and reality principles are not sufficient to account for much of human behavior, Hendrick (1943) proposed a "work principle." In contrast to the behaviors derived from the reality principle, presumably based on libidinal energy, those dependent on the work principle are based on the instinct to master one's environment. The "mastery instinct" in its turn has a biological foundation which is a function of one's attempt to control or change some portion of the environment through the combined use of intellectual and neurological processes. The mastery instinct requires an individual to integrate behavior and develop skill in performing certain tasks. Thus, Hendrick concludes, work pleasure represents gratification of the mastery instinct. Work satisfaction, then, is clearly an ego function since it is not sublimated sexual pleasure.

Several writers have tried to demonstrate how some aspects of career development can be explained in terms of psychoanalytic theory. Using case studies, Galinsky and Fast (1966) attempted to show how the identity problems often seen in young people may frequently be defined in terms of difficulty with vocational decision-making and vocational indecision. In a similar way, Malnig (1967) has developed a psychoanalytic interpretation of the failure to achieve well in school and work; this explanation postulates the notion that competition with one's father, coupled with the possibility that one's achievements might surpass those of the father, is frightening to some people, since parental reprisal might result. Neff (1968) has written a major study of vocational development and behavior with a distinctive psychoanalytic flavor. In his work, Neff describes how psychoanalytically oriented writers have logically shown how adult behavior, including work behavior, is a function of early experience. According to Neff, psychoanalytic viewpoints regarding work have in common a strong emphasis on the role instincts play in motivating behavior, a belief that adult difficulties with work are primarily the result of early shaping of affective processes through the vehicle of early parent-child interaction (a statement reminiscent of Roe), and an underemphasis of the role that culture plays in individual development.

The interests of the work and the reality principles often overlap despite the fact that the reality principle is libido-based while the work principle is based on the mastery instinct. During adolescence, the satisfactions derived from work are more dependent on libidinal energy, whereas during maturity, work mastery (satisfaction of the mastery instinct) is more important as a source of gratification. In terms of human development adolescence is a time when attention centers on sexual growth, whereas at maturity, with sexual needs reduced and competency demonstrated, growth and accomplishment offer a primary source of gratification. Vocational success serves as a likely vehicle for the demonstration of mastery.

The very important psychoanalytic concept of identification also receives emphasis in the vocational choice process. Many writers and a number of investigations have attempted to isolate important ingredients in the process of identification that have relevance for vocational choice. Such questions as whom the individual identifies with assume much significance when assessing the impact of identification on vocational choice. Sommers (1956) analyzed the histories of three therapy cases with respect to the role that conflict in identification assumed in their vocational choices. The cases Sommers reports are so well developed that they deserve some elaboration here. In the first case, a woman suffering from a postpartum depression was shown to be in conflict about her identification with her despised and feared mother. As a child, in response to shame over her economic poverty and to accommodate her feelings toward her overcontrolling mother, the patient developed the technique of high academic accomplishment as a means of trying to reduce her self-hatred. Consequently, she habitually took a logical and intellectual approach to problem solving of all sorts and eventually selected mathematics as a career. After her marriage and the birth of a child, she found her logical approach to be ineffective in resolving her feelings toward her baby. Her anxiety could not be explained intellectually. In the course of therapy, the patient became aware of her similarity to her mother and developed a more positive attitude toward her feminine attributes. She was more able to accept the role of mother and needed less to live the role of mathematician, which had served to masculinize her life. In this case, a career was chosen as a rejection of the feminine role and as a means of facilitating a detachment from the emotional demands of life, both responses which developed from the patient's ambivalence toward the female model available to her for identification during her childhood and adolescent years.

A second case concerned a Japanese-American youth who rejected the Oriental values of his father. As a consequence, the youth came into conflict with his father, adopting rebellious attitudes toward him. Guilt feelings about the rebellion and consequent self-punishment resulted in depression, suicidal tendencies, fear of insanity, sleeplessness, and ulcers. His background at home had been heavily permeated with Oriental culture. He spoke Japanese and his father practiced Buddhism. In his rebellion against his father and Oriental beliefs and customs, the patient rejected his father's wish that he become an engineer (like the father) and instead became an English teacher. The goal of the treatment seemed to be to help the patient to realize his similarities to his father and to accept the ambivalent feelings about these similarities, which had partly caused his rebellion. He was eventually able to continue his professional work in English but without the rebellious and spiteful component toward his father.

The third case is perhaps most striking of all. A young man was seeking relief from symptoms of insomnia, irritability, and tension. Though the patient's current occupation was that of policeman, the therapist was impressed by his timidity and shyness. The patient revealed that his experiences on the police force had made him doubt whether he was aggressive enough to succeed as a policeman. His occupational history included varied jobs in which he was consistently ineffective. He had been unsuccessful as an insurance salesman, a truck driver, a hospital attendant, and a laborer. He concluded that he had never been properly fit for any job he held and, furthermore, he had no idea about what he would like to do.

Interviews with the man revealed that he had been raised by his grandparents. After his prostitute mother died, his bad-tempered father could not handle the responsibility of the child and turned him over to the grandparents. When he misbehaved during childhood he was told he would turn out like his father. The threat was made so frequently that the patient eventually believed the prediction himself. A series of unfortunate experiences in life further convinced him of his unworthiness, and he began to believe more firmly than ever that he was destined to become like his father, to be bad-tempered, aggressive, and "crazy." In all his anxiety and tension was the germ of a fear of homosexuality, the impulses of which his superego would not permit him to accept. Becoming a policeman was the culmination of his efforts to fight off his homosexual fears and to reassure himself of his courage and masculinity. A policeman is a masterful, virile being, and in the act of becoming a policeman himself, the patient denied his homosexual fears. Although the case had an undesirable end, it does illustrate how one man desperately tried to cope with unconscious fears acquired by identifying with a psychopathic father by means of an occupational choice.

The three cases summarized by Sommers give some suggestion of the subtle ways that personality can be woven into occupational events within the psychoanalytic approach to behavior. They also illustrate the complexity of vocational choice within such a framework, point out one way in which such choices can go awry, and suggest some steps that might be taken to correct difficulties in vocational life which are a reflection of basic personality disturbances and which exacerbate the disturbances at the same time that they are symptoms. Oberndorf (1951) suggests another example of the role that work may play in psychopathology. Work, requiring deprivation in the form of delayed gratification, stands in marked contrast to play, which permits prompt gratification of "autoerotic" instincts. In psychopathology, then, one might see "laziness" as the prolongation of infantile behaviors or overwork as an attempt to control infantile libidinal wishes through denial.

The Bordin, Nachmann, Segal Framework for Vocational Development

The most ambitious scheme for defining the process of career development entirely within the psychoanalytic framework and with the appropriate language was proposed by Bordin, Nachmann, and Segal (1963). These three investigators tried to develop the framework of a system based on a few occupations to illustrate the generalizations and the general methods that might be developed for a wide variety of occupations. The three occupations used to illustrate the system were accounting, social work, and plumbing. A number of psychic dimensions or body zones with potential for gratification were assessed for their degree of involvement in each of the three occupations. For example, under the *dimensions* of nurturance were classified "feeding" and "fostering." Only social workers were involved to any extent in feeding, and since they frequently distribute food to their clientele, social workers get a high rating on "feeding" (three on a one-to-three scale). Accountants and plumbers, not involved in feeding their clientele at all, get zero on the "feeding" subdivision of the Nurturance dimension. The *objects* toward which the social workers' feeding activities are directed are the "needs of the clients"; the *Sexual Mode* is feminine, and the social workers' typical defense mechanism is reaction formation. The next subdivision of the Nurturance dimension is "fostering," which the accountants do to some extent (worth a score of one on the involvement scale) in financially advising their clientele, and the social workers do to a considerable degree (earning a rating of three) in encouraging and protecting their clients. The objects fostered by the accountants are the client's financial affairs, and by the social workers, the client's growth and health. The accountants' activity is in a masculine Sexual Mode, the social workers' in a feminine one. The preferred way of handling affect for the accountants is to experience it, while the social workers either experience it or engage in reaction formation.

In the Genital dimension there are subdivisions of Erection, Penetration, Impregnation, and Producing. Only the plumbers have any degree of involvement in the Erection subdivision, and that is only to a slight degree with respect to the use of their hands and tools (mode) for fixing faucets and fixtures (objects). The Sexual Mode is masculine and the typical defense is isolation. In Penetration, again, the plumbers, by virtue of their reaming and coupling (mode) of pipes and joints (objects), are slightly involved; the Sexual Mode is again masculine and the defense is isolation. Impregnation involves only the social workers and then only slightly. The mode is through the prevention or encouragement of family planning (object). It is feminine and the usual defenses are isolation and/or reaction formation. Producing, too, involves only the social workers, with their giving or withholding (mode) of babies for adoption (object); the Sexual Mode is again feminine and the defense is isolation.

If the system is elaborated to extend to a wide variety of occupations, an individual can more accurately identify the significance of a particular area of impulse gratification for a given occupation and the likelihood of satisfying such impulses within that field. Furthermore, inferences may be drawn concerning the sex mode of the field, the occupation's potential for reducing anxiety, and the typical defenses available in the occupational setting.

The analytic conceptualization of career choice emphasizes the techniques of impulse gratification and anxiety reduction which a field offers rather than the interests and abilities a career requires. Assuming, then, that a counselor should wish to base vocational counseling on this framework, a trait-factor approach would be used, but client modes of impulse gratification, psychosexual development, and anxiety level would take the place of interests and abilities. The counselor would try to find the occupation which offered the maximum potential for fitting the client's psychological style. Presumably, psychoanalytic interview methods would underlie the assessment of the individual.

Summary

We have seen that a number of psychoanalytic concepts have implications for vocational psychology and that a few attempts have been made to apply these concepts directly to career development. Generally speaking, the attempts employ the usual analytic methods of the assessment of individuals, such as interviews aimed at assessing the status of psychosexual development and patients' sources of impulse gratification. Career choice is typically construed as a by-product of personality development and consequently is not considered to be worth attention in and of itself. Career development deserves attention only because unusual difficulty in career choice is a symptom of more basic psychological disturbance, or because the choice process itself represents the general status of the individual's psychological development. Aptitudes and interests are of minimal importance in vocational selection (though such writers as Brill give a nod in the direction of aptitudes when they suggest that a man may become a surgeon or a butcher in order to satisfy sadistic impulses, depending upon his abilities, the state of his psychosexual development, and his source of impulse gratification).

Some particular aspects of psychoanalytic theory are more relevant to vocational choice and have been given more attention. For example, the process of identification is a very strong factor in determining vocational behavior, and it is important to know with whom the individual identifies, to what extent, and whether there are conflicts in the individual with respect to the person with whom he or she identified. Another factor of significance in vocational development is ego strength, in terms of the role ego plays in influencing the choice of field, persistence in the choice, and the degree to which it is successfully implemented.

As far as describing the process of vocational development in the normally developing individual, the analytic approach is not detailed. If a person is developing normally in general, presumably vocational life will also proceed according to schedule. If psychological development is not healthy, then one can expect to see some effects of the difficulties in work life. Treatment would presumably follow the general analytic method (or one of the derivatives) and would not focus on the assumption that once the developmental pattern is corrected, vocational life would automatically fall into line. Of course, probably no analyst would treat an individual primarily complaining of vocational difficulty, nor is it likely that a person would seek an analyst for such difficulties alone.

RESEARCH

General Personality Development and Vocational Choice

Several attempts to test hypotheses about vocational choice derived from psychoanalytic theory have been made in the general context of the Bordin, Nachmann, and Segal framework. Most of the research studies antedate the actual publication of the proposal. One of the first was an ingenious study by Segal (1961) in which students of creative writing and accounting were compared with respect to personality development. Several hypotheses about differences in the personality development of writers and accountants were derived from the general principles of psychoanalytic theory. Segal's study was based on the presumption that the personality development of accountants and creative writers differs, that each group has chosen its occupation on the basis of different stereotypes embodied in the careers they prefer, and that the writers' and accountants' choices, based on these occupational stereotypes, are consistent with the developmental history of their personality up to the time of their choice.

As a child, the accountant quickly learns that parental approval may be gained by means of conformity to parental wishes. Conformity to parental demands in exchange for approval is epitomized by the toilet-training period of child development. During this period the child learns to control one set of impulses in return for parental praise and love. It is in exchanges such as these that the superego of the accountant develops and thrives. The child's identification with parents becomes strong, thus serving to reduce the child's fear of the loss of parental love. As a result, a typical compulsive pattern develops, bolstering the child's defense against the anxiety of loss of parental esteem. The compulsive mechanisms to be seen are isolation, reaction formation, and intellectualization. Eventually the child, now growing toward adulthood, generalizes these attitudes from parents to all authority figures. When the necessity for vocational decision-making occurs, in view of the need to conform in exchange for the approval of authority, and the use of compulsive behaviors practical in maintaining conforming behavior, it is natural to select accounting as a career. The stereotype of accounting suggests that the career offers clear and obvious guidelines to behavior.

The background of the creative writer, of course, is very different. As a child the writer learns to rebel rather than conform to the demands of parental authority. The resulting parentally induced frustrations cause the child to identify less with parents. Consequently, the child develops a weaker superego and less acceptance of social norms. As the individual ages attempts are made to resolve the poorly defined identity and to change the social order; given the appropriate abilities, a writing career is a natural way to implement such personality needs. The defenses such a person would erect are likely to be projection, repression, and denial.

Basing his work on this theory, Segal developed several specific hypotheses about personality and behavior, which he tested. His subjects were 15 advanced undergraduate accounting students and 15 advanced and successful creative writing students. Care was taken not to confound the two groups by assuring that SVIB literary scores of accountants were not high, and similarly, that the SVIB accounting scores of creative writers were not high. Furthermore, the general background of each group of subjects was similar, that is, their ages, intellectual levels, and so on were similar. They were administered the Rorschach Inkblot Test and the Bender-Gestalt and were required to write a one-page vocational autobiography.

First, Segal predicted that the general level of adjustment of the two groups would not be different, and the results bore him out. No differences in general adjustment were found. On the basis of his formulations about personality development, Segal then predicted that the accountants would accept social norms to a greater degree than the writers and also that the accountants would attempt to control their emotions more than the writers. On the other hand, the writers would be more sensitive to emotional situations than the accountants. The results concerning this prediction are mixed. On the basis of the observation that accountants chose their career at an earlier age than the writers and that their Rorschach protocols reflected less spontaneity than those of the writers, Segel inferred that the accountants are more concerned with social norms than the writers, who chose careers later than the accountants and whose Rorschach responses suggest concern with "integrating and theorizing" and "less concern with social expectation." The strength of the findings in support of the hypothesis is reduced by the finding that some Rorschach responses that should have differentiated the two groups did not; in fact, no Rorschach differences were found between the groups in the number of popular responses and the percentage of animal response. Differences in age at the time of vocational choice can also be explained in other terms than sensitivity to social expectations. For example, accounting is a more visible occupation than writing, which is likely to result in an earlier age of choice. The Rorschach indicated that the accountants are more emotionally controlled than the writers and the writers more sensitive than the accountants, but the Bender-Gestalt did not support that expectation.

Segal made several predictions about other behavioral differences between writers and accountants. He predicted that accountants would have more compulsive defenses than writers, that writers would show more hostile responses on the tests than accountants, that writers would be able to tolerate ambiguity better than accountants, that the writers would be more skillful in handling complex emotional situations than the accountants, and that the test protocols of the accountants would reflect a rigid, fearful identification while that of the writers would reflect an attempt to "complete multiple identifications." With reference to these hypotheses, the Rorschach results indicated that the writers were more hostile than the accountants and handled emotional and ambiguous situations more adequately than the accountants. Also, there was some evidence for the notion that accountants have a rigid, fearful identification. This was inferred from the autobiographies, which revealed that the most significant occupational influence was some adult figure. It had been expected that the writers would have had a larger number of different occupational choices than the accountants as a reflection of their attempts to implement their "multiple identifications." However, no such differences were found; probably, Segal suggests, because the vacillation of career choice throughout the adolescent population in general obscured the differences between accountants and writers.

Segal concluded that the results in general were consistent with the psychoanalytic model of vocational choice he devised. However, some questions can be raised about the data from which Segal drew his inferences and even about some of the inferences themselves. As mentioned earlier, the assumption that the degree of social concern of an individual is reflected in the age at the time of career choice seems questionable. Using the Rorschach to validate hypotheses about personality development is also questionable, with respect to the reliability and validity of the instrument in such research as well as with regard to the pathological basis of the Rorschach as opposed to the relatively normal process of choosing a vocation. Using students for the sample was undoubtedly convenient, but being a student is a career in itself in some respects, and the strength of the results probably would have been increased had practicing accountants and writers been used as a sample. This last criticism, however, suggests that what differences Segal was able to find between writing and accounting students were minimal. Finally, the very basic question of why people who eventually become accountants should, as children, strive to please their parents while the writers rebel is never really resolved, or even raised.

In another study, Segal and Szabo (1964) retested the hypothesis that accounting students have a rigid and fearful identification and that writing students, in contrast, attempt to complete multiple identifications in their professional choice. Again, 15 students in accounting and 15 creative writing students were used as subjects. They were required to take a Sentence Completion Test which included 16 items particularly relevant to the hypothesis being tested. It was predicted that accounting students would have more positive attitudes toward their parents in contrast to the negative attitudes held by the creative writing students. It was also predicted that accounting students would express more favorable attitudes toward people in general than would the creative writing students. The responses to the 16 relevant completion items supported both predictions. This finding has a more valid behavioral base than Rorschach data, but is also fairly distant from psychoanalytic theory and the basic hypothesis about the differences between the identifications of accounting and creative writing students.

Another investigator (White, 1963) studied the behavior of clerical bank personnel with reference to Segal's general hypothesis that analytic principles of personality are related to vocational choice. Studying three groups of subjects—two groups of experienced clerical personnel in banks and a control group of job applicants at banks (apparently not necessarily for clerical jobs)—White asked two questions: "What would you most like to be if you were not a human being? Why?" and "What would you least like to be if you were not a human being? Why?" The results indicated that the experienced bank clerical workers overwhelmingly disliked the idea of things that were "dirty, sloppy, repulsive, slimy, infectious, and filthy," whereas the control group chose objects on a dimension not necessarily relevant to cleanliness. White concluded that the cleanliness attribute was highly important to clerical workers, a finding consistent with the psychoanalytically based idea that bank clerks are compulsive.

In another study of the relationship between personality and career based on analytic theory, Weinstein (1953) predicted that lawyers, engineers, and social workers would differ in a systematic manner in oral and anal characteristics. He hypothesized that engineers are more anally retentive than lawyers and social workers, that lawyers are more orally aggressive than engineers and social workers, that social workers are more orally receptive than engineers and lawyers, and that lawyers and engineers are more anally expulsive than social workers. Using the Q-technique, the subjects were required to make judgments on 40 anal items and 40 oral items as to the relevance of their ideal self and of their actual self. The items were based on Weinstein's (1953) classification of descriptions of behavior in the psychological literature. The subjects were 20 law students, 20 social work students, and 20 senior engineering students; the samples were not matched but were heterogeneous with respect to age and socioeconomic background.

Weinstein concluded from the Q-sorts that most of his expectations about the personality characteristics under study were supported. He inferred that anal and oral traits are motivating factors in career selection, though no evidence was presented to show how or under what circumstances these traits were developed. Other explanations for the differences in Q-sorts of engineers, lawyers, and social workers might be proposed which would not be invalidated by the results of his study.

Reasoning that because various occupations require different work activities offering diverse potential for needs and satisfactions and that childhood experiences influence the development of needs, Nachmann (1960), using an analytic framework, assessed the question of personality differences between lawyers, dentists, and social workers. One aspect of behavior that should in particular differentiate these three occupational groups is their attitude toward aggressive behavior. In their work lawyers must be verbally aggressive, whereas social workers are not permitted to express their hostility and aggression in their jobs. Dentists, on the other hand, are very aggressive physically in the grinding, drilling, cutting, and inflicting of pain that is inherent in their work. The relationship of these three professionals to privacy is another differentiating feature. Lawyers are permitted a "privileged curiosity" into certain aspects of their clients' lives. The social worker, even more than the lawyer, is allowed unlimited access to the most private parts of a client's life, but at the price of passivity. The dentist is permitted to peer into the mouth, ordinarily a private segment of the body. Such are examples of occupational differences, in analytical terms, that led Nachmann to expect significant differences between the childhood experiences of the three occupational groups.

A number of hypotheses about early experiences were tested by means of data obtained through interviews with 20 graduate students representing each of the three occupations. Most of the hypotheses were supported. Nachmann found aggressive impulses were more accepted in the families of lawyers and social workers and repressed in the families of dentists. She also discovered that in the families of lawyers and dentists the fathers were more dominant and masculine and the discipline more masculine, fairness being emphasized in the lawyers' families and obedience to authority in the dentists'. This was in contrast to the families of social workers, in which the mother was stronger and more dominant, the father either weak or absent, and the discipline less masculine. The fathers of lawyers were more remote physically and emotionally than the fathers of dentists, and a strong male figure maintained more importance in the childhood of lawyers than in that of either dentists or social workers. The home atmosphere of lawyers was warmer and stimulated preschool verbal skills, curiosity, and intellectual development. This was in sharp contrast to the home atmosphere of dentists, in which propriety and conventionality were most dominant and warmth least dominant, preschool verbal skills, intellectual development, and curiosity least encouraged, and physical mastery more rewarded than in the families of lawyers or social workers. The early experiences of social workers included a severe traumatic deprivation prior to age two and emphasis on concern for the feelings and suffering of others; lawyers experienced a less severe trauma at a later age and little emphasis on concern for others, while dentists had no trauma, little emphasis on concern for others, and experienced an event focusing attention on the inside of their bodies, which lawyers and social workers did not. The only hypothesis that was not supported—that sexual curiosity was not satisfied in any group—was most rebuffed in the case of the dentists; this question may have been confounded by the fact that few people of the generation studied had adequate sexual education. From these results, it is evident that Nachmann's findings are impressive support for the utility of psychoanalytic concepts in explaining the personality differences through childhood experiences of at least the three occupational groups she studied. Nevertheless, as with all retrospective studies, the answers of the subjects might have been influenced more by the current events of their lives than by the childhood events influencing current behavior.

Identification

Identification is an important psychoanalytic concept and is consequently important to analytically based vocational choice theory. Crites (1962) has combined the analytic and vocational streams of thought in a recent study which investigated the relationship between occupational interest development and parental identification. Reasoning that identification results in the embodiment of one individual's values and attitudes in another, Crites hypothesized that the degree of parental identification will be reflected in the interest patterns of the offspring. Furthermore, the sex of the parent predominantly identified with should be reflected in the student's interest profile. For a mixed-sex identification, Crites suggests that careers in social work, for example, provide suitable outlets since social work embodies both masculine and feminine stereotyped attributes. Finally, a combination of both the sex of the parent and the degree of identification should produce the particular interest pattern, which will reflect the relevant interaction of stereotyped masculine-feminine interest for that individual.

Using as subjects 350 males, further divided into three groups (100 vocational-educational clients at a university counseling center, 100 more vocational-educational clients as a replication group, and 150 nonclients as a generalization group), Crites assessed the kind, degree, and pattern of parental identification by means of the subjects' responses to semantic differential ratings of "self," "father," and "mother" on nine scales. The scales represented the potency, activity, and evaluative dimensions of meaning. Interest patterns were analyzed by Stephenson's (1961) pattern analysis technique as applied to the Strong Vocational Interest Blank (1943).

The results indicated that the degree of identification with fathers is correlated with the interest pattern on the SVIB, but not the degree of identification with mothers. Sons identifying strongly with their fathers scored high in business detail, sons with slight father identification had high interest scores in the literary area, while sons moderately identifying with their fathers scored high in groups including physical and social sciences. Interestingly, it was observed that as long as some identification with parents existed, predictable interest patterns emerged. Thus, males with male identifications had interests in the business detail area and males with mixed identifications had interests in technical and verbal areas. The findings relevant to the third hypothesis are also as expected: patterns of interests were consistent with the degree and kind of parental identification.

Steimel and Suziedelis (1963) tested the hypothesis that the predominance of perceived influence of one parent will be related to Strong Vocational Interest Blank scores. The expectation was based on a model which suggests that the role of identification with parents in the development of interests is pronounced. They predicted that father-influenced male college students will have different interest patterns on the SVIB than will mother-influenced students. To test this prediction, they administered a perceived parental influence instrument to 198 college freshmen and sophomores and selected 84 subjects whose responses placed them at the extremes in terms of perceived parental influence. The SVIB scores (43 occupational scales and 3 nonoccupational scales) of both groups were compared. The father-influenced boys were significantly higher than the mother-influenced boys on a number of occupational scales and two nonoccupational scales (specifically, engineering, chemist, production manager, aviator, math-science teacher, forest service, YMCA director, personnel director, public administrator, senior CPA, accountant, interest maturity, and masculinity), while the mother-influenced boys were higher on the occupational scales for real estate salesman, advertising manager, and lawyer. While Steimel and Suziedelis did not predict directions in which differences would occur for specific scales, they observed that the differences that occurred were consistent with expected sex differences. Father-influenced boys scored higher on masculine occupations, and mother-influenced boys scored higher on more feminine careers.

Steimel and Suziedelis report several other interesting findings. The father-influenced subjects were more likely to select college majors in the exact sciences, while the mother-influenced subjects leaned toward the liberal arts. More of the fathers of father-influenced subjects were engaged in occupations at the professional level and they had more education than fathers in the mother-influenced group. Furthermore, the fathers of father-influenced subjects averaged almost two years more formal education than the mothers of those subjects, whereas the parents of mother-influenced subjects were about equal in their level of educational attainment.

An interesting question may be raised on the basis of these findings. Is father influence related to the status and respect accorded to fathers by their sons because of their professional and educational achievement, or do well-educated fathers assume a greater role in influencing their sons because of their greater sophistication? Though Steimel and Suziedelis could not answer this question from their data, they did demonstrate that the perception of parental influence is clearly related to vocational interests.

In a study based on Erikson's (1950) hypothesis that the mother in American culture transmits general cultural values to her son, Stewart (1959) tested the hypothesis that the SVIB scores of adolescent males are related to the degree of their identification with their mothers. Reasoning that individuals develop their values by observing respected individuals and that these values would be reflected in interest inventories, Stewart had 97 junior and senior high school boys perform a number of Q-sorts about their self-concept, their ideal self-concept, and their concept of what they thought their mothers would prefer them to be. Fifty-four mothers of the boys in the sample were available to perform Q-sorts on their concept of what their sons were like and how they would like them to be ideally. In addition to the Q-sorts, each student subject took the SVIB and answered a brief questionnaire pertinent to his vocational aspiration.

Stewart found that, in general, the boys were somewhat sensitive to their mothers' ideals for them and that this sensitivity resulted in some behavior pleasing to the mothers. The boys were aware of their mothers' values for them and either acted to please them, or found that their mothers' values were consistent with their own and hence, in implementing their own desires they were pleasing their mothers. Stewart also found that Interest Maturity scores on the SVIB were related to the degree to which boys accepted their mothers' ideal as their own. This, Stewart suggests, is because Interest Maturity is correlated with social sensitivity, which presumably boys learn from their mothers. The closer the identification with the mothers' values, the greater the acceptance of socially sensitive behaviors and the higher the Interest Maturity score.

Also consistent with Erikson's theory was the finding that the Masculine-Feminine (MF) scores on the SVIB were related to the boys' awareness of their mothers' ideal sons. In a finding inconsistent with the theory, however, Stewart found that the closer the boy's identification with his mother, the more likely he was to have an SVIB rejection pattern in a masculine area. Thus, boys who most strongly accepted their mothers' ideals for them seemed more likely to reject masculine occupations. In contrast to this finding is Erikson's expectation that the mother would transmit to her sons her masculine ideal, presumably based on her idealized and overdrawn recollections of her own father. Instead, Stewart's findings suggest she passes on her feminine attitudes.

Crites' (1962) and Stewart's (1959) findings are somewhat at variance, since Crites found that fathers were more influential as identification figures with vocational significance for their sons than were mothers, while Stewart found that mothers influenced their sons' choices by means of the identification process. Of course, Stewart did not study fathers in comparison to mothers, so perhaps the strength of the influence is relative, as Crites' findings suggest, or variable, as Steimel and Suziedelis' results indicate.

White (1959) also studied the relationship between the values of parents and their offspring, but she studied daughters rather than sons. She tested the hypothesis that parents transmit their female ideal to their daughter, by means of assessing the relationship between the vocational interests, self-concepts, and parental identification of college women. She required 81 freshman college women to perform Q-sorts of their self-concept, of their ideal self-concept, and their concept of what they thought their parents would like them to be. In addition, each daughter took the SVIB and provided some personal information. Thirty-four sets of parents were interviewed, and each set also made Q-sorts of their daughter as she is and as they would like her to be ideally. Thus, the design is the same as Stewart's (1959).

White found that the women's sorts were more like those of their mothers than their fathers on most of the self, ideal self, and parental ideal descriptions. Thus, it would seem that the women identify more with their mothers than with their fathers. In addition, high Femininity scores on the SVIB were found for women who showed more agreement between their self-concepts and ideal self-concepts, who had more agreement between their self- and parental ideal concepts, who showed congruence between their ideal and their parents' ideal, and whose parents were both alive (whether living together or not) as opposed to those with one parent deceased.

Hershenson (1965) extrapolated Erikson's concept of identity to the question of perception of self in an occupational role. Hershenson administered a questionnaire to 162 Harvard College juniors to measure the degree to which people feel their occupational choice reflects their abilities, interests, and values and to assess their view of the role a career plays in one's life. Among the observations was the finding that occupational prestige plays an important role for students holding an emergent or "other-directed" orientation.

In another aspect of the same study, Hershenson (1967) tested the hypothesis that the degree of adolescent identity achieved is positively related to the extent that an individual perceives him/herself as fitting into an anticipated occupational role. Hershenson also predicted that the sense of identity that is achieved by adolescents is positively related to the degree of enculturation and that the degree to which adolescents feel they fit into their anticipated occupational role is positively related to their degree of enculturation. Though the results supported the three hypotheses, the data were not clear enough to cause Hershenson to feel confident that the hypotheses were supported in the way Erikson's position would predict.

In another study of the identification process and vocational choice, Sostek (1963) found that girls making sex-stereotyped occupational choices identified more with their mothers than girls who chose masculine-stereotyped occupations. He also found that boys who chose "female-type" occupations identfied more with their mothers than did those boys who chose "masculine" occupations. Finally, he reports that males and females choosing "feminine" occupations identified more with their mothers than with their fathers, and that the males and females who chose "masculine" occupations identified more with their fathers than with their mothers. Of general significance is his finding that identification is facilitated by parental warmth, regardless of sex. Thus, a parent wishing to serve as a model for a child can increase the likelihood of succeeding by generating a warm, close parent-child relationship.

Tipton (1966) tested some aspects of the role of identification in occupational selection. He compared the frequency of having parents who are teachers for groups of education and noneducation majors. No differences in frequency were found. When both student groups were compared with respect to the degree of identification with a teacher by means of response to a rating scale, Tipton found that education majors exhibited stronger identification with the teacher model than noneducation majors. Malnig's (1967) hypothesis that some individuals might avoid competition directly with their parents, discussed earlier, is interesting to consider in the light of Tipton's failure to find offspring of teachers overrepresented in teacher-training programs.

Heilbrun (1969) computed an index of perceived similarity between offspring and their same-sex parent over 15 personality dimensions. Since the possible personality styles could be either "masculine" or "feminine," an individual could potentially identify with a "masculine" or "feminine" father or a "masculine" or "feminine" mother. The results, based on 47 male and 33 female college counseling center clients, indicated that sons' identification with their fathers is correlated with positive vocational interests, sons' identification with a masculine figure (either father or mother) is associated with career interest rejects, and daughters' identification with feminine models of either sex is associated with a high number of career rejects on the SVIB. Heilbrun concludes that identification with a "masculine" father enhances the crystallization of positive vocational interests and of rejects in sons, whereas identification with a "feminine" mother has the opposite effect. However, as is so often the situation, the results are less conclusive for females than for males.

In a similar type of study, Hollender (1972) observed the similarity between SVIB profiles of 31 college and 28 high school male students and those of their parents. Neither group of students showed many high correlations between sons and their parents on the SVIB, in contrast to the findings of many other studies.

The results of these studies seem to imply that identification with a parent or adult model is indirectly important in the vocational choice process, but no direct relationships have been demonstrated, and the findings of the studies are not entirely consistent with one another. Unfortunately, the measures of identification are not powerful, and they have nearly always been related to interest inventory scores rather than other behaviors such as vocational selection or attainment. Even statements of vocational preference might be more revealing in clarifying the relationship between identification and vocational choice than scores on interest inventories.

To further complicate the matter, most of the studies of parental identification and its effects on the career interests of children have been couched in terms of "masculine" and "feminine" sex stereotyped behaviors and careers. Research and thinking in recent years indicates less and less validity to the notion that such sex stereotyping is valid, raising further questions about both the relevance and the validity of much of the research that has been reported above.

Small (1953), exploring personality variables influential in vocational choice, proposed that certain aspects of career decisions are based on ego functioning. He hypothesized that a healthy ego, since it is in close contact with reality, will be able to delay gratification to a much greater extent than a weak ego, which is more distantly removed from reality. Since adjustment is partially a function of ego strength, and according to his reasoning, vocational choice is partly a function of ego strength, reality factors in vocational choice are related to ego functioning. Thus, he predicted that adolescent males who are well adjusted would express realistic first occupational preferences and unrealistic second preferences, while the reverse would hold for poorly adjusted boys.

To test this prediction, he studied the job preferences and reasons for their selection of 50 pairs of 15- to 19-year-old boys, matched on all significant background features except adjustment. The results supported the hypothesis; the choices of the better-adjusted boys reflected participation in their environments, while the choices of the maladjusted boys reflected detachment from their environments and a tendency to act out their impulses and to have feelings of self-deprecation. These findings led Small to conclude that vocational counseling is most effective with people who have strong egos because they are reality oriented, and that those with weak egos need psychotherapy before they can profit from vocational counseling or make realistic vocational plans. Small concluded with the provocative hypothesis that vocationally undecided people are unable to commit themselves vocationally because they have retentive fantasies and do not care to give up any of their career alternatives.

Very and Zannini (1969), testing the Adlerian hypothesis that birth order affects behavior, predicted that a significant number of beauticians would be second born because of the similarity between the personality attributes of the second born (i.e., easygoing, harmony-seeking, and casual, according to Adler) and those of the successful beautician. A significant number of the 210 beauticians Very and Zannini observed were, in fact, found to be second born.

A final study of relevance to the psychoanalytic point of view of vocational choice is Crites' (1960) investigation of the relationship between ego strength and vocational choice. In particular, he was concerned with the correlations between ego strength and occupational interest level and between ego strength and the degree to which interests are patterned. Crites assumed that a strong ego would result in a clearer pattern of vocational interests at a more professional level than would a weak ego. He also predicted that older students, having a stronger ego as a function of more advanced age, would have clearer interest patterns. Using the SVIB occupational level (OL) scale and the number of A and B+ scores on the SVIB as measures of level and patterning, respectively, and the ES scale of the MMPI as an ego strength measure (Barron, 1953), Crites tested his hypotheses on a sample of 100 male college students who had come to a college counseling center for educational-vocational counseling.

The results failed to support the hypothesis that higher occupational levels are related to strong egos, but the data did support the second hypothesis, that interest patterning is related to ego strength in older students but not in younger ones. Unfortunately for analytic theory, other conceptions of maturity might account for greater interest patterning in older adolescents than in younger ones, especially using the Strong Vocational Interest Blank, since the SVIB was developed using mature men as standardization groups. Older adolescents might have clearer interest patterns than younger ones simply because they are more like the criterion groups.

Crites made several suggestions for counseling students who have unpatterned interests. He proposed that vocational-educational counseling for such students be preceded by personal counseling which has as its goal the development of a more adequately functioning ego. To accomplish this task the interviews would apply procedures based on a combination of learning theory and psychoanalysis, similar to the suggestion of the Dollard and Miller formulation (1950).

Evaluation

Considering the general antagonism professionals holding the psychoanalytic point of view have toward vocational counseling, there have been a large number of attempts to test empirically hypotheses about vocational choice stemming from analytic thought. No investigators have attempted to integrate vocational behavior into analytic theory in a complete way; rather, attempts have been made to integrate analytic theory into vocational psychology. The concepts of ego strength, identification, and personality development in general have been especially scrutinized by researchers. Of these processes, ego strength seems to have been studied most carefully and with the greatest success, identification least carefully and with results of a contradictory nature, and personality development within the analytic framework studied too generally to allow it to acquire its potential use in counseling.

The research methods typically have involved the use of Q-sorts to describe some features of the subjects and/or their parents in combination with Strong Vocational Interest Blank patterns of scores. It seems likely that more meaningful results might have been obtained through the use of statements of vocational preference, vocational selection, and possibly vocational attainment rather than through the exclusive use of SVIB scores. The difficulties involved in requiring subjects to do large amounts of Q-sorting are rarely discussed, but it is likely that subjects become careless as they are doing the third sort of 75 or 100 items describing their behavior or someone else's evaluation of their behavior. While most of the investigators report positive findings in studies based on Q-sorts, consideration of the actual meaningfulness of the research tasks for the subjects must be taken in evaluating results of studies.

In nearly all the studies, with the possible exception of Crites' work, the size of the samples used was relatively small, in some cases as low as 15 subjects per group. While that in itself is no error and larger samples are often difficult to obtain, the generalizations to be drawn from such research are of necessity limited. Such limitations are serious since replication of research in vocational development is difficult to accomplish and consequently very unusual. Furthermore, the samples themselves are often not typical of groups of individuals with whom counselors are concerned. It is hard to generalize about mature populations from data based exclusively on student samples. At the same time, the student samples in many cases are not representative of any population outside the particular sample studied, not even other students. College students, especially advanced ones, are not similar to high school youths not planning to enter college.

STATUS

Implications for Counseling

The psychoanalytic view does not suggest any special techniques for vocational psychology other than those used in psychoanalysis in general. The view is presented that career choice is one of several important decisions individuals must make during their lifetime. The normally functioning individual is presumably capable of identifying important vocational factors which will lead to vocational decisions, and will be able to develop the resources to implement those decisions. Indeed, it will be recalled that one-half of Freud's definition of a well-ordered person is the ability to work effectively.

In the disordered person vocational choice may be disrupted along with other major behavioral responsibilities. For such unfortunate individuals the purely psychoanalytic position suggests no shortcuts for intensive analysis designed to identify the snag in development, unravel it, and accelerate the process to the point of maturity. Less orthodox psychologists of an analytic persuasion suggest that analytic concepts may be of use in understanding the motives and developmental history behind the choice of a career. The Bordin, Nachmann, Segal (1963) proposal, for example, might be useful as both an occupational information tool in identifying the potential for satisfying various motives in occupations and as a diagnostic device providing a framework for conducting interviews to appraise vocational suitability.

One proposal Crites offers (1962) is perhaps suggestive of the kind of potential analytic concepts have for vocational counseling. With reference to the question of ego strength and its relation to vocational choice problems, Crites questions the feasibility of trying to help a client develop an appropriate identification in two or three interview hours of vocational counseling. If ego strength is in fact a crucial variable in the development of inappropriate vocational behaviors, Crites' suggestion is that vocational counseling must devote its attention to the strengthening of the ego through the use of personal counseling methods rather than through emphasis on occupational information and the techniques of the trait-factor approach.

Crites talks about career counseling implications as psychodynamic approaches to career development (Crites, 1981). Since the work of Bordin applied best, Crites used that for his example. The diagnostic process for psychodynamically based career counseling breaks down into several categories. First, there are so-called synthetic difficulties, in which there is minimal pathology and conflict and in which the major problem has to do with difficulties in synthesizing choices or achieving cognitive clarity. Second, there are identity problems, in which there are unconscious or semiconscious difficulties in forming a workable self-concept. Third, there are problems called gratification conflicts which grow out of the view that occupations provide opportunities distinctive from each other for psychological gratification. Next are change orientation problems, which have to do with problems the client has with a particular field of work and the struggle to change that work to some other kind. Next are problems of overt pathology, which obviously will disrupt work function because of the symptoms of the pathology. Finally, there are two unclassifiable outcomes, one having to do with problems that involve motivational conflicts and the other having to do with problems that don't involve motivational conflicts.

Once having diagnosed the nature of the problem, the counseling process involves steps called exploration and contract setting, decisions of a critical nature, which include not only career decisions but also alternatives to counseling. Finally, the change process itself is involved, including both personality and career change. Distinctively in the psychoanalytic approach described by Crites, test interpretation involves the client actively in the selection and interpretation of the instruments. Occupational information is also used based on psychoanalytic interpretations of job functions as represented by the Bordin, Nachmann, and Segal (1963) formulation mentioned earlier.

The major strength of the psychoanalytic approach to vocational choice lies in its comprehensiveness and integration with respect to psychological theory in general. To offset this positive attribute, however, several negative ones exist.

First, since psychoanalytic theory essentially concerns psychopathology, the very normal process of vocational choice must be added to the theory as an afterthought, despite the emphasis that Freud placed on the role work plays in a satisfying life. Freud thought work was important, but he did not comment further. Such a limitation is analogous to the criticism made about the Ginzberg theory: the development of vocational choice concepts from a theory of psychopathology is similar to the development of a marital adjustment theory based only on data available on divorced couples.

A very serious limitation of analytically based conceptions of vocational choice is the limited role aptitudes play in psychoanalytic thinking. While it is highly possible that psychology has overemphasized the role of aptitude in vocational theory, it does not seem reasonable to ignore the feedback of experiences people use to guide them in their work selection. If one chooses to use the concept of career attainment as a criterion in career development theory, aptitude would necessarily play a highly important role.

A final problem in the analytical approach to vocational selection is the general failure of psychoanalytic theory to assume a parsimonious position with respect to explanations of behavior and the corollary of this, the difficulty of experimentally validating or refuting analytical concepts. Since the concepts are so intricate, experimental data are often consistent with them but at the same time can usually be explained by other constructs of a simpler and more direct nature.

To date, the analytical model has played only a minor role in vocational psychology, although some aspects of it are highly integrated into the practice of vocational psychology, much as the psychoanalytic method and constructs are intertwined with psychology (especially clinical psychology) in general. Some aspects of the analytical approach are appealing and enrich the understanding of vocational behavior, but others, especially those of more orthodox analysis, are difficult to apply to vocational counseling. It is likely that analytic theory will continue to exert a peripheral though strong impact on vocational psychology, but it does not seem likely that any new, rigorous, or productive formulations will result from the psychoanalytic quarter.

REFERENCES

Barron, F. An ego strength scale which predicts response to psychotherapy. *Journal of Consulting Psychology,* 1953, *17,* 327–333.

Bell, H. M. Ego-involvement in vocational decisions. *Personnel and Guidance Journal,* 1960, *38,* 732–736.

Bordin, E. S., Nachmann, B., and Segal S. J. An articulated framework for vocational development. *Journal of Counseling Psychology,* 1963, *10,* 107–116.

Brill, A. A. *Basic principles of psychoanalysis.* Garden City, N.Y.: Doubleday, 1949.

Crites, J. O. Ego strength in relation to vocational interest development. *Journal of Counseling Psychology,* 1960, *7,* 137–143.

Crites, J. O. Parental identification in relation to vocational interest development. *Journal of Educational Psychology,* 1962, *53,* 262–270.

Crites, J. O. *Career counseling.* New York: McGraw-Hill, 1981.

Dollard, J., and Miller, N. E. *Personality and psychotherapy.* New York: McGraw-Hill, 1950.

Drasgow, J. Occupational choice and Freud's overdeterminism. *Vocational Guidance Quarterly,* 1957, *6,* 67–68.

Erikson, E. *Childhood and society.* New York: Norton, 1950.

Forer, B. R. Personality factors in occupational choice. *Educational and Psychological Measurement,* 1953, *13,* 361–366.

Galinsky, M. D., and Fast, I. Vocational choices as a focus of the identity search. *Journal of Counseling Psychology,* 1966, *13,* 89–92.

Heilbrun, A. B., Jr. Parental identification and the patterning of vocational interests in college males and females. *Journal of Counseling Psychology,* 1969, *16,* 342–347.

Hendrick, I. Work and the pleasure principle. *Psychoanalytic Quarterly,* 1943, *12,* 311–329.

Hershenson, D. B. Some personal and social determinants of occupational role-taking in college students. *Journal of Counseling Psychology,* 1965, *12,* 206–208.

Hershenson, D. B. Sense of identity, occupational fit, and enculturation in adolescence. *Journal of Counseling Psychology,* 1967, *14,* 319–324.

Hollender, J. Differential parental influences on vocational interest development in adolescent males. *Journal of Vocational Behavior,* 1972, *2,* 67–76.

Jones, E. The significance of the sublimating process for education and re-education. In *Psychoanalysis,* New York: Wood, 1923.

Malnig, L. R. Fear of paternal competition: a factor in vocational choice. *Personnel and Guidance Journal,* 1967, *46,* 235–239.

Mowrer, O. H. *Learning theory and personality dynamics.* New York: Ronald, 1950.

Nachmann, B. Childhood experiences and vocational choice in law, dentistry, and social work. *Journal of Counseling Psychology,* 1960, *7,* 243–250.

Neff, W. S. *Work and human behavior.* New York: Atherton, 1968.

Oberndorf, C. P. *Psychopathology of work. Bulletin of the Menninger Clinic,* 1951, *15,* 77–84.

Roe, A. Early determinants of vocational choice. *Journal of Counseling Psychology,* 1957, *4,* 212–217.

Segal, S. A psychoanalytic analysis of personality factors in vocational choice. *Journal of Counseling Psychology,* 1961, *8,* 202–210.

Segal, S. J., and Szabo, R. Identification in two vocations: accountants and creative writers. *Personnel and Guidance Journal,* 1964, *43,* 252–255.

Small, L. Personality determinants of vocational choice. *Psychological Monographs,* 1953, *67,* No. 1 (Whole No. 351).

Sommers, V. S. Vocational choice as an expression of conflict in identification. *American Journal of Psychotherapy,* 1956, *10,* 520–535.

Sostek, A. B. The relation of identification and parent-child climate to occupational choice. Unpublished doctoral dissertation, Boston University, 1963.

Steimel, R. J., and Suziedelis, A. Perceived parental influence and inventoried interests. *Journal of Counseling Psychology,* 1963, *10,* 289–295.

Stephenson, R. R. A new pattern analysis technique for the SVIB. *Journal of Counseling Psychology,* 1961, *8,* 355–362.

Stewart, L. H. Mother-son identification and vocational interest. *Genetic Psychology Monographs,* 1959, *60,* 31–63.

Strong, E. K., Jr. *Vocational interests of men and women.* Stanford, Cal.: Stanford University Press, 1943.

Tipton, R. M. Vocational identification and academic achievement. *Journal of Counseling Psychology,* 1966, *13,* 425–430.

Very, P. S., and Zannini, J. Λ. Relation between birth order and being a beautician. *Journal of Applied Psychology,* 1969, *53,* 149–151.

Weinstein, M. S. Personality and vocational choice: a comparison of the self-conceptions and ideal self-conceptions of students in three professional schools. Unpublished doctoral dissertation, Western Reserve University, 1953.

White, B. J. The relationship of self-concept and parental identification to women's vocational interests. *Journal of Counseling Psychology,* 1959, *6,* 202–206.

White, J. C. Cleanliness and successful bank clerical personnel—a brief. *Journal of Counseling Psychology,* 1963, *10,* 192.

Zilboorg, G. The problem of constitution in psychopathology. *Psychoanalytic Quarterly,* 1934, *3,* 339–362.

CHAPTER THREE
PSYCHOLOGICAL NEEDS, VALUES, AND CAREERS

The concept of the psychological need has a long and distinguished history in psychology. Perhaps the most complex characterization of the operation of needs has been presented by Henry Murray (1938). Since Murray's theory has been elaborately described (Hall and Lindzey, 1957), there is no need for detailed explication here. Briefly, Murray proposed an extensive list of psychological needs involved in a wide variety of human functioning. These needs, in combination with environmental "press," permit the construction of hypotheses to explain individual behavior. Individuals are motivated to behave because of tension states. These may be reduced by need satisfaction. In time, the organism is assumed to associate tension reduction with particular objects and behaviors. When certain recognizable tensions are perceived, the individual knows because of these associations what behavior will reduce the tension and satisfy the motivating need. Thus, tension reduction comes under individual control through the identification of needs and relevant behavior. One group of investigators applied Murray's thinking to the study of motivation for a career in teaching (Stern, Masling, Denton, Henderson, and Levin, 1960).

A psychological needs conception, along with the idea of tension reduction through needs satisfaction, is in many ways ideally suited to explain numerous aspects of career selection and maintenance. Thus, it is not surprising that some years ago Darley and Hagenah (1955), reviewing the research concerning the relationships between vocational interests, occupational preferences and selections, and personality characteristics, concluded that interest patterns represent the various ways that individuals see of potentially meeting their personal needs in careers.

Hoppock (1957) expanded the needs approach to career development. He suggested a theory of occupational choice that was based mainly on the use of occupational information built upon personal needs. The rationale stemmed from the assumption that occupational activities are related to basic needs and that the adequacy of occupational choice improves as people are better able to identify their own needs and the potential need satisfaction offered by a particular occupation. Thus, Hoppock reasoned that "satisfactions can result from a job which meets our needs today, or from a job which promises to meet them in the future." According to the needs reduction approach to career development, a hungry person will take any job to obtain enough to eat. Once the need for food has been reduced, a new job which offers the potential of satisfying other physical and psychological needs will be sought. To the degree that one can find and enter jobs relevant to higher order needs, the more or less satisfied with work one will be.

A number of studies have taken an approach which has explored the role that psychological needs play in determining occupational decisions and membership. Suziedelis and Steimel (1963) compared inventoried needs measured by the Edwards Personal Preference Schedule with inventoried interests measured by the Strong Vocational Interest Blank, to test the hypothesis that certain needs are characteristically found in people who enter particular occupations. A sample of college freshmen and sophomores was tested with the EPPS and then subdivided so that for each of the Edwards needs a group of Ss earned high scores and another group low ones. The frequency of A and B+ scores on each of the SVIB occupational groups was tabulated for each group of subjects. These procedures allowed the identification of interest areas that are systematically related to the Edwards needs.

Some of the resulting correlations are intuitively reasonable. For example, high interest scores in the biological and physical sciences and literary occupations might well be expected to be related to achievement needs, as was indeed found to be the case. Order needs seemed to be negatively related to similarity of interests to those of men in social service and literary occupations. Curious, however, is the failure to find a relationship between order needs and business detail interests and the low correlation between affiliation needs and similarity of interests to those of men in business contact occupations

Though data such as those reported by Suziedelis and Steimel are interesting, little more is understood about personality and career as a result. The correlation between responses on two inventories seems to be too far removed from the real world of both personality and occupational interest to reflect meaningful behavior. At best, the results must be subject to highly cautious interpretation.

In another study of a similar kind, Bohn (1966) related needs inferred from responses to an adjective checklist to Holland personality types. In contrast to Suziedelis and Steimel's findings, some of the resulting matches do *not* seem intuitively correct. For example, the Realistic personality type was found to be high on abasement need and low on dominance and heterosexual needs. Other findings, however, are more in line with expectation: conventional people were high on achievement, order, affiliation, dominance, endurance, and defensiveness needs, and Enterprising subjects were high on achievement, exhibition, affiliation, dominance, and heterosexual needs.

Blum (1961) predicted that a positive relationship between desires for security and choices of highly secure occupations would be found. Blum also examined the relationship between personality (defined in terms of EPPS scores) and the background factors of Ss emphasizing security in their vocational choices. To accomplish these ends he administered the EPPS, a biographical information questionnaire, and a homemade security needs inventory to 513 Ss, which resulted in 346 usable protocols. Blum found that the Ss with the highest score on security desires chose occupations involving a secure setting such as civil service jobs or teaching, while avoiding relatively unstable but high payoff careers such as law.

Some unusual findings occurred, however. For example, business careers were highly sought by the security seekers. Do these latter choices reflect attempts to gain the security of large organizational membership? Security desires were significantly correlated with EPPS needs deference, order, succorance, abasement, and nurturance and negatively related to needs achievement, autonomy, dominance, and change. These correlations seem to be subject to the same criticism as those of the Suziedelis and Steimel (1963) study. That is, what do response-response correlations between two sets of inventory scores mean in a larger behavioral sense?

Dipboye and Anderson (1961) studied the relationship between occupational stereotypes and needs on the assumption that the stereotypes reflect, to some degree, projections of needs relevant to occupational membership. An instrument descriptive of fourteen needs based on EPPS items was devised and administered to male and female high school seniors with instructions to rate each of several occupations on the degree of the accuracy of the descriptions. The resulting stereotypes reflected cultural estimates of the occupations. For example, scientists were seen as having high needs for endurance, achievement, and change, while high school teachers were perceived as high on needs order and intraception. Boys saw engineers as high on achievement and order needs and physicians as high on nurturance, intraception, and achievement needs. Girls perceived nurses as having high nurturance, intraception, order, and endurance needs. The findings are suggestive about the nature of needs as related to occupational selection and membership. Some relevant data will be discussed later in this chapter, revealing needs scores of people in occupations such as nursing and engineering, at which time judgments can be made about the accuracy with which Dipboye and Anderson's subjects made their ratings.

Hall and Nougaim (1968) have studied needs and career development in the context of organizational characteristics. Their observations led them to conclude that the needs individuals exhibit in connection with their careers are not unchanging. Over a five-year period. Hall and Nougaim found that as managers advance, their affiliation, achievement, esteem, and self-actualization needs increase, and their safety needs decrease (these results are consistent with Maslow's theory). In another study, Bradshaw (1970) found similar results for professional men. These results indicate, though tentatively, that opportunities for higher order needs satisfaction in work increase as one moves up the vocational hierarchy.

Needs and Job Satisfaction

It seems reasonable to expect, if one postulates needs as a factor in occupational selection, that needs satisfaction is directly related to job satisfaction. Schaffer (1953) devised a questionnaire designed to measure the strength of each of 12 needs, the degree to which each need is being satisfied in one's job, and overall job satisfaction and administered it to 113 subjects in various industries, department stores, and government agencies. Though the questionnaire was distributed through administrators in those agencies, participation was voluntary, and the questionnaire was completed during the subject's personal time. As a result, only 32 of the 113 questionnaires were completed and returned, raising serious questions about the generality of the findings. Generally, the strongest needs expressed were for creativity and challenge, followed by needs for mastery, achievement, and social welfare. The lowest needs were socioeconomic rewards and the expression of dependency. Examination of the correlations between an individual's needs and the degree to which they are satisfied in his job revealed significant relationships for the three highest needs. More important, the correlation of 0.58 between the mean satisfaction of the subjects' two strongest needs in the job and overall job satisfaction was highly significant.

A study similar in objective was conducted by Walsh (1959). He tested the hypothesis that subjects like or dislike job duties which are consistent or inconsistent, respectively, with their needs. To test the hypothesis he devised a Job Description Questionnaire (JDQ) containing 24 job descriptions with 8 duties each to which Ss were to respond in terms of the appeal the duties had for them. In addition, the Ss, 96 college males in an introductory psychology course, took the EPPS and were asked to recommend two features of each job which should be emphasized and two which should be deemphasized in a recruiting campaign. Correlations were then computed between the EPPS scores and the needs reflected in the duties the Ss selected to be emphasized or deemphasized. Of the 24 correlations that were computed, 17 are significant, lending considerable support to Walsh's hypothesis.

Wolf (1970) has gone so far as to propose a "theory" of job motivation on the basis of the Herzberg, Mausner, and Snyderman (1959) and Maslow (1954) theories combined. According to Wolf, the level of need gratification as defined by Maslow is important to satisfaction-dissatisfaction; the *content* of the activity is involved in the gratification of active needs by means of job-related behaviors, but *context* factors are not so involved.

Orpen and Pinshaw (1975) found results confirming the relationship of job satisfaction to perceived need fulfillment, based on the responses of 100 insurance clerks who were given Porter's Need Fulfillment Questionnaire, Halpern's Job Satisfaction Scale, and an overall 7-point rating scale to measure job satisfaction.

Summary and Evaluation

Knowledge of an individual's psychological needs has been presumed to allow the prediction of his or her desire to enter certain careers which especially satisfy those needs. If the needs are identified with sufficient accuracy and the needs satisfaction potential of the occupation is great enough, contentment with the occupational decision will result. The research concerning the needs satisfaction hypothesis of career choice generally substantiates the idea that different kinds of needs satisfaction potential are perceived in occupations. However, the research leans very heavily on paper-and-pencil personality and interest inventories, which introduces some serious limitations in the degree of confidence with which the hypothesis can be viewed. In order truly to function as a theory, relationships among needs and career decision, behavior, and satisfaction must be identified.

Occupational Values and Careers

Human beings postulate a variety of concepts around which to orient their lives. Some operate within the context of these orientations explicitly, others implicitly, but most people adhere to some anchor points in maintaining the directions of their lives. These anchor points, which typically include religious beliefs, the place of material goods in life, and how interpersonal relations should be conducted, have been formalized by a number of psychologists. Most notably, the ideal "types of men," described by Spranger (1928), have served to combine several fundamental views toward living into one representation.

It has seemed reasonable enough to many people to suppose that these personal values underlie occupational choice and attainment. Surely, it has been reasoned that a person whose main value in life is spiritual will choose different careers and behave differently in them than another whose primary value is economic. Complicating the issue is the fact that values are least stable during the post high school years when many crucial decisions are being made about careers.

It is likely that personal values play a major role in determining human behavior. As a person matures, culture and perceptions of it influence values. These values, in turn, will affect interactions with others; hopes and interests will influence choice of a mate and play a large role in determining occupational choice and attainment. Implicit in the above is the notion that values are not static; they change as they develop. Consequently, the study of the behavioral correlates of values and the forces that shape them, both during early years and maturity, are important in the study of career development.

Some writers have speculated about the role that values and their satisfaction play in job satisfaction. Locke (1970) has presented a formulation of job satisfaction that relates it to work outcomes in terms of the degree to which these outcomes permit the individual to attain and satisfy important job values. In other words, Locke hypothesizes that performance is related to (or "causes") job satisfaction if good performance is seen as significantly involved in the individual's reaching important job values. Mobley and Locke (1970) further examined the relationship between values and job satisfaction-dissatisfaction, emphasizing important values and trying to exclude those which are unimportant. The results of Mobley and Locke's experiment supported the hypothesis. These results led Mobley and Locke to point out that one major difficulty in studying the impact of values on job satisfaction lies in the way the question is asked; an individual asked what is wrong with a job in terms of satisfaction will tell us, but possibly ignore important values that are currently being satisfied. Thus, it is necessary to know what people value highly, how these values operate in their jobs, and how well the values are being satisfied in work in order to establish clearly the relationship between values and job satisfaction.

College Student Occupational Values

An extensive study of occupational values was reported by Rosenberg (1957). Using several thousand Cornell University students enrolled during the early 1950s as his basic sample, he asked questions about the fundamental reasons for their selection of an educational objective. He found that four basic values were expressed: working with people in a helping manner, earning large amounts of money, acquiring social status and prestige, and having the opportunity to be creative and use special talents. These values seemed to be continuous, ranging from the desire to express creativity and originality on one end of the scale to the desire for a stable and secure future on the other.

Rosenberg found that the expression of values by students in different fields varied systematically. For example, architecture, journalism, drama, and art students valued self-expression more than other groups, while students in sales fields, hotel and food studies, real estate, and finance valued self-expression the least. Social work majors, premedical students, and education majors were highest in the desire to help and work with people, while engineering, natural science, and agriculture students were lowest in this value. The real estate, finance, hotel and food, and sales students scored highest on extrinsic reward values, while the social work, teaching, and natural science students scored lowest on this scale.

Rosenberg studied the reliability of occupational values over time. As might be expected, he found that a number of changes in both values and occupational preferences occurred over a two-year period. Where subjects' values and occupational choices changed, the changes generally reduced the disparity between choices and values.

Astin and Nichols (1964) mailed questionnaires concerning life goals to National Merit finalists and Commendation winners and received 5495 usable responses in return (3830 males and 1665 females). A factor analysis of the responses revealed seven factors, subsequently entitled self-esteem, personal comfort, artistic motivation, scholarship, science-technology, prestige, and altruism. With the exception of prospective clergymen, who scored high only on altruistic values, most of the students, regardless of their orientation, were high on altruistic and personal comfort factors. This finding does little to clarify occupational motivation and very likely reflects the tenor of the times during which the study was conducted (the mid-1960s), in the same way that the Rosenberg data reflected their times. The instability of values, in combination with the fact that the Astin and Nichols sample consists of unusually talented students, imposes serious limitations on the generalizations to be drawn from the Astin and Nichols study.

Another study (Miller, 1956), oriented toward objectives similar to the Astin and Nichols survey, compared the vocational values of 60 students classified in each of three vocational categories: those with no vocational choice, those with a tentative choice, and those with a definite choice. The results indicated that the highest single value held by the "no choice" group was security, whereas among the subjects with a definite choice career satisfaction was the highest value category. In other studies of the occupational values of college students, Hammond (1956) and Simpson and Simpson (1960) observed, as expected, that business students valued economic activities and were materialistic and comfort-oriented, whereas education majors and other transmitters of the culture were high on humanitarian values.

Wagman (1965) examined the similarities in occupational values of students and their parents by means of Centers' Job Values and Desires Questionnaire. The subjects, 123 male and 138 female psychology undergraduate students, first responded to the instrument for themselves, then as they believed their fathers, then their mothers, would. Numerous similarities were noted, especially within sex groups (that is, sons were like their fathers, daughters like their mothers).

Fretz (1972) studied the responses to an occupational values questionnaire of 120 preprofessional students heading for law, medicine, engineering, business, and education. The preprofessional groups were distinguishable on the values; it should be noted that such differences are probably underestimates since professional attainment will not parallel choice.

In general, studies of values of college students enrolled in different programs reveal stable value differences associated with vocational objectives.

Occupational Values of Secondary Students

A number of studies have examined the occupational values of junior high and high school students. Dipboye and Anderson (1959) administered a questionnaire concerning the plans and values of high school students in terms of security, prestige, salary, interest, advancement, working conditions, relations with others, independence, and benefits. At the ninth-grade level, girls highly valued matters such as prestige, interest in work, working conditions, and relations with others, while the ninth-grade boys valued independence, salary, and advancement opportunities. Twelfth graders were very similar: the older girls valued the same things as the younger ones with the exception of the stress on interesting work, while the older boys held values similar to those of the younger ones except that their regard for advancement dropped. Looking at the sample as a whole, however, interesting work and prospects for advancement seemed more important to twelfth graders than to ninth graders. It may be that younger boys and girls are less concerned with the need for interesting work than older students because work is not so imminent for them.

In another paper, based on data from the same sample and questionnaire, Anderson and Dipboye (1959) report the results of a comparison between the occupational values of high school students who have expressed a vocational preference as opposed to those without a preference. Occupational values of those students who had made post high school educational or vocational plans were further compared. No differences in the values of vocationally decided and undecided twelfth-grade students were found. For the total sample of ninth and twelfth graders, those expressing a vocational preference were found to value prestige more highly and salary and advancement less highly than the undecided students. At the ninth-grade level, undecided students rated salary and advancement more highly than did the decided students. In a later study, Anderson and Bosworth (1971) found that ninth-grade students in 1970 were somewhat different than their 1958 counterparts in regard to occupational values; in 1970, the ninth graders valued high pay and enjoyable work instead of the stable, enjoyable work their elders had desired.

In a study along similar lines, Perrone (1965) administered a value orientation instrument to a sample of junior high school girls and found that intelligent and high-achieving girls sought careers offering intrinsic satisfaction, whereas lower achieving, less intelligent girls sought educational objectives inconsistent with their abilities and talents. However, since education is highly valued in the American culture and thus something for which many individuals strive, people in lower intelligence levels may be instilled with inappropriate educational goals by the culture itself.

Kapes and Strickler (1975) compared 659 ninth- and twelfth-grade students' occupational values. Findings for five of the seven values measured were different for the two grades. These seemed to be related to curriculum in high school. Salary differed the most, and strong values seemed to grow stronger and weak values weaker. This finding reflects more value changes than earlier studies generally have found.

Summary and Evaluation

The basic procedures followed in the study of values and occupations involve interviewing or administering questionnaires to subjects concerning their goals and objectives vis-à-vis careers. Typically, the samples are large, the research is conducted in a school setting, and the responses to the questionnaire are subjected to factor analysis. Some factors recur in most of the studies, though with somewhat different names: interest in work, satisfaction, and self-expression are three commonly occurring values that appear under various names.

The results of studies of changes in occupational values over time suggest that such values are generally stable for individuals, though subject to some change over time. As a result of cultural influences, the relationship of any particular value to any one occupational group is open to question insofar as significant differences are concerned. For the most part, the values reflect those that are widely held by middle-class American society and thus cut across occupations. Nevertheless, statistical, if not necessarily meaningful, differences between some occupations in certain values have been reported.

The "values" approach to occupational behavior seems to explain little about career motives or behavior. Other concepts are likely to be more useful in understanding career behavior. The studies of occupational values seem to find answers framed in the language of the questions asked, to an extent that limits the resulting information. In counseling, discussions about values with students may be useful in generating self-understanding, but the approach seems limited to the role of an interviewing device and is certainly limited conceptually.

The Relationship Between Interests, Needs, and Values

Because of the character of the measurement approach taken to study interests, values, and needs, some argument has arisen over the distinctiveness of these three concepts. One view asserts that the overlap among the three is so great that no useful purpose is served by trying to distinguish each from the others, while the opposing view asserts that although some commonalities among the three concepts exist, there are several important distinctions that are useful to maintain.

Among those who take the position that interests, needs, and values essentially tap the same pool of questionnaire and behavioral events are Thorndike, Weiss, and Dawis (1968a; 1968b). These investigators used a canonical correlation technique to study the relationship between interests as measured by the SVIB and Minnesota Vocational Interest Inventory, and needs as measured by the Minnesota Importance Questionnaire. The results of the investigations of Thorndike, et al., revealing high correlations between the interest and need measures, convinced them that interests and needs are highly related constructs, possibly indistinguishable. Along the same lines, Siess and Jackson (1970), using a multimethod factor analysis which focuses on "between" rather than "within" correlations, found seven factors which provided evidence that the Personality Research Form and the SVIB jointly define the needs and interests events described by the two instruments. Finally, Kohlan (1968) correlated the results of the SVIB, EPPS, and Minnesota Importance Questionnaire and found many high correlations on the scales of the three instruments.

Arguing from the opposite perspective, however, is Katz (1969), who took issue with Thorndike, Weiss, and Dawis (1968a; 1968b). Katz concludes that although needs and interests are similar, the similarity is the result of the impurity of the SVIB. Baird (1970) performed a canonical correlation of responses from more than 20,000 college students to the Vocational Preference Inventory and their self-ratings in terms of ability, personality, and life goals. Baird concludes that although the relationships among the variables are significant, the results are complex and are not sufficient to indicate that interest measures can legitimately be substituted for measures of goals, self-concepts, or personal potential. Salomone and Muthard (1972) administered the Minnesota Importance Questionnaire and the Vocational Preference Inventory to 333 counselors and performed a canonical correlation. No significant relationships between the two inventories were found, and the investigators concluded that these two instruments measure needs and vocational style independently.

It is possible that needs and values may be subtly related. For example, Meir and Friedland (1971) found support for the hypothesis that since extrinsic needs are not occupationally specific, they do not relate to occupational preferences, but intrinsic needs are occupationally specific and thus apparently are related to occupational preferences.

In general, the question of the independence of interests, needs, and values does not appear to have an answer at this time. The results of research suggest that the instrumentation plays an important role in influencing the degree of relationship to be observed among the three variables. Such results, though they suggest that the item pool may be similar for the three at times, do not necessarily lead to the inference that the concepts are fundamentally the same.

REFERENCES

Anderson, W. F., and Bosworth, D. L. A note on occupational values of ninth grade students of 1958 as compared to 1970. *Journal of Vocational Behavior*, 1971, *1*, 301–303.

Anderson, W. F., and Dipboye, W. J. Occupational values and post-high school plans. *Vocational Guidance Quarterly*, 1959, *8*, 37–40.

Astin, A., and Nichols, R. C. Life goals and vocational choice. *Journal of Applied Psychology*, 1964, *48*, 50–58.

Baird, L. L. The relation of vocational interests to life goals, self-ratings of ability and personality traits, and potential for achievement. *Journal of Educational Measurement*, 1970, *7*, 233–239.

Blum, S. H. The desire for security: an element in the vocational choice of college men. *Journal of Educational Psychology*, 1961, *52*, 317–321.

Bohn, M. J., Jr. Psychological needs related to personality types. *Journal of Counseling Psychology*, 1966, *13*, 306–309.

Bradshaw, H. H., Jr. Need satisfaction and job level in a professional hierarchy. *Experimental Publication System*, 1970, *7*, Ms. No. 264-1

Darley, J. G., and Hagenah, T. *Vocational interest measurement: theory and practice*. Minneapolis: University of Minnesota Press, 1955.

Dipboye, W. J., and Anderson, W. F. The ordering of occupational values by high school freshmen and seniors. *Personnel and Guidance Journal*, 1959, *38*, 121–124.

Dipboye, W. J., and Anderson, W. F. Occupational stereotypes and manifest needs. *Journal of Counseling Psychology*, 1961, *8*, 296–304.

Fretz, B. R. Occupational values as discriminants of preprofessional student groups. *Journal of Vocational Behavior*, 1972, *2*, 233–237.

Hall, C. S., and Lindzey, G. *Theories of personality*. New York: John Wiley, 1957.

Hall, D. T., and Nougaim, K. E. An examination of Maslow's need hierarchy in an organizational setting. *Organizational Behavior and Human Performance*, 1968, *3*, 12–35.

Hammond, M. Motives related to vocational choices of college freshmen. *Journal of Counseling Psychology*, 1956, *3*, 357–361.

Herzberg, F., Mausner, B., and Snyderman, B. B. *The motivation to work* (2nd ed.). New York: John Wiley, 1959.

Hoppock, R. *Occupational Information*. New York: McGraw-Hill, 1957.

Kapes, J. T., and Strickler, R. E. A longitudinal study of changing work values between 9th and 12th grades as related to curriculum. *Journal of Vocational Behavior*, 1975, *6*, 81–93.

Katz, M. Interests and values. *Journal of Counseling Psychology*, 1969, *16*, 460–462.

Kohlan, R. G. Relationships between inventoried interests and inventoried needs. *Personnel and Guidance Journal*, 1968, *46*, 592–598.

Locke, E. A. Job satisfaction and job performance: a theoretical analysis. *Organizational Behavior and Human Performance*, 1970, *5*, 484–500.

Meir, E. I., and Friedland, N. The relationship between intrinsic-extrinsic needs and occupational preferences. *Journal of Vocational Behavior*, 1971, *1*, 159–165.

Miller, C. H. Occupational choice and values. *Personnel and Guidance Journal*, 1956, *35*, 244–246.

Mobley, W. H., and Locke, E. A. The relationship of value importance to satisfaction. *Organizational Behavior and Human Performance*, 1970, *5*, 463–483.

Murray, H. A. *Explorations in personality*. New York: Oxford, 1938.

Orpen, C., and Pinshaw, J. An empirical examination of the Need Gratification Theory of Job Satisfaction. *Journal of Social Psychology*, 1975, *96*, 139–140.

Perrone, P. A. Values and occupational preferences of junior high school girls. *Personnel and Guidance Journal*, 1965, *44*, 253–257.

Rosenberg, M. *Occupations and values*. Illinois: Free Press, 1957.

Salomone, P. R., and Muthard, J. E. Canonical correlation of vocational needs and vocational style. *Journal of Vocational Behavior*, 1972, *2*, 163–171.

Schaffer, R. H. Job satisfaction as related to need satisfaction in work. *Psychological Monographs*, 1953, *67*, No. 14 (Whole No. 364).

Siess, T. F., and Jackson, D. N. Vocational interests and personality: an empirical integration. *Journal of Counseling Psychology*, 1970, *17*, 27–35.

Simpson, R. L., and Simpson, I. H. Values, personal influence, and occupational choice. *Social Forces*, 1960, *39*, 116–125.

Spranger, E. *Types of men*. New York: Stechert, 1928 (translation).

Stern, G. G., Masling, J., Denton, B., Henderson, J., and Levin, R. Two scales for the assessment of unconscious motivations for teaching. *Educational and Psychological Measurement*, 1960, *20*, 9–29.

Suziedelis, A., and Steimel, R. J. The relationship of need hierarchies to inventoried interests. *Personnel and Guidance Journal*, 1963, *42*, 393–396.

Thorndike, R. M., Weiss, D. J., and Dawis, R. V. Canonical correlation of vocational interests and vocational needs. *Journal of Counseling Psychology*, 1968, *15*, 101–106. (a)

Thorndike, R. M., Weiss, D. J., and Dawis, R. V. Multivariate relationship between a measure of vocational interests and a measure of vocational needs. *Journal of Applied Psychology,* 1968, *52,* 491–495. (b)

Wagman, M. Sex and age differences in occupational values. *Personnel and Guidance Journal,* 1965, *44,* 258–262.

Walsh, R. P. The effect of needs on responses to job duties. *Journal of Counseling Psychology,* 1959, *6,* 194–198.

Wolf, M. G. Need gratification theory: a theoretical reformulation of job satisfaction/dissatisfaction and job motivation. *Journal of Applied Psychology,* 1970, *54,* 87–94.

CHAPTER FOUR
OCCUPATIONS
AND
MENTAL HEALTH

There is a long history of interest in the degree to which people engaged in various occupational activities display various forms of psychopathology. For example, folklore associates some occupations with a tendency to alcoholism and others with particular kinds of sexual orientation. There is probably some validity to these notions.

Two lines of investigation, however, appear to be of particular interest with respect to work and mental health. One has to do with the relationship between various kinds of interests and psychopathology (or overall adjustment), the second has to do with the degree to which work settings interact with and produce stresses which cause strains to individuals leading to both work disorder and personal disorder. Recent data also suggest that sometimes these work-related stresses can produce negative effects on overall physical well being (Osipow, 1979).

Certainly, some target populations in society appear to be particularly vulnerable to special work-related stresses. These populations would include women, minority members, the physically handicapped, and elderly workers, all of whom are subjected to additional stresses in work because of their special status and characteristics cause others to reject them at times.

Osipow (1979) makes a case for increasing the involvement of counseling psychologists in the area of occupational mental health, pointing out that occupational stresses frequently result in severe health problems, including prolonged and extensive anxiety, cardiovascular and other physiological deviations, and alcoholism. Osipow (1979) suggests that counseling psychologists need to pay more attention to their roles as consultants to supervisors and company officials in the development of job designs and organizational policies that will reduce stresses and strains on workers. In addition, certain occupations clearly appear to have higher incidences of job-related strain because of the work setting itself. This is true of law enforcement occupations and other jobs in which there are excessive stresses in terms of threats or violence and disorder. Also, many work settings pose problems in terms of overt competition with colleagues, feelings of harassment by superiors, work overload, and faulty organizational arrangements. Personal characteristics carried into the work situation seem, from this literature review, to be less predictive of work stress than the work setting itself.

One study (Colligan, Smith, and Hurrell, 1977) looked at the admissions rate for community mental health centers in the state of Tennessee, categorized by membership in 130 major occupations. The highest-ranking admission rate occupations were, in order, health technologists and technicians, waiters and waitresses, practical nurses, inspectors, and musicians. The absence of many professionals from the list suggests that professionals may not seek mental health assistance in the same way that nonprofessionals do.

People differ in their ability to cope with job stress. Caplan and Jones (1975) looked at how Type A personalities interact with work stresses of various types. Wiener, Vardi, and Muczyk (1981) found that work-related attitudes of professionals and retail-store managers contributed to mental health more that did situational and individual variables, and further that individual and situational variables were more strongly related to work-related attitudes than to mental health. Career and work satisfaction was the strongest contributor to mental health.

Studying the stresses of role ambiguity and quantitative workload and using both Type A personalities and Type B personalities, Caplan and Jones looked at 122 relatively young males (mean age 23) with respect to measures of state of anxiety, depression, and resentment; heart rate; and the average number of cigarettes smoked. The subjects were examined at a time when the plant in which they worked shut down and again five months later. The findings indicated that anxiety, depression, and resentment were positively associated with role ambiguity and that anxiety was the only variable associated with subjective workload. Anxiety was, however, positively related to heart rate. Although Type A persons showed the greatest relationship between anxiety and workload, a similar but not significant trend in anxiety and heart rate showed for all subjects.

French (1976) proposed a theoretical model associated with various hazards that exist in work environments. The model differentiates between the objective and the subjective work environments. The subjective work environment reflects the individual's perception of the environment, or what might be called the psychological environment. French's general hypothesis is that job stresses, especially in the area of person-environment fit, are a major cause of psychological and physiological strain. Strains, in turn, are associated with health and illness. In a study related to this hypothesis, these investigators examined over 2,000 people in a wide variety of occupations with respect to measures involving subjective environmental stress, person-environment fit, social support, strain in terms of depression and anxiety, and a variety of physiological factors such as blood pressure, heart rate, serum cholesterol, thyroid hormones, serum uric acid, and serum cortisol.

One aspect of outcome reported by Caplan (see French et al., 1976) was that blue-collar workers tended to report strain in terms of job dissatisfaction. Unskilled blue-collar workers reported these strains using terms descriptive of boredom, somatic complaints, and to some degree depression. Professional and non-professional white-collar workers, on the other hand, did not report significant strain in terms of job dissatisfaction and boredom. Blue-collar unskilled workers reported stress in terms of underutilization, responsibility, the complexity of their jobs, concerns about ambiguities related to their future, and low social support.

Pinneau (see French et al., 1976) tested the hypothesis that social supports would reduce job stress and result in reduced measures of psychological and physiological strain. The findings showed that support from the home environment had little effect on job stress but support from supervisors and co-workers had a wide variety of effects on stress measures. With respect to the hypothesis that social support would reduce physiological and psychological strain, the finding, again, was that support from home was less often correlated with job dissatisfaction measures than was support from supervisors and co-workers. However, general strains of depression, anxiety and irritation were affected both by home and work support measures. Social support was significantly associated with low levels of psychological strain in many instances.

One problem in studying work stress lies in its measurement. To correct some of the major deficiencies of measuring occupational stress and strain as well as to assess individual coping resources, Osipow and Spokane (1981) have developed three measures which may be useful in (1) identifying sources of occupational stress from a social roles viewpoint; (2) measuring the consequent strain in terms of productivity, interpersonal, affective, and physical disruptions; and (3) identifying the individual's status with respect to four sets of stress-coping mechanisms. Perhaps the greater availability of ways to assess work stress and resulting disruption may increase the awareness of the degree to which work affects mental health.

Klumbies (1967) found evidence indicating that nearly a quarter of 1,500 therapy patients described their work setting as the source of their psychological difficulties. Though the proportion of true work conflict shrank upon closer scrutiny, Klumbies found that work remained a major source of difficulty for 14 percent of the patients. Thus, it is not surprising that a number of investigations into the relationship between occupations and psychopathology have been conducted.

Kuder Preference Record Interests and Adjustment

One of the more clearly established relationships between interests and adjustment has been pointed out by Patterson (1957): maladjusted people tend, in general, to express interests in artistic, literary, or musical careers more often than in scientific or mathematical careers. This statement was further elaborated in a review by Gobetz (1964), who summarized the results of studies which have examined the relationship between interests expressed on the KPR and psychopathology. Most of these studies followed the procedure of identifying a psychoneurotic group, administering the Kuder, and comparing the resulting scores with those of a control group or with the test norms. Some have compared the Kuder scores with scores on a personality inventory for a normal sample. Klugman (1950) studied the relationship between the range of Kuder scores and performance on the Bell Adjustment Inventory. He predicted that the better-adjusted Ss would show both a greater spread and more fields of interest than maladjusted Ss. The sample was composed of 108 counseling clients at a VA Regional Office. With a few exceptions the hypotheses were not supported. A correlation between spread of interest and age, education, and intelligence was found. Also found was a correlation between high scientific and low artistic interest scores and good personal adjustment scores on the Bell Adjustment Inventory.

In another study, Klugman (1960) compared the Kuder profiles of 60 male neuropsychiatric patients and 60 counseling cases. This comparison revealed that the profiles of the two groups were significantly different. The neuropsychiatric group scored higher on literary and lower on mechanical interests than the normal group. Interestingly, in terms of the norms, the NP group's interests were more like those of women than men. Similar findings were reported by Steinberg (1952), who compared the KPR scores of 50 psychoneurotic veterans with those of 100 non neurotic but physically disabled veterans. The nonneurotic veterans' scores were significantly higher on mechanical and lower on musical and literary interests. The only report inconsistent with the tendency for maladjusted Ss to have high literary and musical and low mechanical interest scores was prepresented by Melton (1956), who administered the CTMM and the Occupational Interest Inventory to 324 high school seniors. He found that artistic and personal-social interests were correlated with good personal adjustment, while Ss with mechanical interests had poor adjustment scores.

Newman (1955) predicted that high social service scores on the Kuder Preference Record would be positively correlated with poor personal adjustment. The hypothesis was tested by administering the Kuder to 141 tuberculosis patients previously rated as to their degree of personal maladjustment. The results indicated that a significant number of the subjects with social service scores above the 75th percentile had been rated as maladjusted and that over 53 percent of the maladjusted Ss earned their highest interest scores on the social service scale. Unexplained in terms of the hypothesis, however, was the finding that a significant number of Ss with high scores on the clerical, musical, and computational scales were also maladjusted.

Sternberg (1956) correlated the KPR and MMPI scores of 270 white male students at Queens College in New York. He found a number of moderate correlations of a significant nature between the two inventories, which indicate that aesthetic interests (Kuder scales literary, artistic, and musical) are positively correlated and scientific and technical interests negatively correlated with an inclination toward personal maladjustment. It is again important to recall, however, that the mean MMPI scores of both types of subjects were well within the normal range.

Building on the data of Klugman (1950; 1960) and several others, Drasgow and Carkhuff (1964) observed that literary, artistic, and musical interests are correlated with mental disorder. They administered the KPR before and following psychotherapy and found that in cases judged to be "successful," the artistic, musical, and literary scores decreased, adding further evidence to support the idea that aesthetic interests are in some way related to emotional disorder.

Examining differences among psychiatric patients of various classifications in work history or Kuder Preference Record patterns, Schaffer (1953) found no major differences.

Interest-Interest and Interest-Ability Discrepancies

The idea that discrepancies between interests and abilities indicate emotional maladjustment has often been suggested. Nugent (1961) studied two groups of high school boys, one with a marked agreement between their aptitudes and interests and the other exhibiting a marked discrepancy. The Kuder was used to study interests, the Differential Aptitude Test to measure ability, and the California Personality Inventory to measure personality. No differences in personality adjustment, measured by personality inventory or by judges' ratings, were found between those ninth-grade boys with high and those with low interest-aptitude discrepancy. However, significant differences in personal adjustment were found to exist at the eleventh-grade level. Looking only at the personality scales relevant to personal adequacy and security, Nugen inferred that the relationship between interest-aptitude discrepancy and maladjustment holds not only for eleventh graders but also for ninth-grade boys.

Approaching the matter from another direction, Pool and Brown (1964) postulated a relationship between Kuder and SVIB discrepancies and psychological maladjustment. They administered the SVIB, Kuder, and MMPI to 27 physically handicapped VA male patients who had been referred for vocational counseling. They matched the Kuder and SVIB areas; the mechanical scale on the Kuder was judged to be equivalent to Group IV on the SVIB. Interest scores were classified as either high, medium, or low for each area. Discrepancy points were scored when a subject earned a high score on one test and a medium or low score in the same area on the other test. Degrees of discrepancy were taken into account in terms of the deviation between the scores on the two tests. Thus, a high score in the mechanical area on the Kuder and a low Strong Group IV score earned two discrepancy points, while a medium score for persuasiveness on the Kuder and a high literary group score on the Strong earned only one point. The results showed a correlation of 0.30 ($p < 0.06$) between the number of interest discrepancy scores and MMPI scores with T scores above 65 (still within the normal range). Discrepancies among the interest inventories in the mechanical, computational, and literary scores appeared to be the most sensitive in reflecting MMPI maladjustment. The study is interesting, but the correlation only approaches what is usually considered to be statistical significance; the sample is small and the measurements are gross. The implications of findings such as were predicted are not entirely clear.

Using the MMPI, Munday, Braskamp, and Brandt (1968) examined the psychological adjustment of individuals with undifferentiated SVIB profiles. The subjects were 314 male counseling clients who had taken the SVIB as part of educational-vocational counseling and had also taken the MMPI either as part of programmatic freshman testing or as part of their counseling. The results, contrary to common expectation, do not show any significant relationship between flat SVIB profiles and poor intelligence, age, or maladjustment.

Vocational Conflict and Personal Adjustment

Landis (1963) studied the relationship between emotional maladjustment and interest in particular vocations. Using as an experimental sample 214 male college students who sought help for emotional-personal problems at a college counseling service and, as a control groups, 214 randomly selected college males from the same university, he tested a series of hypotheses predicting that maladjusted students generally are more conflicted about their educational-vocational plans than well-adjusted students. The data were available from the SVIB and a Personal Information Blank, answered by all freshmen and designed to acquire information on, among other things, career choice, certainty, and parental wishes about student career plans. Not one of Landis' seven predictions was supported. Landis observed that maladjusted Ss earn significantly higher SVIB scores than adjusted students on the clinical psychologist, artist, minister, advertising man, author-journalist, and musician scales and significantly lower scores on the farmer, purchasing agent, production manager, and army officer scales. These results are consistent with other findings which reflect a positive correlation between masculine, technical-scientific interests and good personal adjustment, as well as between feminine (for men), aesthetic interests and maladjustment. One might speculate about these persistent findings in terms of the fantasy and the daydreaming component of maladjustment, but also about the possibility that boys with aesthetic interests come into conflict with their culture more readily than boys with typical interests and as a consequence are more prone to become maladjusted.

Carnes (1964) pursued the hypothesis that the vocational interests of psychiatric patients are less varied, less intense, less masculine, less mature, and at an increasingly lower occupational level as the degree of severity of disorder increases. In a study comparing the interests of psychiatric patients with varying degrees of severity he found that although some interests do seem to be correlated in a general way with some aspects of abnormal personalities, more often the interests of psychiatric patients are so varied as to obscure systematic differences by diagnostic category. Some evidence was found in support of the idea that psychiatrically disordered individuals show less interest patterning and are less vocationally mature than more normal individuals.

A related hypothesis about personal adjustment and career goals has been suggested by Roe (1963). Her interest in the lives of scientists led her to speculate about how scientific careers and personal problems influence each other. She suggested that successful scientists encounter during youth a major cultural difference between their home and school environments. The chances are that their school promoted conventional thought while their home environment encouraged individual inquiry and independence. In Roe's opinion, it is important to avoid social isolation during childhood by devising conditions that socially support the young person whose culture has conflict built into it. Cultural problems exacerbate the maladjustment of bright youngsters. An example is the "moral" tone with which concepts are taught in the early grades. Arithmetic, languages, and social conduct are all taught with a sense of absolutism and a rejection of individual judgment. Thus, creativity is discouraged and deviant behavior in the form of repression, withdrawal, or acting out frequently occurs instead.

As the bright "scientist-to-be" grows older, conflicting loyalties occur; organizational and personal (spouse and family) loyalties come into conflict with professional and scholarly interests which can become consuming. Often, interpersonal difficulties arise as a result of professional involvement, as reflected by the not uncommon occurrence of divorce among scientists. Finally, there seems to be clinical evidence for the frequent occurrence of a neurotic basis for scientific work. When that exists, apparent solutions to scientific problems are not seen, and work is often carried on well beyond the appropriate duration. Roe's assessment is interesting, for it might well apply to all intelligent youngsters as well as some ordinary ones and could serve as the basis for understanding the etiology of maladjustment that sometimes seems to go hand in hand with certain endeavors.

Walsh and Russell (1969), using the simple procedure of asking 124 college undergraduates to respond to the Mooney Problem Check List, found that congruent students (those choosing educational majors consistent with their high point code on the Vocational Preference Inventory of Holland) exhibit better personal adjustment than incongruent students. A more complicated study of vocational and personal adjustment was conducted by Osipow and Gold (1968). In this study, the SVIB patterns of 42 male and 23 female personal adjustment counseling cases were compared with the profiles of 53 male and 35 female students selected at random. In comparison with the randomly chosen males, the male counseling subjects exhibited fewer primary interest patterns, more flat profiles, and fewer primary patterns in practical, scientific, and engineering categories and were more likely to reject scientific, engineering, and business detail areas and less likely to reject literary fields. The women counseling clients showed fewer flat profiles, fewer primary patterns in the domestic area, and fewer rejects in sales and education areas than the randomly chosen women. Overall, the results for both sexes indicated that the counseling population is more likely to have interest patterns that are mildly atypical according to sex stereotypes, a finding similar to that of Roe and Siegelman (1964), who observed similar sex role conflicts for male social workers and female engineers. In addition, because the inventoried interests of the subjects in the Osipow and Gold study were different for the counseled and the randomly chosen individuals, while the programs in which they enrolled were similiar, it might be inferred that the students receiving personal adjustment counseling were more likely to be enrolled in programs inconsistent with their interests than the randomly selected students.

In another study investigating SVIB profiles and adjustment, Brandt and Hood (1968) observed individuals who sought counseling during a ten-year period (1955–1964) and had taken both the SVIB and the MMPI. The objective of the Brandt and Hood study was to see how well the SVIB predicted vocational choice for men with normal versus deviant MMPI patterns. All told, some 915 such profiles were available. The results indicated that the SVIB is a better predictor of vocational choice for men with "normal" MMPI profiles than for men with deviant profiles. Furthermore, the vocational satisfaction of the "normal" men was greater than that of those classified as deviant. Of course, as in most of the research examining the relationship between personal and vocational adjustment, it is difficult to determine whether vocational maladjustment causes or is caused by personal maladjustment.

Klein and Weiner (1977) measured self-esteem, life satisfaction, supervisory satisfaction, and overall mental health in 54 middle managers. They found that interest congruency moderated job tenure and mental health. Where high congruency existed, mental health improved as job tenure increased, and this was reflected in self-esteem and life satisfaction. Incongruent jobs and interests were not negatively correlated with job tenure and mental health indices. Klein and Weiner infer that those people who are sensitive to the stresses that incongruence produces are early job leavers.

Summary and Evaluation

Most of the research relating vocational choice and behavior to psychopathology has been conducted at a very simple level. In general, no data exist to suggest a specific relationship between psychopathology and career, though some informed guesses may be made concerning the role occupation may play in exacerbating mental disorder. What does appear to recur in the data is the implication that aesthetic interests in men are associated with personal maladjustment. Whether that observation reflects the attitude of the culture toward men with such interests, or the results of a lifetime of being out of tune with one's contemporaries, or is a manifestation of a rich fantasy life involved in maladjustment remains unclear, but might be a useful area of exploration.

REFERENCES

Brandt, J. E., and Hood, A. B. Effect of personality adjustment on the predictive validity of the Strong Vocational Interest Blank. *Journal of Counseling Psychology,* 1968, *15,* 547–551.

Caplan, R. B., and Jones, K. W. Effects of workload, role ambiguity, and Type A personality on anxiety, depression, and heart rate. *Journal of Applied Social Psychology, Monograph*, 1975, *60*, 713–719.

Carnes, C. D. Vocational interest characteristics of abnormal personalities. *Journal of Counseling Psychology*, 1964, *11*, 272–279.

Colligan, M. J., Smith, M. J., and Hurrell, J. J., Jr. Occupational incidence rates of mental health disorders. *Journal of Human Stress*, 1977, *3*, 34–39.

Drasgow, J., and Carkhuff, R. R. Kuder neuropsychiatric keys before and after psychotherapy. *Journal of Counseling Psychology*, 1964, *11*, 67–69.

French, J. R. P., Jr., Caplan, R. D., Van Harrison, R., and Pinneau, S. R., Jr. Symposium on Occupational Differences, Stresses, and Worker Health presented at American Psychological Association, Washington, D. C., September, 1976.

Gobetz, W. Suggested personality implications of Kuder Preference Record (vocational) scores. *Personnel and Guidance Journal*, 1964, *43*, 159–166.

Klein, K. L., and Weiner, Y. Interest congruency as a moderator of the relationships between job tenure and job satisfaction and mental health. *Journal of Vocational Behavior*, 1977, *10*, 92–98.

Klugman, S. F. Spread of vocational interest and general adjustment. *Journal of Applied Psychology*, 1950, *34*, 108–114.

Klugman, S. F. Comparison of total interest profiles of a psychotic and normal group. *Journal of Counseling Psychology*, 1960, *7*, 283–288.

Klumbies, G. Pathogenic job conflicts. *Psychotherapy and Psychosomatics*, 1967, *15*, 33–34.

Landis, W. A. The vocational interests of emotionally maladjusted male college students. Doctoral dissertation, Pennsylvania State University, 1963.

Melton, W. R., Jr. An investigation of the relationship between personality and vocational interest. *Journal of Educational Psychology*, 1956, *47*, 163–174.

Munday, L. A., Braskamp, L. A., and Brandt, J. E. The meaning of unpatterned vocational interests. *Personnel and Guidance Journal*, 1968, *47*, 249–256.

Newman, J. The Kuder Preference Record and personal adjustment. *Educational and Psychological Measurement*, 1955, *15*, 274–280.

Nugent, F. The relationship of discrepancies between interests and aptitude scores to other selected personality variables. *Personnel and Guidance Journal*, 1961, *39*, 388–395.

Osipow, S. H. Occupational mental health: another role for counseling psychologists. *The Counseling Psychologist*, 1979, *8*, 65–70.

Osipow, S. H., and Gold, J. A. Personnel adjustment and career development. *Journal of Counseling Psychology*, 1968, *15*, 439–443.

Osipow, S. H., and Spokane, A. R. *A preliminary manual for measures of occupational stress, strain and coping*. Columbus, Oh.: Marathon Consulting and Press, 1981.

Patterson, C. H. Interest tests and the emotionally disturbed client. *Educational and Psychological Measurement*, 1957, *17*, 264–280.

Pool, D. A., and Brown, R. A. Kuder-Strong discrepancies and personality adjustment. *Journal of Counseling Psychology*, 1964, *11*, 63–66.

Roe, A. Personal problems and science. In Taylor, C. W. and Barron, F. (Eds.) *Scientific creativity: its recognition and development*. New York: Wiley, 1963.

Roe, A., and Siegelman, M. The origin of interests. APGA INQUIRY SERIES, No. 1. Washington, D. C.: American Personnel and Guidance Association, 1964.

Schaffer, R. H. Job satisfaction as related to need satisfaction in work. *Psychological Monographs*, 1953, *67*, No. 14 (Whole No. 364).

Steinberg, A. The relation of vocational preference to emotional maladjustment. *Educational and Psychological Measurement*, 1952, *12*, 96–140.

Sternberg, C. Interests and tendencies toward maladjustment in a normal population. *Personnel and Guidance Journal*, 1956, *35*, 94–99.

Walsh, W. B., and Russell, J. H. College major choice and personal adjustment. *Personnel and Guidance Journal*, 1969, *47*, 685–688.

Weiner, Y., Vardi, Y., and Muczyk, J. Antecedents of employees mental health—the role of career and work satisfaction. *Journal of Vocational Behavior*, 1981, *19*, 50–60.

CHAPTER FIVE
HOLLAND'S CAREER TYPOLOGY THEORY OF VOCATIONAL BEHAVIOR

In his theory of career development, Holland employs an elaboration of the hypothesis that career choices represent an extension of personality and an attempt to implement broad personal behavioral styles in the context of one's life work. The novel feature that Holland introduces is the notion that people project their views of themselves and the world of work on to occupational titles. By the simple procedure of allowing individuals to express their preference for, or feelings against, a particular list of occupational titles, Holland assigns people to modal personal styles which have theoretical implications for personality and vocational choice.

Holland's conception of career development grew from his experiences with people involved in making career decisions. He observed that most people view the vocational world in terms of occupational stereotypes. Instead of concluding that such stereotyping confuses people and causes vocational counselors extra difficulty, Holland turned the stereotyping process to his advantage by assuming that it is based on the individual's experience with work, thus being based on reality and possessing a high degree of accuracy and utility. Holland hypothesized that where the individual possesses little knowledge about a particular vocation, the resulting stereotype is revealing, much in the manner a projective test presumably exposes personality dynamics. Consequently, Holland set out to develop a list of occupational titles that would be useful as a device onto which a person could project a preferred life style.

THE THEORY

Occupational Environments

Holland's work has been characterized by four attributes: change, simplicity, instrumentation, and data. Holland's original theoretical statement (1959), modified as a result of research testing the theory (1962; 1966a; 1973), proposed that a finite number of work environments exists within the American society. These environments are the realistic (for example, farmers, truck drivers), the investigative (chemists, biologists), the social (social workers, teachers), the conventional (bookkeepers, bank tellers), the enterprising (salesmen, politicians), and the artistic (musicians, artists).

The Developmental Hierarchy

The developmental hierarchy is represented by the individual's adjustment to the six occupational environments. Everyone is required to adjust to each of the environments and develop certain skills with reference to the setting. The six types of adjustment stemming from the developmental hierarchy represent major life styles and patterns of relationships between the individual and the world. The most typical way an individual responds to the environment is, of course, the modal personal orientation. The six orientations were referred to by the same names as the occupational environments in earlier versions of the theory but were renamed by Holland later (1962; 1971). In the following descriptions of the orientations, the original names are in parentheses.

The *Realistic* (Motoric) orientation is characterized by aggressive behavior; interest in activities requiring motor coordination, skill, and physical strength; and masculinity. People oriented toward this role prefer "acting out" problems; they avoid tasks involving interpersonal and verbal skills and seek concrete rather than abstract problem situations. They score high on traits such as concreteness, physical strength, and masculinity and low on social skill and sensitivity.

The *Investigative* (Intellectual) persons' main characteristics are thinking rather than acting, organizing and understanding rather than dominating or persuading, and asociability rather than sociability. These people prefer to avoid close interpersonal contact, though the quality of their avoidance seems different from that of their Realistic colleagues.

The *Social* (Supportive) people seem to satisfy their needs for attention in a teaching or therapeutic situation. In sharp contrast to the Investigative and Realistic people, Social people seek close interpersonal situations and are skilled in their interpersonal relations, while they avoid situations where they might be required to engage in intellectual problem solving or use extensive physical skills.

The *Conventional* (Conforming) style is typified by a great concern for rules and regulations, great self-control, subordination of personal needs, and strong identification with power and status. This kind of person prefers structure and order and thus seeks interpersonal and work situations where structure is readily available.

The *Enterprising* (Persuasive) people are verbally skilled, but rather than use their verbal skills to support others as the Social types do, they use them for manipulating and dominating people. They are concerned about power and status, as are the Conventional people, but differ in that they aspire to the power and status while the Conventionals honor others for it.

The *Artistic* (Esthetic) orientation manifests strong self-expression and relations with other people indirectly through artistic expression. They dislike structure and prefer tasks emphasizing physical skills or interpersonal interactions. They are intraceptive and asocial much like the Investigatives, but differ in that they are more feminine than masculine, show relatively little self-control, and express emotion more readily than most people.

Holland's 1973 book presents lists of adjectives descriptive of each type.

The Role and History of Developmental Hierarchies

The development of the styles corresponds to the general notions of most theorists concerning personality development. Personality is seen as a result of genetic and environmental influences. Such a statement is far too general to be of value in understanding personality development and will not help counselors involved in tasks of correcting misdirected development. Holland does, however, indicate the way in which these modal orientations influence vocational behavior once the orientations have been clearly established. If one orientation is clearly dominant over the others, the individual will seek an occupational environment that corresponds to the orientation.

The "practical, hard-headed" person will thus choose to become an engineer while the aggressive, verbal, ambitious one will easily decide that law is the right career. If two or more orientations are the same or nearly the same in their strength, the individual will vacillate in the selection of an occupational environment. A person characterized by detached thought about problems, avoidance of close interpersonal relations, and a tendency to organize, combined with desire to exert self-control and considerable desire to be emotionally expressive, may one day choose to be a biologist and the next day to be a graphic artist. If environmental factors interfere with the implementation of the first clear-cut orientation, then the individual will seek an occupational environment appropriate to the second strongest orientation. A student blocked in attempts to implement an Investigative choice of oceanography because financial resources are not adequate might well select the field of mechanical engineering, representing the second major orientation, the Realistic. However, if the hierarchy of orientations is not well ordered beyond the first one, then vacillation in the selection of an occupational environment will occur, just as if the first two orientations were not clearly different in their strength.

The Level Hierarchy

The modal orientation exerts a clear influence on the particular occupational environment an individual chooses and whether or not indecision is experienced. The question of the level within an occupational environment that the individual chooses is a function of several other variables, entitled the level hierarchy. The level hierarchy is defined in terms of the individual's intelligence and self-evaluations. Intelligence is inferred from relevant tests and presumably, for the purposes of this theory, has the usual social and genetic antecedents. Generally, the gross manipulations of this variable are outside of the control of the person making the vocational choices. Gross misperceptions of intelligence are possible but would probably enter into the other half of the level hierarchy equation, self-evaluation. The self-evaluation, which might operationally correspond to a scale such as the Occupational Level Scale of the Strong Vocational Interest Blank, is itself a function of the person's life history in terms of social status, economic condition, level of education, and health. It seems, however, that when defined in this way, the factors which contribute to the development of a person's self-evaluations are not independent of the factors which go toward influencing intelligence, and vice-versa.

Interaction Between Level and Developmental Hierarchies

The process, then, is roughly this: a person gradually evolves a modal personality orientation which leads, at the appropriate times, to educational decisions which have implications for a specific occupational environment. As steps are taken to implement the decisions, the level hierarchy developed over the years leads toward a career within the occupational environment that is at a skill level equivalent to the person's abilities and achievements. The adequacy of the decisions and the amount of difficulty encountered in the process of making them are related to knowledge about self and the world of work. If only a vague idea of what occupational environments exist is held, difficulty in selecting one will result. If contradictory self-evaluations are held, vacillation in the level selected will result.

The smoothness of decisions is affected by the clarity of the structure of the developmental hierarchy. Thus, if life circumstances (unspecified by the theory) result in an uncrystallized developmental hierarchy, difficulty will be encountered in selecting an occupational environment, and the individual will change from one environment to another. Other environmental factors will also influence the ease with which an occupational environment is selected, but these are more extra-individual than those already mentioned. Some examples are family factors, such as aspirations and occupational history, which might result in pressures toward a particular occupational environment; financial resources; general economic conditions in society; and educational opportunities. Other factors of a similar sort would exert some influence on the content of the environment eventually chosen.

Not only does the particular dominant personal orientation influence the career choice a person makes, but the *pattern* of the orientations within the individual's hierarchy exerts a significant influence. That is, two students with the same major orientation will choose similar fields, but the stability of their choice is a function of the order of the other five orientations in their personal hierarchy. If the order is consistent and all other factors hold constant, the choice is likely to be stable; if the pattern is inconsistent for that occupational environment, then the choice is likely to be unstable. For example, a research engineer with the order Realistic, Enterprising, Conventional, Social, Artistic, and Investigative is likely to be less stable in the pursuit of his research specialty than another research engineer whose hierarchy is Realistic, Investigative, Artistic, Social, Enterprising, and Conventional. The latter would represent what might be a more typical pattern for research engineers.

Holland originally did not elaborate upon what patterns are typical for certain fields and what patterns are not. Presumably, that is an empirical question and can be answered with respect to patterns indicating stability within the large category of occupational environments, or the more specific cateogry of particular occupations within certain occupational environments. The question of typical versus atypical ordering assumes further importance since, according to the theory, the order affects an individual's success in a chosen field as well as stability. Recent publications of Holland's (for example, *The Job Finder*), in connection with the *Self-Directed Search,* present such pattern data.

Holland proposes that typical patterns of hierarchies for an occupational environment affect, in addition to success, the intensity of the choice and thus provide some predictive data about the potential persistence of the individual in that area. The less typical the pattern of the hierarchy, the less intense the choice and consequently, the less persistent the person is likely to be in efforts to implement it. This feature, however, is not clearly distinguishable from stability.

On Congruence

A very important concept that has been used by many investigators to test aspects of Holland's theory has been the notion of congruence. Congruence is supposed to reflect the degree to which an individual's personal qualities match the environmental demands of the occupational area chosen. It is therefore relatively easy to assess the degree to which the individual matches up to these demands by comparing Vocational Preference Inventory scores or Self-Directed Search scores to the proper personality scores demanded by each of the major occupational areas in a publication such as *The Job Finder*. Congruence is, in fact, one of the principle dependent outcomes associated with Holland's theory.

Other Influences on Career Choice

In addition to the concept of self-evaluation, which, it will be recalled, was one of the two critical variables contributing to the individual's level hierarchy, Holland introduced a concept known as *self-knowledge*. Self-knowledge refers to the amount and accuracy of information an individual has about him or herself. It differs from self-evaluation, which refers to the *worth* the individual attributes to him or herself. However, these two constructs are not clearly differentiated. They seem to be highly interdependent and might well refer to two parts of the same phenomenon. Holland apparently introduces these constructs separately to permit himself to predict the adequacy of vocational choice for people who have self-evaluations based closely on accurate self-knowledge, as opposed to those whose vocational choices are partially based on self-evaluations founded on inadequate self-knowledge.

Holland states that the adequacy of occupational choice is largely a function of the adequacy of self-knowledge and occupational knowledge. The greater the amount and accuracy of the information the individual has about each, the more adequate is the choice. Such a conception is reminiscent of the early, and still useful, trait-factor notion of round pegs fitting best in round holes. He explicitly includes other important environmental features, such as social pressures and opportunities available in society. His theory, however, does not assume that these influence people in random ways. Rather, he suggests that people with well-structured developmental hierarchies will be less affected by outside pressures than people possessing ambiguous hierarchies. Such a notion is an extension of his analysis concerning the effects of the hierarchy pattern on the stability and intensity of the choice and the success the individual has in implementing it. He also notes the importance that social pressures in early adolescence and experiences with parents in childhood (similar to Roe, 1957) have in influencing vocational choices. Since such influences occur before the stable hierarchy of personal orientation develops, they are likely to affect the shape of the hierarchy rather than choices after the hierarchy is developed. His discussion of these early experiences is as close as Holland comes to explaining how personal orientations actually develop.

RESEARCH

Holland's approach to the study of vocational selection is very comprehensive within his theoretical framework. His research has frequently been longitudinal, and he has attempted to assess a wide variety of personal, family, social, and achievement correlates that are pertinent to his theoretical construction. Holland has used responses of Like versus Dislike to occupational titles as projective data about the respondent, on the assumption, probably valid, that vocational preferences represent not merely "what interests" the individual has but also a major facet of his personality (Holland, 1961). Certainly, the history of the use of the SVIB and Kuder Preference Record (KPR) leads to such an inference.

The Vocational Preference Inventory (VPI) (Holland, 1958), actually developed *prior* to the theory, is a personality inventory very intimately tied to vocational interests. Prior to the development of the *Self-Directed Search,* the VPI was the primary tool for the measurement of the personality types. The inventory consists of occupational titles to which the subject is instructed to express interest or disinterest. The scale produces scores on each of the six major personality orientations involved in the theory: realistic, investigative, social, enterprising, conventional, and artistic. The *Self-Directed Search* similarly produces scores on those six characteristics. Versions of the *Self-Directed Search* have been developed for special populations which have difficulty in reading or which may be disabled in certain ways and for cross-cultural purposes. The instrument is similar in rationale to the Vocational Preference Inventory but has more items, includes competence judgments by the respondent, and because of its self-directed administration, has a "process" aspect which serves, according to Holland, as a counseling intervention for a certain proportion of clients.

General Correlates of the Personal Orientation

Holland has published numerous reports of findings in support of the behavioral, educational, and vocational correlates of the Personal Orientations. These are best summarized in his book *Making Vocational Choices: A Theory of Careers* (1973). Since that publication, which represents a compilation of his interpretations of not only his own work but that of many other people through the early 1970's, Holland and others have published numerous papers summarizing the relationships between the constructs of the theory and important vocational behaviors. Two very important papers subsequent to his 1973 book include a paper by Holland, Gottfredson, and Nafziger (1975) and another paper co-authored with Gottfredson and published in 1976.

Over the years there has been a remarkable stability in the degree to which the theory has appeared to generate empirical support. In an early 1962 version, for example, Holland found the following correlates for various personality types: for the realistic type, correlates of unsociability, maturity, "masculinity," extroversion and persistence; for the investigative type, correlates of unsociability, "masculinity," self-sufficiency, introversion, and persistence; for the social, cheerfulness, adventurousness, conservativeness, "femininity," dominance, dependence, responsiveness, and sociability; for the conventional, conformity, conservatism, dependency, "masculinity," playfulness, extroversion, and responsibility; for the enterprising, sociability, dominance, cheerfulness, adventurousness, conservatism, dependency, impulsiveness, extraversion, and playfulness; and for the artistic, immaturity, effeminate behaviors, paranoid characteristics, and introversion. In these early studies, the types were generally found to display behaviors consistent with predictions about how they should behave. The areas of these consistent behaviors included interpersonal relations, selections of occupations, school majors, adjustment patterns, daydreams, and admired figures.

In a four-year follow-up study (Holland, 1963), Holland continued to find substantially the same characteristics as he had found earlier. In another long-term longitudinal study of more than 3,500 male college students from 28 colleges and universities (Holland, 1968), extensive data describing personal competencies by type were reported. The realistic males possessed technical competencies and rated themselves high on mechanical abilities. The other self-ratings were as follows: the investigative males high on scientific competencies and mathematics, the social high on socio-educational competencies and understanding of others, the conventional high on business competencies and conservatism, the enterprising high on leadership competencies and popularity, and the artistic high on artistic competencies and originality. Again, these competencies and self-ratings are generally consistent with the theoretical implications of the various types.

Other variables were investigated, such as hobbies and extracurricular activities (Holland, 1962), vocational daydreams (Holland, 1962; 1963; 1963–64), vocational images (Holland, 1963–64), and academic achievement patterns (Holland, 1962; 1963). Generally, Holland has again found in these kinds of explorations results supporting the internal consistency of the types as they predict a wide range of behaviors in different contexts.

Holland and Gottfredson (1976), updating changes in Holland's position, reviewed the purposes of the theories with the following emphases: What kinds of personal environmental characteristics influence work stability and work level? What concerns with the person and environment characteristics should we have with respect to better understanding career choice satisfaction and achievement? What personal characteristics lead to changing level and kind of work? And what are the reasons why some people make congruent choices, other people make incongruent choices, and other people remain undecided?

In attempts to deal with these questions, Holland has focused heavily on expanding the explanatory modes of the theory. Raising questions about how personal development and work choice come about, Holland points out that parents, schools, and neighborhoods reinforce some work patterns more than they do others, provide models for different kinds of work, lead to differential participation in activities of various sorts, and shape the development of interests. Therefore, environment is considered to be a significant shaper of the development of personal choice.

It would seem that many people maintain more "orderly" careers because they find it easier to continue with existing skills and stereotypes than to alter them. Reasons why people do change jobs include dislike for the particular duties involved, an inability to perform them well, and environmental and personal reasons such as desire to live in a different climate and physical changes in themselves. Their search generally should follow the same principles their previous job search followed and have some relation to their previous choice. As to why some people make incongruent choices and others remain undecided, Holland and Gottfredson suggest that such variations are consistent with the finding that some personality types tend to be better decision makers than others. Data indicate that investigative types make the best decisions and conventional types the worst.

In a 1975 paper, Holland, Gottfredson, and Nafziger (1975) tried to deal with some criticisms regarding the application of the typology to the developmental concept issue. According to Holland and his associates, typologies of persons and environments may be more useful than life stage strategies in developing ways to cope with career problems. One of the positions taken is that coping styles should be predictable as a function of personality style. Holland argues that, although one can speculate about age-related work crises, the weight of the evidence in the literature is on the side perceiving that most people maintain stable work histories, remaining in their jobs or in the same types of jobs for most of their career life. Many of the career changes that do occur seem to be the result of special circumstances that reflect some aspect of the person-environment interaction.

Relations Between Types

Though satisfied with the predictive efficiency of the original classification system, Holland's experience with the data he and others had collected over the years made him attempt to increase the subtlety and sensitivity of the system by moving increasingly to multidigit classifications. He found that his classification system could be extended to two digits and still maintain good predictive validity (Holland, 1966). Over time, however, it has become increasingly clear that the types are related to each other differentially. In a manner very similar to Roe, Holland began to explore the idea that some of the occupational environments are more psychologically similar than others. The results of a major investigation into the relationships between the six types (Holland, Whitney, Cole, and Richards, 1969) indicate that the types may be presented in a crude hexagon. The outer rim of the hexagon reveals the psychological relationship between environments. Highly correlated environments, similar to one another, are closer together than those with low correlations. Realistic is close to Investigative on one side and Conventional on the other (correlations of 0.46 and 0.36, respectively) but fairly remote from Social, which is completely across the hexagon and correlates 0.21. Artistic is next to Investigative and Social (correlations of 0.34 and 0.42) but very distant from Conventional across the hexagon (correlation of 0.11). While the shape would not conform exactly to the hexagon if plotted in scale, it is close enough to be intriguing, and to lend vitality to Holland's attempt to relate the environments to one another differentially.

Wakefield and Doughtie (1973), in studying 300 undergraduate students, found that Holland's six personality types displayed themselves according to the predicted hexagon. In another study, Lunneborg and Lunneborg (1975), also factor analyzing responses of more than 200 college students on the Vocational Preference Inventory and the Vocational Interest Inventory, found results suggesting that a simple two-dimensional circular configuration of types is likely to be an oversimplification of our understanding of the structure of vocational interests. The Lunneborgs suggested that there are four orthogonal dimensions: social versus technical; organizational versus outdoor; science versus business; and artistic. Whether or not these arrange themselves in a manner like the hexagon is, of course, an open question.

Parental Influences on Personal Orientations

Although the statement of the theory did not include a formulation about the events that shape the particular personal orientation that an individual develops, Holland has chosen to investigate classes of events that might bear on the subject. One of the classes of most significance is that of parental influence. We have already studied one theorist who maintains that parent-child interactions are the crucial variable in the development of personality traits which influence later vocational behavior (Roe, 1957). Holland chose to look into parental behaviors in two ways (1962). First, he developed the Parental Attitude Research Instrument (PARI), which was administered to the mothers of the National Merit sample students of 1959. The PARI, based on the work of Schaefer and Bell (1958), assesses the degree to which mothers hold attitudes such as intrusiveness, equalitarianism, martyrdom, and so on. The findings indicated that the students' personal orientations were related to some of the attitudes held by their mothers. For example, students in the Conventional mode had mothers possessing the most authoritarian attitudes, followed in order by those students in the Enterprising, Realistic, Artistic, Social, and Investigative groups. Generally, however, the correlations were low and, except for authoritarian attitudes, generalizations about them are difficult to make.

The approach taken to the study of the fathers' influence on behavior was somewhat different. Each father in the 1959 sample was asked to rank nine goals he held for his child and also his hopes for his child's eventual income. The results indicate that fathers of sons in the Realistic category valued ambition in their sons and hoped their income would be considerable. Fathers of boys in the Investigative category valued curiosity, Social fathers valued self-control, Conventional fathers hoped their sons would be "happy and well adjusted," fathers of boys in the Enterprising group wished happiness and adjustment plus popularity for their sons, and fathers of sons in the Artistic category valued curiosity and independence. Findings for girls, though not as vivid, were in the same general direction.

To test the implicit assumption the theory makes that people with the same personal high point codes should be the product of similar backgrounds, Holland (1962) compared the high point code of the student with that of the father's occupation, parents' education (years), student birth order, and number of children in the family. Only the category of the father's occupation and the category of the son's high point code were significantly related. Other data indicated that father's and son's personal orientations were similar; the father's high-point code was significantly related to son's high point code, though several inversions in the data are evident.

The question of causality recurs when the above data are examined. Thus, while concurrent data about the relationship between parental attitudes and values and student high point codes and personal orientations can be viewed as interesting, they do not clearly demonstrate that parental attitude factors are a primary influence on the particular pattern of personal styles an individual develops. The only rigorous test of such a hypothesis must be predictive in design. Nevertheless, one can speculate from these findings that the behavior of parents creates environments which exert a powerful influence on the personal characteristics of their offspring and that one consequence of this influence is the particular vocational environment the children select. However, such speculation is nothing new in the history of developmental psychology, which has always assigned a major role to the parents. What is new is the shape of the variables Holland chooses to study and the direct connection he tries to make with vocational choice.

Holland did attempt to resolve an issue concerning parental influence with which Roe's theory has difficulty—the question of the effects of parental inconsistency on the vocational behavior of the offspring. Classifying the parents with respect to the degree of authoritarianism or democracy they espouse, he reports that parents who hold consistently democratic ideas toward their children tend to produce sons who are likely to choose scientific careers, while parents holding consistently authoritarian attitudes and values are likely to produce sons selecting Realistic careers, such as engineering or, surprisingly, a Social occupation. It is interesting to recall that Roe and Siegelman (1964) found that male social workers had been more distant from their mothers than engineers and female social workers.

In a more recent study, DeWinne, Overton, and Schneider (1978) found that the personality types of sons and daughters were most similar to those of their fathers. Again, results of this type suggest that relationships between parents and the personalities and career types of offspring are very complicated.

Personal Orientations and Vocational and Educational Choices

The choices made.   Holland's theory leads to the prediction that individuals will choose occupations consistent with their personal orientations. For example, Realistic people will select careers in a Realistic occupational environment. Using career choice instead of career attainment as the dependent variable, Holland studied the relationship between the category of personal orientation and the occupational environment of the field for which a person stated a preference. The assignment of a career field to a particular orientation was made largely on an intuitive basis but, in at least one case, intuition was tempered by empirical findings. Engineering, which intuitively would fit into the Investigative category, was coded as Realistic when it was observed that most engineers' high point codes on the VPI were Realistic rather than Investigative.

Comparing high point code and category of first career choice (Holland, 1962), the results are clear and highly consistent with theoretical expectations. A majority of Realistic, Investigative, and Social subjects chose careers in the appropriate fields. Enterprising Ss chose as many careers in the Realistic area as in the Enterprising, but those two categories constitute a majority of choices for them. Only for the Artistic and Conventional groups does the theory fall down. Artistic Ss chose more Investigative occupations than any other type, not inconsistent with the other findings of similarity between Artistic and Investigative Ss. What is difficult to explain is the finding that Artistic Ss chose Realistic and Social fields more frequently than Artistic careers, and Enterprising occupations as often as Artistic ones. The Conventional group also failed to conform to expectations. They chose a preponderance of Investigative careers, followed by Realistic, Enterprising, Social, in that order, before Conventional. For this finding, explanations are difficult to generate.

What about second and third occupational preferences? Theoretically, these should conform to the principal personal orientation of the chooser. Holland's findings were, by and large, similar to those for first choices and high point code. Most second and third vocational choices were in fields consistent with the major personal orientation of the chooser, and where they were not, they were in a highly related area. As in other parts of his research, Holland found highly similar trends for girls, though his data for girls in the Realistic category are based on an extremely small sample and must be viewed cautiously.

The results of Holland's four-year study (1963) are not clear. It will be recalled that personal orientation in this study was based on the Ss' score on selected SVIB scales. The problem Holland encountered was that his correct predictions, based on the SVIB scores, often did not exceed the predictive efficiency of the base rates of entry into gross occupational categories. For example, he found that about one-third of his sample entered scientific fields, and concluded that predictions of entry rate of subjects into those fields could be made as correctly from the base rate expectation as from SVIB scores.

DeVoge (1975) used the 16 Personality Factor test to study college males during their freshmen year and again during their senior year. He found that the scores for freshmen regarding college majors were not significantly consistent with Holland types, but became so by the time the students were seniors. Judged in accordance with Holland's theory, these results would suggest a general developmental improvement in congruence.

Another long-term predictive validity study of the Holland theory was conducted by O'Neil, Magoon, and Tracey (1978). They followed a sample of investigative male students over a seven-year period. The results indicated that the assignment to an investigative type using the Self-Directed Search is, in fact, predictive over a seven-year period of the actual field of job entry, graduating major, and preferred and projected career plans. These results provide rather striking support for the validity of Holland's instruments and concepts.

Yonge and Regan (1975) conducted a longitudinal study in which Holland's concepts were less strongly supported. Their findings led them to conclude that Holland's constructs are useful in a general way but are not as useful as might be desired in helping to generate highly explicit predictions. Yonge and Regan concluded that personality and college major choice are moderately related and that personality serves as a background factor for these choices, situational demands being more critical in terms of shaping direction for choices.

Stability of choice.   Holland assessed the stability of vocational choices by examining his samples in several ways. He studied the relationship between the student high point codes and successive vocational choices; he compared the high point codes of students who changed majors with those of the students who did not, and he studied the institution's influence on change in the major field. He found that when he examined the first three vocational preferences expressed by the students and grouped the sample into nonchangers (whose three choices all fell into the same environmental orientation) and changers (whose choices fell into two or more categories), his data became more sensitive to the vocational behavior of the students. Thus, if a student had the high point code relevant to the Realistic category and his vocational choice was consistent with it, it was highly likely that his successive occupational preferences would fall into the Realistic orientation. But a student with a high point code in Investigative who said he wanted to be an engineer (Realistic) was likely to express second and third vocational preferences outside of the Realistic environment, presumably in the Investigative area (Holland, 1962).

Other data indicated that when major fields are designated simply as science versus nonscience, boys' changes in major field seem to be a function of their high point code rather than their first choice. Thus, Social Ss change more frequently than other Ss, while Investigative Ss change fields least often, and these changes are independent of field (Holland, 1962; 1963). In a later study (1963), Holland used an *a priori* basis for deciding which combinations of high point codes are consistent with each other and which are not. For example, he says code 12 (Realistic-Investigative) is a consistent code, since Realistic and Investigative people share many interests, activities, and personal traits. However, code 23 (Investigative-Social) is inconsistent because too many differences exist in the environments and characters of these two types. Examining changes of major field in this context, Holland concluded that consistency in code is related to stability of vocational choice.

Another study (Holland and Nichols, 1964) was based on the hypothesis that remaining in a field is associated with the possession of attributes similar to those of the typical student in the field. To test this hypothesis, each vocational group was made to serve, in effect, as its own control. Students were examined as a function of the group which they originally entered, making it possible to identify differences, if any, between those who departed and those who remained. In general, the prediction was supported, though Holland and Nichols point out that the resulting correlations are low and that some inversions exist. Of significance, however, is their final interpretation that change of preferred field is the outcome of a multivariate input combining personality and achievement factors.

Holland's insight into significant variables related to vocational choice stability led him to study student-institution interactions and their effect on the continuity of vocational choice. In his first study (1962), he classified each college attended by Ss in his sample into one of the six environments. These classifications were two-digit codes; the first digit was based on the most common personal orientation of the freshman class vocational choices, the second digit on the second most frequent category. A two-way classification between an individual student's high point code and the institutional code was then made with the expectation that a student in a college with institutional characteristics consistent with his or her personal orientation would receive reinforcement and would thus be less likely to change major field than a student in a college with characteristics inconsistent with his or her personal orientation. Although the findings did not support the prediction, one interesting result did occur. He found that students, whatever the category of their first occupational choice, were significantly more likely to change their major field if they attended an institution with a predominantly Social environment. That is, a science student in a Social college was more than twice as likely to change major field during the freshman year than a student in a Nonsocial college.

In a later study, Holland, further refining his attempts to isolate the influence of colleges on student vocational stability, developed a four-point score which assessed four important features connected with stability and examined the students' stability of choices across these four features. A student received one point for each of the following characteristics that applied: possessing a high point code congruent with the college; having a consistent college code; being a science major; possessing a consistent two-digit code. Classed further under headings of nonchangers and changers, the results indicated a strong relationship between high stability scores and stability of choice. In his sample of males, no Ss scoring four (the maximum) changed field (N = 15); about half of the sample scoring two changed and half did not (N = 46 and N = 42, respectively); twice as many Ss scoring zero changed than did not change (N = 6 and N = 3, respectively). Evidently, then, a third variable must be added to the list of relevant features influencing vocational attainment. The list would then be: achievement, personality orientation, and environmental factors (for example, college characteristics).

In an extensive longitudinal study of more than 3500 male and 4200 female college students in 28 schools, Holland (1968a) was able to draw some generalizations about choice stability defined in terms of college major. In this study, students with Realistic, Social, and Conventional high point codes appear to express very predictable vocational role choices. Overall, when student vocational choice was predicted from the highest VPI score and checked eight months later, the "hit" rate ranged from 21.5 percent to 51.4 percent, while predictions based on the students' original vocational choices and checked eight months later were correct from 63.2 percent to 71.2 percent. Obviously, original choices were better predictors than VPI scores. Holland and Whitney (1968) point out that since about half the males and 60 percent of the females did not change their vocational choice over an 8- to 12-month period in college, one would have a good accuracy rate in predicting that a student's choice would be unchanged. However, the important question is how well the classification system and its instruments permit accurate prediction of choices made by those students who do make changes. If the uncertain students can be sorted out from the more certain ones and predictions made based on their VPI scores, the eventual vocational decisions of these uncertain students may be enhanced.

On the basis of his large longitudinal study of stability of choices, Holland

(1968a) made two other observations of interest. First, he found that for male but not female students, homogeneity or sharpness of VPI profile is related to stability. Inferences about women are difficult to make from this observation (the problems in understanding the career development of women will be discussed in a later chapter). For men, however, it does seem clear that homogeneity of interest is related to crystallization and commitment.

Also, Holland found that the higher a student's choice is in the hierarchy of types in the college, the greater is the probability of satisfaction (and, presumably, stability) of choice. This observation is consistent with results of earlier studies.

Cole, Whitney, and Holland (1971) conducted a study designed to examine the relationship among the occupational groups in the context of Holland's system. One question they specifically asked was whether the congruence of an individual's interests with those of other people in the chosen field was related to vocational stability. The Vocational Preference Inventory was administered to two large samples (6,000 and 12,000); more than half the first sample was followed up a year after original data collection. A principal components analysis of the VPI data was computed. The resulting factor loadings were manipulated to locate the six factor scores over six points; these, in turn, were projected onto the resulting plane, resulting in a two-dimensional representation of the six points. The result of these various manipulations is that occupations can be mapped as a function of their relationship to one another. Cole, Whitney, and Holland used this configuration to define job similarity (the distance between the occupational groups in question on the planar configuration), congruence of an individual and an occupation (again, defined in terms of distances on the configuration), the stability of a vocational choice (the distance between the old and new preference, a large distance indicating instability), and differentiation of interests (a person with a dominating interest pattern would have a profile far removed from the center of the plane, while one with diverse interests would have a profile near the center). With occupational preference stability defined in these terms, congruence and stability were found to be significantly correlated (0.454). In addition, it was found that differentiation of interests was negatively correlated with stability, a finding somewhat inconsistent with the usual expectation that the emergence of a dominating interest pattern will result in an increase in occupational preference stability.

The Level Hierarchy

It will be recalled that the theory included a set of statements which led to some expectations about the occupational level to which a student would aspire. This level hierarchy was hypothetically an additive function of self-evaluation and intelligence. In the 1962 study, Holland tested his formulations about the level hierarchy by predicting a relationship between the student's college major and the sum of his score on the Status scale of the VPI and his Math score on the Scholastic Aptitude Test (SAT). It has been empirically found that certain college majors require more intelligence than others (Wolfle, 1954). Ss with the highest level hierarchy scores, based on the above formula, were expected to choose the more demanding majors more often than Ss with lower level hierarchy scores. Each student was classified into one of nine categories: a 1 to 1 indicated a student whose Status score on the VPI test and SAT Math score both fell into the top third of the sample; a 1 to 2 indicated a Status score in the top third and a Math score in the middle third, and so on. After all the students were so classified, the college major of each student in each category was classified as "high" or "low," indicating whether or not the major required more than "average" intelligence. The general trend of the data supports the hypothesis, though much more clearly for females than for males. The data for the males suggest that the Math score is more significant in influencing the level of the choice than the Status score, while the two seem to operate more equally in influencing the choices the females make.

Evaluation

Holland's investigations based on his theory are impressively extensive. As well as devising ways to test specific hypotheses growing out of his position, he has provided additional information on many aspects of vocational behavior through studies incidental to his tests of his theory. There is considerable evidence from Holland's research that the personal orientations exist much as he described them in his original theoretical formulation and, furthermore, that the types are reasonably stable. The occupational environments also seem to exist as postulated. Most of the predicted characteristics of the types were found to hold, as were a large number of other characteristics and traits that further serve to differentiate the types from one another. Given a student's high point code, an investigator stands a good chance of predicting the student's vocational choice, some personal characteristics, the stability of his/her vocational choice, and to some degree his/her parents' values and attitudes. He also has a good basis for drawing inferences about the student's motives.

The data strongly indicate that personal orientations are related to familial patterns, particularly parents' behaviors, beliefs, ambitions, and goals for their offspring. The data in this sphere are a source of insight into the development of the personal orientations, though large gaps remain and though Holland draws few, if any, conclusions about the direct causal basis underlying developmental hierarchies. The personal orientations have a strong relationship to the vocational choices the students make and relate closely, in combination with other variables, to the stability of the students' vocational choices.

Holland has been sensitive to the data resulting from his investigations and has suggested several modifications of his theory or, at least, pointed to certain weaknesses in it. In two recent monographs, the theory has been revised and updated (Holland, 1966a; 1973), though it remains fundamentally unchanged. As originally presented, Holland's theory was a theory of vocational choice. Proposed were six personal types and six corresponding occupational environments. Following the considerable research he has conducted, Holland chose to broaden the scope of his theory from the relatively narrow context of vocational choice to that of behavior in general. Thus, the six personal types became not merely vocational orientations but styles of life in general, only one facet being vocational. To quote Holland (1962), he has developed "a theory of personal dispositions and their outcomes." Like Roe, he started with a miniature theory to explain vocational choice and shortly arrived at a larger theory of personality.

Other Relevant Research

Holland's work holds up extremely well if judged according to the amount of research his theory has stimulated. The tempo of independent research in investigation of his theory began to accelerate in the middle 1960s and reached very active levels in the early 1970s. The strong interest in testing aspects of Holland's theory partly stems from its simplicity, the available instrumentation, and the attempts Holland himself has made to relate his work to other systems in vocational development such as the *Dictionary of Occupational Titles* and the Strong Vocational Interest Blank.

Level Hierarchy

One of the first studies testing Holland's theory to be reported was by Schutz and Blocher (1961). They sought to test Holland's assumption that the Occupational Level score of the SVIB is a valid index of the self-evaluation concept used as one of the two factors constituting the level hierarchy. Schutz and Blocher constructed a self-attitude instrument which described the similarity between a person's self-description and ideal self-description. The resulting score was called a self-satisfaction score. Their hypothesis, based on Holland's theory, was that a positive relationship exists between Occupational Level scores and the index of self-satisfaction. Using as a sample 135 male high school seniors from a school whose students were more typical of the college-bound population than Holland's National Merit Scholars, Schutz and Blocher first administered the SVIB and then the self- and ideal self-description instruments. After applying statistical transformations to make the data conform to the assumptions of normal statistical analyses, they found a significant product-moment correlation of 0.34 between the Occupational Level and self-satisfaction scores. They concluded, with some caution, that SVIB OL scores may be used to indicate the self-evaluation portion of the level hierarchy in Holland's theory.

Stockin (1964) also investigated an aspect of the level hierarchy in Holland's theory. He studied the correlation between Ss' intelligence and self-evaluation, and level of occupational choices. For intelligence data, he used IQ scores available from school files. To obtain self-evaluation scores, he used three separate scales: the Sims Social Status Scale, the Attitude Toward Education Scale (ATE) of Hieronymus (1951), and the Socioeconomic Expectation Scale (SEE), also by Hieronymus (1951). Sums of scores on these three scales resulted in Stockin's self-evaluation index. The self-evaluation scores of the subjects were then placed into quartiles and combined with the subjects' ranks on the intelligence test. The index from which occupational level could be predicted developed out of these combined scores. The vocational choices of the subjects had already been assigned to a level based on Roe's occupational classification system (1954). The accuracy of Stockin's predictions about vocational choice was then easy to assess by directly comparing predicted preferences with actual preferences.

The findings indicated that a systematic relationship existed between the predictions and the actual choices and, furthermore, that where the predictions were wrong, a large proportion of the careers chosen were in the level adjacent to the actual choice. Stockin also reports that the accuracy of predicting the level of choice is considerably increased by adding self-evaluation to intellectual measures.

However, a study by Fortner (1970) of the level hierarchy does not entirely support this last notion. Using three factors—IQ scores, the Sims Occupational Rating Scale as a measure of self-evaluation, and Wage Earners Occupational Level—to predict levels of occupational choices in 400 junior and senior females in high school, she found a combination of all the instruments was related to level of occupations chosen, but that IQ score alone predicted as well as all three together.

Occupational stereotypes. It should be recalled that a basic assumption underlying Holland's theory is that occupational preferences are based on occupational stereotypes. A number of investigators have chosen to examine occupational stereotypes in terms of Holland's theory. Hollander and Parker (1969) wrote, in terms of the need scales of the Adjective Check List, descriptions of six occupations, each representing one of Holland's six types (auto mechanic, scientist, teacher, bank teller, business executive, and artist). The resulting descriptions were made available to 54 high school sophomores, who were then asked to respond to the Adjective Check List as if they were a member of each one of the six occupational groups. With the exception of auto mechanic and teacher, needs emerged matching the Holland types. Banducci (1970) tested differences in career knowledge of 600 high school boys as a function of their membership in one of the six Holland types. Knowledge was tested in terms of the accuracy of the occupational stereotypes held. Realistic, Investigative, and Enterprising students held more accurate occupational stereotypes than Social, Conventional, and Artistic students. Unfortunately, it is difficult to interpret these results. Do they mean that the three high groups are more in tune with the world of work, or that occupations suitable to their types are easier to stereotype than those of other types, or something else?

Still another study by Hollander and Parker (1972) tested three hypotheses: that adolescent self-concept and stereotypic description of most preferred occupation are positively related, that adolescent self-concept and stereotypic description of the least preferred occupation are not positively related, and that adolescent most and least preferred occupational choices represent different occupational environments. The Adjective Check List and an Occupational Preference List were administered to 54 high school boys. The findings supported all three hypotheses. Hollander and Parker concluded that these results supported Holland's theory since they suggested that individuals "search for situations which satisfy their hierarchy of adjustive orientations."

Indecision, persistence, and change. Holland's theory has been used extensively to orient research concerning career indecision, change, and adjustment in college students. A test of several aspects of Holland's theory was conducted by Osipow, Ashby, and Wall (1966). The first prediction was that subjects would express occupational preferences consistent with their major personal orientation. Second, it was predicted that subjects in the Social category would express greater uncertainty about their vocational preference than would other types of students. Third, it was predicted that subjects expressing a high degree of certainty about their choice would show greater consistency between their first and second choices (the second choice would more likely be in the same occupational environment as the first choice) than Ss whose occupational preferences were tentative. Finally, it was predicted that the same would hold true for the consistency between major personality orientation and second occupational choice (decided Ss would show greater consistency in this regard than would undecided Ss).

A sample of college freshmen was required to rank six personality descriptions they thought matched their behavior. These descriptions were based upon the six personal orientations described by Holland. As part of the ranking procedure, the Ss were required to rate the degree to which each description fit them, so that a measure of the order of the Ss' identification with each type, plus the strength of that identification, was obtained. Information about the occupational preferences of each student was available, and each preference was coded into the appropriate occupational environment according to guide lines set down by Holland in several papers (1962; 1963; 1963–1964). It was thus possible to test the first prediction, that Ss' occupational preferences are consistent with the major personal orientation, by comparing the frequency with which students' occupational preferences were in occupational environments consistent with the major personal orientation. The results concerning this hypothesis supported Holland's theory.

The second hypothesis, concerning the greater uncertainty of Social Ss, was tested by simply comparing the degree of certainty expressed by the Ss in the six orientations on a four-point scale. The results of this analysis did not support Holland's data; Social Ss were no different from other subjects in their occupational certainty.

The Ss in the study had been classified according to the degree to which they were certain of their educational-vocational plans along the dimension of what college they had entered within a large university. (A college for undecided students was available in addition to the traditional academic colleges.) The prediction concerning the greater consistency between the first and second occupational preferences for students certain of their choice as opposed to those uncertain of it was tested by comparing the categories of the choices of students in these two kinds of programs. It was found that Ss with a higher degree of certainty about their plans (as defined by program choice) did show greater consistency in the category of their first and second vocational preferences than did Ss less clear about their plans, thus supporting the prediction.

The final hypothesis was that Ss more certain of their plans, again defined in terms of their college programs as described above, would have second occupational preferences consistent with their major personal orientation, while Ss less clear about their plans would not. This prediction did not receive support. In fact, the second preferences for both groups were not consistently related to their major personality orientation.

Comparisons of the subjects by major personality orientation and SVIB group scores revealed consistency between the SVIB scores and assignment to personality categories. For example, Ss in the Realistic category earned their highest scores, and higher scores than any other personality group, on SVIB groups II and III (science-engineering and practical, respectively), which is exactly what the theoretical statements would lead one to expect. In terms of the degree to which the vocational preferences, when assigned to categories equivalent to those of Holland's theory, fell into appropriate SVIB groups, the evidence is even stronger. From the results it would appear that considerable construct validity exists among the personal orientations, SVIB group scores, and occupational preferences (Wall, Osipow, and Ashby, 1967).

In another study, the same authors (Ashby, Wall, and Osipow, 1966) examined in terms of a number of variables three groups of college freshmen differing in their degrees of educational-vocational certainty. Among the variables were the personality rankings of the earlier study based on Holland's personal orientations. In the later study, it was found that the most highly certain group of subjects ranked themselves significantly higher on the Investigative and Artistic types than the other two groups of less certain subjects.

Baird (1969) has raised in a somewhat different way than Osipow, Ashby, and Wall the question of the degree to which the undecided student is unlike other students. Baird administered a wide variety of questionnaires (the VPI, Preconscious Activity Scale, Interpersonal Competency Scale, the Range of Experience Scale, the Indecision Scale, the Dogmatism Scale, and many others) to more than 6000 male and 6000 female college students. The scores and responses of those students who expressed educational and vocational commitment were compared with those who were undecided about their plans. Male "decideds" rated themselves higher than male "undecideds" on the vocational and academic types and exhibited more achievement drive, expressed more interest in making a scientific contribution, had more scientific potential, and showed more technical competency than "undecideds." For females, "decideds" were more likely than "undecideds" to have a goal involving religious activity and rated themselves higher in homemaking and interpersonal competencies than "undecideds." In another study, reported in the same article by Baird, a comparison of 13,000 undecided students with 43,000 decided students on academic abilities revealed no differences.

Elton and Rose performed several studies of the differences in career and academic development of decided and undecided students. In one study (Elton and Rose, 1970), they tested the hypothesis that immigrants to a major field and persisters should show similar characteristics at the time of graduation. The sample consisted of 530 graduating male students for whom freshmen test data (Omnibus Personality Inventory and the American College Testing Program Battery) were available. The results indicated that senior choice is predictable on the basis of personality and aptitude but even more accurately predicted by the freshman's expressed choice. This finding is similar to Holland's (1968a) observations of predictors of college major 8 to 12 months after entrance into college. Elton and Rose found that most undecided freshmen ended their studies in social or enterprising areas. The results of the Elton and Rose (1970) study tend to support the hexagon model created by Holland, since transfers to fields remote (on the hexagon) from their original choice should have different characteristics from those transferring to adjacent categories.

In another study dealing with the question of whether immigrants to a field might conceal the differences between students who changed from one Holland category to another over time, Elton and Rose (1971) examined the Omnibus Personality Inventory scores of 137 college seniors who were originally vocationally undecided at college entrance as compared to those of seniors persisting in or changing to a major represented by one of the Holland scales. No differences were found, indicating that no personality factors differentiate decided from undecided students. In another investigation with a similar purpose, Rose and Elton (1971) compared 85 freshmen undecided students who persisted to graduation with 88 randomly selected undecided freshmen who left by the fourth quarter. Those who stayed to graduation were less conforming and more masculine on the Omnibus Personality Inventory and had higher ACT scores than those who left. Even though the mean ACT scores of those who left were higher than the mean of the freshman class on the ACT, 72 percent of those students who left prematurely were not in good standing at the time of departure.

Congruence. In terms of Holland's theory, congruence has been defined as the degree of consistency between an individual's high point code and the occupational environment of his preferred or planned field. Several studies have examined both the theoretical and applied implications of congruence in student populations. Morrow (1971), using Holland's theory as a basis for hypothesizing about student satisfaction with college major, predicted that congruent students would express more satisfaction with their college major than incongruent students. To test his prediction, he assigned 86 male and 61 female mathematics majors and 54 male and 122 female sociology majors to personality high point code types on the basis of their Vocational Preference Inventory scores and administered a questionnaire concerning satisfaction with college major. Morrow, assuming that for mathematics majors a high score on the Investigative scale was congruent and all other high point codes incongruent, found support for the congruence-satisfaction prediction. For sociology majors, a high VPI score on Social was considered to be congruent and all others incongruent. The prediction was not supported by the results for the sociology majors.

Southworth and Morningstar (1970) divided 102 freshmen engineering students into three groups according to their status during the junior year: those still majoring in engineering (N = 43), those who had left engineering studies but were still enrolled in the university (N = 33), and those who had left the university (N = 26). The VPI had been administered to the engineering students during their freshman year. Interesting differences in VPI scores were found to occur according to the status of the students' enrollment during their junior year. The "changers" were found to be higher on the Social and Artistic scales than the engineering "persisters," and those who left the university seemed to have lower scores on the Investigative scale than those students who stayed till their junior year. There was also some evidence to indicate that those students who left the university had fewer overall interests. The implication appears to be that students leave engineering to pursue other interests not satisfied by engineering, that students who leave university studies entirely do so because of the lack of a scholarly inclination, and that academic persistence in college may require some minimum development of openness of interest. Taking these results in combination with Morrow's (1971), one might speculate that the mathematics majors were satisfied with their majors because there were no other important interests *uninvolved* in their studies, while the sociology majors' satisfaction was not predictable because the Social environment did not necessarily include all their major activity needs.

Mount and Muchinsky (1978a) administered the SDS to 362 workers in fields representing five types of environment. The results showed that people generally worked in environments congruent with their type. Mount and Muchinsky (1978b) further found that employees classified as working in a congruent occupation by means of the Self Directed Search were more satisfied with their work in terms of work, pay, promotions, supervision, co-workers and overall satisfaction than incongruent employees. This finding supports Holland's theory.

However, the other studies are less supportive of the theory. Robbins, Thomas, Harvey, and Kandefer (1978) examined the work changes of 62 men between the ages of 33 and 54 to see whether or not they changed in a direction more congruent with their Strong-Campbell Interest Inventory codes. In terms of the Dictionary of Occupational Titles codes for the first and second occupations, which were translated into Holland codes, they found that 26 men changed to careers more congruent with personality, 25 to careers less congruent with personality, and 11 made no change. This study does not lend much support to Holland's theory. DOT categories, however, may be too imprecise to adequately test the theory. Gade and Saliah (1975) found that for more than 150 male graduates of a university, expressed choices of occupations that were made as high school seniors more accurately predicted graduating college major and career entry occupation than VPI high point codes.

Spokane, Malett, and Vance (1978) found that person-environment congruence was associated with curricular change in the way one would predict.

Walsh and his students have investigated several other aspects of congruence and career development, always using the VPI and self-reported college major to establish congruence. In one study, Walsh and Russel (1969) found that "congruent" students exhibit better personal adjustment (defined in terms of the Mooney Problem Check List) than do incongruent students. Walsh and Barrow (1971) studied 30 male and 30 female congruent students' and 30 male and 30 female incongruent students' personality characteristics on the California Personality Inventory. No major systematic personality differences were found as a function of congruence-incongruence. Finally, Walsh and Lewis (1972) found, on the basis of the Omnibus Personality Inventory, that congruent male students exhibit more satisfaction with their academic programs, more personal stability, and more stable college choices than do incongruent students. The results of these three studies might suggest that while congruent and incongruent students do not differ in a systematic personal way in the beginning, the different effects of studying a field that "fits" one to varying degrees may have an important impact on one's adjustment as time goes on. Little is known about the factors that enhance the development of congruent choices, though Bodden (1970) reported that cognitive complexity is positively related to expressing a congruent vocational choice.

Holland's theory applied to other settings.   One of the early criticisms of Holland's work was that the data were too dependent, first, on highly talented groups, and second, on student populations in higher education (Osipow, 1968). Since those earlier observations of the theory were made, a number of investigators have extended the Holland theory downward in age and level of talent, outward in terms of moving away from student groups, and upward in terms of applications to older populations, so that the criticism is no longer a valid concern. In one of the early studies of high school students, Rezler (1967a) administered the Kuder Preference Record, the VPI, and the California Test of Mental Maturity to two groups of high school junior and senior females, 33 representing pioneer fields (medicine, mathematics, or natural sciences) and 33 representing the traditional careers in nursing or elementary school teaching. The results indicated that the Pioneers scored higher on Computational, Scientific, and Social Service interests on the Kuder, higher on Investigative and Masculinity, and lower on Social, Self-control, and Status than the Traditionals. The Pioneers also scored higher on CTMM, IQ, and PSAT Mathematics and Verbal scales. Within the Pioneers, the premedical students scored higher on Scientific and Social Service interests than the mathematics and science students and also higher on the Investigative and Social scales on the VPI. The traditionalist nurses scored higher on Kuber Outdoor and Scientific scales and lower on the Computational, Literary, and Clerical scales than prospective elementary teachers, while the future nurses were higher on Investigative than the future elementary teachers.

In a study comparing the work roles and preferred work roles of a 2½ percent sample of clergy in one state association, Osipow (1970) found that most of the respondents were Social types but reported working in Conventional roles more than in Social environments. A student sample, classified by VPI results primarily into the Social category, anticipated Social work roles. Though the VPI results of both the students and professionals apparently confirms that the clergy is a Social type, there is apparently an important discrepancy between the preferred and anticipated role of the clergy and what they do later.

Lacey (1971) attempted to extend Holland's theory to a sample of employed men representing each of the six types described by the theory. Except for those individuals classified as Realistic, the VPI and the occupational activity engaged in by these men were consistent with the theory. Hughes (1972) has also attempted to extend Holland's theory to an employed sample. He tested the hypotheses that individuals are employed in jobs appropriate to their type, that individual occupational level can be predicted on the basis of intelligence and self-evaluation, that individuals give self-ratings consistent with their personal orientation, that individuals with consistent personality patterns change their work less often than those with inconsistent patterns, and that those with consistent patterns are more satisfied with their work than those with inconsistent patterns. Hughes administered the VPI, SVIB, 16 PF, a self-rating personality scale, the Quick Word Intelligence Test, the Sims Occupational Rating Scale, and a personal information sheet to 400 employed men ranging in age from 25 to 35. The results did not support the hypothesis that people work at jobs appropriate to their personality orientation. The level hierarchy prediction, however, was supported in that it was found that intelligence and self-evaluation predicted occupational level. No evidence was found that self-ratings were consistent with personality attributes. No evidence was found that consistent patterns resulted in fewer job changes over time. Finally, no evidence was found to support the hypothesis that occupational satisfaction is related to personality type consistency. Hughes' study is one of the few whose major findings are completely at odds with Holland's theory.

Williams (1972) applied Holland's theory to a graduate student population. She administered the VPI, Allport-Vernon-Lindzey Study of Values, Miller Occupational Values Indicator, and the 16 PF to 145 graduate students representing 18 departments. She concluded that discriminant analysis revealed that the VPI assigned students to their field fairly well, though the Realistic and Enterprising types were marginal, the AVL similarly assigned accurately though the Realistic and Enterprising were not assigned satisfactorily, the Miller OVI assigned adequately only the Social type, and the 16 PF was adequate for all types. Overall, the Investigative and Conventional were most clearly discriminated, Enterprising and Realistic most poorly. Most field selections were congruent with personality type, thus Williams concluded that the theory was supported. However, in another study in a graduate school setting, Frantz and Walsh (1972), found an overriding Investigative orientation in the students which obscured other differences that might have been expected as a function of field differences. It is difficult to know whether this result reflects the impact of environmental press or a flaw in Holland's theory.

O'Reilly (1977), testing the hypothesis that there is a significant interaction between work orientation and appropriate job fit, studied 370 Navy personnel across 10 job categories and found results generally consistent with Holland's theory of person-environment interaction. In a study of 30 clergy Fabry (1975) similarly found validity for the conception of the theory and Vocational Preference Inventory. Fishburne and Walsh (1976) found support, although not perfect, for the notion that Holland's theory predicts as it should for males without college degrees who are employed. Two of the six Vocational Preference Inventory scales and four of the six Self-Directed Search scales accurately predicted the field of employment. Other studies indicating the validity of Holland's theory for employed adults include Helson (1978) for authors and critics, Utz and Hartman (1978) for business school graduates, Salomone and Slaney (1978) for nonprofessional workers, and Spokane and Walsh (1978) for enterprising workers. On the other side, Robbins and Harvey found that the career changes of 62 male managers and professionals were not consistent with what the theory would have predicted (1978). Two other investigators (Folsom, 1969; Osipow, 1969) report studies in which students in baccalaureate or associate degree programs describe themselves in terms generally consistent with the Holland characteristics for their field.

The relation of the VPI to other instruments.　Considerable interest has been shown in relating the VPI to other interest measures, probably because of the value in relating the empirically strong interest inventories to one based on a theory of career development. One approach has been the application of canonical correlation analysis to some combination of interest measures. Navran and Kendall (1971) did a canonical correlational analysis of the VPI, SVIB, and the EPPS based on data from 277 freshmen in a military college. They concluded that the SVIB and VPI are related more to each other than to the EPPS, but that enough differences exist between the two interest inventories to make the use of both worthwhile. Salomone and Muthard (1972) used canonical correlation to relate the Minnesota Importance Questionnaire (a measure of vocational needs) to the VPI, basing their data on 333 counselors. In this study, no significant relation was found between the two instruments, suggesting a need to differentiate between vocational needs and vocational interests. Haase (1971) performed a canonical correlation between the VPI and the SVIB for 176 male college students and found six common factors. Cole and Hanson (1971) attempted to assess the structural relationships between the SVIB, the Kuder Occupational Interest Survey, the VPI, the Minnesota Vocational Interest Inventory, and the ACT Vocational Interest Profile. All these instruments were found to be similar, and some evidence was noted supporting the circular configuration of interests along the lines Roe and Holland each suggest.

Rezler (1967b) compared the Kuder Preference Record and the VPI, using interest data based on the responses of 250 junior and 265 senior females in high school. Performance on the Realistic scale was found to be positively correlated with Kuder Outdoor and Mechanical and negatively with Kuder Persuasive and Literary; Investigative positively correlated with Kuder Science and Outdoor and negatively with Persuasive and Clerical; Social positively correlated with Kuder Social Service and Persuasive and negatively with Outdoor, Mechanical, Computational, and Artistic; Conventional positively correlated with Computational and Clerical and negatively with Outdoor, Literary, and Musical; Enterprising positively correlated with Persuasive and negatively with Outdoor and Scientific; and Artistic positively correlated with Kuder Artistic, Literary, and Musical and negatively with Computational and Clerical.[1]

Some deliberate efforts have been made to relate the SVIB and the VPI. Recent work on the SVIB has resulted in the development of Holland scales on the SVIB. Forerunners of this work are studies by Cockriel (1972), Blakeney, Matteson, and Holland (1972), Eggenberger and Herman (1972), and Lee and Hedahl (1973). The major study is one reported by Campbell and Holland (1972), who describe the procedures followed to provide the basis for the development of each of the Holland scales through the use of SVIB responses. The results of these attempts clearly indicate that the two systems, Holland's and Strong's, can be usefully and logically related to one another. As Campbell and Holland point out in their paper, three levels of classification exist: general categories, such as the Holland types; underlying dimensions, such as the basic interest scales of the Strong; and empirical scales, such as the occupational scales of the Strong. Each may provide a useful and distinctive function. The Hansen and Johansson (1972) paper does the same thing for the women's Strong and the VPI that the Campbell and Holland (1972) paper does for the men's version.

One other study is of some interest in connection with the relation between the Holland system and others. Griffith and Trogden (1969), applying Shaw's (1966) theory, have studied differences between female nursing and music students in self-expressive styles. Shaw has postulated four styles: humanistic, interpretive, promotional, and technological. The Preference Association Survey, developed to measure these styles, was administered to the nursing and music students. Griffith and Trogden predicted that nurses would score higher on the humanistic and lower on the promotional scales than music students while music students would score higher on the interpretive and lower on the technological scales than nursing students. They also predicted that nurses, compared within their group, would score highest on humanistic and lowest on promotional scales, while the music students, also compared within their group, would score highest on interpretive and lowest on technological scales. The Shaw system and the Griffith and Trogden study are of

---

[1]Rezler's (1967) findings are based on females and are of particular interest since there has been controversy about the applicability of Holland's theory and measures to females. For example, Osipow and Ashby (1968) found that two-digit codes for men were far more varied than for women, the latter sex having profiles dominated by a social aspect. Alston, Wakefield, Doughtie and Bobile (1976) found that Holland's theory measured largely the same constructs for both sexes in a college student sample.

interest in that their approach seems similar in some ways to Holland's (though the Shaw system has four types rather than six) and has similar implications. Further research relating Holland's and Shaw's work might be of interest.

Jones, Hansen, and Putnam (1976) found that the six Holland types differed in their degree of vocational maturity between eighth and twelfth grade and in addition that, self-concept differed across the six Holland types.

Environmental aspects of Holland's theory.   In his early work, Holland had little to say about how a person became a particular type or about the events that enhance or influence membership in a type. However, Holland has had much to say about environmental events and their importance in maintaining or shaping type membership once established. A number of investigators have followed the line of research suggested by Holland's emphasis on environment's role in vocational preference and persistence.

Barclay, Stilwell, and Barclay (1972) have taken an interesting approach to the study of environmental aspects in the development of personality types. Barclay studied the effect of father's occupation on, among other things, children's vocational awareness. The Barclay Classroom Climate Inventory was administered to 1386 elementary school children. The occupations of the fathers of these children were also obtained and classified into Holland categories. The results of the BCCI allowed Barclay to make generalizations about the connection between children's behavior and their fathers' particular Holland types as inferred from occupation. The many generalizations are too extensive to be covered here. An example is: having a father as a teacher enhances the child's (both girls and boys) Social, Artistic, and Investigative areas; having a father as a physician or lawyer seems to result in the child's possession of Social and Conventional skills (as perceived and reported by peers). The large amount of data generated from this study and the method and instrumentation introduced offer some promise of filling the gap in Holland's theory dealing with the development of personality.

Elton (1971) examined the effects of environment on personality development in the context of Holland's theory by giving the Omnibus Personality Inventory to three samples of 50 males continuously enrolled in college for four semesters. One of the three samples had moved from an engineering to an arts and science program during the period of enrollment. Scores were "factor change" scores between two administrations of the Omnibus Personality Inventory. Some interesting changes were observed: the nonauthoritarianism score of the transfers to arts and science changed more than that of the engineering persisters; in addition, the transfers to arts and science were more realistic, nonjudgmental, intellectually liberal, and religiously skeptical. These results certainly generate the impression of a changing, open and liberal student moving from engineering to arts and science and of a conservative, stable, and traditional student remaining in engineering, but some limitations should be noted. First, there is really no way to know whether the personality changes seen in those leaving engineering were the result of interaction with the different academic environment or percipitated the change from engineering. In addition, these results must be viewed tentatively because of the small sample and lack of cross validation.

Several studies have examined the impact of environment in terms of student achievement. Barclay (1967), by testing students exemplifying successful performance in certain academic fields, successfully describes both the environmental press enhancing achievement in various fields as well as the personal characteristics required for success according to field. Astin and Panos (1969) report findings which support the idea that, at least in technical and teachers colleges, there is a pressure to conform to the popular majors—students seem unlikely to switch to unpopular majors and highly likely to change to the popular ones. Astin and Panos found, as had Holland himself in another study (1968a), that the best predictor of a student's final major is his or her initial choice of major field. Posthuma and Navran (1970) found, on the basis of the SVIB, EPPS, and VPI scores of 110 students and 44 faculty, some crude evidence to indicate that congruence between the students and their faculty, especially on the SVIB and the VPI, enhances student academic achievement.

Finally, there is a series of studies by Walsh and his students dealing with the impact of collegiate academic environment on the individual student's perceptions of personal change over time. Walsh and Lacey (1969) examined the hypothesis that college students enrolled in a major perceived themselves as changing, over the period of their college years, in a direction congruent with the personal orientation indicated by that major. One hundred fifty-one college male seniors, representing each of the six occupational environments described by Holland, were studied by means of the Perceived Change Inventory. Engineering, chemistry, and fine arts students (representing Realistic, Investigative, and Artistic types) report changes consistent with the typical personality orientation for their field. Psychology, political science, and economics students (representing Social, Enterprising, and Conventional types) did not report consistent changes. In another study, Walsh and Lacey (1970) extended their approach to college women, with generally similar results. Women in Investigative, Artistic, and Conventional fields reported seeing themselves as having changed in a direction consistent with their field's modal personality type. Walsh, Vaudrin, and Hummel (1972) examined the question of whether, over time, college students changed in the direction of their existing personality orientation. Based on the responses of 154 and 165 third-quarter male and female students to the Perceived Change Inventory, some evidence was produced indicating that a modest degree of accentuation of existing personality attributes results from exposure to an environment, a college major being defined as an environment in this study. The longer a student was in an environment, the greater the development of appropriate traits.

Overall, these studies of environmental aspects of personality orientation suggest at least two important influences, family and school. In addition, the results of the Walsh studies, and possibly the Elton study, suggest that at least to some extent, "work" environment can play an important role in changing or maintaining personality characteristics associated with vocational matters.

STATUS

The Implications for Counseling Practice

As is the case with most theorists of vocational choice, Holland did not at first attempt to devise a model for counseling young people and adults with regard to their vocational decisions. However, based on Holland's early writings, inferences which apply to counseling settings may be drawn from the content of the theory and the resulting empirical data testing it. For example, a point that may easily be overlooked is that Holland's theoretical statement denotes a classification of occupations which may be of use to counselors in helping their clientele become oriented to the world of work. Within the context of that occupational classification system the counselor might apply one of various techniques to identify the major personal style of the individual (the techniques used so far are the VPI, selected SCII scores, first occupational preferences, and ranking of descriptions based on the characteristics of the six personal orientations), then identify the particular occupational environment that is relevant and help his or her client locate the suitable level in that hierarchy. This approach is much like the traditional trait-factor approach used for generations in vocational counseling and is best exemplified today in the use counselors make in their practice of the SCII and various ability measures. The advantage Holland's system possesses over the empirical systems (in other words, the nontheoretically derived, such as the SCII) is that the occupational environments may offer a greater potential from which to choose a career field than SCII categories, which are not always internally consistent.

Of significance, too, is the potential that the theory holds for identifying institutional characteristics in terms of the six potential environments of the theory. It will be recalled that some evidence was found indicating that students in schools where the major orientation was congruent with their own major personal orientation were less likely to change fields than those in schools whose major orientation differed from their own. It was also found that orientations of institutions tend to influence the behavior of their constituents in subtle ways. If counselors were to become sophisticated with respect to the identification of modal institutional environments, they could help students to recognize the psychological characteristics of the schools they are considering attending and to add to other factors influencing their decisions some evaluation of this subtle dimension.

The potential of institutional evaluation along the lines of psychological characteristics does not end with universities. There is nothing to prevent professional counselors from systematically studying the psychological characteristics of industries, particular business organizations, hospitals, government agencies, and so on. Such data might well be useful for people advanced in their careers if they are considering changes in their mature years or when they are considering the organization in which to begin their career. It has been suggested that effective organizations play a major role in generating effective careers for individuals, and therefore it is likely that the psychological context an organization provides is a major factor in career satisfaction, progress, and effectiveness. It is a well-known fact that two positions with the same title but in different organizations are likely to be very different because of environmental differences the organizations produce for the persons holding the positions.

There are other uses the counselor may find for Holland's theory. Because of the considerable data that Holland has collected about the features of people possessing different personal orientations, a counselor already has a considerable body of information about a client simply by virtue of knowing his or her major personal orientation to life. The counselor may make some educated guesses about the client's background, parents' behaviors toward and ambitions for the client and the client's goals, values, social relations, motivators, and distractors.

In one paper, Holland (1964b) made some explicit statements about limitations of current practices in vocational counseling and some suggestions about the direction vocational counseling should take in its future development. He is particularly critical about the rigidity of vocational counselors in using interviews with students as the main vehicle to effect change. Holland maintains that few people can be reached in that way and, furthermore, that even those who are reached are only minimally influenced by the things their counselors say to them. Holland proposes as an alternative the use of "environmental programmers and specialists," whose functions are not clearly defined in his mind, but who would generally be concerned with devising techniques through which students could be exposed to real and meaningful occupational experiences. Work-study programs represent meaningful work experiences.

Holland's theory possesses some general utility for counselors in their conceptualization of occupational selection for their clientele, but it offers little specific advice in the way of suggestions about procedures and techniques that the counselors may use in their face-to-face work with their clients. For example, until some questions concerning the antecedents of the personal types are answered, counselors will find it difficult to develop interview procedures based on Holland's theory beyond an empirical trait-factor approach such as is represented by SVIB. That is, counselors might be able to say, "You are a realistic type of person and your intellectual apparatus and personal evaluations place you at a moderate level; thus you might find work as an electronics technician, welder, or draftsman suitable."

As the research effort of a variety of investigators has grown, an impressive amount of data regarding the characteristics and background of members of the various personal types have accumulated. The theory is much more applicable to counseling now than in its earlier stages. Holland has become more directly concerned with applications of the theory and in this regard has developed the Self-Directed Search (Holland, 1971), an instrument which combines the VPI with questions about self-estimates of competency. The goal of this instrument is the stimulation of self-inquiry, which produces a summary statement combining the individual's perception of his abilities and preferences. Holland claims that about half the people who take this instrument find it is all they need to begin the process of vocational selection, while the other half find it sensitizes them to a need for further counseling. The instrument is too new for evaluation and little data are yet available regarding its validity, but it does seem to offer considerable potential value to the counselor and researcher. The occupational classification booklet, listing over 400 occupations, that accompanies the SDS is a useful career exploration adjunct in itself.

Other developments which make the theory more applicable are the publications of VPI norms (Holland, 1968b), the integration with the SCII, and recent applications to the *Dictionary of Occupational Titles* system of classification. Frantz (1972) has shown how Holland's theory can be applied to the problem of counseling an individual with regard to an undifferentiated SVIB profile. Viernstein (1972) has developed procedures designed to extend Holland's occupational classification system to the *Dictionary of Occupational Titles* in terms of the data-people-things relationships described in the DOT. Her data indicate that these data-people-things relationships hold in theoretically predicted ways. For example, involvement with things is higher for Realistic types than for others; Social and Enterprising types are higher on ''people'' involvement than Realistic, Investigative, and Conventional; and only the high Artistic involvement with people seems inconsistent theoretically.

Thus the nature of the theory is such that imaginative counselors might find it possible to generate counseling procedures based on Hollond's theory. Some idea about how difficulties in the choice process develop is given in the theory. For example, problems in the realm of the level of choice are likely to be the result of an inconsistent self-evaluation. Circumstances leading to an ambiguous developmental hierarchy presumably lead also to choice conflicts. Ambiguous developmental hierarchies, in their turn, may develop because of a vagueness about the real world. In such a manner Holland's theory would explicitly account for misdirected vocational behavior or problems in vocational choice. As a result, the theory could be useful to a counselor in diagnosing the underlying factors contributing to vocational indecision.

Evaluation

With respect to the research testing it, the record of Holland's theory is extremely good. The research program has been broad, varied, and comprehensive.

Holland's theory seems to suffer from the problems that are inherent in trait-factor approaches to vocational choice. For example, it is possible for people to change their environments and themselves. The environmental and individual traits that the trait-factor approach tries to match are not only variable but are subject to change by one of the portions of the equation, that is, the individual. Consequently, when a young man discovers that his job as a salesman is not what he thought it would be, he may, and frequently does, exert his efforts at changing his definition and emphasis of his job without changing its title.

_____. A final serious limitation is that the theory, as stated, explains little about the process of personality development and its role in vocational selection. This is a serious deficiency since in this theory an understanding of personality development is crucial to understanding career development. It is one thing to state that people with Investigative orientations are looking for an environment in which they can express their major personality orientation, but it is quite another thing to explain how or why they developed their Investigative orientation to begin with. The data Holland has reported concerning the familial characteristics of people holding the various orientations are suggestive of causal factors, but only very tenuous inferences can be drawn. It is in the area of the growth of these developmental hierarchies that much valuable empirical work can be done with respect to Holland's theory. The effect of these orientations in vocational behavior in later life is also an important area for further study. Indeed, the question as to whether these models of personal styles hold validity for older people is open at present.

As for the overall status, how does Holland's theory rate according to the specific criteria outlined in the first chapter? Certainly, the proposal is comprehensive, covering not only vocational choices but life style in the broadest sense. Tests of the theory indicate its validity in broad outline. Certain aspects are open to rigorous test, while others must of necessity be tested indirectly, or worse, crudely. The theory does not describe the development of the personality types, but does indicate the process of normal choice and misdirected choice from the point of an established personal orientation and beyond. Unfortunately, few suggestions are made for the treatment of problems in career choice and for identifying relevant vocational counseling goals. The theory does logically and parsimoniously account for a good deal of vocational behavior, but falls down somewhat in respect to explanation of why people develop into various types.

It is to be expected that investigators will continue to try to show how early experiences in childhood and adolescence are related to the development of one of the six major personal orientations (for example, Barclay, Stilwell, and Barclay, 1972). Such data will be highly useful to both counselors and researchers in developmental psychology. In a later chapter, an example of how personality and career are intermeshed illustrates how research may uncover the ways personal orientations such as Holland describes evolve (Robert White's *Lives in Progress,* 1952). The number of unanswered and answered questions that remain with respect to Holland's theory, however, suggests that the theory will exert an influence on research in career choice for some time and begin to have a growing impact on counseling itself.

REFERENCES

Alston, H. L., Wakefield, J. A., Jr., Doughtie, F., Doughtie, E. B., and Bobele, R. M. Correspondence of constructs for male and female college students. *Journal of Vocational Behavior,* 1976, *8,* 85–88.

Ashby, J. D., Wall, H. W., and Osipow, S. H. Vocational certainty and indecision in college freshmen. *Personnel and Guidance Journal,* 1966, *44,* 1037–1041.

Astin, A. W., and Panos, R. J. *The educational and vocational development of college students.* Washington, D. C.: American Council on Education, 1969.

Baird, L. L. The undecided student—how different is he? *Personnel and Guidance Journal,* 1969, *47,* 429–434.

Banducci, R. Accuracy of occupational stereotypes of grade-twelve boys. *Journal of Counseling Psychology,* 1970, *17,* 534–539.

Barclay, J. R. Approach to the measurement of teacher "press" in the secondary curriculum. *Journal of Counseling Psychology,* 1967, *14,* 550–567.

Barclay, J. R., Stilwell, W. E., III, and Barclay, L. K. The influence of paternal occupation on social interaction measures in elementary school children. *Journal of Vocational Behavior,* 1972, *2,* 433–446.

Blakeney, R. N., Matteson, M. T., and Holland, T. A. A research note on the new SVIB scales. *Journal of Vocational Behavior,* 1972, *2,* 239–243.

Bodden, J. L. Cognitive complexity as a factor in appropriate vocational choice. *Journal of Counseling Psychology,* 1970, *17,* 364–368.

Campbell, D. P., and Holland, J. L. A merger in vocational interest research: applying Holland's theory to Strong's data. *Journal of Vocational Behavior,* 1972, *2,* 353–376.

Cockriel, I. W. Some data concerning the VPI scales and the SVIB. *Journal of Vocational Behavior,* 1972, *2,* 251–254.

Cole, N. S., and Hanson, G. R. An analysis of the structure of vocational interests. *Journal of Counseling Psychology,* 1971, *18,* 478–486.

Cole, N. S., Whitney, D. R., and Holland, J. L. A spatial configuration of occupations. *Journal of Vocational Behavior,* 1971, *1,* 1–9.

DeVoge, S. D. Personality variables, academic major, and vocational choice: a longitudinal study of Holland's theory. *Psychological Reports,* 1975, *37,* 1191–1195.

DeWinne, R. F., Overton, T. D., and Schneider, L. J. Types produce types—especially fathers. *Journal of Vocational Behavior,* 1978, *12,* 140–144.

Eggenberger, J., and Herman, A. The Strong Inventory and Holland's theory. *Journal of Vocational Behavior,* 1972, *2,* 447–456.

Elton, C. F. Interaction of environment and personality: a test of Holland's theory. *Journal of Applied Psychology,* 1971, *55,* 114–118.

Elton, C. F., and Rose, H. A. Male occupational constancy and change: its prediction according to Holland's theory. *Journal of Counseling Psychology,* 1970, *17,* part 2, 1–19.

Elton, C. F., and Rose, H. A. A longitudinal study of the vocationally undecided student. *Journal of Vocational Behavior,* 1971, *1,* 75–92.

Fabry, J. J. An extended concurrent validation of vocational preferences of clergymen. *Psychological Reports,* 1975, *36,* 947–950.

Fishburne, F. J., and Walsh, W. B. Concurrent validity of Holland's theory for non college degreed workers. *Journal of Vocational Behavior,* 1976, *8,* 77–84.

Folsom, C. H., Jr. An investigation of Holland's theory of vocational choice. *Journal of Counseling Psychology,* 1969, *16,* 260–266.

Fortner, M. L. Vocational choices of high school girls: can they be predicted? *Vocational Guidance Quarterly,* 1970, *18,* 203–206.

Frantz, T. T. Reinterpretation of flat SVIB profiles. *Journal of Vocational Behavior,* 1972, *2,* 201–207.

Frantz, T. T., and Walsh, E. P. Exploration of Holland's theory of vocational choice in graduate school environments. *Journal of Vocational Behavior,* 1972, *2,* 223–232.

Gade, E. M., and Saliah, D. Vocational Preference Inventory high point codes versus expressed choice as predictors of college major and career entry. *Journal of Counseling Psychology*, 1975, *22*, 115–121.

Griffith, A. V., and Trogden, K. P. Self-expressive styles among college students preparing for careers in nursing and music. *Journal of Counseling Psychology*, 1969, *16*, 275–277.

Haase, R. F. Canonical analysis of the Vocational Preference Inventory and the Strong Vocational Interest Blank. *Journal of Counseling Psychology*, 1971, *18*, 182–183.

Hansen, I., and Johansson, C. B. The application of Holland's vocational model to the Strong Vocational Interest Blank for women. *Journal of Vocational Behavior*, 1972, *2*, 479–493.

Harvey, D. W., and Whinfield, R. W. Extending Holland's theory to adult women. *Journal of Vocational Behavior*, 1973, *3*, 115–127.

Helson, R. Writers and critics: two types of vocational consciousness in the art system. *Journal of Vocational Behavior*, 1978, *12*, 351–363.

Hieronymus, A. N. A study of social class motivations: relationship between anxiety for education and certain socio-economic and intellectual variables. *Journal of Educational Psychology*, 1951, *42*, 193–203.

Holland, J. L. A personality inventory employing occupational titles. *Journal of Applied Psychology*, 1958, *42*, 336–342.

Holland, J. L. A theory of vocational choice. *Journal of Counseling Psychology*, 1959, *6*, 35–45.

Holland, J. L. Some explorations with occupational titles. *Journal of Counseling Psychology*, 1961, *8*, 82–87.

Holland, J. L. Some explorations of a theory of vocational choice: I. One- and two-year longitudinal studies. *Psychological Monographs*, 1962, *76*, No. 26 (Whole No. 545).

Holland, J. L. Explorations of a theory of vocational choice and achievement: II. A four-year prediction study. *Psychological Reports*, 1963, *12*, 547–594.

Holland, J. L. Explorations of a theory of vocational choice: IV. Vocational preferences and their relation to occupational images, daydreams and personality. *Vocational Guidance Quarterly*, 1963, *11*, 232–239; 1963, *12*, 17–24; 1964, *12*, 93–97.

Holland, J. L. Explorations of a theory of vocational choice: V. A one-year prediction study. *Chronicle Guidance Professional Service*, 1964. (a)

Holland, J. L. Some new directions for vocational counseling. Paper read at American Educational Research Association Meetings, Chicago, February, 1964. (b)

Holland, J. L. *The psychology of vocational choice*. Waltham, Mass.: Blaisdell, 1966. (a)

Holland, J. L. A psychological classification scheme for vocations and major fields. *Journal of Counseling Psychology*, 1966, *13*, 278–288. (b)

Holland, J. L. Explorations of a theory of vocational choice: VI. A longitudinal study using a sample of typical college students. *Journal of Applied Psychology, Monograph Supplement*, 1968, *52*, 37 pages.

Holland, J. L. A theory-ridden, computerless, impersonal, vocational guidance system. *Journal of Vocational Behavior*, 1971, *1*, 167–176.

Holland, J. L. *Making vocational choices: a theory of careers*. Englewood Cliffs, N.J.: Prentice-Hall, 1973.

Holland, J. L., and Gottfredson, G. D. Using a typology of persons and environments to explain careers: some extensions and clarifications. *The Counseling Psychologist*, 1976, *6*(3), 20–29.

Holland, J. L., Gottfredson, G. D., and Nafziger, D. H. Testing the validity of some theoretical signs of vocational decision making ability. *Journal of Counseling Psychology*, 1975, *22*, 411–422.

Holland, J. L., and Nichols, R. C. Explorations of a theory of vocational choice: III. A longitudinal study of change in major field of study. *Personnel and Guidance Journal*, 1964, *43*, 235–242.

Holland, J. L., and Whitney, D. R. Changes in the vocational plans of college students: orderly or random? ACT Research Report, No. 25, Iowa City, Iowa, 1968.

Holland, J. L., Whitney, D. R., Cole, N. S., and Richards, J. M., Jr. An empirical occupational classification derived from a theory of personality and intended for practice and research. ACT Research Report, No. 29, Iowa City, Iowa, 1969.

Hollander, M. A., and Parker, H. J. Occupational stereotypes and needs: their relationship to vocational choice. *Vocational Guidance Quarterly*, 1969, *18*, 91–98.

Hollander, M. A., and Parker, H. J. Occupational stereotypes and self-descriptions: their relationship to vocational choice. *Journal of Vocational Behavior*, 1972, *2*, 57–65.

Hughes, H. M., Jr. Vocational choice, level, and consistency: an investigation of Holland's theory on an employed sample. *Journal of Vocational Behavior*, 1972, *2*, 377–388.

Jones, O. M., Hansen, J. C., and Putnam, P. A. Relationship of self concept and vocational maturity to vocational preferences of adolescents. *Journal of Vocational Behavior*, 1976, *1*, 31–40.

Lacey, D. W. Holland's vocational models: a study of work groups and need satisfaction. *Journal of Vocational Behavior*, 1971, *1*, 105–122.

Lee, D. L., and Hedahl, B. Holland's personality types applied to the SVIB basic interest scales. *Journal of Vocational Behavior*, 1973, *3*, 61–68.

Lunneborg, C. E., and Lunneborg, P. W. Factor structure of the vocational interest models of Roe and Holland. *Journal of Vocational Behavior*, 1975, *7*, 313–326.

Morrow, J. M., Jr. A test of Holland's theory of vocational choice. *Journal of Counseling Psychology*, 1971, *18*, 422–425.

Mount, M. K., and Muchinsky, P. M. Concurrent validation of Holland's hexagonal model with occupational workers. *Journal of Vocational Behavior*, 1978, *13*, 348–354. (a)

Mount, M. K., and Muchinsky, P. M. Person-environment congruence and employee job satisfaction: a test of Holland's theory. *Journal of Vocational Behavior*, 1978, *13*, 84–100. (b)

Navran, L., and Kendall, L. M. A canonical correlational analysis of the SVIB, the Holland VPI, and the EPPS. *Journal of Counseling Psychology*, 1971, *18*, 514–519.

O'Neil, J. M., Magoon, T. M., and Tracey, T. J. Status of Holland's investigative personality types and their consistency level seven years later. *Journal of Counseling Psychology*, 1978, *25*, 530–535.

O'Reilly, C. A., III. Personality-job fit: an implication for individual attitudes and performance. *Organizational Behavior and Human Performance*, 1977, *18*, 36–46.

Osipow, S. H. *Theories of career development* (1st ed.). New York: Appleton-Century-Crofts, 1968.

Osipow, S. H. Cognitive styles and vocational-educational preference and selection. *Journal of Counseling Psychology*, 1969, *16*, 534–546.

Osipow, S. H. Interaction between occupational environments and personality types. In Bartlett, W. (Ed.), *Evolving religious careers*. Washington, D. C.: CARA, 1970.

Osipow. S. H., and Ashby, J. D. Vocational Preference Inventory high point codes and educational preferences. *Personnel and Guidance Journal*, 1968, *47*, 126–129.

Osipow, S. H., Ashby, J. D., and Wall, H. W. Personality types and vocational choice: a test of Holland's theory. *Personnel and Guidance Journal,* 1966, *45,* 37–42.

Posthuma, A. B., and Navran, L. Relation of congruence in student-faculty interests to achievement in college. *Journal of Counseling Psychology,* 1970, *17,* 252–256.

Rezler, A. G. Characteristics of high school girls choosing traditional or pioneer vocations. *Personnel and Guidance Journal,* 1967, *45,* 659–665. (a)

Rezler, A. G. The joint use of the KPR and the Holland VPI in the vocational assessment of high school girls. *Psychology in the Schools,* 1967, *4,* 82–84. (b)

Robbins, P. L., Thomas, L. E., Harvey, D. W., and Kandefer, C. Career change and congruence of personality types: an examination of DOT-derived work environment designations. *Journal of Vocational Behavior,* 1978, *13,* 15–25.

Roe, A. A new classification of occupations. *Journal of Counseling Psychology,* 1954, *1,* 215–220.

Roe, A. Early determinants of vocational choice. *Journal of Counseling Psychology,* 1957, *4,* 212–217.

Roe, A., and Siegelman, M. The origin of interests. *APGA Inquiry Studies* No. 1, Washington, D. C.: American Personnel and Guidance Association, 1964.

Rose, H. A., and Elton, C. F. Attrition and the vocationally undecided student. *Journal of Vocational Behavior,* 1971, *1,* 99–103.

Salomone, P. R., and Muthard, J. E. Canonical correlation of vocational needs and vocational style. *Journal of Vocational Behavior,* 1972, *2,* 163–171.

Salomone, P. R., and Slaney, R. B. Applicability of Holland's theory to nonprofessional workers. *Journal of Vocational Behavior,* 1978, *13,* 63–74.

Schaefer, E. S., and Bell, R. Q. Development of a parental attitude research instrument. *Child Development,* 1958, *29,* 339–361.

Schutz, R. A., and Blocher, D. H. Self-satisfaction and level of occupational choice. *Personnel and Guidance Journal,* 1961, *40,* 595–598.

Shaw, F. J. *Reconciliation: a theory of man transcending.* Princeton, N.J.: Van Nostrand, 1966.

Southworth, J. A., and Morningstar, M. E. Persistence of occupational choice and personality congruence. *Journal of Counseling Psychology,* 1970, *17,* 409–412.

Spokane, A. R., and Walsh, W. B. Occupational level and Holland's theory for employed men and women. *Journal of Vocational Behavior,* 1978, *12,* 145–154.

Spokane, A. R., Malett, S. D., and Vance, F. L. Consistent curricular choice and congruence of subsequent changes. *Journal of Vocational Behavior,* 1978, *13,* 45–53.

Stockin, B. S. A test of Holland's occupational level formulations. *Personnel and Guidance Journal,* 1964, *42,* 599–602.

Utz, P. W., and Hartman, B. An analysis of the discriminatory power of Holland's types for business majors in three concentration areas. *Measurement and Evaluation in Guidance,* 1978, *11,* 175–182.

Viernstein, M. C. The extension of Holland's occupational classification to all occupations in the *Dictionary of Occupational Titles. Journal of Vocational Behavior,* 1972, *2,* 107–121.

Wakefield, J. A., Jr., and Doughtie, E. B. The geometric relationship between Holland's personality typology and the Vocational Preference Inventory. *Journal of Counseling Psychology,* 1973, *20,* 513–518.

Wall, H. W., Osipow, S. H., and Ashby, J. D. SVIB scores, occupational choices, and Holland's personality types. *Vocational Guidance Quarterly,* 1967, *15,* 201–205.

Walsh, W. B., and Barrow, C. A. Consistent and inconsistent career preferences and personality. *Journal of Vocational Behavior*, 1971, *1*, 271–278.

Walsh, W. B., and Lacey, D. W. Perceived change and Holland's theory. *Journal of Counseling Psychology*, 1969, *16*, 348–352.

Walsh, W. B., and Lacey, D. W. Further exploration of perceived change and Holland's theory. *Journal of Counseling Psychology*, 1970, *17*, 189–190.

Walsh, W. B., and Lewis, R. O. Consistent, inconsistent, and undecided career preferences and personality. *Journal of Vocational Behavior*, 1972, *2*, 309–316.

Walsh, W. B., and Russel, J. H. College major choice and personal adjustment. *Personnel and Guidance Journal*, 1969, *47*, 685–688.

Walsh, W. B., Vaudrin, D. M., and Hummel, R. A. The accentuation effect and Holland's theory. *Journal of Vocational Behavior*, 1972, *2*, 77–85.

White, R. W. *Lives in progress*. New York: Dryden Press, 1952.

Williams, C. M. Occupational choice of male graduate students as related to values and personality: a test of Holland's theory. *Journal of Vocational Behavior*, 1972, *2*, 39–46.

Wolfle, D. *America's resources of specialized talent*. New York: Harper & Row, 1954.

Yonge, G. P., and Regan, M. C. A longitudinal study of personality and choice of major. *Journal of Vocational Behavior*, 1975, *7*, 41–46.

CHAPTER SIX
THE WORK ADJUSTMENT THEORY–LOFQUIST AND DAWIS

Lofquist and his associates in the Work Adjustment Project at the University of Minnesota have developed an approach to the study of job satisfaction and worker adjustment that has implications for career development theory. The approach followed in the program of research directed by Lofquist is a sophisticated trait-oriented study, blending needs (these are the traits) together with environmental demands, to predict such career events as satisfaction, effectiveness, and job tenure. Much of the basic thinking and implications of the theory have been summarized in Lofquist and Dawis (1969). In that volume, Lofquist and Dawis present a list of assumptions underlying their approach. These assumptions may be summarized in several sentences. First, people are seen as motivated to fulfill work requirements and have their personal requirements fulfilled by work. The effort of the individual to maintain this "correspondence" is called "work adjustment" and can be systematically related to job tenure, satisfaction, and effectiveness. The theory concerns itself with defining and explaining the relationships between these various important events. Examples of some of the propositions of the theory are "Satisfaction is a function of the correspondence between the reinforcer system of the work environment and the individual's needs, provided that the individual's abilities correspond with the ability requirements of the work environment," and "Satisfactoriness moderates the functional relationship between satisfaction and need-reinforcer correspondence" (Lofquist and Dawis, 1969, p. 53). A list of nine such propositions is presented, all leading to numerous potential tests of the theory.

The theory is further made operational by the availability of a number of instruments developed in the course of the project. These instruments include the Minnesota Importance Questionnaire, the Minnesota Satisfaction Questionnaire, the Minnesota Satisfactoriness Scales, the Job Description Questionnaire, and a list of occupational reinforcers.

Work adjustment is described by the work personality operationally in terms of abilities, vocational needs, and personality styles. Work environments are described in terms of abilities, requirements, and work reinforcers in relation to environmental styles. A major outcome is job satisfaction which can either be seen as general in nature with respect to the whole job or as specific with respect to particular aspects of the job. Work reinforcers are described, using the Minnesota Satisfaction Questionnaire, in terms of specific sources of job satisfaction. These include needs such as ability utilization, achievement, activity, advancement, authority, company recognition, responsibility, security, social services, social status, supervision in human relations, supervision in technical matters, variety, and working conditions. Vocational needs are assessed by the Minnesota Importance Questionnaire, which measures the relative importance of the same twenty work-related reinforcers that were measured in the Minnesota Satisfaction Questionnaire. Occupational reinforcer patterns (ORP's) describe the systems of work reinforcers that may generally be found in specific work environments. This measure allows the comparison of occupational reinforcer patterns with individual need requirements and predicts job satisfaction. The congruence between occupational reinforcers and individual needs is expected to predict level of job satisfaction (Lofquist and Dawis, 1975).

In another paper, Dawis and Lofquist (1976) describe the work adjustment process by elaborating on work personality and work environment styles. The personality style dimensions that grow out of the theory of work adjustment are flexibility, activeness, reactiveness, and celerity. Flexibility involves the degree to which individuals will tolerate a lack of correspondence between the work environment and their personal environment. To the degree that the person can tolerate a greater lack of work-person correspondence, he or she is more flexible.

Activeness involves the degree to which an individual will try to alter the work environment to increase its correspondence to his or her personal style. An individual responding to work environments by changing the work personality is seen as reactive.

Celerity involves the degree to which people actually differ in the speed with which they try to increase the correspondence of their work to their personality. A work-related profile for these four dimensions could be developed if an instrument existed to assess them. For example, Lofquist and Dawis describe a flexible person as someone who has a history of work that includes a very wide range of situations and jobs as well as of friends. Activeness can be seen in terms of leadership, organizational skills, and achievements; innovative procedures; and a history of taking initiative. Reactiveness is reflected in terms of rule-abiding; following through on assignments; preference for highly structured situations, settings, and groups; and loyalty to groups as a member rather than as a leader. Finally, celerity describes a person who completes assignments early, emphasizing speed rather than accuracy. An absence of celerity would mean deliberateness in response, procrastination, and long response latencies.

Studies examining the measures have indicated stable underlying factor structures. Shubsach, Rounds, Dawis, and Lofquist (1978) found three factors to account for occupational reinforcers: self-reinforcement, environmental and organizational reinforcement, and reinforcement via altruism. Lofquist and Dawis (1978) found six dimensions through factor analysis on the Minnesota Importance Questionnaire: safety, comfort, aggrandizement, altruism, achievement, and autonomy.

Lofquist and Dawis do not ignore the need to develop applications for their ideas. After all, the theory has grown out of a project that is fundamentally applied in nature. For counseling, the theory would lead to the assessment of client needs, the client's vocational and other problems including aspirations, personal history, and various ability levels. From information gleaned above, a number of potential occupational applications could be generated. The individual would then need to make the series of training or job choices that would best conform to abilities and needs in correspondence with the work environment demands, so that work adjustment could be predicted. After job entry, some follow-up is necessary to test the adequacy of the placement. All told, these applications do not sound much different from the tried and true "test them and tell them" approach used by trait factor counselors for years, except that the blend of ingredients of the Lofquist-Dawis approach includes needs, whereas these have tended to be ignored by most other trait-oriented writers in the past.

Considerable research has been conducted on the instruments and the concepts that have grown from the theory. Here only a sample of some studies and their results can be presented, but these will provide a test of what has been done and what might be done in the context of this approach.

Tinsley and Weiss (1971) have studied the validity of various methods of measuring job reinforcers. The perceived job reinforcers of 338 supervisors were compared with those of 381 supervisees, with the finding that the occupational reinforcer patterns of the two groups are generally similar; some differences were found with regard to extrinsic reinforcers, and less agreement between supervisors and supervisees was found regarding reinforcers for lower-level jobs.

Betz (1971) predicted that job satisfaction moderates the degree of job success expected on the basis of high ability scores. Betz studied 352 assemblers divided according to sex into high, middle, and low job satisfaction groups as determined by the Minnesota Satisfaction Questionnaire; abilities had been assessed in another context. Job success was determined by production and by supervisor evaluation. The results of her study tend to support the prediction that success is determined by abilities but moderated by job satisfaction. In another study, Betz (1969) tested the hypothesis that job satisfaction can be predicted in terms of agreement between needs and satisfiers. She administered the Minnesota Importance Questionnaire and the Minnesota Job Description Questionnaire to 186 store employees. The hypothesis was supported for some personnel (cashiers and sales clerks) but not for others (checkers and markers).

Gay and Weiss (1970) tested the hypothesis that work experience is related to vocational needs. The subjects were 1620 vocational rehabilitation clients (1180 men and 440 women) who took the Minnesota Importance Questionnaire. Since 12 out of 20 predictions were supported, Gay and Weiss concluded that work experience tends to be associated with specific vocational needs.

Vandergoot and Engelkes (1977) developed a self-counseling device based on the theory of work adjustment. Subjects were selected by asking 15 counselors to nominate counselees (60 of 67 nominated agreed to participate). Complete data were finally gathered on 56 of these counselees. The procedure involved the administration of a self-directed unit based on a theory of work adjustment. A rationale for vocational counseling was presented, as well as a program learning format and guidelines for self-assessment in terms of needs and abilities and the development of job goals, and these were followed by a knowledge check and instructions for counselor follow-up to determine the accuracy of the self-assessments. Counselees were assigned to two conditions: a control condition involving traditional career counseling and an experimental condition involving self-directed counseling.

Outcome measures involved the administration of the revised scale of employability: counseling as a measure of counselor judgment following conclusion of counseling and the Service Outcome Measurement Form (SOMF) used to assess for clinical judgment of counselors about seven weeks after initial ratings have been made. The SOMF involves scales such as case difficulty, education, economic vocational status, physical functioning, adjustments to disability, and social competence. A third instrument was the structured interview designed for this particular study and involving job-seeking behaviors, knowledge of relevant theoretical concepts, satisfaction with counseling, and items from the Rehabilitation Gains Scale, an instrument sensitive to factors of a person's life that might be changed by counseling services. These items related to vocational, economic, mental, emotional, and social factors. Finally, a knowledge check was administered to all subjects right after counseling. It consisted of ten items measuring the extended knowledge gained through counseling of relevant theory of work adjustment concepts.

Of the more than twenty measures used, not many differences between experimental and control groups were observed. Experimental counselees did better than the control counselors on the knowledge check, importance of theory concepts, general physical health, and the likelihood of gaining a job goal. Overall, self-directed counseling, based on the theory of work adjustment, seemed to have little impact beyond that of traditional counseling. On the other hand, if self-counseling is as good as traditional counseling, it represents a gain in terms of economy of effort. Unfortunately, overall job-seeking behavior did not appear to be very strong no matter what kind of counseling was involved.

Smart (1975) looked at university department chairs in the six environments proposed by Holland, examining the differences that were associated with job satisfaction. Overall satisfaction of chairs was differentially related to predictor variables. Smart concluded that environments serve as job satisfaction reinforcer systems. Such a finding is consistent with the Work Adjustment Theory.

Elizur and Tziner (1977) tested the hypothesis that to the degree that vocational needs and job reinforcements are correlated, an increased level of job satisfaction results. They studied two random samples of female social workers in Israel. A final sample of 85 social workers ranging in age from 22 to 40 was used in the main study. The Minnesota Job Description Questionnaire and the Minnesota Importance Questionnaire were administered. Canonical correlations were computed between the two. The results supported the hypothesis that people strive for correspondence with their working environment and that, when achieved, this correspondence increases job satisfaction.

In a study of one of the measures used to test the theory, the Minnesota Importance Questionnaire, Lofquist and Dawis (1978) found six value dimensions: safety, comfort, aggrandizement, altruism, achievement, and autonomy. As a result of this effort, further investigations of detailed propositions of the theory can be made through the further validation of one of the principle instruments for measuring the performance of the theory. In a similar study, Shubsachs and others (1978) factor analyzed occupational reinforcers and found three principle factors: self-reinforcement, environmental and organizational reinforcement, and reinforcement by means of altruism.

In a recent paper focusing on the elaboration of the theory itself (Dawis and Lofquist, 1978), an attempt was made to integrate the theory into the personality style literature in order to emphasize the dynamic aspects of the theory.

Evaluation

In 1973 it appeared to be too soon to fully assess the adequacy of the impact of the work adjustment theory (Osipow, 1973). At that time it seemed that the theory was well instrumented, had propositions open to testing, and was relatively straightforward and simple. It was not clear whether the approach logically led to any systematic counseling or programmatic interventions.

Since 1973 curiously little has been done to further elaborate the system. A few studies, most of them noted in this brief review, have been conducted. The data from those studies are encouraging. The instrumentation appears to continue to show promise and is increasingly accessible to investigators and counselors. One must wonder why the system has not been further elaborated and applied not only by its proponents but by others. It has still not been put to a fair test.

REFERENCES

Betz, E. L. Aid reinforcer correspondence as a predictor of job satisfaction. *Personnel and Guidance Journal*, 1969, *57*, 878–883.

Betz, E. L. An investigation of job satisfaction as a moderator variable in predicting job success. *Journal of Vocational Behavior*, 1971, *1*, 123–128.

Dawis, R. V., and Lofquist, L. H. Personality style and the process of work adjustment. *Journal of Counseling Psychology*, 1976, *23*, 55–59.

Dawis, R. V., and Lofquist, L. H. A note on the dynamics of work adjustment. *Journal of Vocational Behavior*, 1978, *12*, 76–79.

Elizur, D., and Tziner, A. Vocational needs, job rewards, and satisfaction: a canonical analysis. *Journal of Vocational Behavior*, 1977, *10*, 205–211.

Gay, E. G., and Weiss, D. J. Relationship of work experience and measured vocational needs. *Proceedings, 78th Annual Convention, American Psychological Association*, 1970.

Lofquist, L. H., and Dawis, R. V. *Adjustment to work*. Englewood Cliffs, N.J.: Prentice-Hall, 1969.

Lofquist, L. H., and Dawis, R. V. Vocational needs, work reinforcers, and job satisfaction. *Vocational Guidance Quarterly*, 1975, *24*, 132–139.

Lofquist, L. H., and Dawis, R. V. Values as secondary to needs in the theory of work adjustment. *Journal of Vocational Behavior*, 1978, *12*, 12–19.

Shubsachs, A. P., Rounds, J. B., Dawis, R. V., and Lofquist, L. H. Perception of work reinforcer systems: factor structure. *Journal of Vocational Behavior*, 1978, *13*, 54–62.

Smart, J. C. Environments as reinforcer systems in the study of job satisfaction. *Journal of Vocational Behavior*, 1975, *6*, 337–347.

Tinsley, H. E. A., and Weiss, D. J. A multitrait-multimethod comparison of job reinforcer ratings of supervisors and supervisees. *Journal of Vocational Behavior*, 1971, *1*, 287–299.

Vandergoot, D., and Engelkes, J. R. An application of the theory of work adjustment to vocational counseling. *Vocational Guidance Quarterly*, 1977, *26*, 45–53.

CHAPTER SEVEN
PERSONALITY TRAITS
AND CAREERS

The idea that specific personality traits differentiate people in one occupation from those in another has had appeal for many years and has stimulated considerable research. The rationale underlying the trait-factor approach to the study of personality and careers is simple. It is assumed that because of the inherent differences in the roles that occupations require people to play, the ideal personal characteristics of members of various occupational groups vary. At the same time, perhaps recognizing that most people are not rigidly shaped when they enter an occupation, it is also assumed that exposure to the activities and climate of any given occupation will exert an influence upon an individual's manner of behavior and personality. For example, accountants are often careful, conservative people, partly because their work requires them to be and partly because careful, conservative people are attracted to accounting because of the occupational stereotype. Consequently, the trait-factor approach has as its goal the increasing accuracy of identification of distinctive personality attributes inherent in membership in various careers. The point of view, therefore, is fundamentally research-oriented and empirical.

The trait-oriented approach to career choice and membership is, at least in part, related to Davis' (1965) "birds of a feather" hypothesis, which assumes that members of an occupational group exhibit increasingly homogeneous personality traits over time, leading to the possiblity that the differentiation of potential occupational persisters versus occupational defectors is technically feasible. The "birds of a feather" hypothesis is controversial, however, as witnessed by Watley and Werts' (1969) data indicating that at least in their study, the hypothesis does not hold. Watley and Werts suggest that one flaw in the hypothesis is that it focuses on one trait at a time, whereas in the real world occupational members exhibit a multitude of traits, the combination of which is likely to be significant, rather than the possession of a single trait. The many studies of personality traits and occupational membership or potential membership typically involve an objectively scored personality inventory or a projective test of personality that is administered to a student sample (occasionally an occupational sample). The scores are then compared to those of either a control group of people who represent no particular occupation, or to those of a group of people representative of another career field, or to test norms. Ordinarily, it is assumed that occupational membership results from personality factors rather than the reverse, though a few investigators have considered the latter possibility.

Several major shortcomings of these procedures come to mind. Reports of replications of trait-factor studies are few. The personality measures employed have serious limitations, and inferences drawn from responses to those inventories may have questionable validity. Most of the instruments have a psychopathological basis which is usually inappropriate and inadequate for the understanding of normal behavior. The sampling represented in these studies is very limited. The use of results of personality tests given to students who are considering majoring in various academic fields or the correlation of personality test scores with interest inventory scores are procedures very far removed from the observation of personality differences in members of diverse occupational groups, a practice that is extremely rare. In fairness to the investigators, however, the use of student groups is likely to work against the discovery of spurious relationships between personality and career, since the personality types within student groups are presumably not as "pure" as those that would be found within professional groups which are beyond the screening, training, or education required for vocational entrance.

Super and Bachrach (1957) have pointed out that it is futile to look for personality trait differences among members of different occupations, because too much overlap exists and the occupations tolerate a wide range of personality differences among their members. It is likely to be more profitable to look for factors which influence the sequences of career decisions that people make, which seems to be precisely what the personality style approach, discussed earlier, tries to do. Until an extensive effort is made to analyze occupations functionally and to develop highly sophisticated tests of both personality and aptitude, no serious attempt to match people and careers with a simplistic trait-factor method is likely to be highly successful. Given that caveat, many trait-oriented studies deserve review.

In an early paper, Darley (1941) reviewed the relationship between aptitudes, achievement, and personality, and vocational interests. He concluded that business-contact interests were correlated with economic conservatism, social aggressiveness, and physical robustness; that technical interests were correlated with immaturity, masculinity, and limited social skill; that men with verbal interests could be construed as feminine, and, relatively speaking, not socially inclined; and that men with welfare interests were mature, socially aggressive, liberal, and slightly feminine. This early study of Darley's was the research design prototype that has dominated the trait-factor approach to the study of personality and careers for more than twenty years.

The research generally follows one of several formats. A sample, most desirably a vocational one but more frequently composed of students, is tested with respect to interests and personality and is queried about its vocational plans. Statistical comparisons are made among (1) the personality scores of students expressing different vocational preferences or (2) the personality scores of students with differing interest patterns on some interest inventory. Occasionally, an investigator has factor analyzed the resulting data to suggest several dimensions of personality or interest along which subjects expressing interest or preference for various occupations differ.

Four general methods characterize the trait-factor research on personality and career.

The statistical method is represented by the prototype of the ultimate in the personality trait approach to career selection and preference, Cattell's studies relating his 16 Personality Factor Questionnaire to occupational membership (Cattell, Day, and Meeland, 1956). Cattell and his associates reported the personality scores earned on the 16 PF by small- to moderate-sized samples of athletes, clerks, cooks, editorial writers, executives, nurses, priests, psychological technicians, salesmen, and teachers. Although the results reflected few occupational differences on individual personality scales, a modified discriminant analysis of the occupational profiles could eventually prove to be useful in identifying the likelihood of any one person's membership in a given occupational group.

More typical of the approach is the *factor analytic method,* exemplified by a study reported by Sternberg (1955). He asked whether college students majoring in different fields vary with respect to personality patterns defined in terms of interests, values, and inventories of psychopathology. To answer this question, he administered the Kuder Preference Record, the Allport-Vernon-Lindzey Study of Values, and the MMPI to 270 white male college students majoring in nine different fields (biochemistry or premedical studies, chemistry, economics, English, history, mathematics, music, political science, and psychology). Sternberg factor analyzed the results and identified seven factors: aesthetic communication versus practical science (I), go-getter versus passive aesthete (II), self-expression through art versus the faith in good works (III), the driven extrovert versus the pure scientist (IV), preoccupation with health (V), quantitative detail versus social welfare (VI), and unnamed, not included in data analysis (VII). The factors seemed to fall into four academic combinations. The English and music majors scored similarly on factors I, II, III, IV, and VI, reflecting aesthetic preferences, strong tendencies toward emotional maladjustment, interest in idealistic communication with people, and rejection of business and scientific activities and attitudes. The chemistry and mathematics students had scores similar to each other on all the factors, which mirrors interest in scientific, mechanical, and quantitative activities, avoidance of the aesthetic, business contact, and social service activities, and disinterest in interpersonal communication. The biochemical (premedical) and psychology students were similar on factors II, III, and VI, showing strong scientific attitudes in combination with an interest in helping people, plus a fairly strong interest in accumulating power and prestige. Finally, the economics, political science, and history students formed a group similar to each other in some ways. The political science and history majors were similar on factors I and III, while the economics and political science students were similar on factors II and IV. The latter two groups seemed to be responsive to persuasive interests; the economics students were less concerned with social welfare than the political science and history students.

Though Sternberg concluded that significant differences exist in the personality attributes of college students in different majors, the differences were not of a magnitude to permit the prediction of individual personality profiles. In fact, the dimensions he describes are, considering his instruments, very much like the Kuder Preference Record and the Allport-Vernon-Lindzey scores. The SVIB differentiates among students in various college majors in a similar way and can in that sense be construed to be a personality test.

Using *the work setting method,* Miller (1962) took a somewhat different approach to the question of personality traits and career choice. He suggested that a career is best considered in terms of its work setting and work function rather than as a whole unit. Predicting that people in different occupations vary in personality in a way that is relevant to their occupation, he further predicted that the personality differences are more closely related to the differences in work setting than they are to work function and that the differences in personality become more pronounced as one's length of time in the occupation increases. He studied a sample of 50 men in each of three occupations: (1) YMCA business secretaries, (2) YMCA youth workers, and (3) comptrollers. He reasoned that two of these groups were similar to each other in function (the Y secretaries and the comptrollers) and two were similar in setting (the Y secretaries and the Y youth workers). He compared the three groups on 13 selected variables reflecting personal orientation which were drawn from several personality and interest inventories, such as the MMPI, EPPS, SVIB, and so on.

The results reflected significant differences in personality that seemed to be related to the particular occupation of the subject, supporting the first hypothesis. Looking at the way the three groups were paired on responses, Miller found that four variables reflected similarity of personality based on work setting, two variables reflected similarity on work function, one pair reflected similarity on both function and setting, and two pairs reflected no similarity on either function. Thus, the second hypothesis was only partially supported. Comparison of subjects of longer tenure in a field with newcomers indicated no support for the third hypothesis, that personality trait differences reflecting occupation become more pronounced as tenure increases.

Finally, a fourth approach to the examination of personality and career, *the clinical method,* is represented in a study by Siegelman and Peck (1960). They proposed to develop and test a theory dealing with the underlying need patterns that exist among diverse vocational groups. The approach was based on several propositions: first, that people possess stable and unique personality need patterns; second, that vocations differ in their job-role requirements; third, that people choose vocations because they believe, consciously or unconsciously, that the job-role requirements of the field they select allow them to satisfy some of their dominant personality needs; and fourth, that the job-role requirements of a vocation best satisfy the dominant personality needs of a certain kind of individual. Finally, Siegelman and Peck assumed that as a consequence of all the previous assumptions, most people in a vocation share a common need pattern which differs from the need patterns characteristic of people in other vocational areas.

The specific hypothesis investigated was that the basic personality need patterns of people in different occupations vary systematically. Sixteen chemistry students (15 doctoral candidates and one senior undergraduate major), 16 career military officers on ROTC duty (eight Army and eight Air Force) who had no less than three years of military experience, and 16 theology students (eleven seniors and five ''middlers'') comprised the sample. They were administered the following instruments: the Stern Activities Index, which is a needs inventory based on Murray's personality theory and need system; a homemade sentence completion blank about needs; and a biographical data form eliciting information about early life history. In addition, a structured interview was conducted in which the Ss were asked to describe the personality characteristics they considered to be important or unique to members of their occupation.

On the basis of the interview observations, Siegelman and Peck (1960) wrote the following descriptions of each occupational group:

> Chemist: curious, imaginative, intellectual, creative, relates to objects, emotionally involved in his work.
>
> Minister: nurturant, personally insecure, feels vocationally inadequate.
>
> Officer: values security and variety in associations and living quarters, dedicated to his country, accepts responsibility and authority, concerned with loyalty and honesty.

On the basis of the data obtained through testing with the Stern Activities Index, the following conclusions were drawn: ministers are high on nurturant, impulsive, and idealistic needs, are introspective, and have a strong vicarious sex interest. Of the three occupational groups they are lowest in practical action and the analysis of natural science interests. The chemists have their highest needs in the analysis of natural and social events and in abstract intelligence and are lowest in nurturance, impulsiveness, and idealistic action (almost the direct opposite of the ministers). The officers are highest in practical action, compliance, and determination and lowest in vicarious sex interest, social science analysis, introspection, and abstract intellectualization. Thus, Siegelman and Peck's findings, richer than can be presented here, point suggestively to the coincidence between job roles and personal needs.

In effect, the research strategy has been to study all possible variables and their relation to occupational membership or preference, in the hope that some connection between occupation and personality traits will become evident. Such an approach is useful in an early stage of investigation about a phenomenon because the research may yield results indicating relationships between variables promising for future study. It has the disadvantage of revealing by chance many spurious relationships and as a result possibly diverting attention from fruitful areas of activity. The "shotgun" approach, if persisted in too long, can retard the theoretical development of a discipline.

PERSONALITY STYLE AND
VOCATIONAL BEHAVIOR

A promising approach to the study of occupational psychology is the idea that personality style influences occupational choice and behavior. This approach presumes that individuals engage in modes of behavior which characterize them regardless of the specific nature of the tasks in which they are engaged at the moment. For example, a person whose style leads to a willingness to accept risks is expected by this line of thought to be likely to take risks in such diverse phases of life as the physical, emotional, financial, and vocational. The appeal of the personality style approach lies in its flexibility, since it permits the understanding of career behavior in general rather than in isolation from the rest of an individual's life.

Two kinds of personality variables seem especially suitable for study in regard to career behavior. The first kind are motivational variables, such as the achievement motive, motives growing from fear of failure, and mastery motives stemming from desires to subdue one's environment. The other kind of personality variable with promise for the understanding of career development is response style. Questions are raised about the characteristics of acquiescent or resistive individuals, the personality development of such individuals, and the implications for career behavior.

Achievement Motive
and Fear of Failure

Risk taking.   No systematic theoretical point of view has generated all the research on the effects of personal style on occupational choice and behavior; rather the research has generated the concept. However, Atkinson's formulations (1957) of the role of the achievement motive in behavior have been very influential. One of the first personal styles whose career implications were studied was risk taking. Atkinson (1957) was concerned with the motivational antecedents of risk taking. He proposed that motivation is a function of a specific motive (or drive), the expectancy of success, and the incentive or attractiveness of a goal. Since risk taking is one aspect of motivation, the manipulations of any of these three variables should result in a modification of one's risk-taking propensities. According to Atkinson, both the achievement motive and the motive to avoid failure operate on human behavior. People with an unusually strong motive to avoid failure will frequently set defensively high or low goals for themselves, while individuals influenced more by the achievement motive are likely to aspire to intermediate and attainable goals. There is little risk of a personal sense of failure involved for a poverty-stricken youth who announces plans to become a doctor, because outside circumstances make that goal almost impossible for the youth to achieve. Similarly, a bright youngster who decides not to go to college is likely to avoid career situations where some risk of failure might exist. Hence, people striving vigorously to avoid failure (rather than to achieve) are to be expected either to take unusual risks or to go to great lengths to avoid risk taking, whereas achievement-motivated people are likely to engage in moderate risk-taking activities. Occupational achievement is a very obvious vehicle for social advancement and thus is an ideal context in which to study risk taking.

Several experiments grew directly from Atkinson's proposal. Mahone (1960) took the view that since people with a high fear of failure are likely to avoid even the consideration of information that is high in achievement content, they are unlikely to examine seriously achievement-oriented occupational information. In the case of those who value achievement themselves, this avoidance of relevant information leads to the selection of occupations only distantly related to the main gratifications they value and hope for in their life work. For similar reasons, the fearful person is not likely to possess accurate information concerning his or her abilities and their suitability for the occupation he or she intends to enter. In particular, this lack of realism should evidence itself in discrepancies between ability and judgments about the amount and kind of talent required by a chosen occupation. To test this line of reasoning, the interests and personality attributes of 135 college students were assessed so that judges could estimate the degree to which each subject over- or underaspired occupationally. Mahone found, as expected, that people fearful of failure avoided competitive behavior and thus were generally perceived to be over or underaspiring, while low fear of failure subjects were more moderate in their career expectations.

Using 228 ninth- through twelfth-grade boys as subjects, Tseng and Carter (1970) explored the effects of levels of fear of failure on perceptions of occupational prestige, level of aspiration, and the types of occupations chosen. As a measure of achievement need the TAT was used; the Mandler-Sarason Test Anxiety Questionnaire was used to measure fear of failure, and the Haller Occupational Aspiration Scale was used to assess aspirations. The results of this study extend Mahone's (1960) findings: high achievement and low fear of failure boys differed from the low achievement and high fear of failure group in that the high achievement and low fear group possessed more accurate occupational prestige perceptions, aspired to higher-level occupations, and chose more occupations of high prestige than the low achievement and high fear of failure group.

In another study stemming from Atkinson's formulations about achievement motivation and risk taking, Burnstein (1963) explored the relationship between achievement motive, fear of failure, and aspiration to enter prestigious occupations. Using Thematic Apperception Test scores to measure achievement motivation and test-anxiety scores to assess fear of failure, subjects were divided into four groups representing various combinations of high and low fear of failure with high and low achievement need. Questioned about career preferences, avoidances, and attitudes, these Ss revealed that fear of failure was a strong factor in their selection and avoidance of occupational goals, exerting an influence above and beyond that of talents and interests. As fear of failure increased, Ss were more willing to consider entrance into less prestigious occupations.

Isaacson (1964), assuming that test-anxiety scores represent the strength of the motive to avoid failure, reasoned that Ss with high test-anxiety scores would choose either extremely easy tasks in order to avoid failure or extremely difficult tasks where failure would be relatively less painful since so many others would also be failing. In contrast, Ss high in achievement need were expected to make choices of intermediate difficulty. The prediction that high test-anxiety scores are related to the choice of either extremely easy or extremely difficult fields was supported for male students. In a similar vein, Morris (1966) found that students high in achievement motivation seemed to be making occupational choices that reflected a greater willingness to assume an intermediate degree of risk than Ss low in achievement motivation. Other studies (Minor and Neel, 1958; Meyer, Walker, and Litwin, 1961) reported results supporting the view that high achievement motivation is related to strivings for membership in prestigious occupations and/or competitive situations. Isaacson explained the failure to find the expected results for women in terms of questions about the validity of the use of TAT measures in studying women.

Risk-taking situations.   In an attempt to simulate real conditions of decision making in order to study the role of risk taking in occupational membership and behavior, a number of investigators have contrived situations requiring Ss to make choices possessing somewhat realistic consequences in a controlled situation. The effects of the contrived nature of risk-taking experiments have been explicitly discussed by Williams (1965). First, in such experiments, an assumption seems to be made that risk taking is a pervasive characteristic, that is, some people are risk takers while others are not. As an alternative to this, Williams suggests the possibility that people might assume risks partly as a function of a general tendency within themselves to do so, but also partly as a function of the specifics of the risk-taking situation and the other variables contributing to motivation which were suggested by Atkinson (1957): motive, expectancy, and incentive. Furthermore, Williams points out that the contrived risk-taking experiments are more often constructed around gambling like situations rather than truly chance activities (for example, Hancock and Teevan, 1964). Chance situations in their natural settings have a capriciousness which the individual recognizes and which probably influences behavior in a way different from gambling situations, in which a calculated risk is taken. Vocationally, a tendency to take risks and a lack of concern for job security as inferred by an observer might reflect high self-esteem and self-confidence in ability to manage work demands. As a result, such behavior has different implications and assumes different shapes than the taking of risks in chance situations for minimal stakes, as in a poker game. Because of confidence in vocational skill, a worker may behave differently on his job than in a Tuesday night poker game with friends. These speculations lead to the expectation that vocational risk taking should be related to positive self-evaluations, intelligence (or relevant aptitude), and the utility the risk has for one's self-concept. This is the converse of the predictions made by Mahone (1960).

Ziller (1957) conducted a risk-taking study that seems to minimize the problems outlined by Williams. Ziller reasoned that although the choice of a specific vocation is largely dictated by such things as interests, abilities, economics, and information, the remaining variance is a function of the individual's judgment of chances for success and the price to be paid to accept these chances. Ziller devised a study to test the hypothesis that differences in risk taking exist between college students majoring in different fields. Using as subjects college sophomores enrolled in the ROTC program, he administered an instrument devised to measure the risk-taking propensity of the students. The content of the test was relevant to problems encountered in ROTC studies, but the ability to answer the questions depended on information which the Ss did not actually possess, and they were not able to respond with certainty. Consequently, utility for risk was inferred from the degree to which Ss were willing to make guesses.

The results of this study reflected significant differences in guessing as a function of the college enrollment and occupational plans. Students interested in sales occupations had the highest scores, followed by those of mechanical engineering, education, business administration, chemical engineering, electrical engineering, civil engineering, and undecided students. While there may be no particular reason to expect the groups in the middle of the distribution to be different from one another in risk taking propensities, the groups at either extreme are coincident with expectations. One intuitively expects sales people to be risk takers, while one also assumes that people unable to make decisions find themselves in that predicament at least partly because they cannot take even the minimal risks involved in committing themselves to a course of action. Unfortunately, these fairly clear results were not duplicated in a study (Stone, 1962) partially replicating Ziller's. Slakter and Cramer (1969) also replicated and extended the Ziller study by administering a Ziller-type risk-taking questionnaire (one characterized by a need to answer questions based on insufficient information) to more than 1000 male and 700 female students entering college. Relationships observed between risk-taking scores and vocational preferences were low and often illogical. This result, in combination with Stone's (1962) findings, raise questions about Ziller's results.

That risk-taking has relevance to vocational behavior if not vocational preference seems highly likely. Williams (1965) reports that subjects who score high on a job risk-taking scale express a high degree of concern for promotions, a preference for doing work for which they are most skilled, and relatively little concern for steady employment. Subjects scoring low on the scale report opposite concerns. He also found that when people who are high risk-takers are in jobs with a low probability for promotion, they express more dissatisfaction with their work than low risk takers.

The constructs proposed to explain certain kinds of occupational choices and predict behavior in work settings seem to have a relationship to career events, even though much of the research has a contrived flavor. General personality characteristics related to achievement motivation, fear of failure, and a willingness to accept risks seem to provide a useful personality framework on which to make predictions about the course of vocational events in an individual's life.

Other Personality Characteristics

Mastery.   To contrast the role of risk-taking in occupational behavior with other personality variables, a study conducted by Liberty, Burnstein, and Moulton (1966) must be considered. They were interested in the role that the relationship between the prestige of an occupation and the degree of competency it requires plays in determining the attractiveness of that occupation to the individual. Male college students were required to rate occupations in terms of prestige and the competency required for success in them. Though the resulting correlation between the two ratings was high, those occupations whose prestige was considerably higher than required competency, and vice versa, were selected to become part of two occupational scales that Ss rated on attractiveness. Subjects were also given the Strodtbeck scale designed to measure the value the individual places on competence, mastery, and autonomy (example: "planning only makes a person unhappy since your plans hardly ever work out anyway"), and the deCharms scale purporting to measure the same thing but differing in that it reflects the degree to which a person feels achievement orientation is important.

The occupational preferences that resulted from the ratings Ss made on the occupational scales constructed from prestigious versus mastery occupations were related to the scores Ss earned on the mastery indices. The results indicated that in general Ss who preferred occupations higher on competency requirements than prestige earned higher scores on the mastery index than Ss who preferred occupations that are lower on competency requirements than prestige. The authors speculated that for some people, mastery is a more potent occupational motivator than power and prestige. Obviously, such a possibility should be included in individual counseling in terms of individual assessment and the degree to which occupations vary in their demand for competency. Furthermore, other personality correlates of mastery needs are of interest, as well as the ramifications of differences in mastery concerns on job performance and satisfaction.

Response style.   Couch and Keniston (1960) have proposed the interesting hypothesis that response set—that is, a person's tendency to respond in a particular manner regardless of the specific stimulus complex presented—is based on a personality factor which results in acquiescent or resistant behavior. They coined the terms "yeasayers" and "naysayers" to represent these two types of response set.

That such differing types of response style should be reflected in vocational choices and behaviors is not hard to imagine. Some peripheral indication that acquiescent versus resistant response sets are related to vocational behavior is offered by Lindgren (1962). Postulating a general characteristic of negativism as an indicator of emotional disturbance, Lindgren presented two questionnaires to college students. One questionnaire was a list of 25 male and 26 female jobs, all of a tedious, lowly, and unpleasant nature, the other a list of 39 foods. The Ss were "to indicate which foods they disliked so much they wouldn't eat them and which jobs (appropriate to sex) they would not do under any circumstance." The findings indicated that younger (under age 21) males and females expressed significantly more food and occupational aversions than older subjects. Furthermore, the correlations between the two lists of aversions reflected a tendency for people expressing many aversions in one realm to express many in the other. These observations apparently confirm Couch and Keniston's general hypothesis that two basic response styles exist and further indicate that these styles have implications for vocational decision-making.

The vocational implications may be seen more vividly in a study by Armatas and Collister (1962), who proposed the notion that response sets influence people taking the SVIB to respond in terms of like, indifferent, or dislike responses, according to their personal style and over and above the content of the item. Since the response set may influence the nature of responses when other factors in the item do not exert a strong influence, they can be highly important in determining the resulting interest patterns. Armatas and Collister predicted that the "like" person is socially oriented, impulsive, spontaneous, and flexible, in other words, much like the yeasayer of Couch and Keniston (1960). The "dislike" person is impersonal, object oriented, rigid, suspicious, conforming, passive, and insensitive, like the naysayer, and the "indifferent" responder is unable to cope with the various stimuli found in the world, is indecisive, passive, and ambivalent and tends to procrastinate. A total of 98 Ss exhibiting a marked response set on the SVIB were given the EPPS and the Cattell 16 PF. The results showed that compared to the I and D subjects, the like subjects scored high on social service and business contact SVIB scales and low on physical science SVIB scales, had high EPPS needs of heterosexuality, dominance, and agression and low EPPS needs of succorance and exhibition, and earned scores on the 16 PF which indicated a general tendency to be outgoing.

The dislike subjects scored high on physical science and business contact SVIB scales and low on social service SVIB scales and had high EPPS needs of agression, succorance, and deference and low EPPS needs of heterosexuality and dominance. They generally appeared to be apprehensive on the 16 PF. Finally, the indifferent respondents, in contrast with the others, scored high on social service and physical science SVIB scales and low on business detail SVIB scales. They had low EPPS needs of aggression, dominance, and deference, and may be characterized as aloof, submissive, timid, unconcerned, and silent on the 16 PF. These results in general are suggestive of types of people whose characteristics are very similar to those predicted by Armatas and Collister.

Haakenstad and Apostal (1971) compared the nonoccupational interests of high and low acquiescent individuals. High acquiescent individuals revealed a greater diversity of interests on the SVIB than low acquiescent individuals. These results seem related to those reported by Armatas and Collister (1962) and Berdie (1943) indicating that acquiescent individuals are more open to stimuli than resistant individuals. Berdie (1943) described the relationship between personality test scores and the frequency of like and dislike responses on the SVIB. The greater the number of like responses, the higher the scores on morality, social adjustment, and emotionality, while the greater the frequency of dislike responses on the SVIB, the lower the personality scores on those three variables. Also of interest are the kinds of SVIB patterns generated by responding to a Strong blank exclusively in terms of like, indifferent, or dislike. Dislike responses produced interest patterns high in verbal and language-oriented occupations and low in technical and social welfare fields; like protocols resulted in reject patterns in biological and physical sciences and moderately high scores on the social welfare occupations.

Another study along the same lines is reported by Stewart (1960). He administered the SVIB, the Allport-Vernon-Lindzey Study of Values (AVL), and the Omnibus Personality Inventory (OPI) to a sample of National Merit Scholars (N = 593 males and 238 females). He then correlated the number of like, indifferent, and dislike responses made on the SVIB with the scores on the AVL and OPI. He found that males who might be characterized as likes scored lower on theoretical and economic and higher on social and religious scales on the AVL than other men. Their personality scores reflected enthusiastic warmth and interest in other people, independence of judgment, freedom of expression, and a preference for complexity. Female likes were very similar to the male. The indifferent males scored low on political values on the AVL and appeared to be "conservative, compliant, rigid, responsible, cautious, ready to accept authority and tradition," and to have "a low degree of self-confidence and a liking for overt action." Except for the indifferent females' higher score on theoretical values and their greater tendency to be flexible and permissive in interpersonal relationships, their scores were highly similar to those of the indifferent males. Finally, the male dislikes had high AVL scores on theoretical, aesthetic, and political values and low scores on social and religious ones. They seemed to have little interest in people and might be characterized in general as inner-directed, unsociable, and suspicious of others. Women dislikes differed from likes in that they had high AVL scores only on the aesthetic scale and low scores on the religious scale, and in that the size of the correlations obtained between response set and personality value scales were smaller than those observed in the men. While the correlations underlying these findings are small, Stewart is satisfied that the results cannot be explained away in terms of socially desirable response sets. Instead, he suggests that these findings imply that the differentiation of interests begins through one's awareness of personal dislikes, as Tyler (1951) has suggested.

All of these studies are in general agreement with one another to an extent which demands the serious consideration of the hypothesis that acquiescent versus resistive personal style is a major determinant of career interests. A more general conception of the role of personality style in occupational behavior was proposed by Gough and Woodworth (1960), who suggested that within the scientific community several specific research styles exist which are intimately related to personality. They devised a Q-sort task describing a variety of ways to pursue research as a career, administered it to 45 professional research scientists, and factor analyzed the results. Eight styles of behavior were identified. These types were very descriptively named the Zealot, the Initiator, the Diagnostician, the Scholar, the Artificer, the Aesthetician, the Methodologist, and the Independent.

Kassarjian and Kassarjian (1965) studied still another aspect of personal style and occupational selection. They reasoned that people choose careers in a manner that is related to the degree to which they and the careers are inner or other directed (Riesman, 1950). The investigators deliberately distinguished between occupational *entry* and *preference*, since they correctly assumed that there are factors other than personality attributes involved in occupational entry. Twenty-five male and 25 female students earning the most extreme scores on a scale of inner and other directedness were selected for study and tested with the Allport-Vernon-Lindzey Study of Values and the SVIB.

The findings generally concurred with the intuitive predictions about the relationship between values and interests and social character. Inner-directed males scored higher than other-directed males on SVIB scales such as those for artist, psychologist, architect, physician, dentist, mathematician, physicist, engineer, and chemist, while the other-directed males scored higher on scales such as those for senior CPA, accountant, office worker, mortician, pharmacist, sales manager, and real estate and life insurance salesman. For women, most of the differences between the two groups were similar to those for men. For example, women with interests like those of lawyers were found to be more inner directed than women whose interests are different from those of lawyers, but no such differences existed between inner and other-directed men on the lawyer scale.

Personality and interest stability.   Dunkleberger and Tyler (1961) studied the personality characteristics of people whose scores on the SVIB remained stable over two testings. For male subjects, the only significant differences between the "changers" and "nonchangers" were the higher scores of the changers on the heterosexual scale of the EPPS and on the self-control scale of the CPI. For females, nonchangers had higher nurturance scores on the EPPS, while changers had higher CPI scores on capacity for status, well-being, tolerance, achievement via independence, psychology mindedness, and flexibility.

Cognitive Style in Career Behavior

The research describing the effects of response style on vocational development and behavior has led to the explicit identification of cognitive styles as a variable of potential importance in career development. It has been suggested (Osipow, 1970) that cognitive style might serve as a high-level construct to permit the relation of diverse personality trait variables to vocational preferences and behavior to be seen more clearly. It might be, for example, that a general cognitive style of being "receptive" or "open" to stimuli might cause some individuals to report possessing more interests than others.

Broverman (1960) is among the early investigators of cognitive styles and vocational behaviors. In an early study, Broverman (1964) found that cognitive style is related to distractibility in various types of tasks. Such distractibility could affect scholastic performance and the resulting feedback to the individual and in this way influence the self-concept, task preferences, and, eventually, vocational preferences and selection. In another study, Broverman, Broverman, Vogel, and Palmer (1964) found strong and weak "automatizers" (people who vary in their ability to perform tasks without explicit attention) have different physical attributes. Broverman and his associates hypothesized that these physical differences have an endocrine basis and that these biochemical variables might affect the individual's rate of physical maturation, which, in turn, might affect the development of performance levels. Thus, at the end of a long sequence of events, the individual will receive variable feedback about his stimulus value related to his vocational self-perceptions.

Levine (1968) attempted to demonstrate differences in constricted-flexible cognitive control by means of the Color-Word Test in three vocational groups (physicians, mathematicians, and creative writers). The rationale for this investigation was simply that cognitive differences should be related to the differential functioning of professionals in the three vocations studied. Differences were found, but none that were adequately explained by the constricted-flexible notions of cognitive style. Levine speculated that Color-Word Test performance is related to "molar-adaptive" behaviors such as vocational choice, but not in terms defined by the concept of constricted-flexible control.

In a similar study (Osipow, 1969), a number of cognitive style measures were administered to five groups of college women (nursing, home economics, dental hygiene, special education, and undecided students) and two groups of college men (pharmacy and fisheries-technology students). The cognitive style measures included a measure of associative flexibility (assessing an individual's willingness to see relationships between two stimuli), an object sort (to measure conceptual band width or the tendency to use wide versus narrow notions of similarity between objects in relating to them), a measure of the tendency to respond in extremes, and the Closure Flexibility Test, a measure of field-dependence-independence. The results point up some differences in styles which should be accepted tentatively and interpreted cautiously in view of sampling shortcomings and limitations in the validation of the cognitive style instruments. The nursing students appear to be relatively uncritical, open to stimuli, and moderately field-dependent; the home economics students exhibit a wide equivalence range, are somewhat unresponsive to stimuli, and are field-independent; the dental hygiene students are field-independent; the special education students are field-dependent and display a small conceptual band width; the undecided women students are unreceptive to stimuli and have a wide conceptual band width; the pharmacy students display a narrow conceptual band width; and, finally, the fisheries-technology students appear to be uncritical and avoid the tendency to respond in extremes. However, the data do not indicate that cognitive style variables are related to the ease of vocational development and selection, contrary to predictions.

Kish and Donnenwerth (1969) examined the relationship between interests and sensation seeking. They expected to find that people who seek sensation will display their seeking tendency in connection with their inventoried interests. Forty-one rehabilitation clients took the Sensation Seeking Scale and the Kuder Preference Record. Positive correlations between sensation seeking and scientific interests and negative correlations between sensation seeking and clerical interests were found. Thirty-two male college students took the SVIB and the Sensation Seeking Scale. Here, positive correlations were found between psychologist, physician, psychiatrist, social worker, minister, and musician and sensation seeking, and negative correlations observed between accountant, purchasing agent, banker, pharmacist, and mortician and sensation seeking. Finally, 46 female college students took the SVIB and the Sensation Seeking Scale. A positive correlation between sensation seeking and lawyer and negative correlations between sensation seeking and house-wife, elementary teacher, home economics teacher, and dietician were found. Overall, the results reported by Kish and Donnenwerth suggest that sensation seeking is associated with occupational interests in relatively unstructured tasks.

Using field-dependence-independence as the cognitive style of interest, Gruenfeld and Weissenberg (1970) predicted that differences in field-dependence would be associated with a tendency toward internal versus external sources of job satisfaction. To test the hypothesis, 96 civil service workers were classified into field-dependent-independent categories by means of the Group Embedded Figures Test. Job satisfaction was measured by means of the Wernimont Job Satisfaction Questionnaire. The results, though not exactly supporting the prediction that levels of field dependency are differentially associated with sources of job satisfaction, do reveal that field-independent individuals perceive intrinsic and extrinsic job satisfiers distinctively, while field-dependent individuals view these two sources of job satisfaction in a highly correlated manner.

In a study dealing with field-dependence and vocational interests, Zytowski et al. (1969) predicted that psychological differentiation would be positively related to SVIB scores on engineering scales and negatively correlated with scores on business detail, business contact, and social service scales. Zytowski's predictions were based on the supposition that field-dependent individuals obtain their orientation from their environment and other people to a greater degree than field-independent individuals. Though one of the measures used revealed some modest support for the hypothesis, generally the prediction was not validated by the data.

Some investigators have examined the relation between internal-external locus of control and vocational interests. Zytowski (1967) found that in men Rotter external control scores were positively correlated with "feminine" SVIB scores and aesthetic interests. Tseng (1970) found that locus of control is a useful construct with which to differentiate rehabilitation clients with respect to their work behavior and potential for training.

Kelly's (1955) concept of cognitive complexity has also been used to study vocational behavior. Bodden (1970) found that more cognitively complex individuals were more likely to make congruent occupational choices (defined in Holland's terms) than cognitively simple persons. However, Bodden found no evidence to indicate that cognitive complexity leads to better occupational choices with regard to the use of abilities. Dolliver (1965) went so far as to modify the Tyler Vocational Card Sort using Kelly's theory of personal constructs as a means of organizing client thinking about occupational and nonoccupational activities. However, efforts to apply Kelly's theory to vocational behavior remain rudimentary.

One recent study has found support for the notion that differential career counseling might be appropriate for clients with different cognitive styles. Kivlighan, Hagaseth, Tipton, and McGovern (1981) used a "learning through interaction" counseling approach with half of a "people-oriented" client group and a "learning through individual problem solving method" with the other half, and provided the same treatments to another group of "task-oriented" individuals. Outcomes were found to be superior for individuals counseled with an approach consistent with personality.

In general, while cognitive style has been studied in connection with vocational behavior in a number of ways, the results of these studies are not impressive. Considerable work remains to be done in the definition and measurement of cognitive styles before these behaviors can truly be useful to the study of vocational events.

Summary and Evaluation

The research and theory dealing with personality style and occupational behavior seems to be the most rigorous, both conceptually and experimentally, of all the personality approaches to occupational behavior. It connects psychological theory in general with occupational behavior in an explicit way which has implications for both the selection of careers and eventual career behavior. The notion that acquiescent or resistant response styles influence both career selection and subsequent behavior seems promising. Some questions do remain, however; the definition of risk taking, for example, needs clarification, especially since risk-taking behaviors seem to be very relevant to the consideration of occupational behavior. The personality style approach promises to be very helpful to counselors in the conceptualization of their client's choice process, but somewhat limited as to implications for counseling procedure. For example, a counselor may be able to infer from observation that a client is acquiescent and motivated by fear of failure rather than mastery, but these judgments do not in themselves lead to any distinctive counseling procedures.

REFERENCES

Armatas, J. P., and Collister, E. G. Personality correlates of SVIB patterns. *Journal of Counseling Psychology,* 1962, *9,* 149–154.

Atkinson, J. W. Motivational determinants of risk-taking behavior. *Psychological Review,* 1957, *64,* 359–372.

Berdie, R. F. Likes, dislikes, and vocational interests. *Journal of Applied Psychology*, 1943, *27*, 180–189.

Bodden, J. L. Cognitive complexity as a factor in appropriate vocational choice. *Journal of Counseling Psychology*, 1970, *17*, 364–368.

Broverman, D. M. Generality and behavioral correlates of cognitive style. *Journal of Consulting Psychology*, 1960, *28*, 487–500.

Broverman, D. M., Broverman, I. K., Vogel, W., and Palmer, R. D. The automatization cognitive style and physical development. *Child Development*, 1964, *35*, 1343–1359.

Burnstein, E. Fear of failure, achievement motivation, and aspiring to prestigeful occupations. *Journal of Abnormal and Social Psychology*, 1963, *67*, 189–193.

Cattell, R. B., Day, M., and Meeland, T. Occupational profiles on the 16 Personality Factor Questionnaire. *Occupational Psychology*, 1956, *30*, 10–19.

Couch, A., and Keniston, K. Yeasayers and naysayers: agreeing response set as a personality variable. *Journal of Abnormal and Social Psychology*, 1960, *60*, 151–174.

Darley, J. G. A study of the relationships among the primary mental abilities test, selected achievement measures, personality tests, and tests of vocational interests. In *Studies of higher education*. Minneapolis: University of Minnesota Press, 1941.

Davis, J. A. *Great aspirations: volume one. Career decisions and educational plans during college* (Report No. 90). Chicago: National Opinion Research Center, March, 1965.

Dolliver, R. H. An adaptation of the Tyler Vocational Card Sort. *Personnel and Guidance Journal*, 1965, *45*, 916–920.

Dunkleberger, C. J., and Tyler, L. E. Interest stability and personality traits. *Journal of Counseling Psychology*, 1961, *8*, 70–74.

Gough, H. G., and Woodworth, D. G. Stylistic variations among professional research scientists. *Journal of Psychology*, 1960, *49*, 87–98.

Gruenfeld, L. W., and Weissenberg, P. Field independence and articulation of source of job satisfaction. *Journal of Applied Psychology*, 1970, *54*, 424–426.

Haakenstad, K. W., and Apostal, R. A. Acquiescence and nonoccupational interests. *Journal of Counseling Psychology*, 1971, *18*, 501–502.

Hancock, J. B., and Teevan, R. C. Fear of failure and risk-taking behavior. *Journal of Personality*, 1964, *32*, 200–209.

Isaacson, R. L. Relation between need achievement, text anxiety, and curricular choice. *Journal of Abnormal and Social Psychology*, 1964, *68*, 447–452.

Kassarjian, W. M., and Kassarjian, H. H. Occupational interests, social values, and social character. *Journal of Counseling Psychology*, 1965, *12*, 48–54.

Kelly, G. A. *The psychology of personal constructs* (two vols.) New York: Norton, 1955.

Kish, G. B., and Donnenwerth, G. V. Interests and stimulus seeking. *Journal of Counseling Psychology*, 1969, *16*, 551–556.

Kivlighan, D. M. Jr., Hagaseth, J. A., Tipton, R. M., and McGovern, T. V. Effects of matching treatment approaches and personality type in group vocational counseling. *Journal of Counseling Psychology*, 1981, *28*, 315–320.

Levine, F. J. Color-word Test performance and drive regulation in three vocational groups. *Journal of Clinical and Consulting Psychology*, 1968, *32*, 642–647.

Liberty, P. G., Jr., Burnstein, E., and Moulton, R. W. Concerns with mastery and occupational attraction. *Journal of Personality*, 1966, *34*, 105–117.

Lindgren, H. C. Age as a variable in aversion toward food and occupations. *Journal of Consulting Psychology*, 1962, *26*, 101–102.

Mahone, C. H. Fear of failure and unrealistic vocational choice. *Journal of Abnormal and Social Psychology*, 1960, *60*, 253–261.

Meyer, H. H., Walker, W. B., and Litwin, G. H. Motive patterns and risk preferences associated with entrepreneurship. *Journal of Abnormal and Social Psychology*, 1961, *63*, 570–574.

Miller, S., Jr. Relationship of personality to occupation, setting, and function. *Journal of Counseling Psychology*, 1962, *9*, 115–121.

Minor, C. A., and Neel, R. G. The relationship between achievement and motive and occupational preference. *Journal of Counseling Psychology*, 1958, *5*, 39–43.

Morris, J. L. Propensity for risk taking as a determinant of vocational choice. *Journal of Personality and Social Psychology*, 1966, *3*, 328–335.

Osipow, S. H. Cognitive styles and educational-vocational preferences and selection. *Journal of Counseling Psychology*, 1969, *16*, 534–546.

Osipow, S. H. Some cognitive aspects of career development. In Evans, E. D. (Ed.), *Adolescents: reading in behavior and development*. Hinsdale, Ill.: Dryden, 1970.

Riesman, D. *The lonely crowd*. New Haven, Conn.: Yale University Press, 1950.

Siegelman, M., and Peck, R. F. Personality patterns related to occupational roles. *Genetic Psychology Monographs*, 1960, *61*, 291–349.

Slakter, M. J., and Cramer, S. H. Risk taking and vocational or curriculum choice. *Vocational Guidance Quarterly*, 1969, *18*, 127–132.

Sternberg, C. Personality trait patterns of college students majoring in different fields. *Psychological Monographs*, 1955, *69*, No. 18 (Whole No. 403).

Stewart, L. H. Modes of response on the Strong Blank and selected personality variables. *Journal of Counseling Psychology*, 1960, *7*, 127–131.

Stone, L. A. The relationship of utility for risk to college year, sex, and vocational choice. *Journal of Counseling Psychology*, 1962, *9*, 87.

Super, D. E., and Bachrach, P. B. *Scientific careers and vocational development theory*. New York: Bureau of Publications, Teachers College, Columbia University, 1957.

Tseng, M. S. Locus of control as a determinant of job proficiency, employability, and training satisfaction of vocational rehabilitation clients. *Journal of Counseling Psychology*, 1970, *17*, 487–491.

Tseng, M. S., and Carter, A. R. Achievement motivation and fear of failure as determinants of vocational choice, vocational aspiration, and perception of vocational prestige. *Journal of Counseling Psychology*, 1970, *17*, 150–156.

Tyler, L. E. The relationship of interest to attitudes and reputation among first grade children. *Educational and Psychological Measurement*, 1951, *11*, 255–264.

Watley, D. J., and Werts, C. E. Career selection: turnover analysis and the "birds of a feather" theory. *Journal of Counseling Psychology*, 1969, *16*, 254–259.

Williams, L. K. Some correlates of risk-taking. *Personnel Psychology*, 1965, *18*, 297–310.

Ziller, R. C. Vocational choice and utility for risk. *Journal of Counseling Psychology*, 1957, *4*, 61–64.

Zytowski, D. G. Internal-external control of reinforcement and the Strong Vocational Interest Blank. *Journal of Counseling Psychology*, 1967, *14*, 177–178.

Zytowski, D. G., Mills, D. H., and Paepe, C. Psychological differentiation and the Strong Vocational Interest Blank. *Journal of Counseling Psychology*, 1969, *16*, 41–44.

CHAPTER EIGHT
SOCIAL LEARNING
APPROACHES
TO CAREER
DEVELOPMENT
THEORY

Probably the only significant innovation of the 1970s in career development theory is the application of social learning theory to career decision making. Based on social learning theory as espoused by Bandura (1969), who highlights the roles that "vicarious, symbolic, and self-regulatory processes" play in determining behavior, emphasis is placed on clear specifications of treatments and outcomes. Associated with John Krumboltz and a number of his associates such as Anita Mitchell, G. Brian Jones, Carl Thoresen, Craig Ewart, and others, the principal statements concerning social learning theory approaches to career development are found in two books, *Social Learning Theory and Career Decision Making,* edited by Anita Mitchell, G. Brian Jones, and John D. Krumboltz, and *Career Counseling,* edited by John Whiteley and Arthur Resnikoff. Some of the antecedents for this work appeared in the 1960s and early 1970s as research investigations into the effects on high school students of the reinforcement of a variety of information-seeking and decision-making behaviors (for example, Krumboltz and Schroeder, 1965; Krumboltz and Sheppard, 1969; Ryan and Krumboltz, 1964).

THE THEORY

Like other career development theories, social learning theory applied to career decision making attends primarily to identifying and explicating the personal and environmental events that shape individuals' decisions about careers made at major choice points in life. In general, social learning theory approaches to career development differ from the other approaches by being more explicit about the variables of concern.

143

The theory includes variables familiar to us from other theories. It first concerns itself with inherited attributes such as race, gender, and physical appearance and with special, apparently inherited abilities involving motor, intellective, and perceptual behaviors.

Secondly, the theory concerns itself with environmental events and settings in which these events occur, dealing, for example, with the social climate, individual experiences, the job market, the training options and opportunities available to the individual, and social policies which affect career decisions, such as selection procedures, labor laws, union rules, and retirement policies. Also considered in this context are perceived outcomes and payoffs of various career possibilities, family resources, role models, social and climatic events such as war, natural disasters, technological developments, and educational opportunities and achievements.

Thirdly, the theory concerns itself with learning histories. These are divided into two types. Associative learning experiences are those in which the individual observes relationships between events and is able to predict contingencies. Instrumental learning experiences are those in which the individual operates on the environment directly with observable outcomes.

The last ingredient is the task approach skills. These skills are the result of unspecified interactions among the inherited attributes, environmental events, and the learning histories mentioned above. Through those experiences, the individual develops and learns to apply a wide range of skills, attitudes involving work standards, work values, work habits, perceptual habits, cognitive skills such as attending and selecting, and affective responses to each new task. These behaviors themselves are modified by experience and feedback regarding their outcomes.

Out of the combination of inheritance, environment, learning histories, and task approach skills three consequences are postulated and are considered to be very important. First are self-observation generalizations. These are self-views that the individual learns based on life experiences. (The analogy to the self-concept and to the Holland personality types should be obvious to the reader.) These self-generalizations may be seen in the form of interests expressed by the individual. Social-learning theorists studying career decisions are open to considering the possibility that interests are outcomes of experience rather than the reverse (Osipow, 1972; Osipow and Scheid, 1971).

A second major consequence is the task approach skills mentioned previously. These are characteristic cognitive and affective predispositions that the individual displays in dealing with, interpreting, and predicting the environment.

The final major consequence is the action outcomes. The outcomes are specific, decision-related behaviors that grow out of self-observation, generalizations, and the task approach skills mentioned above. For example, these might include making specific job applications, learning specific job skills, seeing one's way through specific job-training programs, and other activities.

A set of theoretical propositions has been offered to explain how self-observation generalizations are acquired (Krumboltz, 1979). The first three propositions deal with what are called positive influences on self-observations. With increasing degrees of specificity, the first four propositions describe the hypothesis that individuals are likely to express preferences if those individuals have been positively reinforced for engaging in activities associated with the successful performance of a pertinent activity. Methods of reinforcement described in the propositions vary from direct, active reinforcment to observation of reinforcement of a valued model to reinforcement by a valued person who models the activity to, at the lowest level, exposure to positive words associated with the activity. In other words, if someone has been reinforced for studying by praise and good grades, studying behavior will increase. If the most attractive male student has been observed being rewarded for studying, that too will increase the studying behaviors of the observer, but less. If my admired older sibling tells me of the rewards of studying, my studious behavior will also increase, but not as much as if I directly received the rewards or saw my sibling get them.

A parallel set of negative influences is also posed: individuals are considered to be less likely to express preferences and more likely to reject an activity if they have been punished for engaging in those activities, have seen a model being punished for engaging in those activities, have been positively reinforced by a valued person who is negative about those activities, or have been exposed to negative words associated with those activities.

A second set of hypotheses deals with proposed factors that influence career decision making skills. Again, there is a set of positive and a set of negative influences. The positives are expressed in terms of the likelihood that individuals will learn the "cognitive and performance skills and emotional responses necessary for career planning, self observing, goal setting, and information seeking" if they have been reinforced for these behaviors. The second hypothesis is the same except that it involves observing someone else engaging in career decision making behaviors, and the third one is essentially the same except that it involves having "access to people and other resources" who can help in career-decision making.

At the highest level, the negative influences describe punishments resulting from the development of appropriate behaviors for career decision making, the observation of people being punished for such behaviors, or punishment for trying to use materials to develop good career decision making skills.

Finally, a set of propositions to predict factors influencing entry behaviors in relation to schools or careers is posed. The positive influences are described in terms of the probability of an individual taking action to enroll in a school in preparation for work in a certain field or to seek employment in that field. These probabilities are high if the individual has expressed a preference for that activity. The second level involves the probability of an individual taking actions to enroll in a school or seek employment in a field if he or she has been exposed to learning about that school or field, and the third has to do with the probability that the individual will take actions leading to enrollment or seeking employment if skills match the requirements of that activity.

The negative aspect of that set of propositions presumes the individual to be less likely to seek enrollment in a school or employment in a field if the "cost" exceeds perceptions of future gains. The second negative proposition involves the probability of the individual taking actions to seek education or employment in a field if the individual is denied access to the minimum resources needed to enter that field.

The theory may be summarized as follows: People bring a set of genetic and socially inherited attributes to their particular environments. The attributes and environments interact to produce self-views which influence the individual's work-related behaviors. These behaviors are shaped by and may be modified by natural or programmed reinforcements or punishments.

RESEARCH EVIDENCE

Mitchell (1979) has provided a good review and analysis of studies that are pertinent to the social learning approaches to career decision making. The overwhelming majority of the studies Mitchell cites, however, were studies that were conducted independently of the conceptual context of social learning approaches to career decision making.

Mitchell organizes her review in terms of the propositions posed by the theory mentioned earlier. The first of these propositions, it will be recalled, describes the way preferences are shaped. Three relevant studies were noted by Mitchell.

The first set by Osipow (1972) and Osipow and Scheid (1971) experimentally manipulated success and failure ratios that individuals experience in dealing with unfamiliar stimuli. The results of these experimental manipulations revealed that individual preferences for activities dealing with novel stimuli were influenced by the ratio of success to failure that the individual had in dealing with the stimuli. The suggestion of this research is that reinforcement for engaging in certain kinds of activities affects preferences, a finding very consistent with the first proposition of social-learning theory in career decision making. Experimental studies on preferences are rare. The experimental nature is also the major shortcoming of these studies in that they are removed from the real world of preference development.

In another study, Almquist (1974) found that females who selected male-dominated occupations were more likely to mention female role models as significant influences. This finding supports "proposition one," which describes the effect of role modeling on preference development. Finally, Hawley's (1972) finding that nontraditional women perceived significant males to be more encouraging with respect to females' abilities to engage in serious work without impairing their marriage, femininity, or family is consistent with "proposition three" of the theory.

The negative aspects of the propositions are difficult to document. Thus, there are little data to validate the negative propositions. It is always harder to prove a negative proposition than a positive one. However, a finding by Hind and Werth (1969) that low grades have an aversive effect on the development of preferences, along with the Osipow (1972) and Osipow and Scheid (1971) studies noted above, would support the negative aspects of these propositions by inference. With respect to proposition three, which is related to expressed choice predicting actual-choice behavior, perhaps the most convincing data are those reported by Flanagan and

Project Talent data indicating that expressed choice is as good a predictor of college major as test scores. Other sources to support this finding exist as well, such as Dolliver (1969), Astin (1965), Astin and Bisconti (1973), and Whitney (1969).

Betz and Hackett (1981) and Hackett and Betz (1981) have applied self-efficacy theory to the study of career behavior. Self-efficacy concepts grow out of social learning theory (Bandura, 1969). Based on the rationale that cognitions mediate behavior, self-efficacy theory pertains to beliefs about one's performance possibilities. The *level* of self-efficacy expectations refers to the difficulty of the tasks one aspires to achieve, while *strength* of self-efficacy refers to the confidence one has in one's ability to perform a task. Hackett and Betz (1981) applied this model to the career development of women and then studied (Betz and Hackett, 1981) how it operates in connection with understanding the differences in the range and nature of occupations considered by females and males. Studying undergraduates, they found that self-efficacy differences by gender were consistent with occupational "traditionality" in females: females had high self-efficacy levels with respect to traditional occupations and lower levels with "nontraditional" occupations, a pattern different from that observed for males in the sample. It is not hard to imagine how different role models and reinforcement histories might alter self-efficacy level and strength, particularly in females.

Barak (1981) analyzed the development of vocational interests from a social learning perspective. Barak compared the relationship between interest development and variables such as ability, success, and satisfaction. From the logical view that there is a positive relationship between interest and satisfaction, Barak developed a rationale to state that cognitive functions mediate abilities, performance, satisfaction, and interest. His model takes the position that interests result from this mediating process.

Overall, there are data to support social learning approaches to career decisions, but these data are somewhat fragmented, sparse, and unfortunately, (except for the Betz and Hackett work) almost exclusively retrospectively applied to social learning theory. At the moment, the theory requires much more reinterpretation of old data than is desirable, and the research related to the social learning approach smacks too much of "old wine in new bottles" to be convincing. Some earlier studies conducted in the '60's, in which models engaging in information-seeking behavior were displayed to students and information-seeking behaviors were displayed by the observers, are pertinent but somewhat limited in how far they may be generalized (for example, Krumboltz and Thoresen, 1964; Ryan and Krumboltz, 1964). Of course, now that the theory is available it may resolve this shortcoming by generating new studies in the manner of the Betz and Hackett work.

APPLICATIONS

Social learning approaches to career-decision making have a number of possible applications for intervention. Jones and Gelatt (1979) suggest a number of interventions around the basic factors of the theory. With respect to inherited abilities, Jones and Gelatt point out the indirect affects of social policy and social legislation as interventions. Career education, for example, should affect educational opportunities and perceptions. Availability of training funds also affects opportunities which in turn would moderate career choices. Social movements, such as feminism, can offset undesirable sex-role stereotypes which interfere with occupational accessibility for women *and* men.

Similarly, modeling is another way to intervene to offset undersirable aspects of inherited attributes. For example, handicapped individuals can be shown models of other handicapped individuals who are successful; minority group members can be shown successful models for similar purposes, all of these helping to shape a broader range of aspirations to overcome inherited attributes.

Finally, specific programs might be developed to help individuals identify the particular barriers they face by virtue of their inherited attributes, and individuals thus may be helped to overcome these barriers.

Social organization and policy development can indirectly try to affect the environment in order to produce a greater degree of independence and control by individuals over their environment. Policy developments as well as technology should all work to this end.

The individual might be encouraged by social devices such as scholarship programs to change a training program or to move to a geographic region where there are more jobs.

Efforts to improve instrumental learning experiences (the operant approach) might teach people to be more actively in control of their lives, by such methods as helping them to learn the skills needed to explore alternative careers and alternative behaviors, and also by exposing them to the various kinds of work through work-study programs or through simulated-work experiences.

Associative learning experiences, or the respondent type, are affected by traditional methods such as career days and by the observation of models who are making choices at various stages of life. Observing models making choices or seeking information can be very potent, as some research mentioned earlier suggests (Ryan and Krumboltz, 1964).

Stimulating self-observation is critical to the social-learning approach. One must teach self-observation skills and how to synthesize these observations. It is possible to teach people how environment influences their preferences, when one should learn how to analyze present conditions, and how to change them when it is appropriate to do so. Again, programs of the career education type, over a long period of time, can be very efficacious in this respect.

Finally, task approach skills and cognitive and performance skills regarding information processing and goal establishment and implementation can be fostered through simulation kits about work and the completion of workbooks involving self-assessment and exercises about problems, lectures, and social models. Discussion of styles of decision making, using everyday decisions as examples, is also suggested by Jones and Gelatt as a pertinent intervention.

Two of the shortcomings of all of these interventions, however, are their focus on the career decision and their minimal attention to the adjustment of the individual on the job. In addition, these approaches share the shortcoming that they are really not fundamentally new but are rather continuing applications of procedures that have been used for years by many counselors and programs. The social-learning theory overlay seems almost superficial and gratuitous.

The approach lends itself well to individual counseling, however. Krumboltz and Baker (1973) identify a series of steps involved in career counseling which involve defining problems and goals, identifying a variety of "solutions," gathering information about the identified problem, examining possible outcomes of various decisions and reevaluating goals, deciding, and last, generalizing the entire process to new problems as they arise.

Crites (1981) describes career counseling from a behavioral point of view which includes to some extent the point of view of the social learning theorists. The process involves, first, diagnosis in terms of the nature of the problem and second, a decision about the process itself. The process focuses principally on defining goals and examining alternatives and their consequences. The methods are very much the standard behaviorally oriented techniques involving modeling, desensitization, counterconditioning, and the like, these, of course, being varied and adjusted for career counseling settings and concerns. The desired outcomes involve the elimination or reduction of antecedent and consequent anxiety and/or the acquisition of decision-making skills. Tests are minimized because they do not lend themselves well to the stimulus-response model of behavior. Tests and inventories measure individual differences, not individual-environmental interactions, and thus are of minimal usefulness from the behavioral point of view.

Client career problems are often related to the inability of an individual to make a required career-related decision (Krumboltz and Thoresen, 1969). Crites (1981) points out that client problems involved in career counseling typically include some combination (or all) of the following: the absence of a goal; some affective barrier, such as anxiety over the possibility of failure; and choice conflict. Interestingly, these are among the items on the Career Decision Scale (Osipow, Carney, Winer, Yanico, and Koschier, 1976; Osipow, 1980), an instrument designed to measure antecedents of career indecision from a differential-diagnosis—differential-treatment viewpoint.

Using the rubric of behavioral counseling, Crites (1981) presents a case study demonstrating how indecisiveness may be treated using counterconditioning procedures.

Social learning theory in career decision making gives considerable importance to information seeking. However, a study by Barak, Archibald, and Carney (1975) failed to find any evidence that occupational information reduces indecision. While it seems logical that information should help in decision making—and most career theorists and career counselors assume that information does reduce indecision—no real evidence for that assumption exists. Information and choice are not clearly related.

EVALUATION

The positive aspects of the social learning approach lie first in its great explicitness with respect to its objectives and the means to accomplish these objectives, and second in its emphasis on the environment and social influences, an emphasis greater than many other approaches. But the negatives lie primarily in the paucity of new data to validate the idea of the theory and the relative shortage of new ideas or methods to accomplish its objectives. Finally, there is too much focus on the choice itself and not enough on the adjustment process, which is where the ultimate payoff should come. This does not mean that the focus on adjustment could not occur in the context of social learning approaches, but simply that it has not yet done so. In fairness, this is a relatively new approach and such developments are not likely to occur.

Updated research, as well as new methodologies and applications through the adult life span should be secondary developments as the social learning approach matures.

REFERENCES

Almquist, E. M. Sex stereotypes in occupational choice: the case of college women. *Journal of Vocational Behavior*, 1974, *5*, 13–21.

Astin, A. W. Effects of different college environments on the vocational choices of high aptitude students. *Journal of Counseling Psychology*, 1965, *12*, 28–34.

Astin, H. S., and Bisconti, A. S. *Career plans of college graduates of 1965 and 1970.* Bethlehem, Pa.: CPC Foundation, 1973.

Bandura, A. *Principles of behavior modification.* New York: Holt, Rinehart, and Winston, 1969.

Barak, A. Vocational interest: a cognitive view. *Journal of Vocational Behavior*, 1981, *19*, 1–14.

Barak, A., Archibald, R., and Carney, C. G. Relationship between vocational information seeking and educational-vocational decidedness. *Journal of Vocational Behavior*, 1975, *7*, 149–159.

Betz, N., and Hackett, G. The relationship of career related self-efficacy expectations to perceived career options. *Journal of Counseling Psychology*, 1981, *28*, 399–410.

Crites, J. O. *Career counseling: models, methods, and materials.* New York: McGraw-Hill, 1981.

Dolliver, R. H. Strong Vocational Interest Blank versus expressed vocational interests: a review. *Psychological Bulletin*, 1969, *72*, 95–107.

Flanagan, J. C. *Project Talent: five years after high school, final report.* Pittsburgh: American Institute for Research, 1971.

Hackett, G. and Betz, N. A self-efficacy approach to the career development of women. *Journal of Vocational Behavior*, 1981, *3*, 326–339.

Hawley, P. Perceptions of male models of femininity related to career choice. *Journal of Counseling Psychology*, 1972, *19*, 308–313.

Hind, R. R. and Wirth, T. E. The effect of university experience on occupational choice among undergraduates. *Sociology of education*, 1969, *42*, 50–70.

Jones, G. B. and Gelatt, H. D. Illustrations of program interventions. In Mitchell, A. M., et al. (eds.) *Social learning theory and career decision making.* Cranston, R.I.: Carroll, 1979.

Krumboltz, J. D. A social learning theory of career decision making. In Mitchell, A. M., et al. (eds.) *Social learning theory and career decision making.* Cranston, R.I.: Carroll, 1979.

Krumboltz, J. D. and Baker, R. D. Behavioral counseling for vocational decision. In Borow, H. (ed.) *Career guidance for a new age.* Boston: Houghton-Mifflin, 1973.

Krumboltz, J. D. and Schroeder, W. W. Promoting career planning through reinforcement. *Personnel and Guidance Journal,* 1965, *43,* 19–26.

Krumboltz, J. D. and Sheppard, L. E. Vocational problem solving experiments. In Krumboltz, J. D. and Thoresen, C. E. (eds.) *Behavioral counseling: Cases and techniques.* New York: Holt, Rinehart, and Winston, 1969.

Krumboltz, J. D. and Thoresen, C. E. The effect of behavioral counseling in group and individual settings on information seeking behavior. *Journal of Counseling Psychology,* 1964, *11,* 324–333.

Krumboltz, J. D. and Thoresen, C. E. (eds.) *Behavioral counseling: Cases and techniques.* New York: Holt, Rinehart, and Winston, 1969.

Mitchell, A. M. Relevant evidence. In Mitchell, A. M., et al. (eds.) *Social learning theory and career decision making.* Cranston, R.I.: Carroll, 1979.

Mitchell, A. M., Jones, G. B., and Krumboltz, J. D. (eds.) *Social learning theory and career decision making.* Cranston, R.I.: Carroll, 1979.

Osipow, S. H. Success and preference: a replication and extension. *Journal of Applied Psychology,* 1972, *56,* 179–180.

Osipow, S. H. *The manual for the career decision scale,* 2nd Edition. Columbus, Ohio: Marathon Consulting and Press, 1980.

Osipow, S. H. and Scheid, A. B. The effects of manipulated success ratios on task performance. *Journal of Vocational Behavior,* 1971, *1,* 93–98.

Osipow, S. H., Carney, C. G., Winer, J., Yanico, B., and Koschier, M. *The career decision scale* (3rd Revision). Columbus, Ohio: Marathon Consulting and Press, 1976.

Ryan, T. A. and Krumboltz, J. D. Effect of planned reinforcement counseling on client decision-making behavior. *Journal of Counseling Psychology,* 1964, *11,* 315–323.

Whiteley, J. M. and Resnikoff, A. (eds.) *Career counseling.* Monterey, Calif.: Brooks/Cole, 1978.

Whitney, D. R. Predicting from expressed choice: a review. *Personnel and Guidance Journal,* 1969, *48,* 279–286.

CHAPTER NINE
SUPER'S DEVELOPMENTAL SELF-CONCEPT THEORY OF VOCATIONAL BEHAVIOR

In fashioning his theory of career development, Donald Super appears to have been under two strong influences. The first influence, self-concept theory, may be illustrated by the writings of Carl Rogers (1942; 1951), Carter (1940), and Bordin (1943). These writers have suggested that behavior is a reflection of an individual's attempt to implement his self-descriptive and self-evaluative thought. With particular reference to vocations, Bordin (1943) proposed the notion that responses to vocational-interest inventories represent an individual's projection of self-concept in terms of stereotypes held about occupations. A person selects or rejects an occupation because of the belief that the field is or is not consistent with a self-view.

The other major influence on Super's work is Charlotte Buehler's (1933) writings in developmental psychology. She suggested that life can be viewed as consisting of distinct stages. The first is a growth stage, starting at birth and ending around age 14. Following this is an exploratory stage, occurring between ages 15 and 25. The maintenance stage comes next and covers the next 40 years, ending at about age 65, whereupon the final stage, called decline, begins. According to Buehler, life tasks vary according to the stage. Super's conception of career development is built upon the framework of these life stages and based on the assumption that vocational tasks reflect larger life tasks.

While other writers, for example Beilin (1955), have recognized the applicability of developmental psychology to career behavior and have attempted to formulate principles of vocational behavior taking human development into account, no one has so intricately woven developmental hypotheses into career development as successfully as Super.

THE THEORY

Hints of a theoretical basis were evident in Super's research (for example, 1940) in the field of career development many years before the publication of his first theoretical statement. Nevertheless, by his own admission, he was impelled into his first formal theoretical statement by the attempts at theorizing of Ginzberg and his colleagues (1951). Super thought the Ginzberg work had serious shortcomings, one of which was the failure to take into account the very significant existing body of information about educational and vocational development.

Super's theoretical writings have been extensive. His initial formulations were stated in an address before the American Psychological Association (1953) and further elaborated in a book (1957), a monograph (Super et al., 1957), and several papers (most significantly 1963a, 1963b, and 1963c). Super proposes the notion that people strive to implement their self-concept by choosing to enter the occupation seen as most likely to permit self-expression. Furthermore, Super suggests that the particular behaviors a person engages in to implement the self-concept vocationally are a function of the individual's stage of life development. As one matures, the self-concept becomes stable. The manner in which it is implemented vocationally, however, is dependent upon conditions external to the individual. Thus, attempts to make vocational decisions during adolescence assume a different form than those made during late middle age. According to Super, diverse vocational behaviors can be understood better by viewing them within the context of the changing demands of the life cycle on the shape of attempts to implement a self-concept.

In the development of his theory, Super strived to implement a specific stream of thought and research in psychology. The attempt to build a theory on the groundwork laid by previous efforts was deliberate, since Super soundly criticized the Ginzberg theory because of the failure of its authors to use the existing data relevant to vocational choice.

Occupations and Careers

Important to Super's theory is the difference between the psychology of occupations and the psychology of careers. The psychology of occupations is based primarily on differential psychology and on the assumption that once an individual and a career are matched they will "live happily ever after." On the other hand, the psychology of careers, stemming from developmental psychology, rests on the assumption that career development conforms to the general principles of human development, which are fundamentally evolutionary in nature. Vocational psychology is the term Super chose to represent the field of study resulting from the fusion of the two streams of thought. Since the methods and tools of vocational counseling are currently more suitable to the study of the psychology of occupations than the psychology of careers, Super asserts that the latter has been neglected in favor of the former (Super, 1961a; 1964a). He would correct the neglected condition of the psychology of careers by means of his theoretical formulations.

153

The Antecedents of the Theory

Super's theroretical framework is based on three psychological areas. The first is the field of differential psychology. The research related to differential psychology has reached maturity and has contributed much to vocational psychology. On the basis of existing data, Super drew the assumption that any given person possesses the potential for success and satisfaction in a variety of occupational settings. He elaborated on the trait-factor notions that people are differentially qualified for occupations by suggesting that interests and abilities are likely to fall into patterns more consistent with some occupations than others and that people are likely to be more satisfied if they are in an occupation that requires a pattern of interests and abilities closely corresponding to their own characteristics.

The second psychological influence on Super's theory stems from self-concept theory. Super proposed that vocational self-concepts develop on the basis of children's observations of and identifications with adults involved in work. The third influence is the principles of developmental psychology. The concept of life stages suggested by Buehler (1933) led Super to propose that a person's mode of adjustment at one period of life is likely to be predictive of techniques used to adjust at a later period.

Developmental concepts also led Super to the idea of career patterns. From the work of Miller and Form (1951) and Davidson and Anderson (1937), Super expanded the concept of career patterns. The career behavior of people follows general patterns which may be recognized as regular and predictable after study and examination of the individual. These patterns are the result of many psychological, physical, situational, and societal factors which, when accumulated, make up an individual's life. Among the various career patterns are the *stable* pattern, in which a career such as medicine is entered into relatively early and permanently; the *conventional* pattern, in which several jobs are tried, one of which leads to a stable job; the *unstable* pattern, characterized by a series of trial jobs which lead to a temporary stability which is soon disrupted; and finally the *multiple trial* pattern, in which an individual moves from one stable entry-level job to another, and which may be observed in domestic service careers (Super and others, 1957).

The career-pattern concept suggests that the life cycle imposes different vocational tasks on people at various times of their lives. Attention to career choice as a one-shot decision occurring in adolescence reflects only a segment of significant vocational behavior in the life of an individual. To comprehend fully a person's vocational life, the whole cycle must be observed. Super also notes the different roles that environment and heredity play in maturation and brings attention to those aspects of environment that may be manipulated to facilitate vocational maturity.

On the basis of the principles just described, Super (1953) generated ten propositions which should underlie a vocational development theory.

Revised Theory

Despite the considerable research that results from the ten propositions (for example, the Career Pattern Study), the theory remained relatively general for almost ten years. Then, Super and several of his students published a series of papers which provided a more explicit and detailed set of statements about how vocational development occurs. Super began by making the notion of the self-concept as explicit as possible (1963b). Starting with the awareness of self (as differentiated from the nonself) which an infant possesses at birth, Super described a process which leads first to primary self-percepts and then to more elaborate, or secondary percepts. The primary self-percepts deal with raw sensations such as hunger, pain, and temperature. As the child matures and begins to develop secondary percepts, the sensations begin to become ordered and assume a relationship with one another. As maturation continues, the self-percepts become even more complex and abstract, developing into self-concepts and systems of self-concepts. Among the many systems of self-concepts is the vocational self-concept, the system of major concern to Super.

According to Super (1963a), self-concept formation requires a person to recognize himself as a distinctive individual, yet at the same time to be aware of the similarities between himself and others. The self-concept of a well-integrated individual is a continually developing entity, shifting somewhat through life as experiences indicate that changes are necessary to reflect reality. Presumably, the vocational self-concept develops in a similar way. As an individual matures, he tests himself in many ways, most of which have implications for educational and vocational decisions. The process begins with the self-differentiation that occurs as part of a person's search for identity. A child learns that touching a hot stove hurts. In adolescence, the differences between self and others are broadened and one becomes aware of being fat or tall, shy or poised, athletic or clumsy, good or bad in academic matters. These recognitions, in turn, lead to decisions about education and work that are consistent with self-concepts. The athlete makes different decisions than the musically talented youth; the scholar sees the future in different terms than the "dropout."

At the same time that the process of differentiation of self from others is occurring, a process of identification goes on, partly facilitating the differentiation and partly facilitated by it. Beginning with their identification with the like-sexed parent, children develop images of themselves and behavior appropriate to culture gender-role stereotypes. They progress from identification with general models to identification with specific models. Recognizing that his father's life is not ideal, the adolescent male may find other adult males with whom to identify. The grocer's son may model himself vocationally after the neighbor who is an engineer, while at the same time identifying with his father's hobbies and personality traits. Similarly, the young female searches for attractive female role models. If her mother is not an attractive model, the young woman will seek others.

Role playing, stimulated by the process of identification, further facilitates the development of the vocational self-concept. The youth who observes a firefighter will pretend to be one and will play games in which the role of a fireman is acted. Growing older, the role playing becomes more subtle and sophisticated. The budding physician imagines performing great surgery and observes doctors in order to adopt their mannerisms and values. The prospective lawyer may deliberately seek out extracurricular political activities and become involved in school government or even real political campaigns.

Hadley and Levy (1962) have suggested that much of the role playing that occurs to facilitate career development takes place in formal and informal groups. The child evaluates potential roles in the world of work from the point of view of the family, which communicates differential values toward various kinds of work. As the child reaches adolescence, the reference group shifts from the family to the peer group, and vocational role activities, real and vicarious, are evaluated in the context of the teen-age world. In later life, when careers have been embarked upon and established, professional associations and trade unions serve as vocational reference groups. Codes of conduct, modes of behavior, and values are informally or formally set by the vocational group to which a person belongs.

Finally, throughout all of the adolescent period, but actually involved in career development in any life phase prior to decision making, reality testing must occur. Is the hopeful physician a good student? Is the potential musician successful in attempts to extend musical skills? Can the pre-law student earn admission to law school? Does the junior executive perform duties well? Is the scientist able to publish research? Are the consequences of these vocational decisions entirely consistent with the aspirations of the individual? These reality factors must of necessity either confirm or negate tentative educational and vocational decisions and cause them to be modified accordingly.

The various processes in the development of vocational self-concepts are likely to occur in more complex ways than the examples given suggest. While it is possible for an adolescent's identification with a person to lead directly to an educational-vocational decision, it is more likely that the identification will stimulate a chain of events that might not have occurred otherwise and that have vocational implications. Similarly, the adoption of a role may lead directly to a career, but it is more likely that role playing will have immediate consequences which may eventually influence vocational decisions. Talents explored will often lead to talents in new fields that have not been acknowledged previously. Thus, in playing the role of journalist, a student may join the school newspaper staff and meet a teacher who inspires him or her to become a writer. This decision, in turn, may lead to joining a literary club, reading Sinclair Lewis' *Arrowsmith* (1925), and eventually becoming a research scientist.

Vocational Maturity

In a more recent extension of his theory, Super (1963a) elaborated upon the concept of vocational maturity (Super et al., 1957, 1960). Vocational maturity allows the observer to assess the rate and level of an individual's development with respect to career matters. It is to be expected that vocationally mature behavior will assume different shapes depending upon the context provided by an individual's life stage. The vocationally mature fourteen-year-old will be concerned with assessing personal interests and abilities to reach the goal of deciding on an educational plan, while the vocationally mature forty-five-year-old person will be concerned with ways to maintain career status in the face of competition from younger workers. In view of the fluid nature of vocational maturity, Super defined the concept normatively, in terms of the congruence between an individual's vocational behavior and the expected vocational behavior at that age. The closer the correspondence between the the two, the greater the individual's vocational maturity.

Stages of Development

To specify further the process of vocational development, Super (1963c) extended the analysis of life stages with reference to vocational behavior. He proposed the idea that each of the two major stages in the vocationally significant life periods have several substages. The exploratory stage is composed first of the tentative substage, then the transition substage, and finally the uncommitted trial substage. Following these periods is the establishment stage, which is composed of the committed trial substage and the advancement substage. These stages, while not precisely the same as those of the Ginzberg theory, are similar. The names of the stages suggest the gradual nature of vocational concerns, starting in late childhood in tentative probes and questions, becoming stronger stirrings in early adolescence as recognition of the importance of these decisions grows, and finally leading to educational, and sometimes preliminary, vocational decisions. These decisions, in turn, are evaluated, are either modified or crystallized, and lead to the mature stage of elaboration and embellishment of vocational behaviors.

The process occurs by means of five activities which Super has called vocational development tasks. The first of these tasks, crystallization of a vocational preference, requires the individual to formulate ideas about work appropriate for himself or herself. It also requires development of occupational and self-concepts that will help mediate the individual's tentative vocational choice by means of relevant educational decisions. While the crystallization task can occur at any age, as can all the vocational developmental tasks, it most typically occurs during the 14-to-18-year age range. Behaviors involve the awareness, use, differentiation, formulation and planning of concepts to use in determining actions regarding goals, interests and values, and occupations and preferences for each of the four stages: crystallization (14 to 18), specification (18 to 21), implementation (21 to 24), and stabilization (25 to 35).

The next vocational developmental task is the specification of a vocational preference. Here, the individual is required to narrow a general career direction into a specific one and take the necessary steps to implement the decision. Thus, the prospective applied physicist enrolls in an electrical engineering program in college, while the student who likes the outdoors and has a technical bent begins the study of forestry. The specification task is most prominent during the 18-to-21-year age range. Once again, Super has indicated the attitudes and behaviors that are necessary to the successful accomplishment of the specification vocational task. They are similar to behaviors required in the crystallization task, except that they relate to the need for specification rather than crystallization. The third vocational task is the implementation of a vocational preference. This task, well advanced by age 21 and usually complete by age 25, requires the individual to complete some training and enter relevant employment. The necessary attitudes and behaviors for this task call for the individual's recognition of the need to plan for the implementation of a preference and the execution of this plan.

Stabilization within a vocation comes fourth in the list of developmental tasks for career development. Occurring approximately between the ages of 25 and 35, this task is represented by behavior which reflects settling down within a field of work and the use of one's talents in such a way as to demonstrate the appropriateness of the career decisions previously made. It is to be expected that an individual changes *positions* during the stabilization period but rarely changes *vocation*. The final vocational development task Super mentions is the consolidation of status and advancement, which occurs most clearly during the late 30s and mid-40s. Here, the worker becomes firmly established, developing skills and seniority to achieve a secure and comfortable vocational position. The necessary attitudes and behaviors are highly similar to those of the implementation and stabilization tasks. While Super fails to mention the specific task of readiness for retirement and decline in his list of vocational tasks, he has called attention to this task as a final phase in the life cycle in other writings (Super, 1957).

In summary, the individual moves through life stages, each of which calls for vocational behavior of a different sort. The adolescent is cast in the role of explorer searching for career direction. The young adult must translate the direction taken into action through training and job seeking. The more mature adult must find a place within a vocation, elaborate upon it, and secure a position. During each of these phases of vocational development, certain behaviors are more apt to result in growth than others. The degree to which the individual accomplishes the vocational tasks is a function of the adequacy with which the behaviors appropriate to each phase of development have been performed.

Exploratory Behavior

Jordaan (1963), one of Super's colleagues, has attempted to make the concept of exploratory vocational behavior explicit enough to study empirically. Jordaan has suggested that while experimental psychologists have studied the phenomenon of exploratory behavior in general, vocational psychologists have failed to recognize the full potential of research in what he calls "vocational exploratory behavior." He proposes that a complex relationship exists between an individual's exploratory behavior and self-knowledge. Logically enough, Jordaan states that exploratory behavior often leads to experiences in which the outcomes provide information that contradicts the "self-beliefs" the individual may hold. When such contradictions occur, the individual often resorts to the inappropriate mechanisms of repression, suppression, or distortion in order to preserve the values and images held about self and the world. Since new information is necessary for growth and since most important behavioral changes must occur in the context of experiences in which results may contradict old beliefs, it is axiomatic that individuals must engage in "undistorted hypothesis testing" in order to grow psychologically. That is to say, people must be psychologically mature enough to tolerate cognitive dissonance and reduce it by resorting to reality rather than by distorting their experiences if they wish to grow in their ability to cope with the demands life places upon them. While these observations are general in nature, they have a special relevance in vocational psychology.

The exploratory dimensions proposed by Jordaan share the characteristic that vocational exploration is more or less adequate depending upon the degree to which the dimensions are explicit, systematic, overt, and self-initiated. Thus, a person benefits considerably more from exploratory activities if they are purposeful and have external aspects than if they are random and exist only in mental processes. For example, it is more informative to spend a summer working as a camp counselor than to think about how one might enjoy a career working with young children.

According to Jordaan, certain personal traits and environmental conditions may facilitate exploratory behavior. These traits should serve as goals for counselors to consider in working with individuals in the exploratory stages of career behavior. People are more likely to engage in profitable exploratory acts if they are able to tolerate the ambiguity, uncertainty, tension, and frustration that accompany the lack of closure and insecurity that one feels prior to making a decision and starting on a course of action. Furthermore, exploration is most useful if defensiveness is minimal, since new information may be threatening to old self-images and values. Parents may facilitate exploratory behaviors by providing emotional support and an atmosphere which encourages independence. Society influences the outcome of exploration, too, by virtue of the opportunities it provides for exploratory roles, by the amount of time it makes available for exploration, and by the amount of conflict it places on young people in the exploratory stage of development. Counselors would do well to direct their efforts toward the task of teaching their students about the fact that exploration requires the ability to tolerate emotional discomfort, toward helping parents understand their role in facilitating exploration, and toward helping students develop the ability to keep possibilities open through exploration and implement the best dimensions of the exploratory process.

Language and Career

In an effort to make explicit the notions of the translation and incorporation of the self-concept into vocational terms, Starishevsky and Matlin (1963) proposed the idea of two vocationally oriented languages. Their proposal was designed to account for the fact that self-concepts vary from one person to another and that people translate their self-concepts into occupations in different ways. The first language is called *psychtalk*. This is the language an individual uses to think about self. Examples of psychtalk are: I am short; I am musically talented; I am honest; I always try my utmost; I am lazy. Psychtalk can extend to others, so that one may say "he is fat; you are money hungry; she is unethical." The term *occtalk* has been coined for the second language. Occtalk involves both verbal and behavioral expressions of occupational or educational intent. Thus, "I will be a mechanic," or "I am going to apply to law school," or the actual application to law school are examples of occtalk. The two languages, psychtalk and occtalk, can be translated into each other. One person, when saying "I will apply to medical school" in occtalk, may mean "I am compassionate, responsible, intelligent, and desire status and wealth" in psychtalk. Another person may reflect ambivalence about self (psychtalk) in the inability to make any clear vocational commitment (occtalk).

The term *incorporation* has been defined as the degree to which the occupational selection an individual makes is congruent with the self-concept. For example, a person who sees herself or himself as intelligent, strong, and humane (psychtalk) may choose law as a career. In that person's occtalk, lawyers may be described as intelligent, strong, and just. Thus, the choice of law has a level of incorporation of 66.6 percent, since two of the three ingredients of the psychtalk are included in the occtalk. The level can be represented quantitatively provided all the adjectives descriptive of the individual's self-concept and occupational concepts can be collected and then compared.

The logical extension of the scheme described by Starishevsky and Matlin is for the counselor to elicit psychtalk from the client and then verbal and behavioral occtalk, hoping to facilitate the client's ability to match the self-concept and occupational possibilities. Presumably, good matches can be achieved either by helping the counselee modify the self-concept where it appears to be inappropriate, or by helping him or her expand or modify the occupational dictionary, if occupational language appears to be limited or inaccurate.

RESEARCH

Vocational Maturity

As might be expected, the most comprehensive research concerning vocational maturity has been conducted by Super and his associates and students. Many of these studies were conducted within the context of Super's programmatic Career Pattern Study (Super and Overstreet, 1960). Super's purpose was to test the concepts of vocational maturity suggested by the theory. To accomplish this, he selected a group of ninth-grade boys attending school in Middletown, New York and set out to follow their vocational development over the twenty-year period to follow, or until 1971. The Middletown sample was selected because the community and school systems have characteristics that led Super to conclude that they represented a large segment of American culture and thus would allow considerable generalization to be made from the findings. The final number of students actually included in the study of ninth-grade boys, however, was small (142).

Five dimensions of vocational maturity were identified for study. Each of these dimensions was examined by means of several indices. Dimension I, entitled orientation to vocational choice, was assessed by examining the degree to which the student showed concern for vocational problems and the effectiveness of his use of the resources available to him in coping with the decision-making task. Both of these factors were examined by means of ratings made on the basis of interviews conducted with each student. Dimension II, information and planning about the preferred occupation, was assessed by studying the specificity of information possessed by the student about his preferred occupation, the degree of specificity of his planning for the occupation of his choice, and the extent to which the student was involved in planning activities of a vocational nature. Once again, these indices were based on data obtained in structured interviews with the boys.

Dimension III, consistency of vocational preferences, also has three indices, which are the consistency of vocational preferences within fields, within levels, and within families (or fields and levels combined). These indices were based on a modified version of Roe's occupational classification scheme (1956). The student's first two preferences were examined to see the degree to which they were in the same field (Roe's terms) and the same level (Roe's terms) and then to see the degree to which the combination of field and level of the first choice agreed with the combination of field and level of the student's second occupational choice. The data, while objectively scored, were based on the semistructured interviews conducted with the students.

Dimension IV, entitled crystallization of traits, has six indices. Two of these, interest maturity and patterning, were derived from Strong Vocational Interest Blank results. Liking for work, concern for work rewards, vocational independence, and acceptance of responsibility for educational-vocational planning were based on data from the interviews. Patterning of work values was based on scores on the Work Values Inventory, an instrument specifically designed by the staff of the Career Pattern Study. The fifth and final dimension, wisdom of vocational preferences, consisting of indices reflecting the agreement between ability and preferences, compared measured interests with preferences, measured interests with fantasy preferences, occupational level of measured interests with the occupational level of preferences, and the socioeconomic accessibility of the preference of the student. The indices were based on a combination of inventories, such as the SVIB and WVI, as well as interview data.

Six of the indices of vocational maturity were found to be intercorrelated to a significant degree. The particular arrangement of these results suggested that two major factors were relevant to vocational maturity in ninth grade, namely orientation to choice tasks and the use of resources. While the other indices are not necessarily less important as a result of these findings, the relationships among them do not appear to have any systematic basis. Thus, such logical-sounding dimensions as the consistency of vocational preferences, the crystallization of interests and attitudes toward work, vocational independence, and the wisdom of vocational preferences in terms of the consistency between preferences, talents, and socioeconomic factors do not seem to be related to vocational maturity in the ninth grade.

Among the variables important to the development of a useful orientation to vocational choice were those which resulted in behaviors reflecting recognition of the need to make educational decisions that have vocational implications. Also important was the acceptance of the responsibility to plan for these decisions, to collect relevant data toward that end, and actually to make and implement decisions with vocational implications. These behaviors included the effective use of pertinent local resources, such as talking to and observing workers and professionals, reading about vocations, part-time work, and so on.

Super and Overstreet also studied variables that might be associated with vocational maturity. These were classified into several groups:

The first was *biosocial* factors. Taking the vocational maturity index total consisting of factors such as concern with choice, specificity of information and planning, and acceptance of responsibility for choice and planning, or in other words, the "orientation to choice tasks" dimension, and correlating it with such biosocial factors as age and intelligence, Super and Overstreet concluded that vocational maturity is related to intelligence and that age is of less importance in vocational maturity, at least at the ninth-grade stage of development. Of course, since school experiences are structured, grade placement implies greater homogeneity of experience than does age. The difference seems to be primarily a reflection of differences in specificity of planning, which suggests that "bright" youngsters are able to plan more effectively in general than less "bright" ones.

Environmental factors were also associated with vocational maturity. The vocational maturity index correlated positively with parental occupational level, school curriculum (college preparatory versus noncollege preparatory programs), amount of cultural stimulation, and family cohesiveness and negatively with urban background and Protestantism. Most of these relationships are intuitively reasonable, since more enriched family backgrounds are likely to result in greater concern for and skill in planning for a career. The rural boys seemed to be more vocationally mature than the urban ones, possibly because the rural boys had work experience on farms and were likely to follow family farming patterns which were already clear to them. The negative finding with respect to Protestantism, however, is difficult to explain.

The third group consisted of *vocational factors.* The vocational maturity index correlated significantly with vocational aspirations and also with the degree of agreement between aspiration and expectation.

Personality characteristics constituted the fourth group. Vocational maturity was not significantly correlated with any of the personality adjustment or characteristic variables as measured by such devices as the Thematic Apperception Test, Incomplete Sentence Blanks, and a father identification inventory.

The final group of variables was *adolescent achievement*. Some achievements were related to the vocational maturity index. Grades, achievement versus underachievement, participation in school and out-of-school activities, and independence were all positively correlated with vocational maturity, while peer acceptance was negatively correlated.

In all of these five categories, the second major dimension of vocational activity, use of resources, was related only in a negative way with house rating in environmental factors and with achievement-underachievement in the factor of adolescent achievement. It does not appear to be a highly pervasive dimension in vocational maturity, whereas the dimension of orientation to choice is considerably more related to background factors. Super and Overstreet concluded that vocational maturity in ninth-grade boys is related to their degree of intellectual and cultural stimulation, the degree to which they are intellectually able to respond to that stimulation, their aspiration to higher rather than lower socioeconomic levels, and their ability to achieve reasonably well in a variety of activities.

With these results in mind, Super suggested that the school curriculum should "foster planfulness" aimed at helping youngsters become aware of their level of occupational aspiration and the general amount of education required to achieve that level. This self-knowledge could be developed without specifically deciding on an occupational goal, which would be premature in the ninth grade. In fact, rather than restrict occupational possibilities at that age, the school should exert its efforts to broaden occupational perspectives and to teach the student to use available resources for exploration effectively. In this statement lie the roots of the Career Education movement.

In another study, Super (1961) explored the significance of wise and consistent vocational choices at the ninth-grade level in terms of the long-range adequacy of the choice. Reasonable choices held over a long period and from a relatively early age have long been assumed to indicate that good vocational adjustment is to come. In contrast to that assumption is the observed instability of vocational choice in adolescents of all ages. To test the assumption, Super studied 105 ninth-grade boys chosen from his Career Pattern sample. Expressions of vocational preference were obtained by means of taped interviews based on a structured interview schedule. The responses about vocational preferences were then scored with respect to their consistency within fields (that is, the number of different categories, minus one, after statements of vocational preference were coded into Roe's [1956] occupational classification), consistency within levels (the number of different levels, minus one, of vocational preferences expressed, translated into Roe's system), and consistency within families (the sum of both consistency measures stated above).

The wisdom of the vocational choice was defined in several ways. If the agreement between a subject's abilities and preferences was high, the choice was considered to be satisfactory. Thus, if the subject's IQ score was greater than that of the bottom quarter of people in his chosen field, the subject was presumed to possess the required ability to function in the field of his choice.

Of concern was the consistency between stated vocational preferences and Strong Vocational Interest Blank (SVIB) scores. A modified SVIB was scored by means of pattern analysis. When the primary pattern was in the field chosen by the subject he was granted a score of four, while a secondary pattern earned three points, and a tertiary pattern earned two points. Agreement between the occupational level of the preferred occupation and the SVIB Occupational Level (OL) score was also considered. If the SVIB OL score was not more than one standard deviation below the mean occupational level score of the chosen occupation (Strong, 1943, Table 50, p. 192), the subject's OL score was considered to be consistent with his choice. Finally, the occupation of the breadwinner of the boy's family was rated by means of an occupational rating scale and compared with the rating of the occupation of the boy's choice. An index of social accessibility was thus computed. The smaller the index, the more accessible and thus the wiser the boy's choice of vocation.

When Super compared the consistency between fields and levels with the wisdom about vocational choices, he found very slight but statistically significant relationships between the two, but these relationships could hardly be considered practical. Such findings indicate that vocational preferences fail to show much consistency or "wisdom" at the ninth-grade level. Super suggests that at a later point, consistency may begin to reflect the wisdom of the vocational choice. To this writer, however, the lack of a close relationship between various early vocational preferences seems most reasonable, since the closer in time someone grows to vocational selection—the implementation of the first clearly defined steps toward a vocational field—the more consistent vocational behavior is likely to become. Early preferences are almost sure to be imprecise, since as time goes on the individual has an opportunity to evaluate and modify preferences in the light of experience.

One recent report of the Career Pattern Study dealt with the status of the original sample as it approaches age twenty-five (Super, Kowalski, and Gotkin, 1967). Of most interest in the data resulting from this ten-year follow-up, covering the period of the transition from school to college work, is the finding that about half of the sample had engaged in what Super calls floundering behavior and another one-sixth engaged in some floundering combined with stabilization. By age twenty-five, however, when this follow-up occurred, about 80 percent of the sample was engaged in stabilizing behavior. Super, Kowalski, and Gotkin retrospectively related vocational maturity to a variety of criteria. For example, it was noted that vocational maturity generally predicted career satisfaction, self-improvement, and occupational satisfaction, was questionable as a predictor of economic self-sufficiency, was negatively related to early establishment in a career, and was not very effective as a predictor of the ability to get and hold a job. In general, it was found that social status and achievement are effective predictors of vocational behavior. The usual measures found in schools (for example, intelligence tests, parental occupational level, vocational aspirations, curriculum enrolled in, grade-point average, age in grade, and, for seniors in high school, degree of participation in school and out-of-school activities) generally were useful predictors of vocational behaviors. The overall conclusion based on the results of the ten-year follow-up was that vocational maturity, in combination with measures of student status and achievement, is a useful predictor of vocational behavior.

Super and Jordaan (1982) report that by between the ages of 18 and 25 the average subject in the Career Pattern Study had changed job, occupation, or employer six times. When reviewed by trained judges, 85 percent of these changes were classified to be either floundering or trial behavior. Nonetheless, by age 25 the career development of approximately 80 percent of the subjects had stabilized. It was further reported that the 9th-grade data best predicted attained status (educational and occupation level) and career progress (respondent reports feelings about how career turned out), while the 12th-grade data predicted career satisfaction (the respondent expects and desires to continue in present occupation) and attained status.

Vocational Maturity—Other Research

Two investigators, Montesano and Geist (1964) chose to compare the occupational choices made by ninth- and twelfth-grade boys in terms of Super's position. They tested the hypothesis that vocational decisions occur in a developmental context and that the process of vocational development is "predictable and orderly." Sixty ninth- and twelfth-grade boys, equated with respect to reading skills and socioeconomic variables, were required to respond to the Geist Picture Interest Inventory (GPII) and to give their reasons for the responses they made to the inventory. The reasons were classified according to attitudes toward occupational-choice tasks or toward occupations themselves, in terms of categories called simple affect, identified interest, personal need satisfaction, assessment of abilities, assessment of opportunities, assessment of the particular occupation, social value, and ambiguous or evasive.

Montesano and Geist reasoned that if the developmental theory of career preferences has validity, older boys should be more reflective in their reasons for their interests. The findings supported such a view in a general way. Older boys' responses indicated more concern for vocational opportunities, information about careers, and the social value of given careers than did the responses of the ninth-grade boys. The younger boys' responses appeared to show considerable reliance on simple affect ("I would like it") or identified interests.

Gribbons (1964) and Gribbons and Lohnes (1964a; 1964b; 1965) produced a stream of research directed at demonstrating the criteria which are predictable from Readiness for Vocational Planning scores based on an inventory they developed. Their hope was to devise a standard and reliable technique to be used to identify a person's stage of vocational maturity and then introduce experiences to facilitate the growth of aspects of vocational maturity that are not well developed. Such, too, is the end toward which Crites' Career Maturity (1978) Inventory is aimed, as well as the Adult Career Maturity Inventory (Crites, 1979).

Gribbons and Lohnes (1968) published the result of an extensive longitudinal study concerning their attempt to develop an index of readiness for vocational planning. The project was designed to test the hypothesis that occupational choice is a sequential, developmental process. In particular, attempts were made to determine sex differences in vocational development, study the role of the self-concept in vocational decision making in adolescence, and assess the impact of intelligence in the choice, entry, and persistence in an occupation. The results of the Gribbons and Lohnes investigation indicated that although students increased in their awareness of their interests and values in relation to their educational-vocational decisions (during the period from eighth to tenth grade), many educational-vocational decisions continued to be made on the basis of irrelevant information. Also, the results point up the fact that eighth graders can be ahead of tenth graders in their readiness for vocational decisions. The data led Gribbons and Lohnes (1968) to postulate four distinct career processes: the steady pursuit of the first expressed vocational goal (called "constant maturity"); the passage through Super's stages of vocational development (called "emerging maturity"); degeneration, seen as the reduction of aspirations and achievement resulting in individual frustration; and constant immaturity, reflected in a fixation on unrealistic vocational goals. Gribbons and Lohnes (1969) have collapsed the original eight scales into one, which makes them a more convenient way to assess vocational maturity.

Crites (1971) published an integrative review of the work pertaining to the Vocational Development Project. Early work on the Vocational Development Inventory was impressive (Crites, 1961; 1965). Crites (1978) has summarized the extensive body of research on the instrument (renamed the Career Maturity Inventory) to measure career maturity. Recent work has extended it to the adult population with an instrument called the Career Adjustment and Development Inventory (Crites, 1979). This newer inventory is responsive to earlier criticisms that career maturity measured only on adolescents misidentifies the process of career maturity which should rather focus on adjustment, productivity, and satisfaction.

A third investigator, Westbrook (Westbrook and Parry-Hill, 1973) developed still another vocational maturity scale, this one emphasizing cognitive, as opposed to attitudinal, aspects of vocational maturity. Super, Bohn, Forrest, Jordaan, Lindeman, and Thompson (1971) also published the Career Questionnaire, renamed the Career Development Inventory (Super and Forrest et al., 1972), which purports to combine the best features of all these scales. The Crites' Career Maturity Inventory provides the theoretician and researcher with a useful instrument to apply to certain aspects of vocational development.

Dilley (1965) has attempted to evaluate vocational maturity in terms of decision-making ability. He constructed an inventory purportedly measuring decision-making ability and reported its relationship to intelligence, achievement in school, and participation in extracurricular activities, using 174 high school seniors as subjects. He found that more subjects made good decisions (as defined by his inventory) than were predictable by chance and that good decision makers earned higher academic-aptitude test scores, higher grades, and were more involved in school activities than poor decision makers. This positive relationship suggests that a general intelligence factor may be involved in vocational maturity. Wurtz (1969), however, has reanalyzed data in a way that suggests that mental age may be a more appropriate way to assess vocational planning than intelligence. In a way, this finding is similar to Crites' (1965) observation that grade level is more closely related to VDI scores than chronological age, since grade level in general is a better reflection of maturity during adolescence than age level.

Bartlett (1971), reviewing research concerning vocational maturity, reminds us of the two general approaches to its study noted by Crites (1961). The work of Super and Gribbons and Lohnes is called the *absolute* or *relative* approach and is couched in terms of stages of development and the mastery of tasks associated with them, while the *degree and rate* approach, characterizing the work of Crites, uses the individual's own peers as a comparison group in a manner similar to that in which intelligence is measured by the Stanford-Binet or the WAIS. It is interesting to note that both approaches seem to produce valid and useful data, though no direct comparison of the two methods has yet been made. In summary, the research evidence in general indicates that vocational maturity is a reasonable and valid concept which is likely to be of increasing usefulness to our understanding of vocational development.

The accumulated literature on vocational maturity is impressive. Not only has this been summarized in Crites (1978) for the Career Maturity Inventory, but a number of other investigators have written extensively on the topic. Westbrook (1976) examined the correlations between the Career Maturity Inventory subscales. Setting limits of intercorrelations that he thought would be acceptable, Westbrook found that career choice attitudes and competencies correlated more highly than the .30 to .49 range he established as satisfactory. Westbrook also found that the correlations of the competence test subscales correlated mostly in the .60 range, which again is higher than he thought desirable. Finally, Westbrook reports that career choice attitudes and competencies correlated .56, also higher than he thought they should be. Westbrook concluded that the high level of intercorrelation scales of the CMI is not entirely satisfactory and suggests it is a more unidimensional measure than Crites indicates.

Tilden (1978) found that although career maturity scores seemed to be continuous by grade level in high school, as reported by others, that is not so for college students. The Career Development Inventory published by Super et al., (1972) was administered to college students and systematic increases with college grade level were absent. This finding is consistent with studies of the Career Decision Scale (Osipow et al., 1976), which indicates that the career maturation and the decision process of college students may be somewhat different from that of high school students. Tilden concluded that the theoretical positions of Ginsberg and Super are supported by these findings because the process for career development appears to be discontinuous in the post high school years.

Putnam and Hansen (1972) examined career maturity development and self-concept in high school females in terms of Super's theory. High school females who viewed their roles as traditional had lower levels of vocational maturity than those who viewed their roles as untraditional. Putnam and Hansen concluded that the more a young woman accepts the achievement orientation of the culture and strives to fulfill herself by achieving her potential, the better able she is to cope with pertinent vocational developmental tasks.

Vocational Crystallization

Two investigators have scrutinized the crystallization stage. Madaus and O'Hara (1967) inferred evidence of a crystallization of vocational choice in high school students as a result of a study in which occupational preferences were elicited from 979 high school boys and classified into nine groups. The Kuder Preference Record differentiated the nine groups in a way similar to the expressed preferences. These results provide evidence from two vantage points that crystallization of vocational preference occurs during the high school years. Buck (1970) surveyed the career plans and experiences of 120 males entering Stanford as freshmen in 1960 and graduating in 1964. Buck administered the California Psychological Inventory, the SVIB, and the SAT to the students in the fall of 1960. In the spring of 1964, a second administration of the SVIB was executed, along with scales describing the extent and effectiveness of vocational exploration. Although changes in interests reflective of crystallization were observed in the subjects, there was no evidence to suggest that crystallization was enhanced by vocational exploratory behavior. The changes in interest crystallization appear to have been influenced by events other than exploratory ones, such as academic exposure and identification with a popular professor. In addition, crystallization was already under way when the students entered college, and the observed changes in crystallization might well have reflected the continuation of an existing trend.

Vocational Development during High School

The data from the ninth-grade follow-up of the Career Pattern Study (Super and Overstreet, 1960) generally indicate that choices made by boys during their early teen years are neither stable nor well founded. Such a finding naturally poses problems for educators concerned with developing curricula designed to teach vocationally related skills, beginning at about the ninth-grade period, since assignment of students to relatively narrow programs of study is thus questionable. The likelihood that a student expressing a preference for auto mechanics or law at age fourteen will express the same preference at age eighteen is relatively slim.

Research reported by Cooley (1967) and Astin (1967a), based on extensive data collected in the Project Talent Study, is somewhat inconsistent with Super's data, however, and suggests an alternative way of dealing with the dilemma of the timing of curricular decisions. Cooley's data, comparing the educational-vocational interests and choices of ninth- and twelfth-grade boys, indicate that the stated career plan of ninth-grade boys is a relatively good predictor of twelfth-grade plans. One basis for the difference between Super's work and Cooley's might lie in the specificity of classification used in the twelfth-grade criterion. For example, a student might change from planning to be a physician to planning to be a hospital attendant.

Using a criterion of specific careers, his choice is likely to be viewed as having changed substantially; using a larger set of categories, however, such as "health science," his choice has remained stable. It might be that these larger categories are relatively stable during the ninth- to twelfth-grade period, and represent a major portion of the type of output measured by standard interest inventories. Such a criterion might permit planners to develop general curricula oriented around large categories of vocational events which permit students to make commitments that will remain relatively stable (in fact, such programs do exist in some systems, for example, Heilman and Gardner, 1971).

Astin (1967b), further studying the shifts in vocational plans that occur during the ninth grade to post high school period, observed that the shifts tend to move students away from science and technology toward careers in business and education. The most likely explanation offered for this change is that reality factors in terms of chances of success in science and technology careers have increasing impact as the students get older.

Jepsen (1975) found evidence that high school students were able to increasingly specify their career choices between ninth and twelfth grade, generally supporting the tenets of Super's theory.

Kleinberg (1976), using Super's career-pattern data, examined the correlations generated during high school years of occupational stability and change in 148 men who were between the ages of 25 and 35. Overall, a lack of consistent relationship between high school age correlates and adult occupational ability was found. Apparently too many events occur between high school and the 25-to-35 year age range to permit earlier variables to be very useful predictors of occupational stability. The only factor that seemed to be at all positively predictive, and that not very strongly, was high school grades.

Self-Concept Implementation through a Career

To many psychologists, the vital part of Super's theory lies in the formulations made about self-concept implementation by means of vocational activities. Consequently, it is not surprising that a number of studies inquiring into the relationship between self-concept and career choice have been conducted.

Norrell and Grater (1960) tested the hypothesis that subjects who can accurately predict their interests, defined in terms of SVIB scores, are more aware of themselves, awareness of self being defined in terms of scores on selected scales of the Edwards Personal Preference Schedule (EPPS). Fifty-three male college sophomores expressing a variety of vocational preferences were given the SVIB and the EPPS. Those Ss who were able to predict accurately one-half or more of their interests on the SVIB were assigned to a "high awareness of self" group. Twelve of the EPPS scales were judged to possess relevance to self-awareness. For high self-awareness, these were needs achievement, autonomy, affiliation, intraception, dominance, nurturance, change, and heterosexuality; while for low self-awareness, needs deference, order, succorance, and abasement were identified. Subjects in the high self-awareness group were expected to score higher in the appropriate EPPS categories than Ss in the low self-awareness group. The results were all in the expected *direction*, but only scores on two scales, order and succorance, were significant beyond the 0.05 level of confidence. Norrell and Grater concluded that the results support the predictions; however, the failure of the relationships to reach the customary level of significance suggests that some caution should be used before reaching such a conclusion. This caution is not mitigated by Brown and Pool's (1966) replication of the study. Of the four EPPS scales that Norrell and Grater concluded to be significantly different for the high and low self-awareness groups (two at the 0.05 level and two at the 0.10 level), three were found to correlate significantly with interest awareness as reflected on the SVIB, but one was in the opposite direction. The two scales that remained significantly related to self-awareness on replication were again needs order and succorance, the only two that reached the conventional level of significance in the Norrell and Grater study.

Englander (1960) studied the relationship between the degree of agreement between self-perception and perception of people and situations relevant to one's chosen occupation. Englander predicted that prospective elementary teachers would see the personal characteristics of elementary teachers in a fashion more congruent with their own personal characteristics than would Ss choosing other occupations, that they would see the features of elementary teaching as more desirable than would Ss choosing other occupations, and that they would perceive their families and friends as holding more positive attitudes toward teaching than would Ss choosing other occupations.

To test these hypotheses, Englander required 126 female subjects, some elementary education students, some education majors in other areas, and some non-education majors, to perform one Q-sort describing themselves and another, using the same items, describing teaching. The agreement between these Q-sorts was then assessed to test the predictions. The results supported the first prediction, that prospective elementary teachers do indeed see a closer relationship between their personal characteristics and those of elementary teachers than do Ss choosing other occupations. The second prediction, that elementary teachers see elementary teaching as more desirable than Ss choosing other fields, must be amended to include secondary teachers as well. Apparently teaching in general holds no differential appeal to elementary and secondary teachers, at least as far as Englander's sample is concerned. The third hypothesis, too, must be amended to include secondary as well as elementary teachers. Teaching majors as a total group appear to have some consistency in their vocational perceptions and impressions of others' values of teaching which differentiates them from students not in the education area.

A study by Stephenson (1961) examined the occupational self-concept of the premedical student. Stephenson explored the timing of the crystallization of the occupational self-concept of the premedical student with respect to the timing of his application to medical school. The subjects were selected from the rejected applicants to the University of Minnesota medical school emanating from the University of Minnesota undergraduate College of Science, Literature, and Arts for the fall classes of 1947 through 1951, a total of 368 students. Presumably, these rejected applicants had conceptions of themselves as physicians which were fairly well-developed or they would not have applied to medical school. Since they were denied admission, at least to one medical college, the strength of the development of their medical self-concept should be reflected in the persistence they showed in trying to gain admission to medical or medically related occupations. A questionnaire asking current job title and job duties was sent to these applicants. The titles and duties were rated on a medically related continuum, with medical doctor as the positive anchor point, leading through medically related professions, medical services, and related areas, to nonmedically related professions as the negative anchor point. Ninety-three percent of the sample responded to the questionnaire.

The results indicate that almost two-thirds of the sample were in medical or medically related occupations, while somewhat more than one-third were in nonmedically related fields. Approximately two-thirds of the subjects who originally applied to the University of Minnesota medical school between the years 1947 and 1951 were actually admitted to some medical school. Since most of the subjects were in medical or related occupations, Stephenson concluded that the Ss had crystallized their occupational self-concept prior to application to medical school and that they had passed through Super's Exploratory phase and were in the Trial-Establishment substage prior to their application to medical school. Though that is clearly possible, even likely, it is also possible that a large number of rejected medical school applicants entered medically related fields by virtue of the relevance of their college training to the new field. They could have been merely trying to salvage as much as possible out of a misdirected education.

Kibrick and Tiedeman (1961) investigated the role of self-concept in the selection of nursing careers by means of comparing the images of nursing held by nursing supervisors and student nurses. Specifically, they predicted that persistence in nurse's training is a function of the agreement between supervisor and trainee with respect to the image of nursing. Five hundred thirty-eight nursing students from seven different schools, plus three or four supervising nurses from each of the schools, were used as subjects. They were administered a questionnaire concerning the information they had about the nursing program, the activities of the student nurse, the personality characteristics of the ideal nurse, their own personality characteristics, and the rights and obligations of nurses with respect to superiors, peers, and patients. The results indicated a tenuous relationship between persistence in training and the congruence of student and supervisor images of nursing. Probably reducing the relationship is the absence of controls for ability for nursing training. The findings suggest to Kibrick and Tiedeman that "self-concept and learning through role playing may still determine the goal elected when choice is necessary."

Blocher and Schutz (1961), studying the relationship between self-descriptions, occupational stereotypes, and vocational preferences, predicted that a person's vocational self-description and ideal self-concept are similar to the stereotype of a member of an occupation in which he or she is interested. They administered a descriptive checklist surveying self, ideal self, and occupational stereotypes to 135 twelfth-grade boys. The boys also rated 45 occupations represented on the SVIB in order of interest to them. Using the d^2 procedure for profile analysis, Blocher and Schutz observed that the resulting self-concepts, ideal self-concepts, and vocational self-concepts were similar, as had been predicted.

In a similar study, Warren (1961) predicted that changes in a college major field are likely to occur when a discrepancy exists between a person's self-concept and the occupational role he or she expects the college major to prepare him or her for. He measured the self-concept of 525 male National Merit Scholars during the summer prior to their entrance into college, by means of the Omnibus Personality Inventory (OPI), mailed to all Merit Scholars. During the spring of their freshman year, he measured the students' expected occupational roles by having them rate the appeal 13 possible sources of job satisfaction held for them. A measure called self-role discrepancy was based on the agreement between 95 pairs of self-concept and expected role statements. Finally, changes in field were tabulated in several ways. Prior to starting college each subject stated a proposed field of study. During the freshman and sophomore year each student reported his actual major field. The student's field was considered to have been changed if any two of the three expressions of preference were not the same, unless the precollege and sophomore fields were alike. The changes were coded "no change," "minor change," and "major change." For example, a change from physics to geology was rated as no change, from engineering to physics as a minor change, and movement from engineering to music was rated a major change.

The major hypothesis, that changes in major occur more frequently when discrepancies between self-concepts and occupational role expectancies exist, was not supported. A secondary hypothesis, however, did receive support. Warren noted that movement from an extremely inappropriate choice to an appropriate one in terms of self-concept and job-role expectancies, is likely to be difficult to accomplish all in one effort, so he predicted that students who had made two changes would have higher discrepancy scores than those who had made only one change. Warren also found that grade-point average is significantly correlated with change in major while scores on a thinking-introversion scale are correlated with persistence in a field. Thus, one would expect that an academic level of performance that was unsatisfactory to a student might impel the student to consider changing field. It could be that these variables interact, so that a student who might be impelled to make a major change on the basis of his grades might have that impulse moderated by the tendency toward thinking and not acting reflected by a high thinking-introversion score. Such possibilities might have obscured the main effects of Warren's predictions. The use of National Merit Scholars also makes inferences to more typical college students difficult to draw and inferences to noncollege populations almost impossible. Though one might speculate about the impact of performance on changes in academic field, actual observations available from a sample of Merit Scholars are minimal, and thus it is impossible to know if performance overshadows all other variables in bringing about changes in educational and vocational plans.

Morrison (1962) tested the adequacy of the use of Q-sorts in the measurement of self- and occupational concepts. He administered Q-sort tasks to 44 second-semester nursing students and 43 sixth-quarter education students, all females. The nursing students were to sort on their self-concept, their concept of a nurse, and their concept of a teacher. Similar procedures were followed for the sample of education students. Morrison predicted that nursing students would be more likely to report self-perceptions similar to those of nurses than would teachers, while the education students would be more likely to report self-perceptions similar to those of teachers than would nurses. The results supported the predictions.

As part of an attempt to develop and test a "theory" of general satisfaction based on the degree of agreement between self- and role percepts, Brophy (1959) developed several vocationally relevant hypotheses. He proposed a relationship between general satisfaction level and discrepancies between self-concept and ideal self-concept, self-concept and life role, and ideal self-concept and life role. With specific reference to careers, he hypothesized that occupational satisfaction is inversely related to the discrepancy between self-concept and occupational role, ideal occupational concept and occupational role, and self-concept and ideal occupational role concept.

To test these predictions, Brophy used a variety of instruments, most of which he devised. First, the subjects were given a General Satisfaction Scale, on which they were required to rate their general happiness for the past two months, their degree of happiness relative to others of their own age and sex, and their frequency of feeling happy. A Vocational Satisfaction Scale required the subjects to make the same judgments with respect to their jobs. The Bills Index of Adjustment and Values, consisting of 49 trait adjectives rated on a five-point scale, was directed toward eliciting information about self-concept, level of self-acceptance, and ideal self-concept. An Occupational Role Scale, using the same 49 trait adjectives of the Bills Index, was aimed at eliciting data about perceptions of occupational role, level of occupational role acceptance, and ideal occupational role in terms of a specific position. Finally, a Life Role Scale, modifying the 49 Bills Index adjectives in a manner related to life roles, was administered to the Ss. The subjects were 81 female nurses, most of them young, but ranging in age from 20 to 49 years and in professional experience from less than one year to 27 years. Seventy-seven percent of the sample returned usable questionnaires.

Nearly all of Brophy's predictions were supported. The correlations between the scores on the instruments indicated that vocational satisfaction is inversely related to the discrepancy between self-concept and occupational role, ideal occupational concept and occupational role, and self-concept and ideal occupational role concept. The only major prediction that was not supported was between general and vocational satisfaction. Surprisingly, the correlation between those two variables was not significant.

Oppenheimer (1966) studied the hypothesis that a positive relationship exists between an occupational preference hierarchy based on predictions made from the degree of agreement between self- and occupational concepts and the occupational preference hierarchy directly expressed by a subject. He required his subjects, 81 male liberal arts students below the senior year, to rank 70 occupations in order of their preference for them. A modified Repertory Test was administered to permit the subjects to use their own personal constructs to express their self- and occupational ratings. By comparing the occupational rankings with the responses to the Repertory Test, Oppenheimer found support for his prediction that the occupational preferences expressed by people are consistent with their self-concepts.

Another study of relevance to the implementation of the self-concept through vocational choice is reported by Anderson and Olsen (1965). They predicted a positive relationship between the degree of congruence of self- and ideal self-concepts and the ability to make realistic choices of occupational goals. They collected information on first and second occupational choices from 96 high school seniors (51 males and 45 females). In addition, the Flanagan Aptitude Classification Test (FACT) relative to the realism of the choice in terms of four-year versus two-year college plans was administered, and a Q-sort between congruence of self- and ideal self-concept in terms of both positive and negative items was performed. Student choices, then, were classified as to their adequacy in terms of the probability of the student's completion of the academic training necessary for his or her preferred field, two-year or four-year college programs. Anderson and Olsen predicted that students whose self- and ideal self-concepts were similar would make choices more in line with their potential for training then would students whose self- and ideal self-concepts were divergent. The results, however, failed to support such a prediction. There was no systematic difference in the realism of choices made by students of varying degrees of congruence between self- and ideal self-concepts.

James (1965), testing a Super-based hypothesis that lack of congruence between self- and occupational concept will create cognitive dissonance that will result in the individual becoming more congruent with the occupation, found that future teachers who most preferred their anticipated profession changed their ideas about teachers along with their self-expectations when a discrepancy was made known to them. For engineering students, however, such changes in ideas about teachers were not found to occur. These findings support the idea that self-concept implementation is important to career choice, at least for education students.

O'Hara (1966) had 308 ninth-grade and 152 twelfth-grade boys rate themselves on the Kuder Preference Record, the Work Values Inventory, the Allport-Vernon-Lindzey Study of Values, and subtests of the Differential Aptitude Test. Following these self-ratings, the students took the tests and inventories. Four months later, achievement data were gathered in the form of final-year grades in several academic subjects. O'Hara concluded that self-ratings seemed generally related to scholastic achievement, leading to the speculation that achievement might be influenced by self-concept, in which case self-knowledge and self-concept become even more important factors in vocational development.

Pallone and Hosinski (1967) administered a Q-sort of self, ideal self, and occupational self to 168 nursing students. The students represented seven levels of training in nursing, ranging from basic to graduate. The results yielded significant, predicted relationships among the statements for the graduate-level students but not for the others. These results indicate once again that investigations of students are likely to underestimate the true relationship between self-concept implementation and vocational preferences, since by the time students get to the graduate level considerable screening has occurred. The presence of nonscreened students in the lower level samples reduces the clarity of the role the self-concept plays in career preference.

The "level of incorporation" concept was tested by Healy (1968). Paid volunteers—students in medicine, accounting, and engineering—were assessed with repect to general personality traits by means of a modified Kelly Role Concept Repertory Test and some particularly relevant occupations by means of semantic differential ratings on 25 bipolar traits. The SVIB was also administered. The incorporation score was the sum of the differences between the self- and the occupational ratings subtracted from 100. The results indicate appropriate differences in the incorporation scores according to curricular group as well as a correlation between level of incorporation and SVIB scores. Healy also (1973) studied the relationship between social-class membership, self-esteem, and level of incorporation in accounting and nonaccounting majors, and found that high and low self-esteem accounting students had a higher level of incorporation scores on accounting than other business students, and that the high self-esteem accounting majors' incorporation scores were higher than those of the low self-esteem accounting majors. Lower social class accounting students had higher incorporation scores than middle-class accounting students. In another related study, Healy, Bailey, and Anderson (1973) found that high self-esteem veterans exhibit a greater range of incorporation (that is, their self-concept overlapped a greater number of occupations) than low self-esteem veterans.

In a more straightforward test of self-concept implementation in career, Wheeler and Carnes (1968) investigated the similarity between self-concept, ideal self-concept, and ideal and probable occupational stereotypes. One hundred thirty-four college freshmen enrolled in elementary psychology, health education, and general orientation programs responded to a descriptive checklist regarding self- and occupational concepts. The results indicate that self-concept and occupational stereotypes of probable occupation correlate more highly with each other than do self-ideal concepts and occupational stereotypes. In addition, ideal self- and ideal occupational concepts were found to correlate more highly than ideal self- and probable occupational concepts.

Marks and Webb (1969) were concerned with the effects of experience on the accuracy of occupational images. Such accuracy is important to assess since self-concept implementation through career requires adequate knowledge of careers that offer promise for self-expression. In the Marks and Webb study two groups of freshmen, two groups of seniors, and two groups of professionals in industrial management and electrical engineering (along with a sample of freshmen from another university responding in terms of social desirability of the scale) responded to a 95-item trait description covering numerous behaviors and characteristics of occupational importance. All together, including the social desirability sample, 824 individuals served as subjects. In general, the results indicate that the amount of professional experience one has in a field has little effect on the image one holds of the incumbents of that occupation. However, Marks and Webb did note that college freshmen in engineering and industrial management do describe themselves differently, and in ways that correlate appropriately with the images they hold of their respective future occupational peers. This finding would seem to support Super's hypothesis of self-concept implementation through career choice. However, as Marks and Webb point out, it is necessary to be cautious in drawing conclusions about the implications of this study, since little dissatisfaction with a vocational choice would be expected if it allows self-concept implementation, yet it is well known that college majors are frequently changed. It might have been interesting had Marks and Webb pursued the matter of stability in their sample according to congruence between self and occupational field as measured during the freshman year.

Another study testing self-concept implementation through vocational choice was conducted by Ziegler (1970). Ziegler was concerned with the criticism that much of the early research dealing with self-concept implementation and vocational choice was limited to samples of education and nursing students and thus of limited generality. Ziegler, studying 428 male college students representing 39 future occupational areas, compared the students' most- and least-preferred occupational fields against self-concept and most- and least-preferred occupational characteristics on the Adjective Check List. The results indicate greater congruence between self and most-preferred occupational group. In addition, some distinctive and intuitively predictable differences in self-concept characteristics by field were observed.

Greenhaus (1971b) attempted to isolate and examine a variable associated with self-concept implementation in career. He predicted that career salience would be positively related to self- and occupational congruence. A career salience questionnaire consisting of 28 items tapping the areas of attitudes toward work, vocational planning, and the importance of work was administered to 104 male and 273 female college freshmen and sophomores. The results support the prediction that salience and congruence are related in males but not in females. It is easy to speculate about some important differences in sex role that might affect the impact of career salience on career choice as a function of sex.

A study by Schuh (1966) raises some significant questions about the basic logic of hypotheses regarding self-concept implementation and career choice. Schuh, using the semantic differential to measure congruence between self-concept and career, predicted that self- and job ratings would be congruent. In general, based on the responses of 89 graduating college seniors, such congruence is not apparent. Schuh criticizes Super's theory in that it assumes congruence equals satisfaction without dealing with the question of how congruence between undesirable aspects of self should contribute to satisfaction. Logically, a "bad" self-concept congruent with a "bad" occupational concept should produce satisfaction, yet such relations are not found and, on the surface, would seem foolish to predict. It would seem that self-concept occupational congruence provides a meaningful way to predict occupational preference when both are positive but not when either is negative.

Putnam and Hansen (1972), mentioned before, found that vocational maturity in high school females seemed to be related to self-concept issues. Using the Semantic Differential format, Burgoyne (1979) measured self- and occupational concepts in 97 male and 88 female high school students and found that the ideal self-concept plays an important role in vocational preferences.

Overall, considerable convincing research data exist to support the notion that self-concept plays an important role in occupational preference. What appears needed now are additional conceptual links relating the two.

Self-esteem and Career Preferences

One conceptual link that offers some promise as a way of relating self- and occupational concepts is self-esteem. Korman began a series of investigations studying the role of self-esteem in career preferences and vocational development. In one study, Korman (1966) found that high self-esteem individuals are more likely to implement their self-concept through occupational choice than are low self-esteem individuals (a finding that is a logical outgrowth of Schuh's [1966] criticism). In a more complicated study, Korman (1967) tested the hypothesis that self-esteem is related to the perception of the "difficulty" of an occupation, and, as a result, serves as a moderator of occupational choice. One hundred twenty-six college students were administered the Ghiselli Self-Description Inventory as a measure of self-esteem along with a questionnaire to measure perceptions of occupationally required abilities and one designed to measure personal abilities. Vocational choice was also obtained. A discrepancy score between the two highest level occupations (in terms of required abilities) and self-perception was computed. A similar computation was calculated comparing the two lowest occupations and self-perception. The results strongly indicated that individuals with high self-esteem seek high ability demand situations in their work. A "balancing" effect is suggested by Korman; that is, the person who sees himself as competent will seek and enter competence-demanding situations, and vice versa. Korman calls this a closed-loop situation, suggesting that feedback enhances an already existing tendency to accept or reject challenging situations, which feeds back on self-esteem, which then effects the tendency to accept challenge, and so on.

In still another study, Korman (1968) tested the idea that individuals display cognitive consistency in their vocational behavior. In this study, Korman found that task success and task satisfaction are positively related for people with high self-esteem but not for low self-esteem individuals. The former individuals use their own internal frame of reference to determine the value they place on a task and its performance, but the latter look to other individuals to set their standards. Finally, Korman (1969) examined and found support for the hypothesis that self-esteem serves as a moderator variable in that high self-esteem individuals are more likely to seek self-fulfillment in their work than low self-esteem individuals.

Ryan (1969) reports a study in which reinforcement procedures were applied in an attempt to manipulate and enhance the self-concept as an adjunct to improving vocational decision making. Results of several procedures applied to 333 disadvantaged college students indicated that the group with the best scores on self-concept following treatment scored best in terms of the criteria on educational-vocational behavior. This study is one of the few that at least tenuously establishes a relationship between self-esteem and vocational decision making.

Greenhaus and Simon (1976) found that self-esteem and career salience combine to produce an increased likelihood that one's occupation would be viewed to be ideal. They measured self-esteem in 139 college students with Ghiselli's Self-Description Inventory and a modification of Super's Work Values Inventory to measure perceptions of occupations' capacity to satisfy work needs in students. In another study, Lopez and Greenhaus (1978) found that self-esteem and job satisfaction were positively correlated. King and Manaster (1977) studied 98 female undergraduate students' responses to a body satisfaction scale, a self-esteem scale, and in addition, asked them to complete a job interview performance expectation scale. Independent judges were asked to rate the subjects' subsequent interview performance. Job success expectations by subjects were significantly related to satisfaction with body image and self-esteem. Self-esteem was also related to the tendency to over- or underestimate how well one would perform in job interviews.

Fannin (1979) found that predictors of sex-role attitude, work-role salience, atypicality of major field, and self-esteem discriminate among the identity status of achievement, moratorium, diffusion, and foreclosure stages of Eriksen. Bedeian (1977) found a positive relationship between self-esteem and aspiration to high-prestige vocations in male college students. He also found a negative relationship between self-esteem and aspiration for low-prestige occupations, as well as a positive relationship between self-esteem and a willingness to accept vocations less likely to be satisfying than one's perceived upper ability limit. Ohlde (1979) found that middle and high self-esteem subjects in college had more "like" responses on the Strong Campbell Interest Inventory, while low self-esteem subjects more often responded with "dislike" responses. Not only does response set of that type influence inventory results and measured occupational preferences, but it tells us something about the effects of self-esteem on interactions with the world that might be useful.

Not all the research dealing with self-esteem and vocational choice has produced clear results. Resnick, Fauble, and Osipow (1970) postulated that high and low self-esteem college students (self-esteem defined in terms of scores on the self-esteem scale of the Tennessee Self Concept Scale) would differ in vocational crystallization defined in terms of the differentiation of the Kuder Preference Record profiles and self-reported certainty of vocational plans. No differences were found on the Kuder, though the high self-esteem students expressed greater certainty about their plans than did the low self-esteem students. In another study, Greenhaus (1971a), testing the hypothesis that self-esteem is positively related to self- and occupational congruence, did not find results to support his hypothesis.

Korman (1970) has suggested a "balance" approach to explaining the complex relationship between self-esteem and vocational behavior. Korman presents the idea that the self-concept of the individual at the moment is the result of the goals sought and the outcomes that will be satisfying. In other words, people will find maximally satisfying those behaviors which permit them to feel they are behaving consistently. Applied to self-esteem then, "to the extent that an individual has a self-cognition as a competent, need-satisfying individual, then, to that extent, will choose and find most satisfying those situations which are in balance with these self-perceptions." In two experiments designed to test the balance hypothesis, Korman found support for the conclusion that self-perceived competence facilitates task performance and social evaluation of competence seems to become internalized and enhances performance.

The Korman hypothesis has generated a minor controversy among investigators in the field. Dipboye et al. (1978) conducted a study in which they found that high self-esteem physicists displayed significant correlation between their interests and their intrinsic satisfactions in their work, while low self-esteem individuals showed nonsignificant correlations. It was predicted that the same kind of phenomenon would be observed in an engineering sample. Failing to find data to support the prediction for engineers, Dipboye et al. concluded that there is only soft support for the self-consistency—self-esteem notion as a moderator variable. Dipboye (1977) critiques Korman's self-consistency theory pointing out a discrepancy of self-esteem and congruency theory. The theory would predict that people of low self-esteem choose occupations that are not satisfying or are in other ways non-self-enhancing, a hypothesis not yet well substantiated. Related to this criticism is a paper by Barrett and Tinsley (1977) in which a study was conducted to compare the Super and the Korman models in order to explain how self-esteem and vocational decisions are related to each other. According to Barrett and Tinsley, the Super and the Korman approaches lead to a different set of predictions each. Comparing responses on self-concept crystallization and global self-esteem in undergraduates, Barrett and Tinsley (1977) found that degree of crystallization was different across self-esteem levels. The results were interpreted as supporting Super's as opposed to Korman's model. Some support, however, was found for Korman's assumption that high self-esteem people are more likely to see themselves to be "competent and needs satisfying decision makers" than low self-esteem people.

Evaluation

The research and data relevant to the concept of vocational development seem to indicate a steady and reasonably predictable increase in both the amount of sophistication and the attention being given to vocational choice tasks through the adolescent years. The attention culminates, for well-oriented people, in commitment to a position, which is then carried on throughout life, though in varying degrees. It also seems clear that the scholastic aspects of vocational development are closely tied to the educational system. Vocational development exhibits more evidence for the generalization that behavior is a function of the situation in which it occurs. Students seem to make decisions at times that are imposed on them by the structure of the educational system. It is interesting to speculate on the effects of vocational development under the English system of secondary education, in which choice points are imposed at different age levels.

Most of the findings of research support the idea that occupational choice represents the implementation of the self-concept. The results of the research provide an impressive amount of empirical support for the general aspects of the theory proposed by Super. In view of the continuing efforts of Super and his associates to make the theory more explicit (Super, Starishevsky, Matlin, and Jordaan, 1963), even more adequate tests of the theory are apt to be forthcoming.

STATUS

Implications for Counseling

Crites (1981), in comparing approaches to career counseling from different theoretical perspectives, describes the steps involved in developmental career counseling. The diagnostic phase is an appraisal phase which tries to deal with three areas of behavior: problem, person, and prognosis. Tests of various kinds and inventories of various kinds would be heavily relied upon to generate the data for this diagnostic stage.

The counseling process involves, first, identifying the client's life stage and level of career maturity. For an immature client, counseling would concentrate on orientation and exploration phases of development. For more mature clients, counseling focused on decision making and reality testing as well as implementation. Outcomes sought involve helping clients move ahead in their careers through the use of increased awareness and by mastering appropriate vocational development tasks. Essentially, the techniques used involve problem exploration, topic setting, clarification and reflection, the use of tests and occupational information to help clients explore, and nondirective exploration of attitudes and feelings related to careers.

Crites does not deal directly with developmental career counseling of other developmental theorists, such as Tiedeman, Ginzberg, et al. Some similar processes, however, would be likely to be suitable from those perspectives as well as from Super's, which forms the basis for the Crites description of career counseling from a developmental point of view.

One characteristic of Super's theory is its concern for the application to counseling on vocational and personal matters. In an early paper published before the theory was clearly formulated, Super (1951) described the role that self-concept development plays in career development. Super reasoned that although the self-concept is likely to be a function of genetic influences on physical factors, such as glandular structure, and psychological factors, such as aptitudes, it operates in combination with environmental variables, such as social and economic conditions. Thus, a certain portion of the self-concept is open to outside intervention. Such intervention is likely to be most effective in shaping the self-concept during early adolescence, since the concept grows more stable during later adolescence and maturity. Counselors, thus, have access to youngsters during the years of greatest development of the self-concept.

Since vocational decisions require a person to explicitly state self-conceptions, people with accurate information about themselves and the world are most likely to make sound vocational decisions. In other words, Super subscribes to the trait-factor approach to vocational choice. The difference is that Super adds several new ideas to the old ones. Since the data about vocational maturity in ninth graders reflect considerable instability in vocational preferences, Super suggests that counselors should not take expressed vocational aspirations too seriously. More effort and attention should be directed toward the development of vocationally relevant tasks.

In counseling with vocationally mature people, attention should be directed toward the collection and understanding of vocationally and personally relevant information which will serve as a basis for the decisions required. Counseling with the vocationally immature, a more common task, differs in that the vocationally immature know little about the choices to be made, have difficulty framing vocationally relevant questions, and consequently are not in a position to make sound vocational and educational decisions. Counselors, thus, must work to orient such students to the tasks required by their life stage before working on the specifics of the stage itself. The goal of counseling in such situations is to develop a sense of planfulness in the student which will facilitate readiness for choice. To do this the counselor must specifically work on the student's understanding of the relevant factors in vocational choice to increase the effective use of resources for choice and to develop an understanding of the occupational field which most interests the student. When those goals have been accomplished, the student can apply the techniques learned in counseling in the assessment of this field to investigations of other occupations that may be desirable to explore later.

In counseling with a vocationally uncertain individual, the counselor should respond to the client's feeling, in this case to the emotions surrounding the uncertainty. By so doing, attention will be brought to bear on the antecedents of the indecision. In the normal course of the well-conducted interview, data become available about the client's cultural, social, and biological background, which the counselor can help the client to integrate into the decision.

In his early papers, Super reveals his steady interest in using theoretical formulations to guide practice. As he was developing his ideas about career patterns, Super (1954) called for, in general terms, the use of the concept of career patterns in vocational counseling. In another article (Super, 1955), he suggested that a close relationship exists between emotional and vocational adjustment and counseling procedures. This relationship has long been recognized; however, Super's treatment of the question of counseling people seriously disturbed emotionally and vocationally dysfunctional is new. Is a desirable sequence with which to approach these problems known? Traditionally, it has been assumed that if emotional concerns are resolved, other concerns, such as vocational, marital, and so on, will all fall into place. Experienced counselors, however, know that such is not always the case. Consequently, Super's suggestion that resolutions of career dysfunctions may be instrumental in resolving more general psychological disorders is appealing.

Attempting to clarify the role that career patterns play in helping counselors to identify the nature of student problems, Super (1960) states that the task at hand for a counselor working with ninth graders is to aid them to ascertain career alternatives to be explored and to help them to implement exploratory activities. For the older adolescent other assessments must be made, and different counseling techniques might be more appropriate. Super (1964) describes some categories of student concern that might be helpful in identifying relevant counseling techniques.

Operationally, the counseling tasks relevant to the late adolescent period of life are either the facilitation of exploration or of preparation (Super, 1964b). Exploration, either occupationally oriented or nonoccupationally oriented, is aimed at continuing to broaden one's experiences. Preparation, on the other hand, is the result of successful completion of the crystallization stage and the entrance into the specification stage. Thus, counseling the college-bound student in the exploratory stage should include instruction on how to use the facilities of the liberal arts college or general education program, a feat rarely performed.

The student interested in advanced education or training, on the other hand, needs information about which colleges offer compatible programs of study. Thus, the sophisticated counselor will learn to suggest application to one kind of university to the student who needs great academic flexibility, a second kind of university to another student because of its emphasis on theory, still a third kind of university to a highly professionally oriented student, and a two-year technical school to a fourth type of student. According to Super, much of the counselor's work done in the context of the theory must involve the identification of the differential rates of student development, the ability to appraise students with respect to these rates, and knowledge of the alternatives of higher education which fit such varying students. This poses the task of codifying the programs available in institutions of higher education and passing them on to counselors.

Some attempts have been made to apply Super's principles in connection with a computer-based information and exploration system (Minor, Myers, and Super, 1969). In this approach, an attempt has been made to program information regarding career choices and development in sequences built on the stage of vocational development defined in the theory.

The growing sophistication and refinement in the procedures to measure vocational maturity represent another area in which Super's theory can be applied.

The various scales of vocational maturity can be applied as criteria to evaluate career exploration programs (for example, Osipow and Alderfer, 1968) or to counsel for career development or simply to assess a student's progress through the various stages of growth to determine current needs.

Other information for the counselor, growing from the theory, involves differential possibilities for the "early emerger" as opposed to the "late bloomer" (Super, 1964b). The "early emerger" is generally closely identified with the adult world. The counselor should review the important figures in the counselee's life to learn the antecedents of the interests of such a person. The "late bloomer," on the other hand, probably has not identified with the adult world to a sufficient degree and consequently needs an accepting relationship with an adult who is willing to serve as a model and from whom the student can learn acceptable adult outlets for interests and talents.

Other problems are posed by the multitalented and the untalented. Both groups tend to be generalists, but for very different reasons. The multitalented individual has many interests and possibilities and ordinarily moves from one field to another in search of bigger and better opportunities. In maturity, they are the people who succeed in a profession, then move into executive or administrative positions, and frequently end their careers in government, politics, or industry in policy-making activities. When young, such people must be helped to chart a course satisfying to themselves, since often they express no special vocational interests such as are ordinarily demanded of young people. The untalented, too, often express no special vocational preferences. They usually drift from one job to another with little system. Their jobs have little continuity, so one may work as a route salesperson, a laborer, a clerk, and an assembly-line worker in succession. These people need to learn to harness the talents they do possess through some training, so that they will not be completely open to the changing conditions of their local economic situation.

Super also attends to the problem of retirement (1956). He suggests problems facing retirees and differing alternative solutions to these problems, depending upon the career field. Super's description of counseling procedures to be followed with special groups, late bloomers, and talented and untalented students indicates his emphasis on approaches for counselors.

Others have suggested applications of Super's theory. Hummel (1954) suggested that the theory highlights the differences inherent in counseling people at different stages of development, for example, the early adolescent as opposed to the young adult. What must be done is to identify the differential techniques that must be applied for maximum effectiveness to the problems of each stage. These remain to be worked out in detail, though they are further along in development than they were at the time Hummel wrote.

LoCascio (1964) suggested that special attention be paid to misdirected vocational development in the context of Super's theory. Since career development is a continuous process in which a person is successively faced with some vocational developmental task, the outcome of the person's efforts to deal with each task influences not only the context of his later tasks but also the subsequent approaches which the person will have at his or her disposal to deal with vocational problems. Consequently, a well-functioning person faced with a vocational development task applies relevant behavior and learns additional vocationally relevant behaviors as a result. These behaviors are added to the person's knowledge of vocational behavior, and he or she uses this additional learning in dealing with later vocational tasks. At the other extreme is the individual who, when faced with a vocational task, does not apply relevant behavior and learns little as a result, and whose vocational behavior is not only ineffective but who chronically shows little growth. These people present special counseling problems and need special approaches. The following illustrates the sequence: a well-ordered individual might need to select a college to attend. From past experiences it is clear that a school which offers the courses wanted is necessary (for example, engineering courses). Several such schools are identified; the person applies to them for admission, is accepted by some of them, chooses one to attend, and enrolls. The sequence reflects having learned to have several alternatives if possible. The person may also have several alternative plans available should difficulty be encountered in engineering studies, such as changing to another program or another school, acquiring better study skills, and so on. On the other hand, a poorly functioning person might decide to study engineering, apply to a large, highly competitive institution because of its reputation, without regard to personal purposes, and also to a small, local liberal arts college with lenient admission requirements, as a "safety valve." If the person is rejected by the large school and as a consequence is forced to enroll in the small school, he or she may discover that the college fails to provide the desired course of study. Such a person might well continue in the liberal arts school simply out of convenience, without looking for ways to move to a university with programs more relevant to personal interests and goals.

Super's theory, particularly in the developmental component but also in the self-concept idea, is especially compatible with the creation of the career education curriculum. In fact, Super's ideas have so permeated the field of occupational development that it is likely that the architects of career education were both implicitly and explicitly influenced by Super's theory. The career education movement's emphasis on the graded exposure to concepts of self and concepts of work throughout the entire curriculum represents precisely the basic ideas of career development and vocational maturation described by Super (for example, Heilman and Gardner, 1971). It would seem that curriculum development in the area of career education should lean heavily on the vocational developmental tasks described by Super and also that vocational maturity, as measured variously by Super's Career Questionnaire, Crites' Career Maturity Inventory, and Westbrook's Cognitive Vocational Maturity Test, has the potential to serve as one aspect of the criterion for the evaluation of career education programs. It does seem clear that Super's theory emphasizes continuing and simultaneous efforts toward self-awareness and occupational exploration, and these seem to be cardinal elements in career education. The goal of career education, it would seem, is to continuously provide students with information about themselves and the educational-vocational world, so that it may become an integral part of them. Thus, at the time that decisions need to be made, such as the choice of type of high school program, the student has the personal resources to make an intelligent response rather than cast about for a week or two for information and opinions and, very likely, make an ill-founded and impulsive choice that will prove to be unsatisfactory as time goes on.

The Super position seems to present some moderately specific guidelines for the practice of counseling. A counselor operating within this framework would try to appraise the life stage of a client in order to define relevant counseling goals. Attempts would be made to help the client to clarify the self-concept and, within the context of the life stage, be exposed to events both in and out of the counseling situation, which would permit movement toward the implementation of that concept. While Super fails to make explicit statements about particular counseling procedures to accomplish these ends, he does indicate that procedures should be broader than nondirective counseling methods. Among his suggestions are the use of the concept of vocational appraisal, encouragement of the use of experiences out of the counseling office, the use of community resources other than the counselor, and the codification of occupations and colleges to help individuals recognize potentially appropriate steps to take in the decision-making sequence. In some recent work (Super et al., 1963), there is the implication that recommended counseling procedures will grow more specific as the theory matures.

Evaluation

The theory is a well-ordered, highly systematic representation of the process of vocational maturation. It has the virtue of building upon aspects of the mainstream of developmental psychology and personality theory and demonstrating how those two streams can come together to clarify behavior in one major realm of human activity. The original version of the theory was too general to be of much practical value, and even its conceptual value was limited by its sweeping style. Later versions, however, are much more detailed, as Super and his associates have attempted to indicate the parameters of the theory in more specific terms. Consequently, in its current state, it has considerable utility for both practice and research in vocational psychology.

Most of the research reported on Super's theory generally supports his model. The developmental aspects of the theory are well documented, though certain details have been modified as a result of empirical findings such as the specific timing of developmental tasks. The proliferation of names for the various phases and stages makes for some apparent inconsistency in the results and certainly for some confusion, but no serious flaws in the developmental aspects of the theory seem to exist.

The data with respect to the formulations about the role of the self-concept generally agree with the theory. The samples studied in this respect have generally been broadened with respect to career orientation, and the measures of the self-concept are closer to real life and real work situations than before. As additional instruments to measure self- and career concepts are devised, better research designs will result.

With the increasing emphasis on specificity in the theory, Super's concern for applications, and the generally wide empirical support, the future prospects for this approach to career psychology continue to be promising. Still needed are better ways to integrate economic and social factors which influence career decisions in a more direct way than the events described by the theory currently do, as well as to continue the development of specific and rigorous formulations about aspects of career decisions and ways to bring about appropriate behavioral changes which will facilitate vocational maturity.

REFERENCES

Anderson, T. B., and Olsen, L. C. Congruence of self and ideal-self and occupational choices. *Personnel and Guidance Journal,* 1965, *44,* 171–176.

Astin, H. S. Career development during the high school years. *Journal of Counseling Psychology,* 1967, *14,* 94–98. (a)

Astin, H. S. Patterns of career choices over time. *Personnel and Guidance Journal,* 1967, *45,* 541–546. (b)

Barrett, P. C., and Tinsley, H. E. A. Vocational self concept crystallization and vocational indecision. *Journal of Counseling Psychology,* 1977, *24,* 301–307.

Bartlett, W. E. Vocational maturity: its past, present, and future development. *Journal of Vocational Behavior,* 1971, *1,* 217–229.

Bedeian, A. G. The roles of self esteem and achievement in aspiring to prestigious vocations. *Journal of Vocational Behavior,* 1977, *11,* 109–119.

Beilin, H. The application of general developmental principles to the vocational area. *Journal of Counseling Psychology,* 1955, *2,* 53–57.

Blocher, D. H., and Schutz, R. A. Relationships among self-descriptions, occupational stereotypes, and vocational preferences. *Journal of Counseling Psychology,* 1961, *8,* 314–317.

Bordin, E. S. A theory of interests as dynamic phenomena. *Educational and Psychological Measurement,* 1943, *3,* 49–66.

Brophy, A. L. Self, role, and satisfaction. *Genetic Psychology Monographs,* 1959, *54,* 263–308.

Brown, R. A., and Pool, D. A. Psychological needs and self awareness. *Journal of Counseling Psychology,* 1966, *13,* 85–88.

Buck, C. W. Crystallization of vocational interests as a function of vocational exploration in college. *Journal of Counseling Psychology,* 1970, *17,* 347–351.

Buehler, C. *Der menschliche Lebenslauf als psychologiches Problem.* Leipzig: Hirzel, 1933.

Burgoyne, P. H. Concepts of present self, expected self, and ideal self in vocational preferences and expectations. *Journal of Vocational Behavior,* 1979, *14,* 134–144.

Carter, H. D. The development of vocational attitudes. *Journal of Consulting Psychology,* 1940, *4,* 185–191.

Cooley, W. W. Interactions among interests, abilities, and career plans. *Journal of Applied Psychology Monograph,* 1967, *51.*

Crites, J. O. A model for the measurement of vocational maturity. *Journal of Counseling Psychology,* 1961, *8,* 255–259.

Crites, J. O. Measurement of vocational maturity in adolescence. I. Attitude test of the vocational development inventory. *Psychological Monographs,* 1965, *79,* No. 2 (Whole No. 595).

Crites, J. O. The maturity of vocational attitudes in adolescence. *APGA Inquiry Series, No. 2.* Washington, D.C.: American Personnel and Guidance Association, 1971.

Crites, J. O. *Theory and research handbook for the Career Maturity Inventory.* Monterey, Calif.: CTB, McGraw-Hill, 1978.

Crites, J. O. *Career Adjustment and Development Inventory.* College Park, Md.: Gumpter, 1979.

Crites, J. O. *Career counseling.* New York: McGraw-Hill, 1981.

Davidson, P. E., and Anderson, H. D. *Occupational mobility in an American community.* Stanford, Calif.: Stanford University, 1937.

Dilley, J. S. Decision-making ability and vocational maturity. *Personnel and Guidance Journal,* 1965, *44,* 423–427.

Dipboye, R. L. A critical review of Korman's Self Consistency Theory of work motivation and occupational choice. *Organizational Behavior and Human Performance,* 1977, *18,* 108–126.

Dipboye, R. L., Zultowski, W. H., Dewhirst, H. D., and Arvey, R. D. Self esteem as a moderator of the relationship between scientific interests and the job satisfaction of physicists and engineers. *Journal of Applied Psychology,* 1978, *63,* 290–294.

Englander, M. E. A psychological analysis of a vocational choice: teaching. *Journal of Counseling Psychology,* 1960, *7,* 257–264.

Fannin, P. M. Relationship between ego identity status and sex role attitude, work role salience, atypicality of major, and self esteem in college women. *Journal of Vocational Behavior,* 1979, *14,* 12–22.

Ginzberg, E., Ginsburg, S. W., Axelrad, S., and Herma, J. L. *Occupational choice: an approach to a general theory.* New York: Columbia University Press, 1951.

Greenhaus, J. H. Self-esteem as an influence on occupational choice and occupational satisfaction. *Journal of Vocational Behavior,* 1971, *1,* 75–83. (a)

Greenhaus, J. H. An investigation of the role of career salience in vocational behavior. *Journal of Vocational Behavior,* 1971, *1,* 209–216. (b)

Greenhaus, J. H., and Simon, W. E. Self esteem, career salience, and the choice of an ideal occupation. *Journal of Vocational Behavior,* 1976, *8,* 51–58.

Gribbons, W. D. Changes in readiness for vocational planning from 8th to 10th grade. *Personnel and Guidance Journal,* 1964, *42,* 908–913.

Gribbons, W. D., and Lohnes, P. R. Relationships among measures of readiness for vocational planning. *Journal of Counseling Psychology,* 1964, *11,* 13–19. (a)

Gribbons, W. D., and Lohnes, P. R. Validation of vocational planning interview scales. *Journal of Counseling Psychology,* 1964, *11,* 20–25. (b)

Gribbons, W. D., and Lohnes, P. R. Predicting 5 years of development in adolescents from readiness for vocational planning scales. *Journal of Educational Psychology,* 1965, *56,* 244–253.

Gribbons, W. D., and Lohnes, P. R. *Emerging careers.* New York: Teachers College Press, Columbia University, 1968.

Gribbons, W. D., and Lohnes, P. R. Eighth-grade vocational maturity in relation to nine-year career patterns. *Journal of Counseling Psychology,* 1969, *16,* 557–562.

Hadley, R. G., and Levy, W. V. Vocational development and reference groups. *Journal of Counseling Psychology*, 1962, *9*, 110–114.

Healy, C. C. Relation of occupational choice to the similarity between self-ratings and occupational ratings. *Journal of Counseling Psychology*, 1968, *15*, 317–323.

Healy, C. C. The relation of esteem and social class to self-occupational congruence. *Journal of Vocational Behavior*, 1973, *3*, 43–51.

Healy, C. C., Bailey, M. L., and Anderson, E. C. The relation of esteem and vocational counseling to range of incorporation scores. *Journal of Vocational Behavior*, 1973, *3*, 69–74.

Heilman, C. F., and Gardner, R. E. Exploration in careers education. School of Education, University of Oregon, Corvallis, 1971.

Hummel, R. Vocational development theory and guidance practice. *Journal of the National Association of Women Deans and Counselors*, 1954, *18*, 13–18.

James, F., III. Occupational choice and attitude change. *Journal of Counseling Psychology*, 1965, *12*, 311–315.

Jepsen, B. A. Occupational decision development over the high school years. *Journal of Vocational Behavior*, 1975, *7*, 225–237.

Jordaan, J. P. Exploratory behavior: the formulation of self and occupational concepts. In Super, D. E., et al., *Career development: self-concept theory*. New York: CEEB Research Monograph No. 4, 1963.

Kibrick, A. K., and Tiedeman, D. V. Conception of self and perception of role in schools of nursing. *Journal of Counseling Psychology*, 1961, *8*, 62–69.

King, M. R., and Manaster, G. J. Body image, self esteem, expectations, self assessment, and actual success in a simulated job interview. *Journal of Applied Psychology*, 1977, *62*, 589–594.

Kleinberg, J. L. Adolescent correlates of occupational ability and change. *Journal of Vocational Behavior*, 1976, *9*, 219–232.

Korman, A. K. Self-esteem variable in vocational choice. *Journal of Applied Psychology*, 1966, *50*, 479–486.

Korman, A. K. Self-esteem as a moderator of the relationship between self-perceived abilities and vocational choice. *Journal of Applied Psychology*, 1967, *51*, 65–67.

Korman, A. K. Task success, task popularity, and self-esteem as influences on task liking. *Journal of Applied Psychology*, 1968, *52*, 484–490.

Korman, A. K. Self-esteem as a moderator in vocational choice: replications and extensions. *Journal of Applied Psychology*, 1969, *53*, 188–192.

Korman, A. K. Toward a hypothesis of work behavior. *Journal of Applied Psychology*, 1970, *54*, 31–41.

Lewis, S. *Arrowsmith*. New York: Harcourt, Brace, 1925.

LoCascio, R. Delayed and impaired vocational development: a neglected aspect of vocational development theory. *Personnel and Guidance Journal*, 1964, *42*, 885–887.

Lopez, E. N., and Greenhaus, J. H. Self esteem, race, and job satisfaction. *Journal of Vocational Behavior*, 1978, *13*, 75–83.

Madaus, G. F., and O'Hara, R. P. Vocational interest patterns of high school boys: a multivariate approach. *Journal of Counseling Psychology*, 1967, *14*, 106–112.

Marks, E., and Webb, S. C. Vocational choice and professional experience as factors in occupational image. *Journal of Applied Psychology*, 1969, *53*, 292–300.

Miller, D. C., and Form, W. H. *Industrial sociology*. New York: Harper & Row, 1951.

Minor, F. T., Myers, R. A., and Super, D. E. An experimental computer-based educational and career exploration system. *Personnel and Guidance Journal,* 1969, *47,* 564–569.

Montesano, N., and Geist, H. Differences in occupational choice between ninth and twelfth grade boys. *Personnel and Guidance Journal,* 1964, *43,* 150–154.

Morrison, R. L. Self-concept implementation in occupational choice. *Journal of Counseling Psychology,* 1962, *9,* 255–260.

Norrell, G., and Grater, H. Interest awareness as an aspect of self-awareness. *Journal of Counseling Psychology,* 1960, 1960, *7,* 289–292.

O'Hara, R. P. Vocational self-concepts and high school achievement. *Vocational Guidance Quarterly,* 1966, *15,* 106–112.

Ohlde, C. D. Relationship between self esteem and response style. *Journal of Counseling Psychology,* 1979, *26,* 455–458.

Oppenheimer, E. A. The relationship between certain self construct and occupational preferences. *Journal of Counseling Psychology,* 1966, *13,* 191–197.

Osipow, S. H., and Alderfer, R. D. The effects of a vocationally oriented speech course on the vocational planning behavior of high school students. *Personnel and Guidance Journal,* 1968, *47,* 244–248.

Pallone, N. J., and Hosinski, M. Reality-testing a vocational choice: congruence between self-, ideal, and occupational percepts among student nurses. *Personnel and Guidance Journal,* 1967, *45,* 666–670.

Putnam, B. A., and Hansen, J. C. Relationship of self concept and the feminine role concept to vocational maturity in women. *Journal of Counseling Psychology,* 1972, *19,* 436–440.

Resnick, H., Fauble, M. L., and Osipow, S. H. Vocational crystallization and self-esteem in college students. *Journal of Counseling Psychology,* 1970, *17,* 465–467.

Roe, A. *The psychology of occupations.* New York: John Wiley, 1956.

Rogers, C. R. *Counseling and psychotherapy.* Boston: Houghton Mifflin, 1942.

Rogers, C. R. *Client centered therapy.* Boston: Houghton Mifflin, 1951.

Ryan, T. A. Reinforcement techniques and simulation materials for counseling clients with decision-making problems. *Proceedings,* 1969 American Psychological Association.

Schuh, A. J. Use of the semantic differential in a test of Super's vocational adjustment theory. *Journal of Applied Psychology,* 1966, *50,* 516–522.

Starishevsky, R., and Matlin, N. A model for the translation of self-concept into vocational terms. In Super, D. E. et al., *Career development: self-concept theory.* New York: CEEB Research Monograph No. 4, 1963.

Stephenson, R. R. Occupational choice as a crystallized self-concept. *Journal of Counseling Psychology,* 1961, *8,* 211–216.

Strong, E. K., Jr. *Vocational interests of men and women.* Stanford, California: Stanford University Press, 1943.

Super, D. E. *Avocational interest patterns.* Stanford, California: Stanford University Press, 1940.

Super, D. E. Vocational adjustment: implementing a self-concept. *Occupations,* 1951, *30,* 1–5.

Super, D. E. A theory of vocational development. *American Psychologist,* 1953, *8,* 185–190.

Super, D. E. Career patterns as a basis for vocational counseling. *Journal of Counseling Psychology,* 1954, *1,* 12–20.

Super, D. E. Personality integration through vocational counseling. *Journal of Counseling Psychology*, 1955, *2*, 217–226.

Super, D. E. Getting out of an occupation. *Personnel and Guidance Journal*, 1956, *34*, 491–493.

Super, D. E. *The psychology of careers*. New York: Harper & Row, 1957.

Super, D. E. The critical ninth grade: vocational choice or vocational exploration. *Personnel and Guidance Journal, 1960, 39*, 106–109.

Super, D. E. Some unresolved issues in vocational development research. *Personnel and Guidance Journal*, 1961, *40*, 11–14. (a)

Super, D. E. Consistency and wisdom of vocational preference as indices of vocational maturity in the ninth grade. *Journal of Educational Psychology*, 1961, *52*, 35–43. (b)

Super, D. E. Self-concepts in vocational development. In Super, D. E. et al., *Career development: self-concept theory*. New York: CEEB Research Monograph No. 4, 1963. (a)

Super, D. E. Toward making self-concept theory operational. In Super, D. E. et al., *Career development: self-concept theory*. New York: CEEB Research Monograph No. 4, 1963. (b)

Super, D. E. Vocational development in adolescence and early adulthood: tasks and behaviors. In Super, D. E. et al., *Career development: self-concept theory*. New York: CEEB Research Monograph No. 4, 1963. (c)

Super, D. E. A developmental approach to vocational guidance. *Vocational Guidance Quarterly*, 1964, *13*, 1–10. (a)

Super, D. E. Goal specificity in the vocational counseling of future college students. *Personnel and Guidance Journal*, 1964, *43*, 127–134. (b)

Super, D. E., Bohn, M. J., Jr., Forrest, D. J., Jordaan, J. P., Lindeman, R. L., and Thompson, A. S. Career Questionnaire, Form IV. New York: Teachers College, Columbia University, 1971.

Super, D. E., Crites, J., Hummel, R., Moser, H., Overstreet, P., and Warnath, C. *Vocational development: a framework for research*. New York: Bureau of Research, Teachers College, Columbia University, 1957.

Super, D. E., and Forrest, D. K. et al. Career Development Inventory Preliminary Manual. Unpublished test manual. New York: Teachers College, Columbia University, 1972.

Super, D. E. and Jordaan, J. P. *Careers in the making: floundering, trial, and stabilization after high school*. New York: Teachers College Press, Columbia University, 1982. (in press)

Super, D. E., Kowalski, R. S., and Gotkin, E. H. *Floundering and trial after high school*. Cooperative Research Project No. 1393. New York: Teachers College, Columbia University, 1967.

Super, D. E., and Overstreet, P. L. *The vocational maturity of ninth grade boys*. New York: Bureau of Publications, Teachers College, Columbia University, 1960.

Super, D. E., Starishevsky, R., Matlin, N., and Jordaan, J. P. *Career development: self-concept theory*. New York: CEEB Research Monograph No. 4, 1963.

Tilden, A. J., Jr. Is there a monotonic criterion for measures of vocational maturity in college students? *Journal of Vocational Behavior*, 1978, *12*, 43–52.

Warren, J. R. Self-concept, occupational role expectation, and change in college major. *Journal of Counseling Psychology*, 1961, *8*, 164–169.

Westbrook, B. W. The relationship between career choice attitudes and career choice competencies of 9th grade pupils. *Journal of Vocational Behavior*, 1976, *9*, 119–125.

Westbrook, B. W., and Parry-Hill, J. W., Jr. The measurement of cognitive vocational maturity. *Journal of Vocational Behavior*, 1973, *3*, 239–252.

Wheeler, C. L., and Carnes, E. F. Relationships among self-concepts, ideal self-concepts, and stereotypes of probable and ideal vocational choices. *Journal of Counseling Psychology*, 1968, *15*, 530–535.

Wurtz, R. E. Developmental intelligence and vocational development. *Journal of Counseling Psychology*, 1969, *16*, 584–586.

Ziegler, D. J. Self-concept, occupational member concept, and occupational interest area relationships in male college students. *Journal of Counseling Psychology*, 1970, *17*, 133–136.

CHAPTER TEN
THE GINZBERG, GINSBURG, AXELRAD, AND HERMA THEORY

An economist, a psychiatrist, a sociologist, and a psychologist collaborated to produce a rationale describing vocational choice which exerted a substantial influence on vocational psychology during the decade following its publication in 1951. The work was the result of an empirical investigation into the character of events influencing vocational selection. The theoretical formulation was a direct reaction to the absence of elaborate and comprehensive theoretical constructs in vocational psychology. It was the plan of these four investigators to construct a theoretical approach to the matter of vocational choice.

The empirical findings of their own earlier studies and those of other investigators influenced the approach they took to the problem. Ginzberg's group concluded, on the basis of earlier research, that at least four significant variables were involved in vocational choice. The first of the four was identified as the reality factor, which causes an individual to respond to the pressures of environment in making decisions with vocational impact. Then, the influence of the educational process is felt, since the amount and kind of education a person has had will limit or facilitate the flexibility and type of vocational choices he or she makes. Third, emotional factors involved in the individual's responses to his or her environment were considered important, since it seemed, on an intuitive basis, that personality and emotional factors should have vocational concomitants. Finally, individual values were deemed to be important in vocational choice, since they should influence the quality of the choices made, by virtue of the differing values in various careers.

THE THEORY

Ginzberg, Ginsburg, Axelrad, and Herma (1951) construed vocational choice as an irreversible process, occurring in reasonably clearly marked periods and characterized by a series of compromises the individual makes between wishes and possibilities. The three major periods of the process have been entitled the Fantasy, Tentative, and Realistic periods. Probably less is known about the Fantasy period than the other two. Ginzberg and his associates suggest that the chief feature of the Fantasy period is the arbitrary nature of the child's choices and the lack of reality orientation reflected in the occupational preferences expressed during that period.

The Tentative period has been further subdivided into four stages: Interest, Capacity, Value, and Transition. Thus, children begin their vocational considerations by asking themselves what they are interested in and what they like to do. Soon, however, they become aware that there are some things they do more skillfully than others, and thus they temper their unrestrained desires with the notion of abilities. As they grow older, they recognize that certain activities have more intrinsic or extrinsic value than other activities, and they introduce this recognition as a third element in their vocational deliberations. At this point, they are beginning to integrate the four stages of the Transition stage and move into the final period, that of Realistic choice.

The Realistic period, too, has several stages. The first has been called the Exploration stage. Having reached the point of integrating likes and dislikes with capabilities and tempering these two variables with society's and his or her own values, the young adult begins to devise ways to implement the still tentative choices. This stage is distinct from the Tentative period in that the individual evaluates the feedback of his or her vocational behaviors in a highly realistic context such as an entry job or the early years of college. The results of these evaluations gradually blend into the Crystallization stage. Crystallization is characterized by the emergence of some clear vocational pattern based on the success and failures the individual experienced during the Exploration stage. Once this Crystallization is complete it leads to the final stage, entitled Specification. The individual chooses a position or a professional specialty. At this point the process is complete, having occurred over perhaps as much as a 15-year period in the life of the individual.

How is the 10- to 15-year period distributed with regard to the three periods and substages within the periods? Ginzberg and his collaborators take pains to caution their readers that individual variations of timing and degree may be very large. Certain general patterns of timing are evident, however, and are suggested as part of the theory. The Fantasy period seems to terminate at about age 10 or 12. The specific age is partly a function of the rate of emotional and intellectual development of the child. Generally, by age 12 most children have entered the Interest stage of the Tentative period. The three remaining stages of the Tentative period are likely to be concluded by age 17 or 18, though once again considerable variability is likely. Lower-income children are likely to enter the Realistic period at an earlier age than more affluent adolescents who may go to college, mainly because the poorer children are faced with the task of earning a living sooner and partly because the cultural values they are exposed to encourage an earlier assumption of an adult role than the cultural values of upper- and middle-class groups. The latter groups tend to prolong the period of adolescent dependency upon parents. The Crystallization stage of the Realistic period is likely to have a very broad range, though Ginzberg and his associates suggest that for most young people Crystallization occurs between the ages of 19 and 21.

The theory is heavily dependent on general concepts found in developmental psychology. Beyond these basic concepts, however, the work is subtly influenced by the Freudian model of personality development. The theorists assume that the vocational choice process occurs primarily during the adolescent period and is closely linked with the physical changes that occur during adolescence. The authors of the theory further assume that adolescence is in general a period of "storm and stress" and that the storminess of the period influences the pattern of the process of vocational development.

The eventual shape of the theory was heavily influenced by the nature of the students observed. A particular effort was made to select students who represented a population which is relatively unhampered by reality constraints in vocational choice, these constraints being the limits that personal or environmental situations place on the choices one can implement. The assumption made was that such a group would reflect the "purest" features of the vocational choice process. To accomplish this, a sample of white boys of Anglo-Saxon descent of upper- and middle-class Protestant or Catholic background was selected. Both parents were alive and living together. Furthermore, the boys were generally emotionally stable, considerably above average intellectually, and were all ostensibly college bound. Eight subjects at each two-year interval between age 11 and about age 23 or 24 were chosen for intensive study. At the college level, freshmen at Columbia College (the male undergraduate school of Columbia University) who had completed a semester and a half of college work were chosen on the assumption that they had experienced enough of college to evaluate its influence on their career development. At the graduate level, several subjects at the master's degree level were chosen, and several doctoral candidates were also included. No students in professional schools such as medicine and law were included, and special pains were taken to distribute the sample evenly with respect to scientific and nonscientific fields.

The Fantasy Period

The primary task the child accomplishes during the first period of vocational development is part of the general maturational process of changing from a "play orientation" to a "work orientation." According to Ginzberg and his associates, children state clear vocational preferences, and their play reflects what they call "function pleasure" as a motive. As a child grows older and approaches the terminal point of the Fantasy period, a gradual reorientation occurs, reflecting a preference for vocational activity which leads to accomplishments which will result in abstract satisfactions such as pleasing a parent. The ''function pleasure'' principle refers to the observation that very young children delight in activities for the sheer sake of the characteristics intrinsic in the activities. Making mudpies is fun because of the feel of the mud. Later, as the children grow more socialized, they seek out activities that possess potential for extrinsic rewards such as parental approval, success and its rewards, money with which to buy toys, and so on.

Coupled with the developmental change described above is the hypothesis that children are frustrated by a sense of inadequacy and impotency which results from their small size and their relative ineffectiveness as compared to adults. One way that children can attempt to relieve the sense of frustration their size instills is by identifying with and emulating the adults around them. Adult roles are most clearly manifest in work; thus children ''play at'' working and assume make-believe identities in the work roles they pretend to hold. In so doing they try out a variety of adult situations. At this same time they relieve the frustration generated by their feelings of inadequacy and internalize the values of the adult world. During the Fantasy period the children ignore reality, their abilities and potentials, and the time perspective, three of the very important ingredients in the vocational choice process, according to the Ginzberg group.

The Tentative Period

These play activities, nevertheless, help to propel the child to the next period in his vocational selection, the Tentative period. This occurs between the ages of approximately 11 and 18 and is divided into three stages which differ in their vocational developmental tasks. The *Interest stage* is the time, around ages 11 and 12, when the child is beginning to recognize the need to identify a career direction. At this stage, the need is reflected in a growing concern for the identification of activities liked and disliked. Choices are considered in terms of the potential they hold for intrinsic enjoyment. Often these choices reflect a strong identification with the father, but the identification shows signs of ambivalence. The children recognize their instability, a function of the anticipation of physical and emotional changes in adolescence, and accept the need and possibility of deferring final selections until they are older. Nevertheless, they begin circumscribing their arena of choice during the Interest stage. The *Capacity stage*, ages 12 to 14, logically follows the Interest stage. Here, students begin to introduce the notion of ability into their vocational considerations. They begin to evaluate their ability to perform well in areas of interest. There appears to be a decrease in the degree of father identification as an influence in vocational choices and a corresponding increase in the influence of other, more distant models.

In the *Value stage*, following during the 15th and 16th years, students undergo a very marked change in their approach to vocational choice. Of special note is the introduction of the idea of service to society. They seem to become aware that work offers more than the potential for satisfying their own needs and for the first time show signs of choosing careers such as medicine for humanitarian reasons rather than because of its status or intrinsic work activities. Clearer conceptions of differing life styles offered by occupations also emerge during the Value stage. It becomes more evident to students that a salesperson leads a different kind of life than an accountant. It is during the Value stage that the students become more cognizant of the uses to which they may put their special abilities. For example, those skilled interpersonally will begin looking for ways to use that skill in work.

Finally, two significant developments concerning time awareness take place during the Value stage. First, the students begin to develop a broader time perspective than they formerly held. They begin thinking of a career in terms of years of day-in and day-out activities, which will eventually become a life pattern. At the same time, as their time perspective broadens, they become more sensitive to the imminence of vocational commitment. Clearly, by age 16 only a few more years remain before they are almost irrevocably committed to a life pattern, and their recognition of this introduces a sense of urgency in their planning which is frustrated by their continued dependence on their parents.

The *Transition stage* closes the Tentative period. Occurring at about age 17 or 18, this stage is characteristically calmer than preceding stages of the Tentative period. It is during this stage that the individual begins to face the necessity to make immediate, concrete, and realistic decisions about vocational future and furthermore, to assume the responsibility for the consequences of the decisions. This stage differs from the Value stage which preceded it in that during the Transition stage the young person has considerably more independence of action than he formerly possessed. This increased freedom leads to a seeking of new surroundings in which to try out skills and talents. A heightened awareness of the externals of work occurs. The amount and kind of preparation necessary for various careers is studied, recognition of varying financial rewards is keener, and the awareness of the different life circumstances of careers is sharpened. It is during this stage, too, that increasing sexual impulses and the desire for early marriage run headlong into the necessity for delaying marriage in order to pursue the required career training.

The Realistic Period

The Realistic period follows the final stage of the Tentative period and takes place from approximately ages 18 to 22 or even as late as age 24. This period is more variable in its timing than many of the others, partly because of the different training patterns various careers require. While biological maturation and processes exert a strong influence on the rate with which a student progresses through the Tentative period, such physical factors have little to do with the Realistic period. The rate of biological change slows markedly by age 18 or 19, when the Realistic period begins.

The first stage of the Realistic period is the *Exploration stage*. Starting at college entrance, it is marked by narrowed goals in contrast with the broader goals of earlier periods, but maintains a good deal of vocational flexibility. Having moved into a college environment, the students experience much more freedom than they had before, but at the expense of considerable ambiguity. The general indecisiveness continues, partly because their interests are still changing and partly because the reality of the situation does not yet require a specific decision to be made. The principal task during this stage is typically the selection of a path to follow from among two or three strongly held interests. In the face of the selection, the students are fearful of choosing what will eventually be an unsatisfying occupation and are still relatively naive about the specific financial rewards to be expected in certain occupations. They especially feel the pressures of time acutely, since job or graduate-school applications will need to be made at a specified time in the future.

The *Crystallization stage* occurs next. By this time the students have become more or less deeply involved in a specific major field. They definitely have a clear idea of what occupational tasks they wish to avoid. In the face of definite and impending deadlines, by which time decisions must be made, their decisions become firm and the degree of commitment to a choice grows strong. Although most students have reached the Crystallization stage by the time of college graduation, Ginzberg and his colleagues point out that by no means do all students reach Crystallization so early. For some, there is a stage of pseudocrystallization, in which the student thinks and acts as if he has crystallized his decision, though later events indicate otherwise. This is not to say that truly crystallized choices are not subject to change as a function of new experiences or the reappraisal of old experiences. Ginzberg and his associates do not clearly indicate how one is to tell pseudocrystallization and revised crystallization apart. The concept of pseudocrystallization becomes a loophole to explain the behavior of a certain (unspecified) class of students who make late and unpredicted changes in their plans.

The final stage of the Realistic period is the *Specification stage.* For some, this stage never genuinely arrives. It is the final point of career development. The individual here elaborates upon his choice by selecting a specific job or graduate school subspeciality. Once again, however, Ginzberg and his associates suggest the possibility of a pseudospecification, but do not distinguish the pseudoevent from the real one.

Variations in the Pattern

Although the authors of the theory visualize the career choice process as occurring within the framework just described, they recognize that individual variations in the patterns will occur for biological, psychological, and environmental reasons. Such variations will occur in two possible behavioral realms. Individuals will vary with regard to the range of choices they express over time. Some people will select one occupation early in life and never vary significantly from it, while others will make a series of widely diverse occupational choices over the years before eventually implementing one. Ginzberg and his associates suggest that the specific nature of an individual's abilities will partly influence the range of his choices. Thus, if a person possesses a highly developed skill with specific occupational implications and if that skill emerges early in life, it is very likely that he or she will exhibit a very narrow range in choice pattern.

The other dimension of variability is with respect to the timing of the Crystallization stage. Some people make crystallized vocational choices toward the end of the Tentative period, while at the other extreme, Crystallization may occur well into the twenties. In addition to normal variability of patterns of career development, Ginzberg and his collaborators describe certain conditions which differ from normal variations. They consider these conditions to be deviant patterns. The general principle in identifying deviant occupational patterns is that the individual does not conform to age mates in some significant aspect of vocational development. Thus, one might pursue an unrealistic choice far beyond the time when age mates have discarded their earlier and ill-founded choices, or one may approach the end of the Realistic period but be chronically unable to achieve a crystallized choice. Reasons for deviant patterns may be highly variable, but might include severe emotional disorder or unusual personal financial circumstances such as excessive affluence.

Recent Development

Ginzberg (1972), responding to some of the criticisms that have been raised concerning the theory over the years, has suggested three conceptual changes in his theory. First, he would modify his assertion that occupational decisions are a life-span phenomenon, not simply a short-term event restricted to the adolescent and early adult years. Second, the notion of irreversibility has been toned down and is now viewed in terms of the expenditure of time and resources. That is, careers may be redirected in major ways, though there are costs involved, and these costs operate in some ways to make the process irreversible for some people at some times. Finally, the concept of compromise has been changed to one of optimization; that is, Ginzberg proposes that there is a continuing search on the part of the individual for the best fit between the preferred career avenues and the available opportunities. These three changes considerably improve the theory, though the basic style of the conception remains unchanged.

Some General Concepts
of the Theory

Ginzberg and his associates place a heavy emphasis on the role that emotional factors play in career development, though their research has not been notably successful in identifying the specific role played by emotional factors in career choice. In designing their investigations, they went to special lengths to exclude subjects who seemed to be emotionally unstable. Despite the screening, several subjects presented evidence of emotional problems upon intensive interviewing. The observations made of the few emotionally disturbed subjects in the sample led the investigators to conclude that emotional problems were important factors in the deviant vocational choice patterns that they occasionally observed.

The authors of the theory conclude that four important ingredients contribute to the adequacy of an individual's occupational choice process during adolescence. These are reality testing, the development of a suitable time perspective, the ability to defer gratifications, and the ability to accept and implement compromises in vocational plans. Should too many of these ingredients fail to develop properly, a deviant vocational pattern is likely to emerge. It further seems reasonable that should these four traits fail to develop adequately, the youth's overall emotional adjustment is not likely to be effective. Thus, a tie between emotional stability and vocational deviancy seems to exist, but whether of a casual or correlate nature is not clear.

Another critical feature in the career development process is the child's ability to identify with suitable models at appropriate times. During the Fantasy period, children identify with all adults and play games reflecting these many identifications. As they enter the Interest stage of the Tentative period, however, they narrow their models down, so that many students vocationally identify with their fathers at about ages 11 or 12. A vague awareness seems to exist that there may be some things about their fathers' work not suitable for them, and this apparently is involved in the gradual shift in identification from the fathers' field to other, and perhaps more suitable, adult vocational models, such as a teacher or an admired young adult. This latter identification is usually complete by about ages 16 to 18. The identification with emulated adults that occurs during the various stages gives some direction for the vocational planning of the student and actively involves him or her in the task of vocational selection. It is much easier to emulate a specific model than a vague abstraction.

One more important concept about people and work exists in the proposal of the Ginzberg group. They suggest that two basic personality types exist with respect to work, the work-oriented type and the pleasure-oriented one. This does not imply that an individual is in either one category or the other, but merely that one mode characterizes each individual's approach to life. The work-oriented individual can be identified by the ability to defer gratification and to be relatively impervious to deflection from work or occupational goals. On the other hand, the pleasure-oriented person is not likely to defer gratifications for work and is easily distracted from a vocational course by alternatives that seem reasonably desirable. In combination with the work-versus-pleasure orientation, people seem to be either active or passive problem solvers. The active people attack their problems and attempt to solve them, whereas the passive individuals seem to be reactive. Events "happen" to them, which elicit responses from them; rarely do they emit problem-solving responses as do the active people.

The interaction of these two variables exerts an influence on the style with which the young person approaches the developmental task of occupational choice. Active, work-oriented people are likely to behave differently than passive, pleasure-oriented people during the various periods of career development. The particular style, then, influences to some extent the kind of vocational pattern that the individual has during the adolescent period.

Davis, Hagen, and Stouf (1962) compared the frequency of occupational preference stemming from fantasy motives with the frequency of choices having tentative antecedents in sixth-grade students. Based on a paragraph written by the sample of 116 boys and girls ranging in age from 11 to 16 years with a mean age of 12, in which the children described what they wanted to do as adults and the reasons for their choice, Davis and others found that sixth-grade girls are more likely to express choices representing a tentative period than boys and that intelligence and stage of vocational development seem to be correlated. Since the Ginzberg theory assumes that age 11 marks the onset of the tentative period and most of their subjects reported plans consistent with the tentative period, the results support the theory. It would seem, however, that generalizations must of necessity be limited, since the sample was small and confined to a relatively narrow age range. Had the study included younger subjects, evidence might have been found that the tentative period starts even earlier than age 11.

Another study in the framework of the Ginzberg theory and also related to ages when vocational decisions are made was conducted by Tucci (1963). He divided college freshmen into three groups of students: those who were definitely decided about their careers, those who were tentatively decided, and those who were undecided. His sample consisted of 163 male freshmen at Wayne State University. He asked these students how long they had held their current vocational choice. He found that 34 percent of his sample reported themselves to be definite about their vocational plans, another 48 percent said they were tentative, and 18 percent said they were undecided. Of those who said they were definitely sure of their vocational goal, the mean age at which they had made that choice was 14.63 years. The tentative subjects had decided at a mean age of 15.38 years. These ages of decision conflict somewhat with the Ginzberg theory, since the theory suggests that boys' vocational decisions would not really become resolved until considerably later. Two possible explanations for this come to mind: the verbal reports of the subjects may not correspond with reality; that is, while they may report themselves to be definite, many changes might occur in the future, or changes occurring in the past may have been forgotten. It is also possible that a boy may have first thought of becoming an engineer at age 14, and succeeding years may have strengthened that decision. In terms of the theory, however, his original thoughts might well be considered tentative, with the crystallized decision occurring later.

Small (1953), while observing a variety of personality factors which influence vocational choice (which are described in detail in another chapter), touched on several aspects of the career development process that are pertinent to Ginzberg's theory. His data allowed him to assess the hypothesis that reality factors exert an increasing influence in the vocational preferences boys express from age 11 on. No evidence indicating that such an increase occurred was found. This is interestingly similar to O'Hara's observation that the Ginzberg periods may actually be set at age levels higher than they should. Thus, it is possible that reality factors increase in influence prior to age 11 and there reach an asymptote. Small also noted that evidence in support of the compromise aspect of the theory existed. That is, boys included the reality factors in their choices, which led them to make relevant modifications in the preferences they expressed.

In a cross-sectional study of more than 4,600 students in grades six through twelve, Hollender (1967) found that career choices do indeed become more realistic with age (using as the criterion of realism the individual's intellectual adequacy for the occupational preference) thus supporting the Ginzberg group's notion that choices move from fantasy to reality with age.

Kelso (1975), observing a sample of 1,400 male high school students in grades seven through twelve, found that boys who expected to leave school before graduation were more realistic than boys staying in school, suggesting that the progress through stages reflects more than just age.

Finally, as part of a major longitudinal investigation of career development, Gribbons and Lohnes (1968) report finding evidence that the role of values in early vocational decision making predates the timetable suggested by Ginzberg et al.

Evaluation

The empirical evidence in support of the theory is mixed. A thread of data consistent with the major tenets of the theory has been found by several investigators. There does seem to be evidence suggesting that students emphasize different kinds of experiences in their vocational development at various age levels. There also appears to be reason to believe that students must compromise their career preferences in deference to the reality of the world they observe. The evidence is mixed, however, with respect to specifically what the stages are, when they occur, and the order in which they occur.

STATUS

Ginzberg and his associates have proposed a theory which has the significant virtue of being closely related with the broader theoretical structure of developmental psychology. There are, however, some points where the description becomes somewhat diffuse and perhaps excessively broad. Several questions also come to mind with reference to the sample studied. It is difficult to see how the theory was developed from the data base Ginzberg and his associates report in their book. Trends of behavior imputed from interviews with various people can only reasonably be recognized from an already established framework, which causes a reader to suspect that previous reading and research were more influential on the development of the theory than the empirical study reported. The study is more likely to have served to confirm and refine some theoretical expectations than to have shaped them in the first place.

In view of the very serious limitations of the research sample, perhaps it is just as well that the theory seems to have preceded the research. It seems unlikely that such a comprehensive theory could have been developed from the inadequate data base observed. For example, the sample was too small to permit generalizations to be drawn with confidence. In particular, the lower-income male and college female samples were extremely small. No statistical analysis was reported, so that the generalizations were apparently based on the interpretations of the investigators, leaving the readers no basis for independent evaluation.

No older people were studied, only adolescents and a few young adults. Since the major portion of vocational behavior occurs after the adolescent period, ignoring adult career processes is as detrimental to the development of a theory of vocational choice as it would be to the development of a theory of marital adjustment on the basis of the dating behavior of adolescents. In fact, though the theory is concerned with vocational choice, the actual data, with the possible exception of a few of the advanced graduate students and older lower income boys in the sample, are based on educational decisions rather than vocational ones. Even though the theory provides a significant amount of information about the vocational preferences expressed by the subjects, it fails to state the differences between preference, choice, and attainment, thus reducing the clarity of the theory.

Another shortcoming lies in the complete absence of test data. Despite the concern the authors of the theory express about the role of personal and emotional factors in career choice, no tests of any kind were reported to have been used, not even measures of intellectual ability. A study of career development should at least use one inventory of interest measurement.

Some of the assumptions about the principles of adolescent development are crucial to the adequacy of the theory. The position of Ginzberg and his colleagues is that adolescent behavior is characterized by stress and that the conflicts, having a physiological basis, significantly permeate the adolescent approach to vocational choice. That the adolescent period is more stressful than other periods of life for the majority of young people is not a universally held opinion (for example, Kuhlen, 1952). By itself, such a criticism is not crucial, since the authors of a theory are entitled to make certain assumptions upon which to base their position. However, after stating that physical changes are a key part of the adolescent developmental process and that the process in general affects vocational choice, the Ginzberg group says little more about physiological antecedents to vocational problems. The only physiological development they discuss is sexual, and that only with reference to the problems older adolescents face in controlling their sexual impulses while accomplishing the training necessary to implement their career plans. The approach taken by Hulslander (1958) represents the kind of correlation between specific physical development and occupational processes that might be of relevance to this theory.

The concept of the irreversibility of the career development process is stated strongly, perhaps too strongly in the original theory. Obviously, career decisions and early experiences can neither be undone nor erased, yet the direction of the vocational process may be diverted by the sequence of continuing events. In witness of that fact are the many people who change careers in maturity, and the many college students who change majors (often as many as half of freshmen change college major by the time of graduation). A study at Kansas State University (Cross,

1960) indicated that about half of its graduates were working in positions with no direct relevance to their college major. Clearly, some aspects of the career development process are irreversible, but the process is not as inflexible and deterministic as the Ginzberg theory would lead one to expect.

Ginzberg's failure to differentiate clearly between occupational preference, selection, and attainment leads to difficulties in empirically evaluating the theory. At age 12 a youngster is willing to express occupational preferences very readily, since few responsibilities are assumed or consequences incurred as a result. At 18, when entering college, the situation is different, since selection must occur, with real and permanent consequences. The student who selects engineering as a field of study in college to some degree is committing to a career pattern very different from that of a person selecting journalism. Furthermore, immediate consequences in terms of specific course work and associates result. Considering these differences in the meaning of "occupational choice" at ages 12 and 18, how does an investigator rigorously investigate occupational development and yet stay within the framework of the theory? This consideration becomes a difficult problem indeed.

Implications for Counseling Practice

It seems that the theory is too vague to suggest techniques for counselors beyond a general notion that experiences should be arranged for young people that will facilitate their progress through whatever stage they happen to be in (see Katz, 1959, for an illustration of such an approach). If the theory has any accuracy and validity, it can be used to highlight developmental tasks and bring them to the attention of counselors, teachers, and parents. The theory might also be useful in helping a counselor to anticipate problems that might be encountered by students at predicted stages of development. This anticipation would allow the counselor to develop preventive procedures to deal with the expected problems. An example of this might be the tendency of children in the Capacity stage to overemphasize a course grade, a test score, or the opinion of some significant person in evaluating their skills or potentials. Were children alerted to this tendency and to the possibility of evaluating themselves in a variety of ways, some problems might be avoided.

It should also be noted that Tiedeman (1968) has devoted considerable energy toward the development of an information system to foster career development in terms of information gained through exploration. It does seem reasonable that a system such as Ginzberg's could serve as the framework for the practical development of such a computer-based career information-exploration system as Tiedeman proposes.

Evaluation

The absence of data based on older students is a serious limitation. The authors of the theory state that some military veterans had been included in a pilot group of subjects, and the interviews with them revealed that little had occurred

during the few additional years of military life to accelerate the vocational development process. Contrary to this is the observation of many counselors that periods of
employment or military service in the middle of college years may facilitate growth
in the maturity of the individual's attempts at educational and vocational decision
making. Within the limits of the theory, it would seem logical that despite minimal
connections between the job or military activities and the eventual career of the
individual, maturity would be facilitated through more extensive periods of reality
testing, a greater tendency for an appropriate time perspective to emerge, an increase in the interpersonal experience bank of the individual, the decrease in the rate
of physical changes that occur as the youth matures, and the "resolution" of
sexuality. The Ginzberg studies are significantly limited insofar as the original
samples studied consisted exclusively of upper income male-only populations recruited in urban New York City. While some attempts were made to examine some
groups of lower socioeconomic class members, again male only, and while the data
generated from observing these lower-income families largely parallel the data from
the original sample of males, it was noted that probably because of economic
constraints pushing them into the labor market earlier, lower-income male subjects
tended to move through some of the stages at earlier ages than the upper-income
male subjects. With respect to female populations, only a small sample of college
students at Barnard were observed, too few to make any reliable observations or
inferences regarding this theory. Clearly, at the time Ginzberg and his associates
conducted their research and did their theoretical writing, a very sexist attitude was
predominant in thinking about careers, and so, little attention was given to female
career development. Ginzberg and his associates should not be singled out for
criticism in this regard, however, since in the early 1950s theirs was the common
practice rather than the exception.

Does the theory contain the general features attributed to a good theory of
vocational counseling? Certainly, the theory seems to rate well on its comprehensiveness and its relationship to what is known about human development. The
process of normal vocational development is clearly evident in the theory, and, to a
lesser extent, patterns of deviant vocational behaviors are also described. Thus, it is
possible for a counselor to have expectations about the development of an individual
along vocational lines from the theoretical statement. The theory also permits a
counselor to develop some expectations of the problems in career development
when confronted by an individual with a deviant vocational pattern.

In another paper, Ginzberg (1972) explicitly discusses some of the implications the theory has for vocational counseling. First, he suggests that the theory
provides a counselor with normative information about vocational process, so that
young people who do not appear to be developing according to usual patterns of
maturation can be identified. Thus, a counselor can identify those students who
perhaps need extra or special kinds of attention to facilitate their growth in the
career development area. Ginzberg also states that the theory suggests a particular
type of counseling for the student. A student stalled in the Interest phase of development would need counseling with respect to interests, not information about aptitudes. Similarly, questions about values might be appropriately discussed with a

young person obviously in the Value stage who is not progressing toward a career goal as expected.

The theory does not, however, suggest corrective measures when deviant patterns are observed, nor does it give any specific techniques for counseling to facilitate occupational development, but some possibilities may be inferred from the nature of the theory, primarily with respect to the developmental stages. As a corollary to the absence of counseling techniques, no counseling goals are suggested beyond that of facilitating the individual's growth in the four basic features of major vocational growth: the reality testing, adequate time perspective, the deferment of gratification, and the ability to compromise.

It would seem that certain specific features of the theory are open to testing in that certain behaviors should distinguish students in one stage from those in another and should appear approximately at predictable times. One limiting feature in the testability is the problem presented by the pseudocrystallization and pseudo-specification stages which the authors allow themselves, but these do not affect the stages that come earlier in the process which could be tested independently of the validity of the advanced periods.

Perhaps the most useful purpose the theory has served for vocational psychology is its stimulation of interest in the development of theoretical foundations for the study of career development. While the Ginzberg group may not have developed the first attempt to formulate a system of understanding vocational choice, the attempt was timely, widely circulated, and stimulated considerable thought about career development. Certainly, the theory has heuristic value (the stages seem valid in a general way and correspond to a view of reality in adolescent development) and has exerted its influence on later theorists in vocational psychology. It is likely that as such, its purpose has been served, and its general concepts will be modified many times by other approaches that attempt to explain and describe vocational choice processes.

Summary

Ginzberg and his associates have developed a conception of career development which construes the vocational choice process as a specific behavior, one of many based on the adolescent development pattern. They further have proposed a systematic and predictable series of tasks that face young people as a function of the changes that occur during adolescence. These tasks culminate during the early twenties in a specific vocational choice, the adequacy of which is related to the adequacy of the accomplishment of the various other tasks which adolescents encounter along the way.

REFERENCES

Cross, K. D. *Comprehensive occupational survey of 1947 and 1952 Kansas State University graduates.* Manhattan, Kans.: Kansas State University Placement Center, 1960.

Davis, D. A., Hagen, N., and Strouf, J. Occupational choice of twelve-year-olds. *Personnel and Guidance Journal,* 1962, *40,* 628–629.

Ginzberg, E. Toward a theory of occupational choice. *Occupations,* 1952, *30,* 491–494.

Ginzberg, E. Toward a theory of occupational choice: a restatement. *Vocational Guidance Quarterly,* 1972, *20,* 169–176.

Ginzberg, E., Ginsburg, S. W., Axelrad, S., and Herma, J. L. *Occupational choice: an approach to a general theory.* New York: Columbia University, 1951.

Gribbons, W. D., and Lohnes, P. R. *Emerging careers.* New York: Teachers College Press, Columbia University, 1968.

Hollender, J. Development of a realistic vocational choice. *Journal of Counseling Psychology,* 1967, *14,* 314–318.

Hulslander, S. C. Aspects of physical growth and evolution of occupational interests. *Personnel and Guidance Journal,* 1958, *36,* 610–615.

Katz, M. R. *You: today and tomorrow.* Princeton, N.J.: Cooperative Test Division, Educational Testing Service, 1959.

Kelso, G. I. The influence of stage of leaving school on vocational maturity and realism of vocational choice. *Journal of Vocational Behavior,* 1975, *7,* 29–39.

Kuhlen, R. G. *The psychology of adolescent development.* New York: Harper & Row, 1952.

Small, L. Personality determinants of vocational choice. *Psychological Monographs,* 1953, *67,* No. 1 (Whole No. 351).

Tiedeman, D. V. Information system for vocational decisions. Project Report No. 12, Cambridge, Mass.: Harvard Graduate School of Education, 1968.

Tucci, M. A. College freshmen and vocational choice. *Vocational Guidance Quarterly,* 1963, *12,* 27–29.

CHAPTER ELEVEN
TIEDEMAN'S DEVELOPMENTAL THEORY

David Tiedeman, stimulated by developmental writers like Super and Ginzberg, has produced his own special version of developmental notions of careers. With his colleague Robert O'Hara, Tiedeman (1963) built upon the somewhat simple concepts described by Ginzberg and his associates, creating a more complex and probably, thus, a more realistic system. The approach stresses the role of the self-concept in negotiating developmental stages and includes a complicated and sophisticated set of developmental notions.

THE THEORY

Briefly stated, Tiedeman and O'Hara view career development as a function of the developing self, becoming increasingly differentiated and comprehensive. The critical ingredients of this emerging self include situational and social factors as well as biological. The self is seen as an entity which is always either expanding or contracting and for which crucial decisions occur at points of discontinuity with the past, for example, graduation from high school and/or college; marriage; and taking one's first full-time position.

The decision-making process involves anticipation, implementation, and adjustment. The system describes anticipation in terms of the following sequence of events: exploration, crystallization, choice, clarification, induction, reformation, and incubation. The entire sequence is characterized at first by somewhat disorganized thinking by the individual about occupational fields, followed by the development of clearer distinctions among fields, accompanied by judgments about their advantages, disadvantages, and relative values.

On the basis of this evaluative process, some preliminary decision making occurs, followed by a refractory period, in which the individual has an opportunity to express doubts regarding the choice and to further elaborate the decision. Following this, the individual is "inducted" into a group during which time it is possible to identify closely with the purposes of this new group. Later, the individual begins to question those same purposes and may try to change the group somewhat (reformation period). The final stage, integration, involves a process by which the individual resolves the conflicts of individuality with the group's demands and in some way manages to integrate the two.

Kroll, Dinklage, Lee, Morley, and Wilson (1970) have taken the Tiedeman and O'Hara position and added further points of emphasis. First, they have added the notion that career development represents a balance between changing the environment to fit oneself and changing oneself to fit the environment. Considerable weight is given to the importance of self-evaluation in the learning of one's areas of competence and incompetence. Descriptions of this learning process during childhood and adolescence are provided, largely stemming from the framework of Piaget and Erikson.

In some ways, the work of Tiedeman and O'Hara stands as a bridge between the developmental formulations of Ginzberg and his group and the work of Super. All these writers share the view that career development is an aspect of general development in that self-concepts interact with career decision making. In addition, it appears to be assumed that individuals with inaccurate self-evaluations are more prone to make inappropriate or inadequate career decisions than those with accurate self-evaluations. Finally, all these writers seem to assume that the ability and motivation to evaluate oneself realistically can be enhanced through education and counseling.

In a recent publication, Dudley and Tiedeman (1977) have further amplified and revised Tiedeman's position. Elements in career decision making are considered. These elements include the environment and the individual, and of particular interest is the way these two interact with each other.

The environment is seen as affecting the individual in terms of the ways the person reacts to the environment, the support the environment provides, and the definition of conditions the environment provides. Tiedeman and Dudley use the term *function* to describe how the systems interrelate, the term called *structure* to describe the mechanisms that discharge repetitive functions that maintain the larger system, and the term *concepts* to refer to constructs the individual uses to understand the relationship between self and environment. Tiedeman and Dudley consider the criterion of career decision making to be a "personal construct" which involves both work and nonwork activities. The individual serves as a so-called operator controlling his or her own career.

This volume represents probably the best and most recent comprehensive treatment of Tiedeman's theoretical contributions. It is based on his and Dudley's incorporation of the nineteen years of Harvard Studies in Career Development projects which Tiedeman conducted at Harvard until the late 1960s. While some of this volume represents Tiedeman's own notions of different points of view of various theorists in career development, parts of it represent his own viewpoint. According to the introduction to Chapter Two, one of the impetuses for the Harvard studies in career development was a new statistical procedure called "multiple discriminant analysis." Using this procedure, a number of studies dealing with questions such as prediction of choices or group membership, the application of such information, and the development of methods to exploit the situations in which career events occur without career decision making and career development. Thus, the studies examining the structure of decision processes, the self-concept, and the notion of "purposeful action" resulted.

According to Dudley and Tiedeman, the major notions involved in the process of decision making in careers include the following:

1. Career development is built on ego identity continuously differentiating based on experience;

2. Among the ways this differentiating begins include the individual's problem solving set;

3. This "condition of rational differentiation" is important because a) it represents a higher-level form of differentiation and b) its rationality forms the basis on which counseling and guidance practices are designed.

Dudley and Tiedeman (1977, p. 205) describe the information system for vocational decisions. Extending Tiedeman's work, this sytem used several assumptions and objectives.

First, it places occupation into vocational development as a "single instance of vocational expression." It requires people to take responsibility for their choices not only in work but in marriage, leisure, and education. It extends preparation for choosing into the elementary grades and past retirement.

This system was built on one devised by Gribbons (1965). Gribbons' system focused on initiating problem-solving behavior between kindergarten and grade 3; between grades 4 to 6 it focused on developing the independence of choice, including things like planning, exploratory behavior, and the accumulation of self-knowledge. Grades 7 to 9 focused on realistic self-appraisal in terms of abilities, interests, and values and relating these to careers and decisions. Grades 10 to 12 focused on the noncollege-bound student in terms of making and executing plans to enter the job market. Then the system focused on the first job and helping people become stabilized in terms of being qualified or dealing with instability.

O'Hara and Tiedeman (1959) were interested in studying the relationship between aptitude, interest, social class, and values in the Ginzberg model and the development of a vocational self-concept. For this study, over a thousand students of a private Catholic day school in Boston were tested on the verbal reasoning, numerical ability, mechanical reasoning, space relations, and abstract reasoning subtests of the Differential Aptitude Test and the Kuder Preference Record. Further, the social class of these students was estimated by means of the Home Index developed by Gough (1949), their general values were assessed by the Allport-Vernon-Lindzey Study of Values (1951), and their work values measured by means of Super's Work Values Inventory (1955). Finally, each student was required to complete a self-estimate questionnaire devised by O'Hara and Tiedeman to reveal the self-concept with respect to interests, aptitudes, and values. The sample included 160 students in the senior year in high school, 264 in the junior year, 276 sophomores, and 321 freshmen.

The design thus permitted data about aptitudes, interests, and values to be compared with the self-estimates of these attributes by a group of subjects representing the age range of the last half of the Tentative period. Only the variable of social class failed to show an increasing relationship between self-estimates and tested findings over the four-year age period represented in the sample. Social class was fairly constant and students probably become aware of their own class when relatively young. Thus, it is not unreasonable to infer that no change occurred over time in the ability of the students to estimate their social class. Correlations among the other variables (aptitudes, interests, general values, and work values) and self-estimates, however, reflected increasing congruence through high school. By inferring that increasing vocational clarification is reflected in the increasing congruence of tested attributes and relevant self-estimates, O'Hara and Tiedeman concluded that a view of vocational clarification as a developmental process is very likely.

O'Hara and Tiedeman also attempted to discover if stages in the development of vocational choices, such as those described by Ginzberg, do indeed exist. Examining the correlations between the self-estimates and test estimates they were able to infer the termination of a period of development. For example, the correlations between the self-estimates and tested estimates of interest were 0.70, 0.81, 0.79, and 0.83 for the freshman through senior years, respectively. The period of greatest increase occurred between the freshman and sophomore years, when the correlation increased from 0.70 to 0.81. O'Hara and Tiedeman inferred from these data that the interest period ended in their sample after the tenth grade. Applying the same reasoning to the other variables, they concluded that aptitudes and general values continuously increased in congruence; thus no real aptitude or general values period seemed to exist (within the age range they studied). They also observed an increase in the growth of work values occurring between eleventh and twelfth grades. Although O'Hara and Tiedeman did not attempt to compare directly the timing of the stages of development, they found a degree of agreement with those predicted by the Ginzberg theory. More significantly, however, O'Hara and Tiedeman suggest that while students may *talk* about their vocational plans in a manner which indicates they are concerned with one sphere of development, the *quality* of their estimates of their progress in these spheres is erratic.

In a pilot study, O'Hara (1959) examined the age at which values begin to serve as a focus for vocational preferences. Studying a sample of 15 boys, three boys in each of the first, third, fifth, seventh, and ninth grades, chosen to represent superior, average, and below average intelligence, he inquired into the development of the boys' interests, their self-descriptions, their current and past occupational preferences, and their reasons for making and for subsequently discarding the choices. His findings suggest that boys engage in reality testing at an earlier age than the theory of Ginzberg and his associates predicts. Thus, he found boys talking about the possibility of implementing their plans as early as the third grade. Compromise, according to the theory, should occur around ages 16 or 17. In this study, O'Hara observed that boys were planning compromises as early as 12 or 13 years of age. He found evidence that the Tentative period, which theoretically should begin about age 11, may occur as early as age 9, since many of the "fantasy" choices made by boys during the third grade and later actually have a rational basis. Finally, he observed that while interests are a major basis for preferences in these younger boys, values and aptitudes are significant forces in the formation of these preferences at much earlier ages than Ginzberg's group suspected. O'Hara observed that values are involved in preferences as early as fifth or sixth grade instead of tenth or eleventh as the theory suggests, and that capacity assumes importance even to third or fourth graders instead of at the lower limit of eighth or ninth grade as the theory proposed.

Despite the shortcoming that only boys were studied, the results of O'Hara's study are useful. The periods of development all seem to occur much earlier than expected, yet the periods as predicted do actually seem to occur—and in the order expected—at least insofar as they might occur in the age range O'Hara studied.

Harren (1966) developed a Q-sort designed to assess Tiedeman and O'Hara's (1963) formulation of the stages of vocational choice and based on the notion that choice is a cognitive process of differentiation and integration. On this basis, he predicted that a difference would be discernible between those decisions made by individuals regarding choice of major and those involving occupations. The response of male undergraduate liberal arts students indicated that most saw college major and occupational choices as the same and that those who did not equate educational and vocational choice either treated the two as separate problems or failed to see the two as pieces of the same chain of events. One might guess that observations of more vocationally oriented groups, such as those involved in engineering, would even enhance these findings. However, some question can be raised regarding the logical development of Harren's predictions from the constructs of differentiation and integration as described by Tiedeman (1961).

Other Related Approaches

Another developmental approach to career development has been proposed by Knefelkamp and Slepitza (1976). Knefelkamp and Slepitza developed a so-called cognitive developmental model based on schemes developed by William Perry (1970) which are themselves an outgrowth of Erikson's (for example, 1963) views of life-stage development.

Knefelkamp and Slepitza developed their approach based on what they call nine areas of qualitative change: 1) a shifting from an external to an internal *locus of control;* 2) the ability to break a subject down into its parts (*analysis*); 3) the ability to put a subject back together again in a complex form by *synthesis;* 4) the ability to deal with the nature of language in concept use (synthetic structure)—an ability that with development becomes increasingly open as opposed to absolute in nature (*semantic structure*); 5) the ability to become increasingly aware of the factors that define one's self (*self-prophesy*); 6) increasing openness to alternative perspectives; 7) ability to assume responsibility; 8) ability to assume new roles; 9) ability to take self-risks, largely in terms of exposing one's self-esteem to risk.

Given these nine areas of qualitative change, each of which represents increasing maturity, Knefelkamp and Slepitza talk about the stages individuals encounter as they move toward the mature end of the continuum. Dualism is seen in simple and dichotomous thinking about career decision making. Here the individual relies heavily on others for making career decisions and experiences some anxiety resulting from awareness of the possibility of making "right and wrong" decisions. Following this comes a stage called "multiplicity," or stage three, in which individuals recognize more clearly than before that they may make so-called "right and wrong" decisions and, as a consequence, experience even more conflict anxiety and recognize that their development and decisional processes are more complex than they thought. In this stage, they begin to engage increasingly in analysis. (See point 3 of qualitative change, above.)

The fourth stage involves a complex weighing of the components that are related to career decision making, and in this stage, multiple career possibilities are increasingly recognized by the respondent.

The next stage is relativism. Here the student has not yet shifted from an external to an internal point of reference, but is trying to involve the exploration and implementing that is necessary with the multiple possibilities perceived. The stage ends with a sense of motivation to create some order and to clarify the process and decision.

Stage six is described by Knefelkamp and Slepitza as involving choice as a way to move out of a chaotic situation. Here the respondent must deal with commitment and must take responsibility for the process.

Stage seven involves integrating oneself and one's career roles; stage eight involves being open to the experiencing of the consequences of the commitment; stage nine involves the expansion of the self-created role and the recognition that the role interacts with life in general, not just careers.

In their paper, Knefelkamp and Slepitza describe two studies conducted, one at Maryland and one at Ohio State. In these studies, data collected through interviews and written protocols revealed that university freshmen and sophomores seem primarily to be in stages two and three; university seniors primarily were in stages three, four, and five; and first year master's students in educational psychology were in stages three, four, and five; while advanced graduate students in educational psychology were in stages six and seven. Furthermore, a study conducted at Ohio State and summarized in the same paper by Knefelkamp and Slepitza indicated that thirty-five students in a career development class were asked to write statements about themselves from which career stage classifications could be inferred. The results of the class facilitators' evaluations of the responses were also interpreted to support these areas of qualitative change used as a basis for the model. Data were interpreted by Knefelkamp and Slepitza to support the notion that there is developmental movement from dualism to relativism. However, these data are not really fully reported for either study, and the reader is left with a somewhat slender information base on which to evaluate the process, as well as a somewhat slender operational basis on which to do so.

Knefelkamp and Slepitza acknowledged the preliminary nature of their efforts, and one might reasonably expect more work to be forthcoming.

As with many of the developmental, phenomenological views, however, the data, as well as the outcomes and interventions, are essentially "soft" and difficult to measure.

SUMMARY AND EVALUATION

Tiedeman's system is very complicated, quasi-mathematical, and hard to understand. Furthermore, there seem to be serious problems in making the system operational. Although the original attempt to develop a computer-based information system growing out of Tiedeman's views is extremely operational in nature, one has to question both the availability of that computer-based information system and its rational relationship to the system itself. There seem to be some gaps in allowing observers to see how the theory relates to the system.

Another problem is the lack of adequate instrumentation for the theory. Even though Harren (1977) has developed the Assessment of Career Decision Making Scale in terms of Tiedeman's stages, little other instrumentation that even remotely pertains to Tiedeman's theories exists.

The Tiedeman system has produced some potentially useful offshoots such as the Perry system, and it is related to the approach of Mosher and Sprinthal (1971) (Deliberate Psychological Education), but aside from the information systems based on computers, which have not been notably successful, it has few practical applications. It seems more generally philosophical than career development oriented.

REFERENCES

Allport, G. W., Vernon, P. E., and Lindzey, G. A. *A study of values* (Revised Edition). Boston: Houghton-Mifflin, 1951.

Dudley, G. A., and Tiedeman, D. V. *Career development: exploration and commitment.* Muncie, Ind.: Accelerated Development, 1977.

Erikson, E. *Childhood and society* (2nd Edition). New York: Norton, 1963.

Gough, H. C. A short social status inventory. *Journal of Educational Psychology*, 1949, *40*, 52–56.

Gribbons, W. D. *Notes on procedures for implementing the making of vocational decisions.* Cambridge, Mass.: Center for Research in Careers, Harvard Graduate School of Education, 1965.

Harren, V. A. The vocational decisional making process among college males. *Journal of Counseling Psychology*, 1966, *13*, 271–277.

Harren, V. A. Empirical Evidence for the Tiedeman and O'Hara Decision Making Paradigm. Paper presented at the Americal Personnel and Guidance Association, Dallas, 1977.

Knefelkamp, L. L., and Slepitza, R. A. A cognitive developmental model of career development—an adaptation of the Perry Scheme. *The Counseling Psychologist*, 1976, *6*(3), 53–58.

Kroll, A. N., Dinklage, L. B., Lee, J., Morley, E. D., and Wilson, E. H. *Career development: growth and crisis.* New York: John Wiley, 1970.

Mosher, R. L., and Sprinthal, N. A., et al. Psychological education: a means to promote development during adolescence. *The Counseling Psychologist*, 1971, *2*(4), 3–82.

O'Hara, R. P. *Talks about self—The results of a pilot series of interviews in relation to Ginzberg's theory of occupational choice.* Harvard Studies in Career Development No. 14. Cambridge, Mass.: Center for Research in Careers, Harvard Graduate School of Education, 1959.

O'Hara, R. P., and Tiedeman, D. V. Vocational self concept in adolescents. *Journal of Counseling Psychology*, 1959, *6*, 292–301.

Perry, W., Jr. *Intellectual and ethical development in the college years.* New York: Holt, Rinehart and Winston, 1970.

Tiedeman, D. V. Decisions and vocational development: a paradigm and its implications. *Personnel and Guidance Journal*, 1961, *40*, 15–21.

Tiedeman, D. V., and O'Hara, R. P. *Career development: choice and adjustment.* New York College Entrance Examination Board, 1963.

CHAPTER TWELVE
ASPECTS OF
ADULT CAREER
DEVELOPMENT

The developmental theorists interested in careers have typically focused on the adolescent and early adult periods of career life, largely because social institutions and historical emphasis have been concentrated on the initial selection and implementation of vocational choices. Strangely, despite the fact that most vocational activities occur after the school years are over, only recently has interest developed in providing a conceptual basis and empirical data to describe adult career development. It has recently become widely recognized that vocational selection and implementation is simply the vestibule for career life. Recognizing that disproportionate attention has been paid to the choice and prevocational processes in comparison with what actually happens to people in their work lives, many recent theorists and writers have devoted a great deal more attention to what happens after the implementation of the first work choice through establishment into the middle career period and into the retirement period.

Sarason et al. (1975) made a number of interesting points about maturation:

1. The process of choosing careers is a major confrontation with aging, because it is done so with the expectation that the choice will determine how the rest of one's life will be ''filled in.''

2. The variety of choices and need to hone them down as required by the educational system place an unwanted pressure on the student and further focuses his or her attention on the process of aging.

3. Beginning a lifetime in a field which is acutally a second, third, or even lower choice, as many people do, is tragic because it impinges drastically on one's sense of self-worth. People who cannot pursue their ''primary'' interest—an increasing number—are likely to be very frustrated and unhappy.

4. More and more people are changing their career fields. As in the institution of marriage, where people are inclined to change spouses, in the field of work people are inclined to change careers. When as many as 20 percent of physicians express dissatisfaction with their careers, it is cause for concern and gives pause for thought. The longer people live, the more changes of career and spouse are to be expected. No one wants to be saddled with an unsatisfactory career or spouse; it's bad enough to live unhappily to sixty or sixty-five, but it's intolerable (for some) to live unhappily into their eighties.

A New Stage

Murphy and Burck (1976) proposed that a formal developmental stage in career life occuring at the midlife period be added to Super's developmental stages of careers. Murphy and Burck have marshalled a considerable amount of evidence to justify the fact that such a stage exists. For example, among the common concerns of middle-aged men that were found in the study by Levinson (1974), there was considerable anxiety over aging and death, a strong amount of questioning about the basis of their lives, and a need for affirmation of self by society through success in career. These middle-aged men shared in common stock-taking behaviors, the realization and acceptance of differences between early goals and present achievements. As a consequence, in their middle 40s they entered a stage of stability which emphasized the fulfilling rather than the unfulfilling aspects of their lives.

However, other studies have indicated that in their early forties men in general experience considerable dissatisfaction with life and a reduction in self-esteem (Horrocks and Mussman, 1970). Still other studies show considerable boredom occurring during the period between ages forty and fifty, along with the fear of the consequences that may occur when one changes one's life significantly (Bischoff, 1969). Overall, there is considerable data to indicate that middle age is the most negative period in life in attitudes towards marriage, parents, self, and leisure (Armstrong and Scotzin, 1974).

Murphy and Burck have inferred from these data that a "common inner experience" can be inferred, this including a decrease in self-esteem, questions about the meaning of life, a reexamination of personal values, and overall dissatisfaction with life in combination with a general stock taking. Externally, (Neugarten, 1968) there is the impact of children leaving the home, the attainment of one's highest career position and economic success, the reaction to job threats from younger people using new techniques, and the problems and responsibilities associated with aging parents. Developmental tasks, Murphy and Burck suggest, that would be associated with this mid-life period include setting new milestones, reassertion of control over one's development, stock taking, reactivation of control over one's future, and self-acceptance in the face of growing limitations in terms of decreased energy levels and changing family relations.

Entrekin and Everett (1981) examined more than 670 responses from academicians in Australian universities. Using a variety of statistical techniques, a number of factors were isolated and analyzed with respect to age trends. Several stages were identified: a stage called settling in, starting from about age 30 and running on a relatively even keel to the middle 40s; followed by a stage called reaching out between about age 45 and 49 which appeared to be a period of considerable disruption and restlessness, demand for change, and so on; then a settling down stage from age 50 to 54; and last, a so-called finishing stage from age 55 on. The 45 to 49 stage appears to represent the mid-career crisis and is precipitated by the individual belief that it is the last point at which the individual can change careers.

This concern for mid-life career as a stage is shared by Golumbiewski (1978). Golumbiewski suggests in general that a mid-life career transition occurs between 35 and 43. Even though some people are hardly affected by this period and transition, many experience a great torment. According to Golumbiewski, the transition affects both sexes at about the same age, but with significant differences regarding the nature of onset and how the individual handles the stress. Depression is the common "toxic" reaction, particularly with respect to professionals in their mid-30s. It has been observed that they raise questions about the importance and fulfillment of what they are doing. In addition to depression, high rates of alcoholism, suicide, and divorce are also seen as evidence of disruption.

The mid-life period, according to Golumbiewski, also involves becoming one's own "man" in the 40s, the rejection or mollifying of relationships with mentors and, in fact, mentoring one's self. The mid-life transition involves a disparity between one's achievements and aspirations, and it includes awareness of bodily decline, a great sense of morality and aging, and, for men, the emergence of the more feminine aspects of the self.

On a more positive note, Golumbiewski suggests that the outcome of this period of stress and transition can involve a restabilization with a new life structure that is even better than the one that existed before. The point is made, incidentally, that the mid-life transition may be more observable now than formerly, not only because more people are alive during that period of life than ever before, but also because, since our life span has been increased, the quality of the middle period of life is of greater concern to us than it had been before. People who survive beyond their 40s generally are healthy enough so that they maintain substantial vigor beyond the years during which they might have expected to maintain it in an earlier generation. This increased vigor and longer life creates the possibility of serial life styles. Middle-aged people with raised standards of what is acceptable to them and to other people are likely to experience some of the same kinds of causes of distress that young people have been observed to experience when they make their career entry and implement choices in late adolescence.

Career Change in Mid-Life

One obvious outcome of this mid-life career transition period has to do with career change. Perhaps first it should be noted that career change can occur in many ways. According to Sarason (1977), for example, one can display "horizontal" career change, in which one moves dramatically from one career field to another;

one can also display vertical change, in which one advances within one's career field to levels of greater managerial responsibility or supervisory responsibility; last, one can experience substantial multiple vertical changes in which movement can be seen several times within one's career field. Thus, horizontal change might be displayed by an attorney who opens up a bookstore, vertical change might be displayed by an engineer who becomes a plant manager, and multiple vertical change might be exemplified by a minister who becomes a seminary professor and then subsequently the president of the seminary. Some of these may not be perceived as clearly as changes as others, yet the functional, institutional, and behavioral contexts or events associated with these events may be very substantial. Many university counseling professors began their careers as counselors, then moved to university teaching and research; while they may consider themselves to have continued along in the same career line, actually they have experienced a very substantial psychological career change.

The motivations for career change have been examined by many writers. Heddesheimer (1976) has examined the environmental and self-generated pressures for career change. Some of the obvious environmental pressures identified include family changes, such as divorce, widowhood or widowerhood, and the departure of children from the home. Job changes, such as are reflected by mandatory retirement or loss of job, are also included here, as are societal changes such as increased freedom for middle-aged people to do the things they really desire to do.

Some of the self-pressures Heddesheimer points out include a search for greater satisfaction, an attempt to generate greater financial freedom, response to chronic unhappiness with one's present job, attempts to improve social status and income, finding work that is not boring, and so on. In addition, developmental stages may serve as a self-pressure because of the series of biological changes that usually occur. Heddesheimer postulates that people who experience high self-motivated reasons for changing are more likely to be vocationally mature than those who are less self-directed in these changes.

Driskill and Dauw (1975) examined the reasons people changed careers during the mid-life period. They sent questionnaires to 780 men who were over the age of forty and who were seeking jobs. Of these men who were voluntarily looking for jobs, about one third were seeking greater pay, about 40 percent were concerned with increasing their promotional prospects, about 66 percent felt their abilities were not well used, and about 50 percent wanted to do things in a way different from the way managerial philosophy of their present employer allowed. About 25 percent described a personality clash with a significant supervisor. All of these observations were significantly different from those of people who were not seeking jobs on a voluntary basis. These motivations for change should not be surprising and probably do not significantly differentiate motives for finding other employment in any generation.

Mills (1970), focusing on religious careers, has tried to extend the idea of vocational developmental tasks from adolescence through the middle years. Mills suggests three specific tasks for this period. The first is to set one's own milestones.

In the middle years, institutions no longer provide clear guidelines of progress or clear identification of transition points, as are provided in earlier years by events such as graduation ceremonies, acquisition of privileges to purchase liquor, voting rights, and so on. A second task of mid-life is the need to reassert control over one's self-development. Mills suggests an increased need to reassert control over one's progress and become active again in controlling one's future, rather than passively following a course of action set in motion some years before. Finally, Mills points to the problems associated with the acceptance of self, particularly in the face of adjustments to growing limitations including a decrease in energy level, changing relationships with the family (for example, children leaving home, becoming grand-parents), and the fact that the time for accomplishment is running out.

Some empirical studies touch on these issues. Vroom and Pahl (1971) have demonstrated that age is negatively correlated with risk-taking behavior among managers and with value placed upon such behavior in business. Hirt (1964), studying GATB earned by various individuals during various decades of life, found that older people tend to score lower. This finding should be viewed cautiously, however, because the study was cross-sectional in nature; there is no reliable way to be sure whether the differences in GATB scores between older and younger workers represent deterioration in older people or changes in culture that differentially affect the older workers.

Sheppard (1971) tried to adapt Crites' Vocational Development Inventory to adults. Applying the modified inventory to a sample of 200 unemployed men, 100 vocational trainees, and 100 graduate students, he predicted that the student group would score higher, followed by the trainees, with the unemployed males lowest. The results confirmed his expectations. These results, combined with item analysis and cross-validation data, suggest that the instrument might have some potential usefulness in studying vocational maturity in adults. Crites' (1979) Career Adjustment and Development Inventory describes and measures career adjustment through the adult span of life.

Taking a sociological approach, Gottfredson (1977) looked at career stability and change in a very large sample of 21- to 70-year-old men and women workers over a five-year period. As might be expected, career stability was observed to increase with age. People who were initially working in occupations predicted to be stable and in which there were consistent environments were more stable than those who were in occupations which were expected to be inconsistent in their demands and environments. For example, "realistic-social" is an inconsistent personality correlate, and people of that type change career more often than people with highly consistent codes. One might view this shifting about in mid-life as a reflection of attempts to adjust initially inappropriate choices and implementations, but it could simply represent changes in personality as a function of development.

Vaitenas and Weiner (1977), in their study of 78 young and 27 older career changers in business and managerial occupations and 45 young and 40 older voca-tionally stable controls, found that developmental processes do not seem to be involved in career change. The results indicated that adult career change results from events such as interest incongruity with occupation, lack of consistency and differentiation of interests, fear of failure, and emotional problems, and not as the result of life-span development processes. This observation suggests that some individuals are destined to have difficulty with their careers because of predisposing factors rather than crises, although crises were exacerbated over the life span.

Satisfaction in Career in Adults

Clearly, job and career dissatisfaction seems likely to play a part in mid-career change process, but the data do not indicate that it is as significant as one might imagine. A literature review indicates that young workers in their teens and 20s seem to enjoy high levels of job satisfaction, but these levels decline drastically until about age 30, followed then by a steady increase throughout most of the rest of the work life. For example, a study by Schwab and Heneman (1977) examined the relationship between age and job satisfaction. Age appeared to be related to work satisfaction of an intrinsic nature and generally not related to the extrinsic satisfiers such as pay, working conditions, and the nature of supervision. This observation was based on a sample of 350 employees of both sexes in their middle 30s. Schwab and Heneman used the Minnesota Satisfaction Questionnaire and the Cornell Job Description Index to measure satisfaction and intrinsic-extrinsic satisfiers. Their results indicated that intrinsic scores are positively related to age in males, but for females the Minnesota Satisfaction Questionnaire intrinsic need scores appear to be related to age. None of the extrinsic scores were significantly related to age for either sex.

Wright and Hamilton (1978) conducted a study designed to examine three possibilities regarding age and job satisfaction. The three possibilities were the following: 1) a generation of workers subscribes to a set of views which contradicts the demands of the industrial system and therefore causes greater worker discontent; 2) the standards of older workers are systematically eroded by their years in the system, and they have learned to be satisfied with less in their job; and 3) older people simply have better jobs because of job development through seniority.

Wright and Hamilton collected data sampling a large number of workers through the Michigan Survey Research Center in the early 70s. Respondents were divided by age and social class and were excluded if there were missing data on either occupation or age, if they were self-employed, or if over age 65. Furthermore, the analysis was restricted to men because the conditions affecting working women seemed substantially different from those affecting men. The sample, therefore, is based on economically active, salaried males between the ages of 16 and 64. The results indicate that job satisfaction increases with age and that age is a better predictor than social class for job satisfaction. These three findings are consistent with those of other studies.

Hall and Mansfield (1975) tried to identify the development of needs and age in a sample of engineers and scientists. They found that the amount of security needs seems to increase with age, with a peak occurring at about age 50. Self-actualization appears to become less important with age. This study differs from other studies, however, in that self rather than other ratings of performance were used. Van Mannen and Katz (1976) examined the satisfactions in four different kinds of careers over time: administrative, professional, clerical, and maintenance. They studied about 2,500 employees over career stages ranging from less than a month to almost 25 years. Sex differences were negligible. Van Mannen and Katz concluded that one must be very tentative in concluding *a priori* that staged careers are more satisfying than unstaged careers. Furthermore, they suggest that we must not assume that most careers are "front loaded" in that the most important changes in perspective do not always occur relatively early in the person's career. In fact, data indicate a great deal of change is apparent throughout the entire career life. Finally, it is noted that special attention must be paid to the interaction of the person, the work, and family variables. Not surprisingly, linear models are often very inappropriate ways to think about careers.

Gold (1979) studied job complexity and satisfaction over the life span. Generally, findings indicate that strong positive relationships between job complexity and work satisfaction exist from ages 20 to 29. Job complexity is positively related to job performance from ages 30 to 44, and work satisfaction is positively related to job complexity.

Changes in Occupational Values with Age

Mention of the effect of maturation on the development of values leads to the consideration of several studies devoted to identifying the changes in occupational values occurring over time. In an attempt to answer the question of what changes in occupational values occur in individuals as they grow older, Miller (1954) administered the Occupational Values Indicator to 196 male college students, whose ages ranged from 17 through 30. No differences by age groups were found, though individual values were observed to vary considerably but unsystematically as far as age groupings were concerned. In general, career satisfaction seemed to be the most highly valued occupational attribute and prestige the least. This study would have been more conclusive if the younger men had been college students and the older ones in business or professional life instead of all the subjects being students. The homogeneity of college life may have reduced differences in values that ordinarily occur as men grow older and assume mature responsibilities.

Another study concerning the values of people at different stages of development overcomes the shortcomings of the Miller study to some extent. Wagman (1965) compared the values of groups of high school and university students on Centers' Job Values and Desires Scale. The results of Centers' studies (1949) also provided an adult comparison group, but it must be remembered that the Centers' adult group represents values expressed in an earlier decade. Attending only to the high school and college student samples, a number of differences were evident. The high school students preferred jobs which offered security and independence while the college sample valued interesting work most highly. The difference could be an outgrowth of socioeconomic differences between high school and college students. The former probably have lower socioeconomic backgrounds more commonly than the college students, which in turn might lead to greater concerns for security. The age differences between the college and high school samples might also be related to the finding that the younger group was more concerned with matters of independence. High school students are probably still fighting an independence battle with their parents to a greater extent than college students.

Gordon and Mensh (1962) explored the changes in values of medical students as they progressed through their professional training. Gordon's Survey of Interpersonal Values was administered to all students in the first through fourth year of medical training in a large midwestern school. Examining the data obtained from male students only, Gordon and Mensh found that desire for support from others rose significantly, desire for recognition and independence increased, and leadership remained unchanged. Although it is easy to infer that medical training influenced these changes, other factors can easily be identified that might have been involved. For example, maturation might result in similar value changes over the same four-year period out of the context of medical school.

Summary and Conclusions

It has become increasingly apparent that there is an irreversibility in the narrowing of options involved in vocational development and its dimensions, variations, and deviation as people grow older. The associated events are usually talked about in terms of maturity, the accumulation of information, and the development and shaping of the self-concept. The changes are usually evaluated in terms of how they affect the quality of career decisions people make and their timing.

Often overlooked is the fact that maturation involves decline as well as growth. Mid-life career issues are related to several particular kinds of problems. What are the developmental tasks in mid-life? As has been pointed out, problems include dealing with diminishing personal resources; the accumulation of commitments and material resources; the Mount Everest phenomenon (how many times must it be climbed?); the physical effects of aging and its consequences on work productivity and satisfaction, in terms of diminishing energy and physical capacity; disappointment; the illnesses and demises of family members and friends; and, ultimately, the loss for most people of status attained through work and financial reverses.

Other features important to consider in life-span careers include the differences in occupational life spans themselves. Of importance are the different ages of entry for various occupations, variations in the number of years of productivity, and occupational differences in age of retirement. Age of entry is clearly related to entry rules associated with apprenticeships, required formal training, and credentialing (which is often irrelevant to skills and performance). Age of retirement, until recently, had been moving down, but now there are variations in the trend, fostered by government policies and concerns about economic implications for retirees, in terms of both social and personal well being. Some occupations require early retirement, for example, sports, certain theatrical occupations, and certain creative fields. Other occupations are not open to young people, for example, the learned professions, government, and senior levels of administration. Super (1957) has described early entry, normal leaving occupations, such as assembly work; early entry, late leaving occupations like gardening and landscaping; normal entry, early leaving occupations such as work as flight attendants and military officers; normal entry, normal leaving fields such as teaching and accounting; normal entry, late leaving, such as banking; late entry, normal leaving such as counseling, high level college teaching and medicine; and late entry, late leaving, involving judges, politicians, and night security personnel as examples. These entry and departure patterns are related to earnings. Usually, normal entry, normal leaving occupations are not high earning fields, but early entry, early leaving ones often tend to produce high earnings.

Productivity is another feature. The controversial Lehman studies (1953) indicate that years of major productivity seem to vary by professional field. Granting that this is based on retrospective analysis, the notion Lehman proposes is intuitively attractive. Thus, for example, chemists are presumed to make major contributions in their late 20s, surgeons and psychologists in their 30s, instrumental composers in their late 20s, poets in their middle 20s, college presidents in their 50s, senators in their 60s, and justices in their 70s.

Clearly, attention to mid-career transition is burgeoning. Many interventions have been devised to try to help people deal with the associated stresses and strains. These interventions remain to be proven with respect to their effectiveness. What does appear to be clear is that the cultural determinants that have indicated career stages and development in younger people seem as they get older to operate to produce predictable stages in many people, at least in professional and managerial levels and very likely in other levels as well. Probably these events are subject to continual revision as a function of changes in society and the continuing reorganization of its work structure, as well as demands for different kinds of human resources.

REFERENCES

Armstrong, B. N., and Scotzin, M. M. Intergeneralizational comparison of attitudes toward basic life concepts. *Journal of Counseling Psychology,* 1974, *87,* 94–304.

Bischoff, L. J. *Adult psychology.* New York: Harper & Row, 1969

Centers, R. *The psychology of social class.* Princeton, N.J.: Princeton University Press, 1949.

Crites, J. O. *Career Adjustment and Development Inventory.* College Park, Md.: Gumpert, 1979.

Driskill, T., and Dauw, D. C. Executive mid-career job change. *Personnel and Guidance Journal,* 1975, *54,* 562–567.

Entrekin, L. V., and Everett, J. E. Age and mid-career crisis: an empirical study of academics. *Journal of Vocational Behavior*, 1981, *19*, 84–97.

Golumbiewski, R. T. Mid-life transition and mid-career crisis: a special case for individual development. *Public Administration Review*, 1978, *38*, 215–222.

Gold, S. H. Job complexity, satisfaction, and performance. *Journal of Vocational Behavior*, 1979, *14*, 209–223.

Gordon, L. V., and Mensh, I. N. Values of medical school students at different levels of training. *Journal of Educational Psychology*, 1962, *53*, 48–51.

Gottfredson, G. D. Career stability and redirection in adulthood. *Journal of Applied Psychology*, 1977, *62*, 436–445.

Hall, D. T., and Mansfield, R. Relations of age and seniority with career variables of engineers and scientists. *Journal of Applied Psychology*, 1975, *60*, 201–210.

Heddesheimer, J. Modal motivations for mid-career changes. *Personnel and Guidance Journal*, 1976, *55*, 109–111.

Hirt, M. L. Aptitude changes as a function of age. *Personnel and Guidance Journal*, 1964, *43*, 174–177.

Horrocks, J. and Mussman, M. C. Middlescence: age related stress periods during adult years. *Genetic Psychology Monograph*, 1970, *82*, 119–159.

Lehman, H. C. *Age and achievement*. Princeton, N.J.: Princeton University Press, 1953.

Levinson, D. J., et al. The psychological development of men in early adulthood and in the mid-life transition. In B. Ricks, et al., (Eds.) *Life history in psychopathology*. Minneapolis: University of Minnesota, 1974.

Miller, C. H. Age differences and occupational values of college men. *Journal of Counseling Psychology*, 1954, *1*, 190–192.

Mills, E. W. Career development in middle life. In Bartlett, W. E. (Ed.) *Evolving religious careers*. Washington, D.C.: CARA, 1970.

Murphy, P., and Burck, H. Career development of men at mid-life. *Journal of Vocational Behavior*, 1976, *9*, 337–343.

Neugarten, B. L. (Ed.) *Middle age and aging: a reader in social psychology*. Chicago: University of Chicago Press, 1968.

Sarason, S. B. *Work, aging and social change*. New York: The Free Press, 1977.

Sarason, S. B., Sarason, E. K., and Cowden, T. Aging and the nature of work. *American Psychologist*, 1975, *30*, 584–592.

Schwab, D. P., and Heneman, H. B., III. Age and satisfaction with dimensions of work. *Journal of Vocational Behavior*, 1977, *10*, 212–220.

Sheppard, D. I. The measurement of vocational maturity in adults. *Journal of Vocational Behavior*, 1971, *1*, 399–406.

Super, D. E. *The psychology of careers*. New York: Harper & Row, 1957.

Vaitenas, R., and Weiner, Y. Developmental, emotional and interest factors in voluntary mid-career change. *Journal of Vocational Behavior*, 1977, *11*, 291–304.

Van Mannen, J., and Katz, R. Individuals and their careers: some temporal considerations for work satisfaction. *Personnel Psychology*, 1976, *29*, 601–616.

Vroom, V. H., and Pahl, B. The relationship between age and risk taking among managers. *Journal of Applied Psychology*, 1971, *55*, 399–405.

Wagman, M. Sex and age differences in occupational values. *Personnel and Guidance Journal*, 1965, *44*, 258–262.

Wright, J. D., and Hamilton, R. S. Work satisfaction and age: some evidence for the job change hypothesis. *Social Forces*, 1978, *56*, 1140–1158.

CHAPTER THIRTEEN
THE SITUATIONAL
APPROACH

The social systems approach to the consideration of career choice and occupational behavior differs from the other points of view examined in this book primarily in its emphasis. The sociological approach is fundamentally based on the notion that elements beyond the individual's control exert a major influence on the course of life, including educational and vocational decisions. Supporters of this view suggest that the degree of freedom of occupational choice a person has is far less than might at first be assumed and that one's self-expectations are not independent of the society's expectations. Society, in turn, is assumed to present occupational opportunities in a manner related to class membership, a matter that has been extensively studied by interested sociologists.

Related to the sociologist's belief that circumstances impose choices on individuals is the proposal that chance plays a major role in occupational decisions. That is to say, being in the "right place at the right time" may have more to do with the vocational decisions people make than systematic planning and vocational counseling. The chance theory of vocational selection is more at home in the social systems chapter than in any other chapter in this book. The psychological theories of career decision making do not exclude the possibility that chance factors influence decisions, though psychologists do not often discuss the effects of chance factors on careers explicitly. What differentiates the sociological and psychological approaches to the chance issue is a matter of emphasis. To psychologists, the chance variable represents an irritant, hopefully to be minimized so that better decisions can be made and brought more under the control of the individual. The psychologist strives to understand the nonchance variables better in order to reduce the effect of chance elements on predictions. The sociologist, on the other hand, is likely to focus attention on chance (extraindividual) variables themselves and seek to understand the forces that operate in that dimension, in order to introduce some systematic organization of these apparently unsystematic aspects of life. Both disciplines might agree as to the proportion of chance involved in a given decision, but the psychologists are likely to be annoyed with chance variables and ignore them if possible, while the sociologists are more likely to be interested in the phenomenon of chance and study it. Hart, Rayner, and Christensen (1971), although reviewing the career histories of sixty men from the psychologists' point of view, found evidence indicating a clear relationship between occupational level and vocational planning behavior. On the basis of these observations, Hart and his associates urge the theorists to take the role of "chance" in thinking about vocational development more seriously than at present, in that so much of what appears to determine career entry, especially for lower-level occupations, is unplanned. The suggestion is reminiscent of Osipow's (1969a) suggestion that a principle of "least resistance" in career development operates and that program planners be mindful of the principle and design training programs that permit easy access and exit. Salamone and Slaney (1981), however, note that more than 900 male and female nonprofessional workers report that they believe chance played a minor role among factors influencing their career choice.

While impersonal and chance social factors may represent a major portion of the interest of the social system view of career decision making, the organization of society itself represents another, more systematic social aspect which influences individual career behavior in a way that is not directly under personal control. One must also consider the influences of the economic opportunities and general situational elements surrounding the individual as a function of social class membership and the organization of society. The social and the organizational environments with their economic implications are the dimensions upon which we shall consider the social systems approach to career choice and subsequent occupational behavior. The ideas and research discussed in this chapter represent several diverse streams of thought. Some of the concepts and data were developed specifically with career development theory in mind, whereas other work was conducted independently of career development theory but has been included here because it has relevance to our study.

THE SOCIAL ENVIRONMENT

Social organization in America is not without class strata. These social class distinctions, which have grown up over the past two or three hundred years, are continuously changing in order to keep in tune with the expanding economy. Because of the changing nature of the social structure and the geographic mobility open to Americans, the effects on behavior of social class membership have sometimes been overlooked.

Social class membership both influences and is influenced by occupational membership. Hollingshead's study of Elmtown's youth (1949) is a classic investigation of the role social class plays in human development in general. Although the details reported by Hollingshead may seem somewhat outdated now, his generalizations about the social and ethnic background factors that influence occupational expectation and selection probably remain true today. Hollingshead reported that, when queried about career goals, 77 percent of Class II adolescents aspired to professional or business careers, while only 7 percent of Class V youth had such high aims. About one-quarter of Class V adolescents aspired primarily to service trades, while virtually no Class II adolescents had such plans.

Unquestionably, an interaction between personal characteristics, transmitted relatively independently of the culture, and social factors results in occupational choice. Havighurst (1964) described several hypothetical case studies to illustrate the process through which boys in different social milieus mold their life styles. The values in the home, the adult models available and identified with, and the differential rewards for work versus play and for enterprise versus academic achievement all contribute to the career of a given individual.

Some sociological writers have suggested how the world might be if occupational selection were highly subject to social manipulation and selection. In *Brave New World,* Huxley (1946) described a technique of control whereby each individual is trained for a place in society. Young, in *The Rise of the Meritocracy* (1961), produced a fascinating, satirical characterization of life in a culture where people "rise to the top" exclusively on the basis of their talents, with no advantage as a result of family connections, money, or irrelevant personal characteristics. In our own world, it is clear that the idea of complete freedom of occupational choice is exaggerated and that many constraints operate to limit the choice (Cherevenik, 1956–1957). Even the young people making these choices seem to know that complete freedom of choice is lacking, as evidenced by Hollingshead's (1949) data presented above, showing that the occupational aims of most lower-class adolescents are consistent with their social class.

Two social anchor points exist to fix a person's occupation (Caplow, 1954). At one extreme is the society in which occupation is hereditary; offspring follow parents, or at least the parent's career and life style impose rigid limits on the variety of careers children consider. At the other extreme lies the society in which occupational choice is the exclusive result of the individual's personal characteristics. Young's *Meritocracy* (1961), mentioned earlier, represents such a culture. In the Western world, occupational choice lies somewhere in between the two anchor points. At what particular point on the continuum the choice is made depends on the specific area of the culture.

In American society, the inheritance of occupation is most likely to occur where the older generation has large capital investments to pass along to its offspring. Family-owned businesses, such as retail stores and farms, are good examples of this kind of career heredity. It is interesting to speculate about the role that the production of large families in farming communities has played in the gradual transition in American society from farming to manufacturing. Only the oldest sons could inherit enough farmland to make their efforts profitable. The others were required to leave the farm and find other means of support, contributing to the urbanization and mechanization of the society, which, cyclically, created opportunities in cities for future farm-born generations.

The inheritance of occupation is also likely to occur where the parent works in a state of relative isolation from other people. Isolation may be either physical, such as in careers in the farming, lumbering, or fishing industries, or psychological, such as in medicine, the military, or religious occupations, which set their members apart from the community at large and, in the case of the latter two, add to the psychological isolation by requiring frequent moves from place to place. Counterbalancing these influences toward the inheritance of work in American society is the fact that most parents whose occupational and class status are below Class I hope that their children will exceed their own occupational achievements. Thus, marginal storekeepers might encourage children to go to college to become accountants, or the skilled machinist might hope for a child's success in engineering. Both of these parental careers might have some hereditary characteristics, the first in the real property involved, the second in access to the union, yet parents in subprofessional fields usually hope that through education their children will do better than they did.

Education is the main element in individual choice and the primary agent of occupational mobility. Educational decisions, though often made rather casually, effectively commit a person to certain courses of action by eliminating other possibilities. Frequently, educational decisions which are made in a school setting but which have occupational implications are based on tenuous assumptions about the world of work. Because the choices are made *for* but not *in* work, the students usually find it difficult to make the decisions. Once made, the decisions are far from final (Caplow, 1954). A study done at the Pennsylvania State University revealed that approximately 20 percent of entering freshmen changed their college of enrollment before registering for their first class (Osipow, 1969b). A study conducted at the Kansas State University (Cross, 1960) revealed that relatively few graduates were employed in work directly related to their major field of study in college. To the degree that parents influence the educational decisions of their offspring and to the degree that social class influences parental attitudes toward and capability of providing educational opportunities, social class factors are highly important in educational-vocational decisions.

The scholastic goals of a student are a function of the particular set of experiences. The resulting values stem, at least in part, from the beliefs of parents, of neighborhood, of other children in the neighborhood, and so on (Slater, 1957). One is not likely to find a heavy emphasis on academic training in a low socioeconomic neighborhood where hard physical work is the norm and people are admired and respected for their physical skills and strength.

Lipsett (1962) has summarized the role of social variables in vocational development. Social class membership influences the particular choices of career that adolescents make. Sewell and Shah (1968) make a similar point regarding college plans. Although the sequencing of the educational-vocational decisions probably does not differ basically from class to class, the timing is likely to be different. The higher-class youth make their decisions when older than their lower-class counterparts, and the specific careers they choose are different from those made by the lower classes. The career decisions influence and are influenced by educational decisions and opportunities. Both the home and community stimulate the adolescent. To place pressure on students to make certain choices, parents provide or deny certain contingencies accordingly. For example, the availability of the family car may depend upon school grades in one family while in another no such restrictions may exist. While in one community going to college is the normal activity for an 18-year-old, in another that may be seen as frivolous, and instead most parents may insist upon work after high school graduation. All of these factors operate to influence the role the student perceives himself or herself as likely to play when an adult and the degree to which effort is expended to fulfill expected roles.

The research strategy most commonly used to study social factors underlying career behavior has been to interview large numbers of students with respect to their occupational preferences and selections and relate these to their familial background. Frequently, parental occupation, family income, and parental educational background have been broadly translated into social class terms.

In a comprehensive work, Blau and Duncan (1967) analyzed many sociological factors influential in determining occupational entry and functioning in America. The fundamental question raised by Blau and Duncan is what determines occupation. The answer is, simplistically, the beginning social level, since the lower one is at the beginning, the more likely is movement up the social-occupational scale. More complexly, however, Blau and Duncan draw conclusions similar to those drawn by Lipsett (1962) and Sewell and Shah (1968), that variables such as race, parents' occupation, gender, marital status, family income, place of residence, and family status (for example, broken versus complete), interact with significant variables and affect opportunities as well as training and preparation. According to Blau and Duncan, even more important than family status in determining occupational entry and achievement is one's training and early experience. However, as noted above, training and experience are not independent of family-based factors.

As illustrations of the findings of Blau and Duncan, consider that people from small families start their careers higher than those from large families and that even when differences in the allocation of family resources in large versus small families are taken into account, people from small families are seen to attain more occupationally in the long run than those from large families. The positive effect of small family size on occupational attainment is especially pronounced for "only" children. Furthermore, boys from small families go farther in school than boys from large families, until observations are made at the graduate level, where boys from large families seem to have an advantage for some apparently inexplicable reason.

Rosenberg (1957) reported some interesting data concerning the relationship between parental class and student career expectations. In particular, father's income seemed to be highly related to the kinds of choices students made. In proportion to their numbers, very few prospective teachers came from families where the earnings exceeded $20,000 (in 1950 dollars). On the other hand, families with such incomes produced more than their share of physicians and lawyers, as might be expected in view of their ability to afford the training. Interesting too is the finding that the future earnings expected by students correlates very highly with fathers' income level. It is as if students expect to lead a style of life very similar to the ones led by their parents while at the same time maintaining generally upward mobile hopes. Family income thus seems to exert a major effect on student expectations of income, opportunities, and specific choices.

Vander Well (1970) used an interesting method of classifying occupational choices into crystallized versus exploratory categories by virtue of the degree of occupational specificity associated with the chosen field. For example, medicine would be considered to be a crystallized choice since it is fairly specific, whereas psychology, which does not specify an occupational activity, is not considered a crystallized choice. The results of Vander Well's study revealed that second-year college students qualifying for financial aid reflected a greater degree of crystallization in their educational major and vocational goals than other students.

A study by Hewer and Neubeck (1962) examined the socioeconomic backgrounds of all freshmen entering the University of Minnesota in 1959. As might be expected, the upper socioeconomic levels were overrepresented in the class. More than 14 percent of the freshmen came from professional and technical level families and over 25 percent from families where the main wage earner was a manager or owner, while fewer than 6 percent came from families where the main worker was an "operative" and less than 3 percent from families of laborers. All these figures are disproportionate to the representation of these categories in the general population.

Werts (1968) classified the occupational preferences of more than 70,000 college freshmen into SVIB categories along with the occupations of their fathers and found three general patterns of similarity between sons' and fathers' occupations. First, where fathers were in social sciences, social science fields were overchosen (chosen more often than chance would predict) by the sons (for example, teachers' sons overchose college professor, clergymen's sons overchose professor, missionary, and social worker). Second, where fathers were engaged in occupations in the physical sciences, the sons overchose physical science fields (for example, chemists' sons overchose mathematics and physics, and biologists' sons overchose architecture). Third, physicians' sons overchose medical professions (for example, sons of medical doctors overchose medicine as a career, and dentists' sons overchose medicine and dentistry).

Generally, the results of studies comparing the occupations, or occupational levels, of fathers and sons reveal that children generally follow careers that resemble those of their fathers, within the context of a general upward striving in American society (Samson and Stefflre, 1952; Beilin, 1955; Porter, 1954; Jenson and Kirchner, 1955; Gunderson and Nelson, 1965; Krippner, 1963; Clark, 1967; Hollingshead, 1949; Miller and Form, 1951; Werts, 1968). Thus, some upward movement may be seen, but generally it is slight and is usually statistically offset by the corresponding slight downward social movement, a movement largely ignored by the general public.

The few studies reporting exceptions to this finding deserve some mention. Stewart (1959) studied the relationship between occupational perceptions and socioeconomic background, observing the responses of fifth-grade boys to a vocational "guess-who" test comprised of nine pictures of men representative of a variety of occupations: judge, teacher, scientist, mechanic, police sergeant, salesman, laborer, bellboy, and newsboy. The subjects were asked to identify the occupations depicted and then to rank the occupations with respect to earnings, housing, admiration and respect, and education. The resulting rankings were much as might be expected, except that the police sergeant was rated somewhat higher and the salesman somewhat lower than predicted. Of most interest was the finding that the rankings revealed little differences as a function of the occupations of the fathers.

Mowsesian (1966) studied and classified the occupational preferences by level of 147 Wisconsin high school students who were participating in a study of the superior student. Information about fathers' occupations was also elicited. The results indicated that most students possessed professional aspirations higher than those of their fathers and that there was a trend away from the fathers' fields.

A number of studies have examined heredity and occupation. Vandenberg and Stafford (1967) examined the Minnesota Vocational Interest Inventory scores of 53 pairs of fraternal and 71 paris of identical twins. The results suggested the presence of a hereditary component in the possession of nonscientific interests, which Vanderberg and Stafford speculate operates on behavior by means of personality variables.

Grotevant, Scarr, and Weinberg (1977) compared the responses of 114 biological families and 109 adoptive families on the results of the Strong-Campbell Interest Inventory. Parent-child correlations of biological families ranged from −.13 to .40; 15 of the 24 scale correlations were significantly correlated. Only two of the adoptive parent-child correlations were significantly correlated, with a range from −.15 to +.25. Biologically related pairs were observed to have interest profiles more significantly correlated than adoptive families. Same-sex biological siblings were more like each other than opposite-sex siblings or parent-child pairs, a finding similar to that of Vandenberg and Stafford (1967). The suggested explanations concerning how genetic influences on interest might occur include the possibility of a correlation between inherited abilities and interests. It could be, it is suggested, that genetic factors have an effect on personality which relates them to interest through tempermental factors. It is also suggested that the same personality factors influence the kinds of activities which a person engages in and enjoys. Another possibilitiy is that individuals inherit rates of maturation, which in turn are related to social experiences, which in their turn influence interest development. All of these speculations notwithstanding, it is still hard to understand how correlations between responses to as specific a stimulus as an interest inventory could be influenced by genetic factors.

Goodale and Hall (1976) observed that "student preceptions of parent interest in school work and hope for children's attendance in college mediated work values, while perceived pressures and involvements from parents did not.'' A path analysis suggests that parental background led to student college plans, which led to student occupational plans holding for male but not for female subjects. This kind of finding confuses the genetic hypotheses but does not eliminate them because of the differences between biological and nonbiological relationships found by investigators such as Grotevant et al. and Vandenberg and Stafford.

Using Roe's occupational classification system as an index of socioeconomic status, Lunneborg and Lunneborg (1968) found that father's occupation enhanced the accuracy of predictions of success in various curricula such as a law (if the father was in an organizational career) or architecture (if the father was in a business contact field it detracted from the probability of the son's success). The Lunneborgs suggest that socioeconomic status relates to a broad array of attributes that are relevant to occupational choice and attainment.

Mulvey (1963), in a study of the career patterns of women over approximately a twenty-five-year period following their graduation from high school, found that although the subjects' own level of education was highly related to the nature of their career patterns, parental socioeconomic status was apparently unrelated to and exerted little influence upon the patterns followed by the women in her sample. Possibly, a woman's career pattern is more significantly affected by her husband's social standing than that of her parents, though it is to be expected that parental status will influence marriage prospects.

Another research approach to the study of social class factors in occupational level is represented by a study of Hewer (1965). She studied the relationship between SVIB scores and the socioeconomic background of the freshman class entering the University of Minnesota in 1959. Socioeconomic class was determined by the assessment of the occupation and education of the students' fathers. The SVIB scores of the students were compared, scale by scale, with nine socioeconomic levels that resulted from the analysis of parental educational and vocational classification. The comparison revealed a relationship between scientific and technical interests on the SVIB and relatively lower socioeconomic social antecedents. It should be kept in mind, however, that Hewer and Neubeck's (1962) findings indicated that most of the freshmen at the University of Minnesota come from the upper half of the social strata.

Hyman (1956), in a similar design, classified high school seniors into social class groups and compared their standing with scores earned on the Kuder Preference Record. When the social class alone was considered, no differences were found in Kuder scores. When intelligence was also included in the analysis (by means of scores on the Otis Self-Administering Test of Mental Ability), upper-class students in the ''normal'' range of intelligence scored higher on the mechanical scale than upper-class ''superior'' intellect students. Middle- and lower-class ''superior'' students scored higher than upper ''superior'' students on the social service scale. It is interesting to speculate about the kind of family experiences that permit a bright lower-class youngster to develop a social service interest and compare those experiences with the kind that inhibit the development of the same interests in an upper-class adolescent with similar intellectual talents. The bright youngster from a socially prominent family would probably be encouraged to use talents to maintain family's status while the lower-class youth might develop a sense of mission to help others financially, especially the socially disadvantaged.

A study by Pierce-Jones (1959) correlated scores on the Kuder Preference Record with socioeconomic ratings obtained through the Gough Home Index rating. Based on a sample of eleventh graders, Pierce-Jones found that for boys the home rating was positively correlated with high literary and musical scores and negatively with outdoor interests. For girls, high home ratings were negatively correlated with clerical and mechanical scores. Not surprising is the finding that high socioeconomic status is positively correlated with IQ scores and school grades for both boys and girls. Thus, socioeconomic status may well have an effect not only on the development, nurture, and acceptability of certain interests but also on the likelihood that the student will achieve well enough academically to keep a wide range of choices open to himself.

Some investigators have examined the differences between social classes in their expectations of work and their approach to it. As Miller and Form (1951) have described the occupational expectations of the various social classes, upper-class members come from families where the parents are owners or managers, where much stress is placed on the maintenance of ''contacts'' designed to uphold the family's high status. Middle-class youth stem from white-collar families. The principal task for these youngsters is to learn to manipulate other people interpersonally. Parents of this class expect their children to work hard and advance in work that pays well and is ''clean.'' The lower-class family, largely blue-collar or manual, passes on to its children the attitude that they are not going to advance socially to any significant degree. Instead, the main job goals are, realistically, security, respectability, and pleasant and loyal interpersonal associations on the job. The children are taught that as long as one can provide well for one's family and enjoy life one is considered successful.

Other investigators have observed substantially the same things about occupational expectations. Centers and Bugental (1966) interviewed men and women in a cross section of occupations to investigate various motivations for work. They observed that the motives of white-collar workers are more intrinsically related to their work while the motives of blue-collar workers are more extrinsic. Contrary to this, however, Champagne (1967) found that for underprivileged adults intrinsic job factors were more important to job satisfaction than context factors. Stephenson's (1957) finding that lower-class youth are disproportionally represented among student who express no particular vocational choice is probably related to the lower-class students' recognition that they have relatively little control over the work they will actually perform. Thus, they are likely to disengage themselves from involvement in any particular work and instead remain undecided until specific opportunities present themselves. In contrast to this is Forrest's (1961) finding that National Merit Scholars were less concerned with the practical factors in career choice than most college students. Forrest speculated that the difference may reflect the higher socioeconomic status of Merit Scholars and the consequent lesser importance of concern with practical matters.

Friedlander (1966) investigated the importance of work compared to other aspects of life in blue-collar, white-collar, high, and low occupational status groups. He found that work content, context, church, education, and recreation were important in that order for all groups. Only when the white-collar versus blue-collar status was examined in connection with work status was Friedlander able to isolate any systematic differences in the importance of life activities. Friedlander concludes that work is a major environmental variable that leads to significant courses of satisfaction for most people. Friedlander's conclusion, however, is challenged by the work of Strauss (1963), Dubin (1956), Dubin and Goldman (1972), and Whitehill (1964), who disagree with the often-made assumption that work is a central life interest and that people strive for self-actualization through their work.

A distinctive method of studying one aspect of occupational membership has been reported by Laumann and Guttman (1966). A stratified sample of men was interviewed concerning a number of social and occupational matters. In particular, each subject was asked to state his own occupation, his father's, father-in-law's, those of his three closest friends, and of his two neighbors. The relationship between the social status of the subject and the statuses of his associates could then be determined. Through the use of a three-dimensional analysis, variables contributing to associations with others were identified. Laumann and Guttman predicted that occupational prestige alone was overemphasized in other research as a dimension determining interpersonal association. However, the results of Laumann and Guttman's study suggest that of the three major dimensions involved, the most heavily weighted one is highly correlated with occupational prestige.

REFERENCES

Beilin, H. The occupational mobility of a rural 1924 high school group. *Personnel and Guidance Journal*, 1955, *34*, 18–20.

Blau, P. M., and Duncan, D. D. *The American occupational structure* New York: Wiley, 1967.

Caplow, T. *The sociology of work*. New York: McGraw-Hill, 1954.

Centers, R., and Bugental, D. E. Intrinsic and extrinsic job motivations among different segments of the working population. *Journal of Applied Psychology*, 1966, *50*, 193–197.

Champagne, J. E., and King, D. C. Job satisfaction factors among underprivileged workers. *Personnel and Guidance Journal*, 1967, *45*, 429–434.

Clark, E. T. Influence of sex and social class on occupational preference and perception. *Personnel and Guidance Journal*, 1967, *45*, 440–444.

Cross, K. D. Comprehensive occupational survey of 1947 and 1952 Kansas State University graduates. Kansas State University Placement Center, 1960.

Dubin, R. Industrial workers worlds: a study of the "central life interests" of industrial workers. *Social Problems*, 1956, *3*, 131–142.

Dubin, R., and Goldman, D. R. Central life interests of American middle managers and specialists. *Journal of Vocational Behavior,* 1972 *2,* 133–142.

Forrest, A. L. Persistence of vocational choice of the Merit Scholarship winners. *Personnel and Guidance Journal,* 1961, *39,* 466–471.

Friedlander, F. Importance of work versus nonwork among social and occupationally stratified groups. *Journal of Applied Psychology* 1966, *50,* 437–441.

Goodale, J. G., and Hall, D. T. Inheriting a career: influence of sex, values, and parents. *Journal of Vocational Behavior,* 1976, *8,* 19–30.

Grotevant, H. D., Scarr, S., and Weinberg, R. A. Patterns of interest similarity in adoptive and biological families. *Journal of Personality and Social Psychology,* 1977, *35,* 667–676.

Gunderson, E. K. E., and Nelson, P. D. Socioeconomic status and Navy occupations. *Personnel and Guidance Journal,* 1965, *44,* 263–266.

Hart, D. H., Rayner, F., and Christensen, E. R. Planning, preparation and chance in occupational entry. *Journal of Vocational Behavior,* 1971, *1,* 279–285.

Havighurst, R. J. Youth in exploration and man emergent. In Borow, H. (Ed.), *Man in a world at work.* Boston: Houghton Mifflin, 1964.

Hewer, V. H. Vocational interests of college freshmen and their social origins. *Journal of Applied Psychology,* 1965, *49,* 407–411.

Hewer, V. H., and Neubeck, G. Occupations of fathers and mothers of entering University of Minnesota freshmen, fall, 1959. *Personnel and Guidance Journal,* 1962, *40,* 662–627.

Hollingshead, A. B. *Elmtown's youth.* New York: Wiley, 1949.

Huxley, A. L. *Brave new world.* New York. Harper & Row, 1946.

Hyman, B. The relationship of social status and vocational interests. *Journal of Counseling Psychology,* 1956, *3,* 12–16.

Jenson, P. G., and Kirchner, W. K. A national answer to the question, "Do sons follow their fathers' occupations?" *Journal of Applied Psychology,* 1955, *39,* 419–421.

Krippner, S. Junior high school students' vocational preferences and their parents' occupational levels. *Personnel and Guidance Journal,* 1963, *41,* 590–595.

Laumann, E. O., and Guttman, L. The relative associational continuity of occupations in an urban setting. *American Sociological Review,* 1966, *31,* 169–178.

Lipsett, L. Social factors in vocational development. *Personnel and Guidance Journal,* 1962, *40,* 432–437.

Lunneborg, P. W., and Lunneborg, C. E. Roe's classification of occupations in predicting academic achievement. *Journal of Counseling Psychology,* 1968, *15,* 8–16.

Miller, D. C., and Form, W. H. *Industrial sociology.* New York: Harper & Row, 1951.

Mowsesian, R. Superior students' occupational preferences and their fathers' occupations. *Personnel and Guidance Journal,* 1966, *45,* 238–242.

Mulvey, M. C. Psychological and sociological factors in prediction of career patterns of women. *Genetic Psychology Monographs,* 1963, *68,* 309–386.

Osipow, S. H. What do we really know about career development? In Gysbers, N., and Pritchard, D. (Eds.), Proceedings of the National Conference on Guidance, Counseling, and Placement in Career Development and Education-Occupational Decision-Making, Columbia, Missouri, 1969. (a)

Osipow, S. H. Student appraisal of a college preregistration counseling program. *Journal of College Student Personnel,* 1969, *10,* 47–51. (b)

Pierce-Jones, J. Vocational interest correlates of socioeconomic status in adolescence. *Educational and Psychological Measurement,* 1959, *19,* 65–71.

Porter, J. R. Predicting vocational plans of high school senior boys. *Personnel and Guidance Journal,* 1954, *33,* 215–218.

Rosenberg, M. *Occupations and values.* Glenco, Ill.: The Free Press, 1957.

Salomone, P. R., and Slaney, R. B. The influence of chance and contingency factors on the vocational choice processes of non-professional workers. *Journal of Vocational Behavior,* 1981, *19,* 25–35.

Samson, R., and Stefflre, B. Like father . . . like son? *Personnel and Guidance Journal,* 1952, *31,* 35–39.

Sewell, W. H., and Shah, V. P. Social class, parental encouragement, and educational aspirations. *American Journal of Sociology,* 1968, *73,* 559–572.

Slater, M. Perception: a context for the consideration of persistence and attrition among college men. *Personnel and Guidance Journal,* 1957, *35,* 435–440.

Stephenson, R. M. Realism of vocational choice: a critique and an example. *Personnel and Guidance Journal,* 1957, *35,* 482–488.

Stewart, L. H. Relationship of socioeconomic status to children's occupational attitudes and interests. *Journal of Genetic Psychology,* 1959, *95,* 111–136.

Strauss, G. The personality-versus-organizational theory. In Sayles, L. R. (Ed.), *Individualism and big business.* New York: McGraw-Hill, 1963.

Vandenberg, S. G., and Stafford, R. E. Hereditary influences on vocational preferences as shown by scores of twins on the Minnesota Vocational Interest Inventory. *Journal of Applied Psychology,* 1967, *51,* 17–19.

Vander Well, A. R. Influences of financial need on the vocational development of college students. ACT Research Report No. 36, Iowa City, Iowa: American College Testing Program, 1970.

Werts, C. E. Paternal influence on career choice. *Journal of Counseling Psychology,* 1968, *15,* 48–52.

Whitehill, A. M. Cultural values and employee attitudes: United States and Japan. *Journal of Applied Psychology,* 1964, *48,* 69–72.

Young, M. D. *The rise of the meritocracy.* Baltimore: Penguin, 1961.

CHAPTER FOURTEEN
EFFECTS OF
"MINORITY GROUP"
MEMBERSHIP[1]

It seems clear, based on the work of Blau and Duncan (1967), for example, that variables such as race interact with social class membership in ways that significantly affect occupational membership and attainment.

Neff's (1968) concept of work "psychopathology"[2] is in many ways relevant to the career development of disadvantaged and minority group members. Neff has postulated several types of work psychopathology, three of which apply to many minority group members. In type 1, work is perceived in a negative fashion; the individual exhibits little work motivation and finds little or no reinforcing value in work. In type 2, work elicits fear and anxiety, possibly the result of a lack of experience in work and confusion about work roles and rules. In type 3, the individual's response to work is characterized by hostility and aggression, and he or she is easily angered and, as a result, frequently comes into conflict on the job. This last type is potentially highly relevant to explaining the work behavior of minorities who display anger toward the existing social system.

---

[1]The phrase "minority group" membership does not adequately describe the members of groups whose social-ethnic class membership interferes with their occupational life because of discrimination or poverty. An argument can be made that it is not their minority group status that is most significant (cf. the situation of women, operationally a "minority" but actually, of course, in the majority) but rather the poverty and discrimination, along with their consequences, that such groups are exposed to that is important to consider. However, since the usage "minority group" is commonly accepted, it shall be followed in this discussion.

[2]The use of the term "psychopathology" may not be most appropriate here because of the connotation of mental illness which does not seem relevant to this writer. However, Neff uses the term, and the *behaviors* described by the types do appear to be relevant.

Certainly, anger would be appropriate if the hypothesis of Walsh (1975) is valid. In his book entitled *Dirty Work, Race, and Self-esteem,* Walsh discusses how self-esteem factors associated with working in low-level occupations (like garbage collection) can affect self-esteem; or one might consider the literature review of Smith (1975), which is generally critical of vocational development theories as applied to blacks.

Certain perceptions of the world of work of blacks and whites appear to be similar. For example, Dixon-Altenor and Altenor (1977) found that a sample of 15 black college women expressed occupational prestige rankings remarkably similar to those found by Hakel, Hollman, and Dunnette (1968). These findings are similar to those of Plata (1975), who found only small differences between the occupational prestige rankings of 117 Anglo and 129 Mexican Americans. Overall the stability of occupational prestige seems well established. For example, Fossum and Moore (1975) found that 100 undergraduate students described occupational prestige hierarchies very much like those found by investigators in 1927, 1947, 1968, and so on. The results of the Plata and Dixon-Altenor studies indicated that the same stability applies to minority group members as well.

It is, thus, tempting to go on from this point to explain all of the vocational behavior and career development of minority group members in these pathological terms. However, to do so would be inappropriate and oversimplified, because the work behavior of minority group members is complex and differentiated. For example, it would be grossly inaccurate to characterize the career development of minority group members as ineffective. Campbell and Parsons (1972) found that although the vocational maturity (measured by the Vocational Development Inventory) of disadvantaged students in junior high school was not as great as that for nondisadvantaged students, the mean scores on vocational maturity earned by the disadvantaged students were above the norms developed for the VDI.

Gradually, a data base from which to understand the current career development process of minority group members is being created. However, understanding of the situation is changing. Feingold (1968) wrote that work-study programs and a wide range of occupational information techniques should be applied to counteract the deprivation of the disadvantaged. In the early 1970s, the emphasis on minority group membership was seen as less a matter of overcoming disadvantage (still important, however) than as a matter of enabling minority group members to apply the unique aspects of their background to the world at large.

One study of interest, conducted by Pallone, Rickard, and Hurley (1970), asked 161 black and 218 white high school students in grades eleven and twelve what they expected to do (vocationally) and who was the major influence in this choice. For black males, white males, and white females the major influencer was a person who actually held the job chosen. For black females, a job holder was the second most common influence and mothers the most common influence, while for white females mothers were the second most common influence. For black males, second most influential were parents, while for white males, second place was occupied by fathers. Least important influencers, except for white females, were neighbors and friends; for white females, relatives were least often indicated as important influencers on careers. What is interesting about this study is the similarity between the races in source of influence in career. It is possible to classify investigations concerning the career development of minority group members into those whose results indicate that few differences exist between minority and "majority" group members versus those studies which indicate that many differences exist.

Differences between minority and majority members in career development. Dole and Passons (1972) compared 66 black male and female graduating high school seniors with 276 white graduating high school seniors with respect to post high school plans and goals. (In this study, minority group membership refers to race.) Black students were higher than white students with respect to altruistic values and the influence of school and science on their plans. Clark (1967), using the Vocational Apperception Test, compared 159 male and 139 female elementary students, mostly black inner-city children, with 206 male and 204 female suburban, middle-class, and mostly white children with respect to vocational preferences and perceptions. The results indicated that middle-class boys more often chose professional careers and less often "government" jobs than inner-city boys; middle-class girls more often chose business or teaching and were less often uncertain about jobs than the inner-city girls. Asbury (1968) compared 63 low-income Kentucky Appalachia students with 601 Iowa students on the Vocational Development Inventory (measuring vocational maturity) and found the Appalachia students scored lower than the Iowa students. Schmieding and Jensen (1968) compared 39 eleventh- and twelfth-grade Indian students in a "control" group with 39 eleventh- and twelfth-grade Indian students in an occupations class and 39 white high school students on the Vocational Development Inventory and the Vocational Tenacity Test. On the VDI the white students scored significantly higher than the Indians, with the Indian students in the occupations class scoring second. No differences among the three groups were found on Vocational Tenacity. Slocum and Strawser (1971) compared black and white CPAs in job attitudes and found significant differences in the sources of needs satisfaction: blacks were less satisfied with respect to social needs, self-esteem, opportunity for independent thought and action, opportunity for growth and development, and financial compensation. The "need importancies" hierarchies for the two groups, however, were very similar. Shappell, Hall, and Tarrier (1971) compared 186 ninth-grade males and females from inner-city and suburban neighborhoods on the Hall Occupational Orientation Inventory and found a number of significant differences reflecting social class membership.

Several studies have been conducted examining the relationship between racial membership and Holland's theory of career development. In one study, Doughtie, Alston, Chang, and Wakefield (1976) examined the possibility that racial differences are a basis for differences in scores on the Vocational Preference Inventory. The instrument was administered to 115 black and 122 white college freshmen and sophomore males and females. Differences in scores by race were found: blacks scored significantly higher on the social scale, the conventional scale, the enterprising scale, and a number of the nonoccupational scales. No differences were found on realistic, investigative, or artistic scales. In another series of studies, Bingham and Walsh (1978), Matthews and Walsh (1978), and Ward and Walsh (1981) found that congruence existed between the work environment and personality for black females with and without college degrees.

Wakefield, Yom, Doughtie, Chang, and Alston (1975) studied whether the VPI and Holland's theory were generally applicable to black people. There was a general correspondence to Holland's model in their study, but not as close as for white students. Particular weaknesses lay in the fact that the relationships between realistic and investigative scores, between social and enterprising scores, and between conventional and investigative scores were all not as close as one would have expected.

Sewell and Martin (1976) compared a sample of 97 black male juniors and seniors in high school with a sample of 200 junior and senior white students in a suburban academic sample and 255 junior and senior white male rural students. A general rural sample of 100 white males of about 17 or 18 years of age and a nonacademic sample of about 100 male seniors was also studied using a variety of interest and other measures. It was generally found that the black students in the sample had fewer interests than did white students, that the black students tended to score higher than the other students, and that the black students tended to score higher than the other groups in artistic interest and lower in scientific, technical, mechanical, and outdoor occupational interests. Gackenbach (1978) found that black women who were not employed outside the home possessed traditional sex-role attitudes to a greater degree than did white women, but had the same sex-role attitudes about working as did white women. Finally, Dole and Passons (1972) found that black students were higher than white students in altruism of occupational values.

Similarities between minority and majority members in career development.   Ansell and Hansen (1971) examined 375 eighth- through twelfth-grade boys, representing lower-class white, lower-class black, and middle-class white groups, on the Readiness for Vocational Planning Scales. Differences existed, but seemed to be related more to social class membership rather than race. Lower-class whites and blacks did not differ, but were different from middle-class whites. Unfortunately, these conclusions are somewhat tenuous in the absence of a sample of middle-class blacks to compare with the middle-class white sample. Maynard and Hansen (1970) compared 180 white, 180 black male students from the inner city with 90 white suburban male students on the VDI. Significant differences were found on Vocational Maturity, but these differences disappeared when controlled for intelligence. Campbell and Parsons (1972) compared 2370 disadvantaged and nondisadvantaged junior high school students from four large, geographically distinct communites with respect to a large number of vocational planning variables. Most of the students, disadvantaged as well as nondisadvantaged, exhibited a readiness for vocational planning, though the nondisadvantaged students scored high on vocational maturity on Crites' VDI. Compared to the VDI norms, however, the mean scores of the disadvantaged students on Vocational Maturity were above the means for their grade levels. Most of the students from both groups seemed to feel they had some control over their future occupation, were engaged in some planning behaviors, and aspired to relatively high occupational levels; male and female nondisadvantaged and female disadvantaged students most frequently chose service occupations while male disadvantaged students most often chose technical fields with service occupations second most frequently chosen. One of the most important variables affecting planning and choice was the community variable, which seemed to override sex and advantaged-disadvantaged status in influence.

Vriend (1969) developed a vocational maturity rating scale entitled the Vocational Education Survey, based on the following dimensions of vocational maturity: school achievement, relation between aspiration and expectation, educational-vocational planning, vocationally related self-knowledge, general job knowledge, and participation in in-school and out-of-school activities. The survey was administered to 112 college preparatory and 168 inner-city youth, the latter group enrolled in a special two-year program of structured career development. The results indicated that the inner-city students earned higher vocational maturity scores than the college preparatory students. On this basis, Vriend concludes that vocational maturity can be fostered.

Bergland and Lundquist (1975) studied sixty junior high school males in three treatment groups: vocational exploration, vocational exploration without interaction, and a control group. They found no differences after providing job information and awareness, concluding that counseling programs do not require significant racial adjustments. Wakefield, Alston, Yom, Doughtie, and Chang (1975) compared two samples of white and black students on six career scales and five other scales of the VPI and found relatively little in the way of racial differences. Yom, Doughtie, Chang, Alston, and Wakefield (1975) further factor analyzed these findings by race and again found a great similarity between the races.

Turner and Horn (1975) used the Kuder Occupational Interest Survey to classify 400 Mexican Americans with respect to Holland's theory. They computed in multiple, discriminate analysis using Guilford-Zimmerman scores and found that the personality characteristics involved in the Holland theory generalized to Mexican American males.

Implications of research on career development of minority group members. Unfortunately, since this is a topic of critical social significance, the information dealing with minority group career development is both confusing and inconsistent. This appears to stem primarily from a lack of consistency in the definition of minority group membership and an absence of any clear conceptual basis for most of the research. In general, the studies have confounded race, social class, ethnicity, educational levels, and economic variables. This confounding of variables contributes to the confused and conflicting picture that has developed concerning the status and needs of economically disadvantaged and minority group members with respect to their career development.

REFERENCES

Ansell, E. M., and Hansen, J. C. Patterns in vocational development of urban youth. *Journal of Counseling Psychology*, 1971, *18*, 505–508.

Asbury, F. A. Vocational development of rural disadvantaged eighth grade boys. *Vocational Guidance Quarterly*, 1968, *17*, 109–113.

Bergland, B. W., and Lundquist, G. W. The vocational exploration of group and minority youth: an experimental outcome study. *Journal of Vocational Behavior*, 1975, *7*, 289–296.

Bingham, R. P., and Walsh, W. B. Concurrent validity of Holland's theory for college-degreed black women. *Journal of Vocational Behavior*, 1978, *13*, 242–250.

Campbell, R. E., and Parsons, J. L. Readiness for vocational planning in junior high school, a socioeconomic and geographic comparison. *Journal of Vocational Behavior*, 1972, *2*, 401–418.

Clark, E. T. Influence of sex and social class on occupational preference and perception. *Personnel and Guidance Journal*, 1967, *45*, 440–444.

Dixon-Altenor, C., and Altenor, A. The role of occupational status in the career aspirations of black women. *Vocational Guidance Quarterly*, 1977, *25*, 211–215.

Dole, A. A., and Passons, W. R. Life goals and plan determinants reported by black and white high school seniors. *Journal of Vocational Behavior*, 1972, *2*, 209–222.

Doughtie, E. B., Alston, H. L., Chang, W. N. C., and Wakefield, J. A. Black white differences on vocational preference inventory. *Journal of Vocational Behavior*, 1976, *8*, 41–44.

Feingold, S. N. Presenting educational and occupational information to the disadvantaged. In Amos, W. E., and Crambs, J. D. (Eds.), *Counseling the disadvantaged youth*, Englewood Cliffs, N.J.: Prentice-Hall, 1968.

Fossum, J. A., and Moore, M. L. The stability of longitudinal and cross-sectional occupational prestige rankings. *Journal of Vocational Behavior*, 1975, *7*, 305–311.

Gackenbach, J. The effect of race, sex, and career-goal differences on sex role attitudes at home and at work. *Journal of Vocational Behavior*, 1978, *12*, 93–101.

Hakel, M. D., Hollman, T. D., and Dunnette, M. D. Stability and change in the social status of occupations over 21 and 42 years period. *Personnel Guidance Journal*, 1968, *46*, 762–769.

Matthews, D. F., and Walsh, W. B. Concurrent validity of Holland's theory for non-college-degreed working women. *Journal of Vocational Behavior*, 1978, *12*, 371–379.

Maynard, P. E., and Hansen, J. C. Vocational maturity among inner-city youths. *Journal of Counseling Psychology*, 1970, *17*, 400–404.

Neff, W. S. *Work and human behavior*. New York: Atherton, 1968.

Pallone, N. J., Rickard, F. S., and Hurley, R. B. Key influences of occupational preference among black youth. *Journal of Counseling Psychology*, 1970, *17*, 498–501.

Plata, M. Stability and change in the prestige of occupations over 49 years. *Journal of Vocational Behavior*, 1975, *6*, 95–99.

Schmieding, O. A., and Jensen, S. F. American Indian students: vocational development and vocational tenacity. *Vocational Guidance Quarterly*, 1968, *17*, 120–123.

Sewell, T. E., and Martin, R. P. Racial differences in patterns of occupational choice in adolescents. *Psychology in the Schools*, 1976, *13*, 326–333.

Shappell, D. L., Hall, L. C., and Tarrier, R. B. Perceptions of the world of work: inner-city versus suburbia. *Journal of Counseling Psychology*, 1971, *19*, 55–59.

Slocum, J. W., and Strawser, R. H. Racial differences in job attitudes. *APA Experimental Publication System*, June, 1971, *12*, Ms. No. 471-12.

Smith, E. J. Profile of the black individual in vocational literature. *Journal of Vocational Behavior*, 1975, *6*, 41–59.

Turner, R. G., and Horn, J. M. Personality correlates of Holland's occupational types: a cross-cultural study. *Journal of Vocational Behavior*, 1975, *6*, 379–389.

Wakefield, J. A., Jr., Alston, H. L., Yom, B. L., Doughtie, E. B., and Chang, W. N. C. Personality types and traits in the vocational preference inventory. *Journal of Vocational Behavior*, 1975, *6*, 19–26.

Wakefield, J. A., Yom, B. L., Doughtie, E. D., Chang, W. N. C., and Alston, H. L. The geometric relationship between Holland's personality typology and the vocational preference inventory for blacks. *Journal of Counseling Psychology*, 1975, *22*, 58–60.

Walsh, E. J. *Dirty work, race, and self-esteem*. Ann Arbor, Mich.: Univ. of Michigan, Wayne State Inst. of Labor and Industrial Relations, 1975.

Ward, C. M., and Walsh, W. B. Concurrent validity of Holland's theory for noncollege-degreed black women. *Journal of Vocational Behavior*, 1981, *18*, 356–361.

Vriend, J. Vocational maturity ratings of inner-city high school seniors. *Journal of Counseling Psychology*, 1969, *16*, 377–384.

Yom, B. L., Doughtie, E. B., Chang, W. N. C., Alston, H. L., and Wakefield, J. A., Jr. The factor structure of the Vocational Preference Inventory for black and white college students. *Journal of Vocational Behavior*, 1975, *6*, 15–18.

CHAPTER FIFTEEN
CULTURAL ORGANIZATION AND CAREER

It must be kept in mind that social organizations and culture did not develop independently of a physical context. Geography and climate contributed to the emergence of community structure. The isolated, small family-size farm developed because of the availability of cheap land and the time saved by not commuting to the fields from villages. Hilly lands encouraged dispersed communities; plains encouraged nucleated settlements where farmers commuted from villages to their fields. Similarly, urban centers developed around manufacturing, which is interrelated with market factors, accessibility of labor, power, raw materials, capital, and transportation (Finch et al., 1957). Social organizations often persist long after their reason for being has been modified. Thus, attention to ecology is critical if we are to identify which social institutions should be changed, how they may be changed, and what the effects of these changes may be on other aspects of human behavior.

In this section, attention is devoted to the role that the person's setting plays in career behavior. Psychological theories about careers and career decisions give little emphasis to matters of situational "accident." Sociological theories, on the other hand, provide some basis for understanding the interplay between the person and the world. Caplow (1954) has suggested that the crystallization of a career choice may occur at any age, the particular timing that is observed usually reflecting one's culture.

Blau and his associates (1956) have devised a complex and comprehensive scheme with which to conceptualize occupational choice in the cultural framework. According to Blau and his group, social structure exerts an influence on vocational choice through both the role it plays in the personality development of the individual and in its influence upon the economic and social conditions that prescribe the choice. The resulting choice made by the individual is the consequence of his estimate of the probability of the attainment of a particular career goal in combination with an evaluation of the career. Blau and his group assumed that people develop a hierarchy of career evaluations and estimations of the probabilities of career attainment, much as Holland (1959) assumed.

Thus, the occupational decisions people make are seen as a compromise between the two judgments. Accordingly, for the most part, people should select their most highly evaluated career possessing a reasonable probability of attainment. What varies from person to person is the definition of reasonable probability. The evaluations, as might be inferred from studies of occupation prestige hierarchies are relatively similar from one person to another. The effectiveness of the view Blau and his associates proposed is based on the degree to which people are aware of the various career possibilities open to them. Sound occupational information, in the broadest sense, is crucial to good decision making in this framework.

The Blau group has proposed that a double chain of events determines occupational entry. One chain, based on individual characteristics, includes biological and psychological factors, while the other chain is concerned with conditions affecting the economic opportunities facing the individual, such as geography, social resources, opportunities for mobility, cultural labor conditions, variations in potential rewards, and so on. Both the individual and social chains interact in a manner which shapes the eventual occupational choice. The career development of a young man growing up in New York City who is well endowed intellectually and highly skilled in physical coordination and strength will be different from that of a similar young man living in rural Wyoming. The urban boy is much more likely to rely on his intellectual characteristics than his rural counterpart because of the greater number of educational institutions in the city. At the same time, it is clear that two youngsters with different temperaments and physiques growing to maturity in Pittsburgh will not necessarily both enter the steel mills. Parallel situations should exist for young women growing up in different settings.

Information about the occupational organizations of American culture is likely to be more effective in bringing occupational information to life than the current methods of disseminating career information. Descriptions of the sociological elements of various careers, such as have been written by a few investigators and agencies (Danskin, 1955; 1957; U.S. Department of Labor, 1965; the descriptions written by the Research Department of the Vocational Guidance and Rehabilitation Services in Cleveland, Ohio), are more effective in producing the flavor of life involved in a given career than the relatively sterile information about education, income, and necessary special talents such as are often all the information that is available. Samler (1961) has suggested the use of a scheme such as Murray's environmental press and needs theory (1938) to describe career environments.

A Social Type Based Theory of Career Development

Gottfredson (1981) has proposed what she calls a developmental theory of occupational aspirations, which appears to combine both development and social systems views about careers. It is built on the assumption that all social groups share occupational images and that these can be represented in a "cognitive map of occupations." Occupational preferences are viewed as developing in terms of self-concepts in a series of four stages. These are orientation to size and power, orientation to sex roles, orientation to social values, and orientation to the internal unique self. Ultimately individuals are required to compromise in making choices among conflicting goals.

Critical variables involved in developing occupational images and preferences involve such things as how successful an occupation is perceived to be, what occupational alternatives seem to be accessible and acceptable, and how large that range of alternatives actually is.

Variables of significance in developing occupational aspirations and in their accessibility involve occupational prestige, perceptions of the sex type of the occupation considered, and the particular kind of traits perceived to be held by the occupation's inhabitants. This leads to the so-called occupational map mentioned earlier.

The developmental issues seem reminiscent of those of other developmental personality theorists and involve dimensions such as concreteness-abstractness, the interaction between self-concept and vocational preferences, overlapping differentiation and incorporation sequences, and what is called the "irreversible progressive subscription or elimination of alternatives."

The first stage involves orientation to size and power, which occurs in very young children three to five years old. Following that is the orientation to sex roles, ages six to eight, and then orientation to social evaluation, ages nine to thirteen, occurs. The last stage of orientation, internal unique self, begins around age fourteen.

According to Gottfredson's theory, the perception and the attractiveness of occupations at different levels is a function of social class membership. For example, lower-class individuals see lower-level class jobs more positively than do higher socioeconomic class individuals. Parental aspirations also differ. Parents prefer to see their children obtain high-level jobs, but their views about what constitutes failure differ—the lower social class mothers are willing to accept lower levels of jobs than their offspring.

Job accessibility perceptions and the implementation of aspirations are related to one another. It is assumed (without data) that people differ in how they perceive opportunities. People take into consideration what they think is possible before they express an occupation preference.

How to compromise goals? Age is a factor; people are fairly realistic about their job levels because, according to Gottfredson (1979) by age thirty both higher and lower social class members, at least males, have obtained the job levels that they aspire to as adolescents. On the other hand, we do know that people aspire to specific fields of work out of proportion to the availability of jobs in those fields. People frequently aspire to scientific and medical careers but the frequency of these aspirations moderates as people become older, while aspirations for enterprising occupations, such as in management and sales work, increase because they are more available.

Gottfredson suggests some principles which govern the compromise process, such as, 1) "Some aspects of self-concept are more central than others and will take priority when compromising occupational goals." 2) "Exploration of job options ends with the implementation of a satisfactory choice, not necessarily the most optimal potential choice." 3) "People accommodate psychologically to the compromises they make."

In summary, Gottfredson's work represents a new integration of the social systems and developmental approaches. It suffers the obvious shortcomings of being so new as to require reliance on the reinterpretation of existing data for support (for example, Gottfredson, 1979) rather than to present new data. It is also vague in terms of the kinds of instrumentation that would be necessary to test its assertions, assumptions, and hypotheses. Nonetheless, it is useful to have a new stimulus for research in thinking about careers from the social systems development point of view.

Environmental Press

The ability of a situation to exert an influence on behavior is well known. Ford and Urban (1965) have shown how significant the modification of student living situations can be in the decision and opportunity to complete a college program. Similarly, Osipow and Grooms (1970) have demonstrated how the analysis of the situational context of a problem may provide suggestions about techniques to modify behavior in desirable ways. Super and Bachrach (1957) have suggested a social systems approach to the study of career development based on the interaction between the individual and his society. Presumably, the society dictates the developmental sequence and timing of vocational behavior and requires the individual to make career decisions within the framework of the social system. The social system itself includes the press of the larger culture, its various subcultures, and the community, as well as personal sources of influence such as the home, family, school, and so on. The individual must make a choice which reflects a compromise between the self and the requirements of the social system.

Murray's writings of the 1930s provided the basis for the concept that environment exerts a "press" upon the individual which interacts with personality, affecting the consequent behavior. In an academic context, the experimental prototype of this proposal is Pace and Stern's (1958) study of the psychological press of different college environments. Pace and Stern devised an instrument to measure environmental press, administered it to students in five collegiate institutions, and were able to write statements illustrative of the environment of each of the schools.

Other investigators have conducted similar studies of academic environments. Thistlethwaite (1960) studied the influence of the college environment on the academic plans of 1500 highly talented students who had completed their junior year. He found that faculty behavior was highly influential in stimulating certain changes in educational plans. A warm and informal faculty seemed to attract students to the social sciences, arts, and humanities, while an enthusiastic and permissive faculty attitude seemed to attract students to the natural and biological sciences.

Astin (1965) also studied the effect of college environment on vocationally related educational decisions but attempted to take into account two other classes of data as well, which were criterion data, that is, the student's vocational choice at the time of graduation, and control data, or the student input characteristics of the institution. The results indicated that the students' career choices at the time of their graduation were highly similar to the choices they expressed when they began college. Realistic and Enterprising occupational choices were correlated positively with Realistic and Enterprising college environments and negatively with other environments, suggesting that choices may be reinforced by the atmosphere at a given college. However, the talents of the subjects (Merit Scholars) introduce a flexibility not likely to exist for more typical students, namely, the ability to exercise their preferences and not be concerned with limitations in ability to any major extent in college. It seems likely that many changes in educational and vocational plans made by students in college reflect achievement problems, not genuine modifications in preference. Preferences may change afterward, possibly to reduce cognitive dissonance.

Herr (1965) applied the environmental press concept to the study of high school students' behavior. He administered a modification of Stern's College Characteristics Index, renamed the High School Characteristics Index, to high school students. Differences were found in student perception of school press associated with academic performance, school grade, public versus parochial elementary school enrollment, IQ score, father's occupation, and parental educational level. These results are suggestive of the interaction of social experiences and consequences of social class attributes with the perception of the environment, which combine to influence behavior.

Most of the emphasis of the environmental approach is based on the recognition that educational and vocational choices reflect a compromise between the individual's basic inclinations and those possibilities that the culture opens to him or her. Unfortunately, little research has been conducted outside of the educational system concerning the effect of the interaction between the individual and environmental press on career decisions. Systematic research on the effects of environmental press on occupational behavior in industry would be interesting to examine.

Industrial Organization

Though the effect of environmental press of industrial organizations on career development has not been studied directly, considerable data about organizational effects on behavior are available. One leading writer, Gross (1964; 1967), suggests that it must be recognized that organizations affect career behavior in four general ways. Although there are a great number of small businesses in Western society, large organizations employ more people than do the more numerous small firms because of the large numbers of people employed in a single firm. Consequently, most people adjust to the particular problems of life in large organizations. These problems include learning how to deal with authority, satisfying security needs appropriately, accommodating to work that is routine, resolving the conflict between the need of the organization for creativity and its demand for conformity, coping with the distance in interpersonal relations that most large organizations require, and the acceptance of the fact that social mobility in large organizations may be, at retirement, downward rather than upward.

Also, the particular organization in which a worker is employed largely determines the character of the people with whom he or she interacts. Since interpersonal relations are highly important to vocational success, the character of one's associates may become even more important to a worker than the physical surroundings within which the work takes place. The organization within which one is employed plays a major role in one's job and influences income and material style of life. A worker's income determines consumption of goods, a major factor of modern American life. The car one owns and the vacations one takes depend upon one's income and social expectations, both of which may be largely determined by one's job and institution. The effect of institutional life on noninstitutional behavior has been aptly described by Whyte (1956).

Finally, Gross suggests the notion of the occupational career within organizational structures. Even though one may change jobs several times, it is still possible to have a "career." Consequently, organizational life requires its workers to avoid becoming too well suited to one job or work setting, since a career pattern may require several job changes as the career matures. A promotion may require one to give up old friends; a promising job may necessitate a cross-country move. A personal knowledge of the problems in production acquired in younger days may inhibit an executive's ability to detach him or herself from the managerial decisions required when there are wider responsibilities in a more mature career phase.

The four organizational effects imply that people must plan for career cycles which require them to maintain occupational flexibility and ability to adapt to new friends, communities, and ways of life. It also implies that the career decision-making process must be sharpened and that people must strive to identify as many career alternatives as possible at any given point in their career progression, recognizing that they may maximize their chances of choosing wisely but not expecting perfection or finality to result from their decisions. Discussing organizational careers further, Slocum (1965) points out that occupational decisions are not exclusively the province of the chooser but are subject to the demands of society and the opportunities available. Career choices have many causes such as skills, interest, sex, values, and so on.

Other writers have commented on life in organizations (Miller, 1964) and the way organizations affect work. Wilensky (1964) has pointed out that although people complain about their work to one another, when they are asked in a variety of ways whether they are satisfied with their work, most indicate that they are. Few says their work is dull and few would choose another line of work if they were able to start again, although the frequency of satisfaction with work decreases as the respondents move from upper- to lower-class status, and most say they would continue working even if they suddenly became financially independent of their jobs. Curiously, however, despite the evidence for satisfaction, most people express the hope that their children will do better vocationally than they did.

Related to organizational factors in occupational behavior is occupational sociology. Generally, occupational sociology applies itself to the description of such factors as occupational status and mobility, the relationships between ethnicity and career and between occupation and personality, occupational images and stereotypes, occupational culture and ethics, and client-professional relations (Smigel, 1954). It has led to many interesting studies of occupational stereotypes (for example, Grunes, 1956; O'Dowd and Beardslee, 1960). These investigators showed, by different methods and based on different samples, that vivid occupational images are held by the majority of youth in the process of making entry decisions about careers. Their findings suggest very strongly that these sterotypes provide a large basis for the kinds of occupational decisions that are subsequently made. Although the stereotypes may have considerable validity, as Holland's (1959) theory suggests, for any individual a career decision based on a cultural stereotype of an occupation may prove to be unfortunate.

Another aspect of occupational sociology has been the development of occupational information literature based on sociological data on occupations. True to life descriptions of work and living conditions afforded by membership in certain careers can be very useful to students involved in making entry vocational decisions or educational-vocational decisions (Danskin, 1955; 1957; U.S. Department of Labor, 1965).

Cross-cultural studies of occupation.   Sociologists and anthropologists have studied various cultures extensively. One concern, usually not the primary one, of their studies has been the vocational activity that occupies the inhabitants of the culture. The occupational implications of the many different cross-cultural studies that have been conducted deserve a book to themselves. However, some of these studies and their major implications for vocational behavior may be mentioned briefly here.

Early studies concerning human development across cultures have been reported by Margaret Mead (1930; 1937; 1939), who studied the behavior of islanders in the South Pacific. These studies of the Samoans, Manuans, and New Guineans revealed, as might be expected in primitive cultures, that work was begun at a very early age and was assigned according to the individual's general capability. Although beginning work as young children in these three cultures had its disadvantages, some genuine advantages appeared to exist. Most significant of these was that the work the children did was real and important in marked contrast to the work that children often perform in middle- and upper-class segments of American society. The artificiality of work for children in American culture may well generate unwholesome attitudes toward work which may interfere with effectiveness later in life. Furthermore, the children who inhabit these primitive cultures had the advantage of relatively easy identification with their like-sex parent, which facilitated the acquisition of work skills and helpful attitudes, once again, a feature missing from the daily experience of most American youth.

Mead's work (1937; 1953) also reveals some interesting aspects of cultural organization on work-related behavior. The degree to which a society is based on cooperative versus competitive effort among its members may be highly related to physical characteristics of the land they inhabit, such as the climate, topography, and geography. All of these influence customs about property, which in turn affect the way work is organized, the division of labor among the sexes, and the response to the modification of work procedures from primitive to modern techniques. For example, the difficulty Hindu cultures have in adapting to technical change is predictable from an understanding of Hindu philosophy toward living and working (Mead, 1953).

Other writers, such as Ruth Benedict (1946) and Anne Roe (1956), have extensively discussed work in various cultures. Roe has shown how the complexity of a society influences and in turn is influenced by the variety of work available to the members of the society. Ross and Ross (1957) studied the American Apache Indians to determine some of the background factors in the vocational decisions made by these people. Though the sampling was not representative and thus limits generalizations to be drawn from the results, the findings reveal, much as would be expected, that younger tribe members earned higher IQ test scores than older members and that artistic and clerical interests generally were stronger than scientific ones, a finding not surprising in a culture with a strong artistic tradition and no scientific one.

Remenyi and Fraser (1977) replicated Osipow's (1962) study of the effects of occupational information on occupational perceptions. They found very similar results in an Australian sample seventeen years after Osipow's study was conducted in a United States sample. The fact that the results were replicated across culture and across time is impressive and does suggest that there may well be some strong cross-cultural similarities in career development. Certainly, elsewhere we have seen many studies done in other countries using instrumentation developed in the United States and concepts developed in Western culture which seem to generally apply elsewhere.

In this section we have reviewed the idea that the physical and social environment creates institutions whose particular arrangement exerts a significant influence on occupational behavior. It seems likely that a comprehensive approach to career development theory must include the effects of the social organization on the individual's personality characteristics.

REFERENCES

Astin, A. W. Effects of different college environments on the vocational choices of high aptitude students. *Journal of Counseling* Psychology, 1965, *12*, 28–34.

Benedict, R. *Patterns of culture.* New York: Mentor, 1946.

Blau, P. M., Gustad, J. W., Jessor, R., Parnes, H. S., and Wilcox, R. S. Occupational choice: a conceptual framework. *Industrial Labor Relations Review,* 1956, *9,* 531–543.

Caplow, T. *The sociology of work,* New York: McGraw-Hill, 1954.

Danskin, D. G. Occupational sociology in occupational exploration. *Personnel and Guidance Journal,* 1955, *34,* 134–136.

Finch, V. C., Trewartha, G. T., Robinson, A. H., and Hammond, E. H. *Elements of geography: physical and cultural (4th ed.).* New York: McGraw-Hill, 1957.

Ford, D. H., and Urban, H. B. College dropouts and social strategies. *Educational Record,* 1965, *46,* 77–92.

Gottfredson, L. S. Aspiration-job match: age trends in a large nationally representative sample of white young men. *Journal of Counseling Psychology,* 1979, *26,* 319–328.

Gottfredson, L. S. Circumscription and compromise: a developmental theory of occupational aspirations. *Journal of Counseling Psychology Monographs,* 1981, *28,* in press.

Gross, E. The worker and society. In Borow, H. (Ed.), *Man in a world at work.* Boston: Houghton Mifflin, 1964.

Gross, E. A sociological approach to the analysis of preparation for work life. *Personnel and Guidance Journal,* 1967, *45,* 416–423.

Grunes, W. F. On perception of occupations. *Personnel and Guidance Journal,* 1956, *34,* 276–279.

Herr, E. L. Differential perceptions of "environmental press" by high school students. *Personnel and Guidance Journal,* 1965, *43,* 678–686.

Holland, J. L. A theory of vocational choice. *Journal of Counseling Psychology,* 1959, *6,* 35–45.

Mead, M. *Social organization of Manua.* Honolulu: Bernice P. Bishop Museum, 1930.

Mead, M. (Ed.). *Cooperation and competition among primitive groups.* New York: McGraw-Hill, 1937.

Mead, M. *From the South Seas.* New York: Morrow, 1939.

Mead, M. (Ed.). *Cultural patterns and technical change.* Paris: UNESCO, 1953.

Miller, D. C. Industry and the worker. In Borow, H. (Ed.), *Man in a world of work.* Boston: Houghton Mifflin, 1964.

Murray, H. E. *Exploration in personality.* New York: Oxford, 1938.

O'Dowd, D. D., and Beardslee, D. C. College student images of a selected group of professions and occupations. Cooperative Research Project No. 562, U.S. Office of Education, Wesleyan University, Middletown, Connecticut, April, 1960.

Osipow, S. H. Perceptions of occupations as a function of titles and description. *Journal of Counseling Psychology,* 1962, *9,* 106–109.

Osipow, S. H., and Grooms, R. R. Behavior modification through situational manipulation. In Osipow, S. H., and Walsh, W. B. (Eds.), *Behavior change in counseling: readings and cases.* New York: Appleton-Century-Crofts, 1970.

Pace, C. R., and Stern, C. G. An approach to the measurement of psychological characteristics of college environment. *Journal of Educational Psychology,* 1958, *49,* 269–277.

Remenyi, A. G., and Fraser, B. J. Effects of occupational information on occupational perceptions. *Journal of Vocational Behavior,* 1977, *10,* 53–68.

Roe, A. *The psychology of occupations.* New York: Wiley, 1956.

Ross, W. T., and Ross, G. V. B. Backgrounds of vocational choice: an Apache study. *Personnel and Guidance Journal,* 1957, *35,* 270–275.

Samler, J. Psycho-social aspects of work: a critique of occupational information. *Personnel and Guidance Journal,* 1961, *39,* 458–465.

Slocum, W. L. Occupational careers in organizations: a sociological perspective. *Personnel and Guidance Journal,* 1965, *43,* 858–866.

Smigel, E. O. Occupational sociology. *Personnel and Guidance Journal,* 1954, *32,* 536–539.

Super, D. E., and Bachrach, P. B. *Scientific careers and vocational development theory.* New York: Bureau of Publications, Teachers College, Columbia University, 1957.

Thistlethwaite, D. L. College press and changes in study plans of talented students. *Journal of Educational Psychology,* 1960, *51,* 222–234.

U.S. Department of Labor, *Sociological studies of occupations.* Washington, D.C.. Manpower Division, U.S. Government Printing Office, 1965.

Wilensky, H. L. Varieties of work experience. In Borow, H. (Ed.), *Man in a world at work.* Boston: Houghton Mifflin, 1964.

CHAPTER SIXTEEN
THE CAREER
DEVELOPMENT OF WOMEN

Perhaps the most significant area of concern for advocates of equal rights for women is that of careers, especially as these rights concern equality of opportunity, treatment, remuneration, and advancement, but also as they concern the general social attitude toward women's careers and marriage and family responsibilities. For many years, questions of career development concerning women were ignored or given cursory treatment, partly out of a lack of general social interest and partly because the confusing nature of career development in women made the topic difficult to study. That gender affects career development in numerous ways as a result of social organization seems to be generally agreed (Fidell [1970], showed data reflecting how employment opportunities are affected by sex), and thus, the variable of sex becomes a legitimate one to consider in this disucssion of social systems and careers.

It seems to be well established that despite the mythology to the contrary, professional women do not surrender their vocational identity lightly. Giuliani and Centra (1968) found that women veterinarians engage in professional practice 78 percent of the total possible years open to them, that 90 percent intend to continue in or return to professional practice, and that 92 percent of the female graduates since 1952 of the veterinary school studied were in active practice. Studying a sample of women dentists in Israel, Meir, Camon, and Sardi (1967) found that professional goal attainment, in combination with the degree to which dentistry satisfied intrinsic needs, predicted women dentists' persistence in professional practice. Astin (1967) reports that 80 to 90 percent of women doctorates are in the labor force.

The activity of women in the labor force over the past half century has noticeably changed. U.S. Department of Labor statistics from 1940 to the early

1970s, for example, have indicated that while the proportion of single women in the labor force has remained relatively stable, the proportion of women who are married and living with their husbands while participating in the labor force has quadrupled. Furthermore, even the number of women with children under age 18 engaged in the labor force has substantially increased. Examining overall proportions, the data indicate that in 1940, 48.1 percent of women in the labor force were single, while in 1972 the corresponding figure was 54.9 percent. In 1940, 14.7 percent of married women living with their husbands were in the labor force, while in 1972 that group represented 41.5 percent of employed women. Widows, divorcees, and women living apart from their husbands constituted 35.4 percent of employed women in 1940 and 40 percent in 1972. Overall, the number has gone from 13.9 percent of women employed in 1940 to 32.9 percent employed in 1972. This represents a remarkable increase that clearly justifies the attention now being given to women in the work force.

Over the last decade a number of major publications have appeared dealing with the issue of women's careers. A number of papers in a volume edited by Osipow (1975) deal with the factors involved in the career development of women, such as women's interest development, parental factors, personalogical factors, the interaction of marriage and work for women, sex-role stereotyping, and barriers that women face in working with their careers.

More recently, Fitzgerald and Crites (1980) point out both similarities and differences in the areas of career development of women and men. Fitzgerald and Crites assume that women's career development is more complex than that of male career development because of a differential combination of attitudes. Although Fitzgerald and Crites conclude that traditional career development theories have a contribution to make to the understanding of women's career development, the theories may be "necessary, but not sufficient" to explain women's career development fully. Fitzgerald and Crites suggest, for example, that achievement motivation may be viewed to be important to women, particularly because women seem to be more differentially influenced by virtue of sex-role socialization in the area of achievement orientation.

In addition, counselors' perception about careers may be distorted, and these distortions are reflected in problems in measuring women's interests as well as in dealing with potential counselor bias in working with women about their career problems.

The Development of Work Images in Women

A number of investigators have tried to study how occupational stereotypes develop in children, in order to better understand sex-role perceptions of work roles. Pratt (1975) had over 200 women judge 18 occupational titles, half of which commonly involve women and half of which are less likely to involve women, on 26 semantic differential scales. The resulting profiles are interesting in that they offer concrete descriptions of the stereotypes that women hold about the occupations. In addition, the results have potential utility as a research tool for other investigators. In a similar vein, Shinar (1975) examined sex stereotypes by measuring them in three different ways. These were the judgments of respondents about the proportion of males and females in occupations, the judgments of the respondents about the functional requirements of work as stereotyped by sex, and the judgments about the masculinity and femininity of occupations without any additional instructions. Shinar found few differences as a function of these three different ways of measuring sex stereotypes. Sex stereotyping of occupations was found to be very evident and similar across both sexes. The consequence of her study was the development of a mean rating on sex stereotype for 129 occupations, creating yet another potentially useful research tool Finally, Suchner and Moore (1975) had 113 college students evaluate stereotypes with descriptions that were biased by sex and prestige information. They found that gender has an important effect on occupational stereotypes.

The evidence seems clear that gender is a major factor in the way that people see occupations. The question remains of how these stereotypes develop. A number of investigators have studied this issue. Tibbetts (1975) looked at sex-role stereotyping in 42 early elementary school children aged 7 to 11, 21 of whom were boys and 21 girls. A sex-role attitude test was administered which asked questions about work roles to which the children were to indicate whether males, females, or either sex should appropriately perform. Even at the young ages of the subjects in Tibbetts' study, sex-role-stereotyped responses were generally observed to exist. Kriedber, Butcher, and White (1978) tried to replicate studies by Looft (1971a, 1971b). Kriedber et al. found that sex-role stereotypes were observable in the vocational aspirations of young children but began to be moderated in the aspirations of adolescent females. From the few studies that exist, it is clear that the literature is divided, in that some studies show that sex-role stereotypes are established by the early grade school years and other studies show that those attitudes are not established early.

Lerner, Benson, and Vincent (1976) found that the sexes are similarly egalitarian in social perception. For fourth, fifth, and sixth graders, Lerner et al. found that male personal vocational perceptions were most closely associated with traditionally valued male roles, while for females, personal perceptions were associated with traditional female roles. O'Bryant, Durrett, and Pennebaker (1978) found that fifth and seventh graders and high school and college students gave lower ratings to workers in nontraditional than in traditional jobs in terms of prestige and importance, in particular in terms of money and education. The subjects agreed by gender on job ratings, but boys gave higher ratings to male jobs on respect and importance to the community, while girls gave higher ratings to female jobs. Barnett (1975) studied over 2500 young people between the ages of 9 and 17 years, of whom about 1500 were male and 1000 female. From a list of 24 occupations, subjects were asked to indicate the two they most liked and the two they least liked. Correlations were computed between these preferences and occupational prestige and age. It was found that occupational prestige and preference were more highly correlated for males than for females at all ages. For females at all ages, the correlations between prestige and occupational aversion were higher than those between occupational prestige and preference. Do these results suggest that women learn that they should not aspire to prestigious positions?

Hoult and Smith (1978), in a study of 646 children aged 11 to 17, found that a U-shaped curve existed, as a function of age, in the number of choices expressed about careers. There was a high point at age 13 followed by a slight decrease to age 16. Males listed a greater range of choices and a greater range of preferences, as compared to females, but the range of aspirations was similar for both groups. O'Bryant, Durrett, and Pennebaker (1978) found that both genders become less stereotypic in their occupations from fifth grade through college. As children mature and become increasingly aware of their environment, they tend to choose high-status nontraditional jobs with greater frequency than low-status traditional jobs, an observation even more true for females than for males.

The only study that gives an empirical hint about how these preferences develop is a study by Knell and Winer (1979). They found that reading content had an affect on occupational sex-role stereotypes. When children were read stories that portrayed a sex-stereotyped occupational relationship, the girls in their study became more stereotyped in their responses. Knell and Winer concluded that reading content can therefore reinforce attitudes and ideas, although there wasn't anything in their study to indicate that reading could counteract already existing ideas.

The folklore (and probably the reality) is that a whole combination of events operate to socialize children at a fairly early age to "appropriate sex-type behaviors." These appropriate behaviors include attitudes toward work and definitions of what is proper and improper work for males and females. While these attitudes may be established early, they are apparently not impervious to change, as witnessed by the change in proportions of women in various occupations over the past twenty to thirty years.

Motivations for Work in Women

Eyde (1968) followed 51 women college graduates of the class of 1953 and 55 more of the class of 1958, five and ten years after graduation, respectively. She required the women to complete "desire to work" and "ranked work" scales. The first instrument measured the relative commitment of the woman to work as compared to other tasks (for example, childbearing), while the second instrument measured the idea that women and men work for a variety of motives (for example, money, interpersonal development, and interest). The results indicated that mastery-achievement work values do not decline in the period between the fifth and tenth year after graduation (a finding in contrast to Baruch's [1966]). In addition, also contrary to much existing literature, Eyde found that the older alumnae indicated a stronger desire for independence than the younger women, suggesting that the desire for independence in women may have a developmental aspect. Astin

(1967) identified the major factors associated with doctoral level women working and found that early commitment to work was a major discriminator relative to working or not. Harmon (1971) asked 1100 first-year college women to indicate those occupations (from a list of 135) they had at some time considered, along with their age when these were considered. The resulting list was very limited during early years. Altogether, the results indicated that college women are homogeneous in the occupations they express interest in at early ages, and that though this restrictiveness loosens with age, the later choices tend to be primarily in "typical" women's fields, suggesting that one motive operating is the smooth combination of work and marriage.

Of course, in such a rapidly changing area one must be cautious about concluding that these data reflect current thinking among young females regarding their future careers. Rand and Miller (1972), however, have data which might speak to this point. They conducted a cross-sectional comparison of women at three educational levels in order to assess the differential cultural and developmental effects on career attitudes. There were twenty females each from the junior high, senior high, and collegiate levels. The results indicated that the desire for marriage was present and an important career variable in the junior high girls and that by the time they went to college it had become an important aspect of plans. Almost all the girls' plans included combinations of work, marriage, and family responsibilities. Occupational choices were fairly consistent across age levels, with teaching being the most frequently chosen. At all levels, the females seemed to choose stereotyped "women's" occupations. Thus, Harmon's general data are reinforced and are probably likely to continue to reflect the range of occupations considered by young women for at least the near future.

Achievement Motivation

A major area of interest in studying women's career adjustment has been focused around achievement orientation. Lenney (1977) has provided a useful literature review related to women's attitudes in achievement-oriented situations. Lenney's general observation is that women display less self-confidence than do men across almost all achievement situations studied. While that may be an oversimplification of the research findings, it is generally an accurate observation. It should be noted, however, that there are some achievement situations in which women do not appear to have less self-confidence than men. Such circumstances seem characterized by the difference in the situational variables, such as particular abilities that are required, the available feedback, and the emphasis upon evaluation and comparisons with other people. Lenney concludes that attention needs to be paid to the contextual aspects of the achievement situation for women rather than simply assuming that women have less self-confidence in achievement-oriented situations than do men.

Esposito (1977) studied 221 male and female white and black college freshmen with respect to their vocational choices and their "motive to avoid success." A significant gender difference was found on motive to avoid success in both black and white women who scored significantly higher than did males on that variable. In addition, it was found that females with high motives to avoid success engaged in significantly more traditional occupational daydreaming than women with low motives to avoid success. A curious correlation between motive to avoid success and high educational aspirations was found in white males. That observation did not hold for females, in fact it was somewhat the opposite. For black males no relationship of that type was found at all. For black females who clearly had a high motive to avoid success, lower educational aspirations were found than for subjects with low motives to avoid success.

Sedney and Turner (1975) compared two models of career orientation of women. The first was called the Compensatory Model, which proposed the notion that females' inadequacies in developing sexual associations led to high need achievement, which orients particular women to particular careers. The alternate hypothesis was the Enrichment Model, which suggested that a woman's high achievement need would lead to high career orientation, therefore decreasing heterosexual orientation. To test this hypothesis, 92 white females and 26 white males were studied with respect to affiliation behaviors, need for achievement via affiliation, and career orientation. Sedney and Turner concluded that the data more closely supported the Enrichment than the Compensatory Model.

Janda, O'Grady, and Kapps (1978) compared success imagery in males and females in a variety of sex-linked occupations. The results indicated that males had the greatest fear of success imagery in response to nursing stimuli, while females showed the greatest fear of success imagery in response to engineering stimuli, suggesting that there is an important interaction effect between subject gender and occupation as it relates to fear of success imagery.

Bedeian and Touliatos (1978) found that women with favorable self-esteem scores were significantly higher in achievement need and power need than other women and also were higher in affiliation needs. In general, these results suggest that self-esteem is related to work motives in women. Burlin (1976) studied the relationship between locus of control and ideal versus real occupational aspirations of adolescent females. One hundred thirty-nine eleventh-grade females ranging in age from 14 to 16 were given the Internal-External Scale and two Occupational Aspirations Scales, one measuring real and one measuring ideal occupational aspirations. It was found that internal-locus-of-control subjects were more likely to display agreement between ideal and real occupational aspirations. A considerable number of exceptions, however, were found for internal-locus-of-control women. Finally, a study by Fannin (1979) indicated that sex-role attitude, work-role salience, atypicality of major field, and self-esteem seem to discriminate among the identity stages of achievement moratorium diffusion and foreclosure. Fannin concluded that career development is closely related to other aspects of growth, both for women and for men.

Is the Career Development of Women Like That of Men?

Data exist to indicate that the process of career development in women is both similar to and different from the process for men. On the negative side, indicating differences in the process as a function of sex, are the results of numerous studies. Lewis, Wolins, and Yelsma (1967) demonstrated that women have different educational goals and reactions than men; Greenhaus (1971) and Masih (1967) found that careers occupy a more salient position in the lives of men than in the lives of women; Dole and Passons (1972) found more sex differences than racial differences in a study of educational-vocational goals and values; Fortner (1970) found that girls tend to choose more high-level occupations than boys; Ace, Graen, and Dawis (1972) found sex to be the most influential variable affecting work attitudes; and White (1970) points out the special problem of professional isolation as a result of part-time employment or spaces between employment for women. Lewis (1968), making many generalizations about sex differences in career behavior, asserts that girls make vocational choices earlier than boys; that girls prefer people-oriented to object-oriented jobs and service fields to professional fields; that girls give more consideration to job characteristics than boys do and are less likely to value pay and advancement in their job selection than boys and that girls' choices are more likely to be based on short-term objectives than are those of boys (possibly a response to the need for women to plan careers in the uncertain context of interweaving marriage and career, a task not demanded of men). Walsh and Barrow (1971) found that females are more concerned with status and prestige in work than males, an observation not entirely consistent with that of Gribbons and Lohnes (1968), who observed that boys ranked salary and prestige high for work values, while girls ranked personal contact and social service as important job values.

Evidence indicating that men and women do have essentially the same career development process is provided by several studies. Diamond (1971) found evidence that sex differences in occupational interests are minimal at upper occupational levels though clearly obvious at lower levels. Saleh and Lalljee (1969) found no sex differences in intrinsic versus extrinsic job orientation in samples of university students and public school teachers and found differences for technical employees only when job level was not controlled. Helson (1967) found that "creative young women" possess personality characteristics similar to those of "creative young men." Osipow and Gold (1968) and Roe and Siegelman (1964) report results indicating that the antecedents and adjustment problems of members of both sexes are similar when they cross into occupational activities stereotyped for the opposite sex.

Rose and Elton (1971) predicted that no interaction would be found between sex and occupational category (in Holland's scheme) as a way of examining the need to develop separate theories for men and women. Sex differences along with occupational category differences on the Omnibus Personality Inventory were found, and furthermore, these differences interacted in such a way as to indicate that they were not the same for both sexes. Rose and Elton concluded that while the

Holland system might be modifiable to include women, it needs revision or otherwise some new theory of career development for women is necessary.

A number of studies have examined differences between the sexes in a variety of career-related variables such as interest development. Lunneborg and Gerry (1977) tested the hypothesis that there is less sex stereotyping in occupational choice for people in a college population than in a general population and that this is even more true for women as compared with men. Studying 150 students of each gender on the Strong-Campbell Interest Inventory, they found no differences between the sexes on the general themes and basic interests in occupational scales, except for a greater attraction toward art among females than among males. Compared with a general population, male students seeking career counseling had more artistic and fewer realistic and enterprising interests. This finding is reminiscent of Osipow and Gold's (1968) findings. College females and women in general were basically the same. What differences did exist were those between college men and men in general, which suggests curiously that vocational interests in women do not seem to be changing generationally as a function of the women's movement, but that interests do appear to be changing slightly for males. Is it possible that males are somewhat freer to behave in a less stereotypically male way than formerly? Certainly that has been suggested as one possible outcome of the women's movement.

Richardson (1975) compared women college seniors on self-descriptions, ideal self, and career and homemaking interests, measuring career orientation with Eyde's Desire to Work Scale. Results indicated that self- and career congruence were significantly correlated with marriage values and that self- and homemaker congruence was significantly correlated with marriage, career, and occupational field, as well as level. For the self-and-homemaker-congruent group significantly negative correlations were found between high and medium differentiations and the desire to work as well as between the importance of marriage and career. As expected, the results indicate that women who see themselves as homemakers are not career oriented and that self- and career-role concept similarity is not highly associated with career orientation. This raises questions about the degree to which self-concept implementation through work occurs for women.

Harmon (1981) conducted a long-term follow-up of plans of young adult college women. Three hundred ninety-one women were followed up six years after they entered college. It was found that more than 40 percent were no longer pursuing a bachelor's degree, that almost 66 percent were married, and that almost 50 percent planned to combine family life with a career. More than 70 percent of these women were employed and almost half of them in their chosen careers, which were usually in some kind of social, medical, or clerical area. They had considered an average of nine occupations for themselves since they were high school students, and the "traditional choices" that were popular with these women when they were freshmen in college were still popular but had been joined by other, less traditional choices. Harmon concludes that these results do not support the notion that women of the college and young adult generation have turned in substantial numbers to the nontraditional career areas.

A number of studies have examined gender issues related to career satisfaction. Weaver (1978), replicating samples of U.S. workers three times, found that no sex differences existed in overall level of job satisfaction, despite the typically lower job prestige and the typically lower wages women experience in the workplace. In another study, Weaver and Holmes (1975) tested the hypothesis that work satisfaction would vary with full- versus part-time employment and full- versus part-time homemaking. They questioned more than 600 white females, of whom about half had jobs and about half were full-time homemakers who reported being satisfied with their work. Results suggest that satisfaction with career or homemaking is itself more related to individual variables than to the work setting itself. Sauser and York (1978) tested the hypothesis that sex differences in job satisfaction are usually associated with a number of variables associated with gender membership. The usually observed differences associated with job satisfaction, such as promotion, disappeared when age, organizational tenure, and position tenure were held constant through covariance. Covariance analysis, however, magnified sex differences in satisfaction with variables such as pay, indicating that women are more satisfied with less pay than are men. Since women in the sample studied had lower pay grades and less education than did the males in the sample, the findings indicating a difference in job satisfaction according to gender are likely to reflect these input variables instead of sex-related personality traits. Covariance analysis results revealing that women are significantly more satisfied with their pay than are men is difficult to interpret with confidence, but the investigators suggest that if women are more satisfied than males with respect to their pay as a function of expectancy, this should change as the women's movement increases its impact on the world of work and self-income discrepancies begin to disappear.

The study of "central life interest" has been applied to women in the workplace. Taveggia and Ziemba (1978) examined more than 1000 male and female employees in manufacturing settings and compared them on their work interests. Males were found to be more work oriented than were females, who were found to be more extrinsically oriented to their work. Gender differences in occupational status and opportunities for work mobility seem most related to gender differences in overall life interest.

Finally, Blum (1975) studied the desire for security in careers of men compared with women and found no differences. Some differences, however, in subsamples were found. Men and women in business were different from subsamples of men and women in education in their desire for job security. Therefore, the usual conclusion that occupation rather than gender leads to differences is again supported.

Parental Matters

Sorensen and Winters' (1975) review of parental influences on women's career development summarizes the literature very effectively, and raises many of the issues that have been considered with respect to how women's career choices are influenced by their parents. Sorensen and Winters indicate that the career perceptions and attitudes of daughters are influenced by identification with their mothers and awareness of their mothers' work history. However, the nature of this influence is by no means clear. Furthermore, since we are in a period of social transition, findings of earlier studies may not have validity when extrapolated to current populations. Overall, it is difficult to be conclusive about the results of studies reviewing the effects of fathers on their daughters' careers, but the literature does suggest that fathers influence their daughters' careers at least through the socio-economic status that their own work has generated.

Burlin (1976) studied the relationship between daughter's occupational aspirations and father's education, as compared with the relationship between daughter's occupational aspirations and mother's occupational status. He described mother's occupational status in several ways, for example, as traditional or nontraditional in nature. Burlin found that both of the variables were significantly related to the aspirations of adolescent females.

Oliver (1975) compared homemaking versus career-oriented college women. She found that fathers were more important than mothers in determining the career orientation of daughters. Career-oriented college women perceived their fathers differently from the way they perceived their mothers.

In a study of a younger population, Weeks, Little, and Thornburg (1977) tested the hypothesis that five-year-olds exposed to nontraditional work-role models will become less traditional in their vocational role preferences. The treatment involved a two-week curriculum exposing the children to people working in nontraditional careers. No treatment was given to a control group. The results indicated no effect on attitudes after the two-week curriculum. Overall the children were fairly traditional in their work-role attitudes. Of course, a two-week intervention is not very powerful, but that weakness is counterbalanced by the youth of the subjects, who presumably are more susceptible to such an intervention because of the relative permeability of their attitudes at age five.

These few studies indicate the general disarray and lack of conclusiveness of the literature on parental influences on career development in women. It is a truism that parents influence their children in general and particularly in their career choices. Lacking are the details of how this influence occurs. Much of the belief about the influence appears at the moment to require faith rather than data to support it.

Toward a Theory for Women

A reading of the similarities and differences between men and women in their career development suggests that while there are some similarities between the sexes in the career process, enough substantial differences exist to warrant attempts to develop distinctive theories for each gender, at least until such time as true sexual equality of career opportunity exists and the results have permeated society at all levels. Efforts to set the stage for the development of such independent theories have already been made. Zytowski (1969) proposed a set of postulates designed to stimulate research and thought in women's career development. These postulates may be summarized by asserting that although most women are homemakers, the frequency and singularity of this role is changing, and that when a careful observation of women's life roles is made they are seen to be orderly and sequential. Zytowski takes the controversial position that the homemaker role for women is exclusive because its impact on entry into and persistence in the labor market, as well as the level of the work the woman performs in her career. Psathas (1968) makes the point that important elements in women's career development (marriage, timing of children, and spouses' attitudes) are just not considered in theories of career development for men, and thus, separate concepts to explain the process in women are essential.

As Levitt (1971) has pointed out with respect to the vocational development of professional women, several problems exist in our approach. Some questions exist regarding the role of interests. What is the role interests play in predicting career commitment in women? There is lack of agreement among researchers on what constitutes career orientation in women. Finally, how can women who plan to combine marriage and work (or are already doing so) be distinguished from those who plan to engage in either homemaking *or* work as full-time activities. To some extent the following sections deal with these questions.

Aptitudes, Interests, and Achievement in the Career Development of Women

Tyler (1964) reports one of the early studies of interest development in females. One small aspect of a longitudinal study of a small number of career- and non-career-oriented girls, defined in terms of their interest scores on the SVIB, revealed that distinctive interests in females begin to develop prior to age 14, an observation confirmed by Astin's (1968a) Project Talent data. Astin found that ninth-grade interests, plans, and aptitudes were good predictors of twelfth-grade educational-vocational choices. In an extensive report of the study which examined subsamples of girls included in Project Talent, Astin (1968b) found that girls who changed their choices from science, teaching, or some other professional activity generally possessed lower aptitude and achievement records than those girls who persisted in those choices. Furthermore, those girls who originally planned to be housewives but later changed plans earned higher scores on achievement and aptitude tests than girls who persisted in the original choice of housewife. In addition, girls who changed their field of choice were observed to have had lower interest scores in their original field than those who persisted. Once again, as for males, females' choices appear to be substantially influenced by personal abilities, achievement, and possibly interests. However, in a five-year follow-up to the original Project Talent study, Astin and Myint (1971) found that events such as marriage, and scholastic aptitude and socioeconomic status proved, retrospectively, to be the best predictors of occupational activity in women.

Harmon (1970a), looking at a group of women 10 to 14 years after college entrance, found similar results. Most of the events that assumed a significant role in distinguishing career and noncareer women from one another seemed to occur after age 18. Variables such as the number of years of college, age at first marriage, number of children, and age when first child was born, were the kind of variables that separated the two groups. Generally, the "career" women had more years of college, married later, had fewer children, and were older when the first one was born than the "noncareer" women.

In another study, Harmon (1972) followed the careers of 72 nursing students, 32 medical technology students, and 56 social work students, all women, over a two-year period. She found that persistence in the original curriculum was related to SVIB consistency with the choice, being firstborn, and having a mother who worked during the child's early years.

The results of the series of studies by Astin and Harmon suggest that social factors, though not the only important variables in women's career development, loom importantly in a way that is distinctive from the way they do for men. This may be demonstrated, for example, in a study reported by Thomas and Stewart (1971). These investigators had school counselors listen to tapes of girls talking about themselves in an interview setting and then rate the girls on a number of dimensions. The counselors tended to evaluate conforming (traditional career) vocational planning as more positive than "deviant" (pioneer career) vocational talk. Counselors perceived girls with such "deviant" plans as more in need of counseling than girls with conforming plans. As might be expected, female counselors were more accepting of so-called deviant as well as conforming female clients than male counselors. Such evaluations, if widespread, are bound to exert a subtle influence on the career decisions made by women, a factor not likely to be operating on males in the same way. Another study reported by Hawley (1971) tested the hypothesis that "women are influenced in their career development by their perception of what men think is appropriate female behavior." To test this hypothesis, she constructed a career attitude instrument for women yielding five factor analytically derived scales, measuring woman as partner, ingenue, homemaker, competitor, and knower. The scale was administered to 33 homemakers, 30 women in "female" type careers, and 23 women in androgynous or "male" careers. The androgynous women did not see men as possessing ideas about proper career sex roles for women, but the other two groups did. In addition, unmarried women tended to perceive men's attitudes toward women's careers as "separatist" to a greater degree than married women did. Hawley concludes that the "guesses" women make about what men think about careers for women influence female career development substantially. Since such behavior is pervasive and starts early, women's attitudes toward their own careers are likely to be shaped in important ways while the women are still very young girls.

Pioneer Versus Traditional Women

Numerous studies have chosen to classify women into one of two groups, pioneer women, or those engaged seriously in career activities, versus traditional women, or those participating in full-time homemaking activities. One of the early studies displaying such an approach was conducted by Hoyt and Kennedy (1958). Hoyt and Kennedy investigated the two hypotheses: (1) career-oriented and home-making women differ on the housewife, stenographer-secretary, office worker, and elementary teacher scales of the SVIB, and (2) personality differences (not specified) exist between homemakers and career women. A total of 407 freshman women at Kansas State College were given the SVIB and EPPS and then queried about their interests. Of the original sample, the authors formed two groups, a career-oriented group composed of 30 women and a homemaking group consisting of 71 women all of whom were highly oriented toward marriage.

The results revealed a great many significant SVIB differences between the two groups of women. The findings, however, seem somewhat circular. Homemaking women, assigned to a homemaking group in the first place by means of inquiries about their plans, had homemaking interests on the SVIB, while career-oriented women, selected because they had career plans, were found to have interests on the SVIB similar to those of career women.

The results of the EPPS comparisons were more meaningful, however. Career women were found to score higher on needs achievement and intraception, while homemakers had higher needs on heterosexuality and endurance. Thus, the career-oriented woman may be viewed as seeking to prove her worth through vocational accomplishments. The homemakers, on the other hand, seemed to be more highly motivated by needs for affection and acceptance, which are more readily available in marriage than in a career.

Wagman (1966) replicated and extended the Hoyt and Kennedy (1958) study. His findings substantially duplicated those of the early study. The career-oriented women had higher theoretical and lower religious scores on the Allport-Vernon-Lindzey Study of Values than the homemakers. Three interest patterns for the career women on the SVIB were tentatively identified: a verbal-linguistic pattern, including lawyer and social worker; a science-technical pattern represented by physician, nurse, and author; and a combination pattern including psychologist and several other occupations that overlapped the two major patterns. In contrast only one pattern was found for the homemaking women: dietician, housewife, and home economist.

Career versus marriage orientation in women is obviously an important variable to be studied in connection with female career development. Watley and Kaplan (1971), examining the career aspirations of more than 800 female National Merit Scholarship winners, found that most (85 percent) indicated they had plans for a career, but important differences in the fields and the timing of these careers were evident. Nearly half planned on marriage *and* an immediate career, about one-third planned on marriage and a deferred career, and the remaining one-fifth was evenly divided between plans for marriage only, career only, and indecision. Not entirely surprising was the finding that those women planning on immediate careers (or careers only) were more likely to be found in the humanities and arts, while the marriage and deferred career women were commonly found in education fields. Farley (1970) has shown that career women differ from noncareer women in a number of important ways: career women desire fewer children, are more willing to use child-care facilities, are less willing to give priority to their husband's career, and are more likely to intend to work while their children are preschoolers than noncareer women.

Other investigators have reported differences between pioneer and traditional women. Rezler (1967), defining pioneers as females who wanted to study medicine, mathematics, and the natural sciences and traditionals as girls who wanted to study nursing or elementary teaching, compared 33 high school juniors and seniors of each type on the Kuder Vocational Preference Record, the Vocational Preference Inventory, and the California Test of Mental Maturity. Pioneers were found to be higher on computational and scientific and lower on social service interests, higher on the intellectual and masculine and lower on the social, self-control, and status scales of the VPI, and higher on CTMM IQ. Rand (1968), comparing the responses of 828 pioneer and traditional college freshwomen on the American College Survey, found evidence to indicate a "masculine" orientation in career women. Of course, numerous questions have been raised about the meaning of masculinity and femininity as these are usually scaled (for example, Diamond, 1971), so it is hard to interpret Rand's findings. Along a similar line, Elton and Rose (1967) found two discriminants on the basis of the Omnibus Personality Inventory (OPI) and the American College Test administered to over 600 college women. One dimension was called scholarly-practical, the other masculine-feminine, and these were related to curricular choices. Other studies (for example, Parker, 1966; Gysbers, Johnston, and Gust, 1968) have also demonstrated that psychometric and demographic differences between traditional and homemaking women can be identified. This effort seems to have culminated in an effort by Schissel (1968) to develop a career orientation scale for women based on the SVIB-W. On the basis of comparisons between career-oriented women (defined as those who had worked for five consecutive years) and noncareer women (who did not work within two years of leaving school, before or after marriage), Schissel found that career women do have interests different from noncareer-oriented women. The most discriminating scales were production manager and, once again, masculinity-femininity. The problems with Schissel's scale, however, lie in the lack of cross-validation data and the fact that the career-noncareer definition may not really represent an important distinction.

Several studies have approached the study of career versus traditional women by assuming that three, not two types of women exist with respect to vocational development: the homemaker, who exhibits no out-of-home work activity; the traditional career-oriented woman, who works but in a female-dominated or accepted work setting; and the pioneer career woman, who works in a male-dominated field where women are either not commonly found or well accepted or both. Nagely (1971) studied the responses of two groups of twenty women each, all mature, married, and mothers, to a TAT-like instrument, an attitude scale, and a biographical questionnaire. One group of women was working in traditional women's fields, the other in nontraditional fields, but both groups were "career-oriented" in the sense that they were committed to out-of-home vocational activity. One particularly interesting difference was found between these two groups. The women in nontraditional careers seemed more career-committed than those in traditional careers, yet seemed to have more successfully integrated their working and family roles than the women in the traditional fields.

Working independently, Wolkon (1972) divided women into two groups, pioneer and traditional, on the basis of their responses to two scales: the Desire to Work Scale and the Ranked Work Scale. The resulting data, however, indicated that really three groups exist: homemakers, traditional career women, and pioneer career women. An interesting aspect of the pioneer women was the fact that they were less concerned with economic motives in their work than with the satisfaction of mastery and independence motives.

Kriger (1972) also compared two groups of career women, calling those in female-dominated occupations "homemakers" and those in male-dominated occupations "career women." Based on the adaptation of Roe's (1957) theory, she predicted that women in female-dominated occupations would report perceptions of their parents' child-rearing attitudes as overprotective, and that women in male-dominated occupations would report perceptions of child-rearing attitudes as accepting and casual. The results indicated that career orientation is a function of parental practice. The field and level of each woman appeared to be a function of her achievement motivation, which in turn seemed to be related to her perception of her parents' treatment of her as a child. Kriger presents the interesting idea that instead of using the notion of an orientation toward or not toward people to account for career development (mostly in men) later in life, examination of parental treatment of daughters should be used to predict orientation toward homemaking or toward a career for women. Kriger suggests that parental overcontrol leads to a homemaking orientation, while parental casualness leads toward a career orientation.

A significant question that remains, not nearly satisfactorily answered is what events influence a woman's career direction. Baruch, Segal, and Handrick (1968) used a structured projective technique to study career motivations in women and tentatively concluded that married working women identify with male figures while housewives identify with female figures. Matthews and Tiedeman (1964) found data which suggest that girls' career-marriage attitudes are a function of their developmental stage. Such observations, however, still seem to raise more questions than they provide answers. And, finally, occasionally a truly puzzling result is encountered. Harmon (1967), comparing the SVIB profiles of women whose lives outside the home had been permanently interrupted by marriage with those of women who had worked outside the home consistently during the same twenty-year period, found no differences!

Counseling Women about Careers

Controversy has arisen concerning whether or not career counselors display their sex stereotypes and thus contribute to the difficulties women have in career development. Ahrons (1976) administered 326 semantic differential questionnaires to counselors in school and found that the counselors generally held the traditional view of female work roles involving home-career conflict. Since these counselors operate, at least implicitly, out of a sex-stereotyping context, some influence on how they deal with high school female students making career decisions is likely. Lunneborg (1978), on the other hand, found no sex differences between high school and college samples regarding style of decision making, vocational decisiveness, and vocational self-concept and concluded that gender-based differential career counseling does not seem appropriate. Though these two observations are not on a continuum, they do suggest that while there is nothing inherently different about career decision making in women that requires different counseling, nevertheless, if counselors display bias, they can create some problems for the young women who are trying to get help from counseling professionals.

Similarly, the study of Moreland, Harren, Krimsky-Montague, and Tinsley (1979) found that for both men and women sex roles and self-concepts were related to decision-making styles. This is consistent with Lunneborg's conclusion that processes seem to be similar for men and women, although the Moreland et al. study found that women tended to use both rational and intuitive styles, while men tended to use only rational styles. Donahue and Costar (1977) conducted a study to document counselor bias toward females. Their results, based on responses to a case-study analysis presented to 300 randomly selected senior high school counselors, led to the conclusion that perhaps counselors recommend occupations for their female clients that pay less money, require less education, and are more closely supervised than for males. This conclusion was roundly criticized by Smith (1979), who asserted that a number of major limitations exist in the Donahue and Costar study. Smith concluded that more than ten years of research on sex bias have not produced results which allow the conclusion that counselors discriminate against women. Thus, the gender bias controversy continues.

Another study done by Price and Borgers (1977) required 13 counselors to rate the appropriateness of courses taken by more than 3400 students in high school. The results indicated that not only did the male and female counselors not differ in their judgments about the appropriateness of the choices made by male and female subjects, but that female students made more appropriate choices than males. However, it is impossible to conclude that this finding does not reflect counselor bias, because the fact that the females made "better" or "more appropriate" choices than males could be attributed to greater vocational maturity in females than in males. It could also be attributed to the possibility that females were fitting into sex-role stereotypes and expectations better than their male counterparts.

It is difficult to conduct well-designed studies to test the gender-bias hypothesis, and perhaps the best that can be done now is to alert counselors to the possibilities of bias in themselves and at the same time to avoid automatically assuming that all counselors are biased regarding work choices made by female clients. What does seem to be clear is that outside of the bias issue the processes of career development and the necessary counseling that results appear to be the same for both genders.

Barriers to Women's Careers

Gold (1978) reviewed a number of the barriers confronting women who are trying to implement careers. These appear to boil down primarily to sex-role stereotyping and value conflicts. In another extensive review of the literature, Mishler (1975) also examined a variety of factors that interfere with women's career development. For example, gender-related ability differences have been thought to account for sex differences in work. However, there are few documented innate sexual differences in abilities which would impose barriers to women's career development. It is generally agreed that women are not as powerful as men in muscular strength because of hormonal differences, which result in differences in musculature, but even those differences apparently can be moderated to a significant degree by training, even though perhaps such training has not frequently been done. Intellectual differences between the sexes are for the most part minimal. Some data exist to suggest that the rate of development of verbal, spatial, numerical, and analytical abilities is different across gender, but it is hard to know whether these differences are innate, whether there is a developmental difference, or whether both these possibilities are confounded with social stimuli.

A major barrier for women in work has to do with attitudes toward career and marriage. Women in general still give careers second place to marriage and even highly career-oriented professional women have different kinds of expectations and pressures with respect to their marriage roles than do men. While dramatic examples of expectations are noted in the popular media, they still remain relatively infrequent and most spouse pairs still have sex-stereotyped role assignments which work to the disadvantage of women implementing career objectives. Another variable, of course, is the sex-role stereotypes which further exert pressure to keep men in "men's jobs" and women in "women's jobs" and thus restrict the range of work activities of the sexes. Other factors that Mishler mentions that interfere with women's ability to implement career preferences and abilities include psychological services which may be biased; self-defeating behaviors of women; what Mishler calls the masculine mandate, for example, the perception that women's attitudes and behaviors are all to be interpreted in the context of masculine desires and values; sex typing of work; formal as well as informal discrimination; role conflict and overload; and time and vocation constraints placed upon women because they live where it is convenient for their husbands to live with respect to work, more often than where it is convenient for themselves.

Marriage is a major constraint on women's career development. In one study, Hall (1975) sampled a group of college women, in which graduations at each of the five-year points between 1948 and 1968 were represented. He found that pressures from home and work, as well as from self, vary significantly with family stages. Personal variables of children and responsibilities from home are clearly involved. Miyahira (1975) reviewed a number of studies dealing with marriage and women's work, concluding that in general work effectiveness and satisfaction was negatively correlated with marital satisfaction. Summarizing the review, Miyahira points out several generalizations, as follow: 1) Career-committed women remain marriage oriented even though they may marry later than women who are traditionally oriented. 2) Marital satisfaction related significantly to women's attitudes toward working and the rewards they get from homemaking. 3) Husbands' attitudes are one of the most important factors affecting whether their wives are employed and, if so, the kind of work they do. 4) The younger the children at home, the less likely women are to be working outside the home. 5) Family income influences when wives are employed and for how long. 6) As might be expected, career-oriented women have more education in general than noncareer-oriented women.

Summary

The most apt way to summarize current understandings about the career development of women is to make several assertions. First, the study of women's careers is a highly timely endeavor. Second, there are data which indicate that women's careers are not substantially different from men's, and at the same time, data exist suggesting just the opposite conclusion. One hypothesis might be that at the extremes of vocational levels certain similarities exist: the career of the woman functioning vocationally at very high professional levels and the woman at the unskilled level may bear more similarities to their male counterparts than the large mass of women in the middle-level careers. Even so, there are likely to be important sex distinctions between men's and women's careers and their perceptions of their careers, as well as in the way they perform their duties in the same positions. It does seem clear that women frequently face obstacles that affect the pay they receive, promotions, and the accessibility of certain positions as a function of sex, and these discriminations naturally would be expected to exert an influence on female career development not experienced by men. A third and final assertion that might be made about women's careers is that so much social change is occurring in the area of sex and vocation that any theoretical proposal made now is likely to be premature, as would be any generalization about women's career development.

REFERENCES

Ace, M. E., Graen, G. B., and Dawis, R. V. Biographic correlates of work attitudes. *Journal of Vocational Behavior*, 1972, *2*, 191–199.

Ahrons, C. R. Counselor's perceptions of career images of women. *Journal of Vocational Behavior*, 1976, *8*, 197–207.

Astin, H. S. Factors associated with the participation of women doctorates in the labor force. *Personnel and Guidance Journal*, 1967, *46*, 240–246.

Astin, H. S. Career development of girls during the high school years. *Journal of Counseling Psychology*, 1968, *15*, 536–540. (a)

Astin, H. S. Stability and change in the career plans of ninth grade girls. *Personnel and Guidance Journal*, 1968, *46*, 961–966. (b)

Astin, H. S., and Myint, T. Career development of young women during the post high school years. *Journal of Counseling Psychology Monographs*, 1971, *18*, 369–393.

Barnett, R. C. Sex differences and age trends in occupational preference and occupational prestige. *Journal of Counseling Psychology*, 1975, *22*, 35–38.

Baruch, R. The achievement motive in women: a study of the implications for career development. Unpublished doctoral dissertation. Harvard University, 1966.

Baruch, R., Segal, S., and Handrick, F. A. Constructs of career and family: a statistical analysis of thematic material. *Journal of Counseling Psychology*, 1968, *15*, 308–316.

Bedeian, A. G., and Touliatos, J. Work-related motives and self-esteem in American women. *Journal of Psychology*, 1978, *99*, 63–70.

Blum, S. H. The desire for security in vocational choice: a comparison of men and women. *Journal of Psychology*, 1975, *91*, 277–281.

Burlin, F. D. The relationship of parental education and maternal work in occupational status through occupational aspiration in adolescent females. *Journal of Vocational Behavior*, 1976, *9*, 99–104.

Burlin, F. D. Locus of control and female occupational aspirations. *Journal of Counseling Psychology*, 1976, *23*, 126–129.

Diamond, E. E. Occupational interests: male-female or high level-low level dichotomy. *Journal of Vocational Behavior*, 1971, *1*, 305–315.

Dole, A. A., and Passons, W. R. Life goals and plan determinants reported by black and white high school seniors. *Journal of Vocational Behavior*, 1972, *2*, 209–222.

Donahue, T. J., and Costar, J. W. Counselor discrimination against young women in career selection. *Journal of Counseling Psychology*, 1977, *24*, 41–46.

Elton, C. F., and Rose, H. A. Significance of personality in the vocational choice of college women. *Journal of Counseling Psychology*, 1967, *14*, 293–298.

Esposito, R. P. Relationship between motive to avoid success and vocational choice. *Journal of Vocational Behavior*, 1977, *10*, 347–357.

Eyde, L. D. Work motivation of women college graduates: five year follow-up. *Journal of Counseling Psychology*, 1968, *15*, 199–202.

Fannin, P. M. The relation between ego identity status and sex role attitude, work role salience, atypicality of major, and self-esteem in college women. *Journal of Vocational Behavior*, 1979, *14*, 12–22.

Farley, J. Graduate women: career aspirations and desired family size. *American Psychologist*, 1970, *25*, 1099–1100.

Fidell, L. S. Empirical verification of sex discrimination in hiring practices in psychology. *American Psychologist*, 1970, *25*, 1094–1098.

Fitzgerald, L. S., and Crites, J. O. Toward a career psychology of women: what do we know? What do we need to know? *Journal of Counseling Psychology*, 1980, *27*, 44–62.

Fortner, M. L. Vocational choices of high school girls: can they be predicted? *Vocational Guidance Quarterly*, 1970, *18*, 203–206.

Fried, M. A. Is work a career? *Trans-action*, 1966, *3*, 42–47.

Giuliani, B., and Centra, J. A. The woman veterinarian. *Personnel and Guidance Journal*, 1968, *46*, 971–975.

Gold, A. R. Re-examining barriers to women's career development. *American Journal of Orthopsychiatry*, 1978, *48*, 690–702.

Greenhaus, J. H. An investigation of the role of career salience in vocational behavior. *Journal of Vocational Behavior*, 1971, *1*, 209–216.

Gribbons, W. D., and Lohnes, P. R. *Emerging Careers*. New York: Columbia University, Teachers College Press, 1968.

Gysbers, N. C., Johnston, J. A., and Gust, T. Characteristics of homemakers and career-oriented women. *Journal of Counseling Psychology*, 1968, *15*, 541–546.

Hall, D. T. Pressures from work, self, and home in the life stages of married women. *Journal of Vocational Behavior*, 1975, *6*, 121–132.

Harmon, L. W. Women's working patterns related to their SVIB housewife and "own" occupational scores. *Journal of Counseling Psychology*, 1967, *14*, 299–301.

Harmon, L. W. Anatomy of career commitment in women. *Journal of Counseling Psychology*, 1970, *17*, 77–80.

Harmon, L. W. The childhood and adolescent career plans of college women. *Journal of Vocational Behavior*, 1971, *1*, 45–56.

Harmon, L. W. Variables related to women's persistence in educational plans. *Journal of Vocational Behavior*, 1972, *2*, 143–154.

Harmon, L. W. The life and career plans of young adult college women: a follow-up story. *Journal of Counseling Psychology*, 1981, *28*, 416–427.

Hawley, P. What women think men think: does it affect their career choice? *Journal of Counseling Psychology*, 1971, *18*, 193–199.

Helson, R. Personality characteristics and developmental history of creative college women. *Genetic Psychology Monographs*, 1967, *76*, 205–256.

Hoult, P. P., and Smith, M. C. Age and sex differences in the number and variety of occupational choices, preferences, and aspirations. *Journal of Occupational Psychology*, 1978, *51*, 119–125.

Hoyt, D. P., and Kennedy, C. E. Interest and personality correlates of career motivated and homemaking motivated college women. *Journal of Counseling Psychology*, 1958, *5*, 44–48.

Janda, L. H., O'Grady, K. E., and Kapps, C. F. Comparison of success in males and females in sex-linked occupations. *Sex Roles*, 1978, *4*, 43–50.

Kaldor, D. B., and Zytowski, D. G. A maximizing model of occupational decision-making. *Personnel and Guidance Journal*, 1969, *47*, 781–788.

Knell, S., and Winer, G. A. Effects of reading content on occupational sex role stereotypes. *Journal of Vocational Behavior*, 1979, *14*, 78–87.

Kriedber, G., Butcher, A. L., and White, K. M. Vocational role choice in second and sixth grade children. *Sex Roles*, 1978, *4*, 175–181.

Kriger, S. F. Need achievement and perceived parental childrearing attitudes of career women and homemakers. *Journal of Vocational Behavior*, 1972, *2*, 419–432.

Lenney, E. Women's self-confidence in achievement settings. *Psychological Bulletin*, 1977, *84*, 1–13.

Lerner, R. M., Benson, P., and Vincent, S. Development of societal and personal role perception in males and females. *Journal of Genetic Psychology*, 1976, *129*, 167–168.

Levitt, E. S. Vocational development of professional women: a review. *Journal of Vocational Behavior*, 1971, *1*, 375–385.

Lewis, E. C. *Developing women's potential*. Ames, Iowa: Iowa State University Press, 1968.

Lewis, E. C., Wolins, L., and Yelsma, J. J. The academic interests of college women: a factorial study. *Personnel and Guidance Journal*, 1967, *46*, 258–262.

Looft, W. R. Sex differences in the vocational aspirations of elementary school children. *Developmental Psychology*, 1971, *5*, 366.

Looft, W. R. Vocational aspirations of second grade girls. *Psychological Reports*, 1971, *28*, 241–242.

Lunneborg, P. W. Sex and decision-making style. *Journal of Counseling Psychology*, 1978, *25*, 299–305.

Lunneborg, P. W., and Gerry, M. H. Sex differences in changing sex stereotype vocational interest. *Journal of Counseling Psychology*, 1977, *24*, 247–250.

Masih, L. K. Career saliency and its relation to certain needs, interests, and job values. *Personnel and Guidance Journal*, 1967, *45*, 653–658.

Matthews, E., and Tiedeman, D. V. Attitudes toward career and marriage and the development of life style in young women. *Journal of Counseling Psychology*, 1966, *11*, 375–383.

Meir, E. I., Camon, A., and Sardi, Z. Prediction of persistence at work of women dentists. *Personnel and Guidance Journal*, 1967, *46*, 247–251.

Mishler, S. A. Barriers to the career development of women. In Osipow, S. H. (Ed.), *Emerging woman: career analysis and outlooks*. Columbus, Ohio: Charles E. Merrill, 1975.

Miyahira, S. D. Marriage and the employment of women. In Osipow, S. H. (Ed.), *Emerging woman: career analysis and outlooks*.

Moreland, J. R., Harren, V. A., Krimsky-Monague, E., and Tinsley, H. E. A. Sex roles, self-concept, and decision making. *Journal of Counseling Psychology*, 1979, *26*, 329–336.

Nagely, D. L. Traditional and pioneer working mothers. *Journal of Vocational Behavior*, 1971, *1*, 331–341.

O'Bryant, S. L., Durrett, M. E., and Pennebaker, J. W. Developmental and sex differences in occupational preferences. *Journal of Social Psychology*, 1978, *106*, 267–272. (a)

O'Bryant, S. L., Durrett, M. E., and Pennebaker, J. W. Student ratings of occupational dimensions of traditionally male and traditionally female occupations. *Journal of Vocational Behavior*, 1978, *12*, 297–304. (b)

Oliver, L. W. The relationship of parental attitudes and parent identification to career and homemaking orientation in college women. *Journal of Vocational Behavior*, 1975, *7*, 1–12.

Osipow, S. H., (Ed.). *Emerging woman: career analysis and outlooks*. Columbus, Ohio: Charles E. Merrill, 1975.

Osipow, S. H., and Gold, J. A. Personal adjustment and career development. *Journal of Counseling Psychology*, 1968, *15*, 439–443.

Parker, A. W. Career and marriage orientation in the vocational development of college women. *Journal of Applied Psychology*, 1966, *50*, 232–235.

Pratt, A. B. Exploring stereotypes of popular and unpopular occupations among women in general. *Journal of Vocational Behavior*, 1975, *6*, 145–164.

Price, G. E., and Borgers, S. An evaluation of the sex stereotyping effect as related to counselor preceptions of courses appropriate for high school students. *Journal of Counseling Psychology*, 1977, *24*, 240–243.

Psathas, G. Toward a theory of occupational choice for women. *Sociology and Social Research*, 1968, *52*, 253–268.

Rand, L. M. Masculinity or feminity? Differentiating career-oriented and homemaking-oriented college freshmen women. *Journal of Counseling Psychology*, 1968, *15*, 444–450.

Rand, L. M., and Miller, A. L. A developmental cross-sectioning of women's career and marriage attitudes and life plans. *Journal of Vocational Behavior*, 1972, *2*, 317–332.

Rezler, A. G. Characteristics of high school girls choosing traditional or pioneer vocations. *Personnel and Guidance Journal*, 1967, *45*, 659–665.

Richardson, M. S. Self-concepts and role concepts in the career orientation of college women. *Journal of Counseling Psychology*, 1975, *22*, 122–126.

Roe, A. Early determinants of vocational choice. *Journal of Counseling Psychology*, 1957, *4*, 212–217.

Roe, A., and Siegelman, M. *The origin of interests*. APGA Inquiry Series No. 1, Washington, D.C.: American Personnel and Guidance Association, 1964.

Rose, H. A., and Elton, C. F. Sex and occupational choice. *Journal of Counseling Psychology*, 1971, *18*, 456–461.

Saleh, S. D., and Lalljee, M. Sex and job orientation. *Personnel Psychology*, 1969, *22*, 465–471.

Sauser, W. I., Jr., and York, C. M. Sex differences and job satisfaction: a re-examination. *Personnel Psychology*, 1978, *31*, 537–547.

Schissel, R. F. Development of a career orientation scale for women. *Journal of Counseling Psychology*, 1968, *15*, 257–262.

Sedney, M. A., and Turner, B. E. A test of causal sequences in two models for development of career orientation in women. *Journal of Vocational Behavior*, 1975, *6*, 281–292.

Shinar, E. H. Sexual stereotypes of occupations. *Journal of Vocational Behavior*, 1975, *7*, 99–111.

Smith, M. L. "Counselor Discrimination" based on client sex: reply to Donahue and Costar. *Journal of Counseling Psychology*, 1979, *26*, 270–272.

Sorenson, J., and Winters, C. J. Parental influences on women's career development. In Osipow, S. H. (Ed.), *Emerging woman: career analysis and outlooks*. Columbus, Ohio: Charles E. Merrill, 1975.

Suchner, R. W., and Moore, D. M. Stereotypes of males and females in two occupations. *Journal of Vocational Behavior*, 1975, *6*, 1–8.

Taveggia, T. C., and Ziemba, T. Linkages to work: a study of the "centralized interest and work attachments of male and female workers." *Journal of Vocational Behavior*, 1978, *12*, 305–320.

Thomas, A. H., and Stewart, N. R. Counselor response to female clients with deviate and conforming career goals. *Journal of Counseling Psychology*, 1971, *18*, 352–357.

Tibbetts, S. L. Sex role stereotyping in lower grades: part of the solution. *Journal of Vocational Behavior*, 1975, *6*, 255–261.

Tyler, L. E. The development of career interests in girls. *Genetic Psychology Monographs*, 1964, *70*, 203–212.

Wagman, M. Interests and values of career and homemaking-oriented women. *Personnel and Guidance Journal*, 1966, *44*, 794–801.

Walsh, W. B., and Barrow, C. A. Consistent and inconsistent career preferences and personality. *Journal of Vocational Behavior*, 1971, *1*, 271–278.

Weaver, C. N. Sex differences in the determinants of job satisfaction. *Academy of Management Journal*, 1978, *21*, 265–274.

Weaver, C. N., and Holmes, S. L. A comparative study of the work satisfaction with full-time employment and full-time housekeeping. *Journal of Applied Psychology*, 1975, *60*, 117–118.

Weeks, M. O., Little, L. S., and Thornburg, K. R. Impact of exposure to nontraditional vocational role models on vocational role preferences of five-year-old children. *Journal of Vocational Behavior*, 1977, *10*, 139–145.

White, M. S. Psychological and social barriers to women in science. *Science*, 1970, *170*, 413–416.

Wolkon, K. A. Pioneer versus traditional: two distinct vocational patterns of college alumnae. *Journal of Vocational Behavior*, 1972, *2*, 275–282.

Zytowski, D. G. Toward a theory of career development for women. *Personnel and Guidance Journal*, 1969, *47*, 660–664.

CHAPTER SEVENTEEN
APPLICATIONS

Career development theory has become increasingly useful. A broad range of interventions and assessment techniques has become available and is centered around helping people identify, select, enter, and function effectively in careers. While these methods include diverse procedures ranging from career education to computer-assisted counseling, the heart of the field lies in career counseling.

CAREER COUNSELING

A spate of writing concerning career counseling has occurred over the last decade. The increase in the quantity of specific suggestions and research evaluations of career counseling in the 1970s and 1980s, compared with earlier decades, is quite remarkable. Part of the increase is represented by several full-length book treatments dealing with career counseling (for example, Crites, 1981; Whiteley and Resnikoff, 1978; Seligman, 1980; Healy, 1974; 1975; and 1982), as well as a number of major papers dealing with career counseling (for example, Vetter, 1978; Fitzgerald and Crites, 1979). In addition to those major treatments of career counseling techniques and procedures, a number of major papers have appeared concerning career counseling research and evaluation (for example, Oliver, 1979; Fretz, 1981; Osipow, 1982, in press; and Spokane and Oliver, 1983, in press). Finally, a major new description of career counseling problems through the life span has also appeared, one which leads to the development of a major taxonomy to use in the diagnosis of adult career problems (Campbell, Cellini, Shaltry, Long, Pinkos, and Crites, 1979; Campbell and Cellini, 1981). The status of career counseling is still emerging but increasingly looks like a professional speciality with its own armamentarium.

Effects of Counseling on Educational-Vocational Adjustment

Most of the studies of the role of educational-vocational counseling in career decision (for example, Gonyea, 1962; 1963; Hewer, 1966; Apostal, 1960; Marks, Ashby, and Ziegler, 1965; Marks, Ashby, and Noll, 1966; Hill and Grieneeks, 1966) have raised serious questions about the effect of counseling on educational performance or vocational decisions, or at least have challenged the common criteria called into use in evaluating counseling. Typically, criterion studies have compared the performance or decisions of groups of students receiving counseling with those who have not been counseled or who might have been counseled in different ways. Inferences were drawn about the adequacy of the performance or decisions and the ways counseling may have contributed to the adequacy or shortcomings of the behavior observed.

Three problems seem to be inherent in this technique. First, the actual counseling procedures to which individuals are exposed are rarely described in an explicit fashion, and thus it becomes exceedingly difficult to identify genuine differences in experiences of counseled or noncounseled groups. Second, the outcomes are frequently evaluated in highly specific terms. Did the subject choose to major in engineering after counseling and was he or she an engineer five years after college? How many and what kinds of changes in academic major occurred after counseling? This type of question fails to recognize that entering engineering at college graduation may have been very appropriate at the time, but that in the normal process of career development, an individual may quite properly change to another field. One's exposure to engineering studies may contribute crucially to one's later career in city planning, in government, or in management.

A study by Hollender (1971) illustrates some of the problems involved in considering the outcomes of vocational counseling. Hollender examined the hypothesis that vocational decisiveness increases with age by studying a cross section of 5200 students in grades six through twelve. He found that about 30 percent of his sample entered adolescence undecided about vocational plans and about 30 percent finished high school undecided and concludes that no change in decisiveness about career plans occurs during adolescence. The critical point is whether or not the 30 percent undecided when entering adolescence is the same 30 percent undecided at high school graduation. Obviously, since Hollender's study is cross-sectional, the two are not the same, and in that light it is potentially misleading to draw the conclusion that no changes in decisiveness occur during adolescence. In a similar way, averaging outcomes regarding decisions about careers following counseling may mask important individual changes.

Third, the sources of judgments made introduce irrelevant bias. In Hewer's study (1966) it was observed that counselor judgments about the realism of client career choices made at the completion of counseling did not agree with student judgments about the appropriateness of their current work and the decisions they had made some years earlier. In fact, the clients saw more relation between their current jobs and past decisions than did the counselors, suggesting, quite reasonably, that they had sources of information connecting the events in their lives in a more meaningful way than did the counselors. Career development theory is intimately bound to research in career decision making and its effectiveness. To improve current research efforts, a number of steps might be considered: first, a broadening of the sampling usually obtained and an increase of follow-up data; second, greater willingness to use interview data in combination with more objective data-collection techniques; third, the use of experimental designs which avoid the effects of biases in sampling resulting from the study only of people coming to counseling centers for help and which would also facilitate replication and allow the introduction of treatment procedures in sequence much as Crites (1964, p. 305) has suggested; finally, more explicit description of input variables, experimental conditions, and expected and observed outcomes.

Two questions may be raised with regard to applications to practical matters: what should vocational counseling attempt to accomplish, and how should it go about its tasks? Related to the first question is the additional question of the degree to which vocational counseling should attempt to be preventive and facilitative in nature versus corrective or rehabilitative. It would probably be widely agreed that the development of facilitative programs for career behavior is the most efficient approach in the long run, but given our imperfect world and its imperfect inhabitants, the fact is that the development of some people will become disrupted and efforts to correct problems in their development will be necessary.

Most career development theories are written descriptively so that either a facilitative or rehabilitative approach is possible. However, most counseling theorists have grown up in the tradition of problem-centered counseling, and thus most thought has been given to the corrective aspects of career counseling. Many clinical techniques and concepts have been applied directly, and sometimes inappropriately, to the matters of career development.

Clinical Procedures and Career Development

Ivey and Morrill (1968) have taken the interesting point of view that "career process" is an aspect of mental health and general development and, as a result, suggest that counseling activities should deemphasize career choice and intensify the emphasis placed on helping individuals become aware of the continuity that runs through their lives. The point of view expressed by Ivey and Morrill represents only one aspect of the impact on thinking about vocational counseling that clinical psychology has exerted. Also growing out of the clinical tradition is the recognition of the importance of identifying the client's problem and deciding what might be done to best resolve the difficulty. In simple terms, Pepinsky's (1948) list of client problems summarizes the variety of career problems presented to counselors. The problem areas, labeled lack of assurance, lack of information, lack of skill, dependence, self-conflict, and choice anxiety, are general in nature, yet suggestive of treatment procedures once the problem is clearly defined. In a more general way, Super (1957) has called for a three-pronged appraisal including assessment of the problem and of the individual and predictions about the outcome.

Many client problems fall under the rubrics suggested by the Pepinsky scheme: mistakes about the parameters of a career; discrepancies between antici-pated rewards and actual events; inappropriate extrapolations of past experiences; misevaluation of skills; faulty labeling of interests; undifferentiated, multiple, adient, or avoidant interest patterns; and interests having no known vocational application. Once so assessed, however, these attitudes are resistant to change on the basis of information and frequently recur at later choice points. Many indi-viduals fail to seek counseling help because they can live with the inefficient decisions they make. Furthermore, these assessment procedures fail to take into account the developmental nature of career behavior. Might it not be more profit-able to develop programs that would educate people to career patterns and career decisions so that they make sound decisions and develop techniques to continue to make them as required during life?

Even though there may be a lack of research evidence to substantiate the use of the "dynamic" model of career counseling (McCabe, 1965) as compared to the trait-factor approach, it must be recalled that the trait-factor approach is limited to specific immediate decisions and that the "dynamic" models, building on the trait-factor approach, try to prepare the individual to make a series of specific decisions (Nachmann, 1965).

Making Vocational Counseling Operational

That counseling is rapidly approaching the need to face the decision of *what* behavior should be changed is demonstrated by a study reported by Krumboltz and Schroeder (1965), who devised a way to assess the use of reinforcement counseling in educational-vocational information gathering. They found that the kind and amount of information-seeking behavior of a student could be influenced by the type of reinforcement procedure followed.

What is critical about this study is the fact that differences in behavior as a function of counseling techniques could be observed and measured. It appears to be possible to get people to change their behavior during interviews in a manner which influences their out-of-interview behavior in significant ways. Now that the rudi-ments of technology to produce change exist, shall they be used to extend informa-tion-seeking behavior or on more socially significant and recurring patterns of behavior? Yabroff (1969), Magoon (1969), and Krumboltz and Sheppard (1969) have described applications of behaviorally oriented techniques to the process of vocational counseling and development. The behavioral methods generally deal with overt, explicit behaviors that can be measured and on which progress can be charted. In addition, the behavioral approaches frequently use simulation techniques to effect the desired growth in individual behavior. Crites' plan for the development of the Career Maturity Inventory (1961) represents another way that a concept critical to career development may be made operational in terms of expected tasks at discrete points in development.

Too often the implications of relevant observations from psychology at large have been overlooked. For example, Izard (1960) observed that individuals who score high on the personality traits of autonomy and dominance on the Edwards Personal Preference Schedule were unlikely to be convinced to change a concept. If the influence of such traits were found to be general, there might be implications for the development of different kinds of counseling procedures on the basis of the personality patterns of the clients, even though the general reason the clients seek counseling might be the same.

Hershenson (1968) has attempted to integrate some of the developmental theories of vocational choice into a single framework. He suggests that five stages exist: an awareness stage, a control stage, a directed stage, a goal-directed stage, and an invested stage. The five stages have the following corresponding vocational modes, respectively: being, play, work, occupation, and vocation. Also, the stages ask the following questions, respectively: "am I?", "who am I?", "what can I do?", "what will I do?", and "what will it mean?" Finally, the stages are measured differently as follows, again respectively: by socialization, attitudes and values, abilities, interests, and satisfaction. In another paper, Hershenson (1969a) has tried to relate these life stages to specific vocational techniques designed to promote progress through the stages. However, a good data base underlying the stages appears to be lacking, and the methods themselves seem to be at a level of abstraction which makes them difficult to apply.

Morrill and Forrest (1970) have summarized approaches to counseling for careers by asserting that four types of methods seem feasible: counseling oriented toward producing a specific vocational decision (traditional counseling), counseling designed to teach decision-making skills so the individual can make good vocational choices throughout his life, counseling which views career development as a process rather than a point in time and focuses on continuity and growth rather than choice, and counseling oriented to helping individuals use their assets to reach their own goals and influence the options open to them.

The literature on career counseling has become so voluminous it is clearly not open to summary as part of a chapter in a book on theories of career development. Selected studies of career counseling, however, may be useful to review in this context. Flake, Roach, and Stennid (1975) used the Career Maturity Inventory as a criterion measure in studying 87 tenth-grade students who were exposed to a short-term counseling intervention over three sessions. Compared with students in control groups, students exposed to counseling increased significantly in their scores on the CMI scales of attitudes and self-appraisal, leading to the conclusion that even brief interventions can be reflected in improvements in measures such as the CMI. Yates, Johnson, and Johnson (1979) used a vocational exploration group process over a five-week period, comparing the outcomes with those of a control group that received no treatment concerning career development. The junior high-school students scored higher on the attitude scale of the CMI in three of the five subtests in the vocational exploration group, compared with none in the control group. Talbot and Birk (1979) examined the degree to which a programmed intervention in vocational exploration is effective compared with other structured interventions. The three structured interventions studied in this investigation (Vocational Exploration Insight Kit, Self-Directed Search, and Vocational Card Sort) all had similarly small effects on women's vocational thinking in terms of the number of occupations considered as possibilities, the proportion of nontraditional occupations considered, and the number of nontraditional occupations considered. Overall, the number of occupations the individual considered to be possible in the group was significantly different for the three approaches compared to a no-treatment control. Counselor free techniques can be helpful and obviously are inexpensive, but do have some limitations based on the results of this study.

Farmer (1978) reviewed research on internal versus external locus of control as it relates to career decision making, largely basing her observations on a study reported by Phares (1976). Some of the summary data concerning locus of control and career choice process have important implications for counseling. Farmer's report indicates that internally oriented people with high self-esteem choose career goals promoting intrinsic satisfaction and tend to choose careers consistent with their values, interests, competencies, and potentials, while externally oriented low self-esteem people tend to be more diffused about their low-range career goals. High self-esteem internal people engage in moderate risk taking related to high achievement motives, while low-esteem external people tend to select tasks that are highly risky in order to have excuses for failure. High self-esteem internal people seem willing to try out new behaviors and persist at them more than do low self-esteem external people. The moral of these findings seems to be that some identification of whether an individual is high or low in self-esteem and externality and internality would be useful before deciding on a counseling program.

Brandt (1977) proposed a complicated outline for delivering career counseling services in a college context. One dimension he used is descriptive of the amount of counselor-client interaction during counseling. A second dimension describes a service in terms of development goals. Such a scheme could be useful in determining treatment in program plans for different kinds of clients.

Krivatsy and Magoon (1976) studied the differential effects of three career counseling treatments in a sample of 113 college students. They compared the effects of Self-Directed Search, Individual Vocational Planning, and Traditional Career Counseling, along with the effect of the absence of career counseling on a control group. The three treatments were apparently equally effective in terms of their outcome, and the absolute levels of outcomes were generally favorable. Krivatsy and Magoon concluded there was some advantage for self-administered counseling methods which seem to leave the subjects feeling more closure about their career decisions than other treatments. Since the methods were supervised by paraprofessionals and involved less student time, they were also more efficient.

Finally, as another variation of career counseling, Morgan and Skovholt (1977) describe the use of what they call inner experience in career counseling. In their procedure individual fantasies and daydreams are used to help people explore career possibilities. They describe methods for both the spontaneous fantasy and guided fantasy approaches and indicate some of the benefits as well as some of the difficulties in the use of such procedures.

Group Methods

Although group methods have a long history in counseling, some resistance has always been expressed to their use, since counseling has been seen as a way to individualize large and impersonal educational institutions. Nevertheless, some imaginative uses of group techniques have been suggested. Ford (1962) has pointed out that responses elicited from individuals by procedures in group settings may be modified in individual settings at a later time. In fact, there may even be some advantages to presenting information in one setting and modifying it in another. People might be inclined to dissociate the source of stimulation from the counselor who sees them later, and the time delay may provide a fruitful incubation period.

Courses dealing with the proper approaches to and information about career decision making have been continually improved and go a long way toward decision-making effectiveness (for example, Salinger, 1966). Group approaches toward alleviating career indecision now seem to be the norm.

Ideas about group methods such as those suggested by Ford (1962) and Magoon (1964) were the forerunners of programs designed to facilitate career development. Magoon (1964), concerned about a shortage of counselors and the general inaccessibility of occupational information, suggested programmatic ways of disseminating career and educational information. Ford (1962) proposed that since educational-vocational counseling attempts to elicit responses relevant to the decision-making task and modify them through the use of the interview, it is theoretically feasible to elicit these responses and response modifiers in group settings, thus saving staff time. Furthermore, experience suggests that group settings thus have unique features which result in greater effectiveness in modifying responses than the individual interview. Other group members are often more potent response eliciters and modifiers than counselors.

Pritchard (1962) suggested an approach to career decision making that discards the use of tests and checklists because they are too stimulus bound. Instead, he suggests a greater emphasis on occupational sociology to provide information about work settings. A program derived from his approach would emphasize the choice process rather than the choice and would aim for closer agreement between occupational and self-exploration by means of real or vicarious work experiences. Such a program would necessarily result in an increasing emphasis on the differences of work settings *within* occupations to bring about a greater tolerance between client and career. Procedures showing people how their general goals might be implemented personally would be a strong move in the direction of increasing individual control over the career development process.

Similarly, programs aimed at prevention of error, correction of difficulties, and the facilitation of growth through planned professional intervention exist. One example is the career education movement. In part, this movement is the result of efforts at theory building in career development and draws heavily on research and ideas in career development theory. Career education is designed to be a system-wide, kindergarten through college education that has vocational choice and development at its heart. The rationale is to make education relevant to career life. Part of the implementation of this rationale involves enhancing career and self-exploration, awareness, and attitude development during childhood and adolescence, the shaping of decision making as well as educational and career-related skills, training, and eventually job placement, all within the context of the curriculum. Formerly, such efforts, where they occurred, tended to be outside the mainstream of school activities. Career education has not been adequately evaluated, but it has influenced those working in the field of career development theory to extend the data base of their work as well as to make their efforts increasingly applied in nature. It is entirely possible in the long run that the effects of career education will change the shape of thinking about career development.

CAREER INDECISION

A good deal of the concern of occupational development theorists has to do with the process of career decision making and the problem of career indecision. A long history of research into the question of the antecedents and cures of career indecision exists. Out of that history of research a variety of conceptions to explain career indecision have been produced as well as a number of interventions. Before these are considered, some review of the major findings dealing with career indecision is in order.

Many studies have compared decided and undecided students with the hope of identifying substantial differences between the two groups in order to better understand both. The results of these studies are mixed. For the most part the data reveal few systematic reliable personality or ability factors involved in whether an individual is decided or undecided about a career. For example, Rose and Elton's results (1971) along with those of Ashby, Wall, and Osipow (1966) suggest that being decided about a career might have something to do with one's achievement and performance pattern, but the data do not suggest the nature of this influence. On the other hand, it should be kept in mind that Baird (1969), in a study based on a much larger sample than either the Rose and Elton study or the Ashby et al. study, did not find *any* ability differences between decided and undecided students.

Clearly, large numbers of students are undecided. Lunneborg (1975) found that 24 percent of more than 1600 college students were undecided about their careers, and that their major difference from the more decided students had to do with ability measures and academic achievement. Interests appeared to have relatively little to do with indecision. Titley et al. (1976) studied career changers in school in an attempt to differentiate between decided and undecided students.

Logically, they found that students who had just changed majors were more able to be specific about their probable career choices than they had been about their previous career choice. However, Titley and his associates also noted a decline in the proportion of students who were able to be specific about their job choices as they moved across the college class years. This finding is apparently paradoxical because, presumably, increasing choice specificity should occur over time. The authors try to explain their finding in terms of the differentiation-integration concept of the Tiedeman and O'Hara theory discussed earlier. In another study, Lunneborg (1976) compared 127 undecided college graduates with college graduates who were decided about their careers. In this study, Lunneborg found that undecideds had significantly lower grade-point averages than did decided students, as well as having fewer plans involving graduate school after college or career activities in general after college, and overall, reported less satisfaction with what had happened to them in college.

One of the hypotheses that has been developed about career indecision is Goodstein's (1965) notion that indecision and undecidedness are different. Specifically, Goodstein suggests that career indecision results from limited experience. McGowan (1977) tested this hypothesis by means of the Self-Directed Search. Sixty-six males and sixty females, selected out of a larger sample of undecided students, took the SDS. Half of those using the SDS arrived at a career choice without the aid of a counselor, leading McGowan to conclude that the SDS appeared to be capable of reducing career indecision. No differences among experimental and control vocationally decided, indecisive, and undecided groups in terms of anxiety level and vocational maturity were found, leading McGowan to conclude that the Goodstein (1965) hypothesis that career indecision and indecisiveness differentially related to anxiety in vocational maturity was not supportable.

Another variable related to the Goodstein notion, and one believed to be valid by counselors in general, has to do with the role of information seeking in reducing career indecision. In one of the few studies examining this variable specifically, Barak, Carney, and Archibald (1975) compared students enrolled in two different kinds of career-oriented workshops. A very complex relationship was found between vocational information-seeking behavior and decidedness. The study does not lend support to the notion that the more occupational information sought by an undecided individual, the more decided such a person will become. It therefore supports the relatively unpopular notion that information is not a panacea for a career-undecided individual.

A different kind of approach was taken by Greenhaus and Simon (1977). They studied the relationship between vocational indecision and level of career salience. Studying 153 students, it was found that a positive correlation existed between low career salients and high frequency of vocational indecision. In addition, they found that vocationally undecided students seem to place less value on intrinsic work values than students who were committed to a field. They conclude that there may be two kinds of vocational indecision—high career salience individuals with high value for intrinsic rewards and low career salience people who do not value intrinsic rewards.

In a major study trying to tease out theoretical implications of vocational decision-making ability, Holland, Gottfredson, and Nafziger (1975) examined a large sample of high school and college students along with employed adults on the Self-Directed Search, the Career Maturity Inventory, a task of decision making, and a number of scales involving vocational choice, identity, anomie, originality, and interpersonal competency. They found that signs that should theoretically predict good decision-making ability did predict scores in the decision-making task better than other predictors. Out of the studies such as Holland's, increasing evidence is developing to suggest that it might be possible to build a picture of a career-undecided individual at a particular time in that person's development. The literature also suggests, however, that individuals change and that these signs are not necessarily stable over a long period of time.

One expected relationship, that indecision is negatively related to occupational interest differentiation, does not appear valid. Lowe (1981) found that the differentiation of interests as measured by the Vocational Preference Inventory was not related systematically to indecision scores measured by the Career Decision Scale. Apparently more is involved in career indecision than uncrystallized career interests.

One of the conceptions that has developed about career indecision is based on decision theory. While the use of decision theory has not been developed extensively by career development theorists and counseling psychologists, one such approach has been reported by Mitchell and Beach (1975). Mitchell and Beach reviewed the research on expectancy in decision models in the context of career choices. They concluded that the empirical results substantially support the use of models, such as decision models, in understanding career decision making. The models assume that individuals will choose careers believed to result in greatest personal benefit, provided the individuals believe that there is a good probability that they can actually obtain a position in that career. This leads Mitchell and Beach to conclude that if people have accurate information about jobs and their work outcomes, adjustment is increased and turnover is reduced. A counseling technique that Mitchell and Beach suggest is to require people to list career alternatives, their pros and cons, and their personal importance. Mitchell and Beach conclude that such a procedure would enable people to consider a wider range of alternatives, which in turn would modify previous evaluations and minimize discomfort with the choice eventually made. One of the reasons that it is likely that these approaches have not been widely used in counseling and by career development theorists is their mathematical base, as well as the spotty development of instrumentation to make external the subjective estimates of probability of success so inherently involved in decision theory.

This discussion would not be complete without mentioning a number of instruments that have been developed over the past decade to further help deal with questions involving career indecision. One measure by Kohen and Breinich (1975) is a standardized measure of occupational information. The instrument, which measures knowledge of the world of work, seems to be adequate in terms of its internal consistency, its ability to discriminate among appropriate groups, and its level of difficulty. A second measure is the Career Decision Scale (Osipow, Carney, Winer, Yanico, and Koschier, 1976). This instrument is designed to identify barriers that prevent individuals from making career decisions. It is based on the rationale that a finite number of relatively discrete circumstances are responsible for problems people have in reaching appropriate closure in implementing career decisions. This Career Decision Scale has been in use for several years and appears to have substantial reliability and reasonable levels of validity for its purposes (Osipow, 1980). A measure by Holland and Holland (1977) takes a slightly different approach to indecision than the Career Decision Scale. It measures indecision as an aspect of personal and vocational identity and suggests that indecision may be interpreted as the outcome of an "indecisive disposition." It sees undecided students as "multiple subtypes" who need different kinds of treatment, a concept inherent in the development of the Career Decision Scale. Finally, Harren's (1976) Assessment of Career Decision Making is a measure of aspects of career indecision that relate to the Tiedman theory of career development. This instrument is often used in both counseling and research and its manual suggests that it possesses a reasonable degree of reliability and validity.

For the interested reader, several additional summaries of career indecision literature are available—Crites' (1981) book on career counseling deals with career indecision extensively. A study by Mendonca and Siess (1976) deals with aspects of career indecision and appropriate literature that might be useful to the reader; Osipow's *Manual for the Career Decision Scale* (1980) also summarizes aspects of the career decision literature.

In sum, the status of knowledge about career indecision has advanced substantially over that of a decade ago. It appears to be increasingly clear that subtypes of career indecision exist, that a variety of treatments can be useful in helping individuals deal constructively with their indecision, and that if people move from one stage of career indecision to another that is not necessarily a bad progression, since each stage is likely to move the individual further toward effectively implementing a satisfactory career life. Conceptually, while our knowledge of career indecision has substantially advanced in recent years, much remains to be learned about the antecedents and interventions that are theoretically plausible as far as career indecision is concerned.

CAREER COUNSELING
RESEARCH

Career counseling research has lagged behind other kinds of counseling research largely because for many years little systematic intervention was done in career counseling aside from the old-fashioned "test them and tell them" approaches. As more sophisticated interventions and assessments have been developed, however, increasing concern has existed about examining the effects of career counseling interventions. This increased interest led Oliver (1978; 1979) to examine the adequacy of outcome measures that had been used in evaluating career counseling research.

Oliver identified a set of outcome measures that relate to career decision making. In the course of her review, she identified many more outcome measures than might have been thought to exist. Unfortunately, however, many of these outcome measures are fairly marginal in nature, having minimal demonstrated validity and reliability. Many of the measures involved rely on self-knowledge as a dependent variable. Many also involve appropriateness of choice as a dependent variable, mostly based on a judge's ratings of the suitability of career choices. In addition, some of the measures are based on instrumental behaviors such as information seeking, with attention to its variety, frequency, and amount. Some are based on interviews or structured questionnaires like the Vocational Exploratory Behavior Inventory. Some of the measures involve attitudes toward career choice, such as commitment, decidedness, career salience, certainty satisfaction, and so on, most of these being measured on a variety of scales. Other outcome measures involve performance, such as test information, occupational information, academic performance, completion of programs or graduation from them, knowledge of careers, and career information accumulated in a variety of ways. Finally, adjustment measures, such as the level of incorporation and self-concept, are also included. Counseling satisfaction ratings, measuring counselor helpfulness, client "feeling tone," usefulness of test data, and helpfulness of information, are also some of the outcome measures often used in evaluating career counseling.

Since the list has been so varied, Oliver concludes that these criteria should be considered in terms of two other criteria: how immediate versus long term they are, and whether or not they rely on behavior change.

Building on the work of Oliver, Fretz (1981) has written a major treatment of the effectiveness of career counseling interventions. Fretz concludes that there is a need to be more specific and systematic in the way we describe the treatments that we use as interventions, the relationships between these treatments, the characteristics of the clientele to which they are applied, and the relationship among the treatments, the clientele's attributes, and the measures we use to assess outcome. Fretz concludes the following: 1) when reporting studies of career intervention, investigators need to be much more explicit and specific about the nature of the intervention and the participants and the outcomes; 2) it would be useful if the costs of each study were reported; 3) at least two or more interventions should be compared in each study; 4) at least four treatment groups should be presented in each study so that there are at least two levels of two different treatments examined; and 5) as many outcome criteria as possible should be used. Fretz's requirements are demanding, but clearly are necessary in order for the field of career counseling to progress substantially.

One of the problems in studying career counseling in the research context is the definition of career counseling (Osipow, 1982, in press). Fretz (1981) clearly alludes to this difficulty when he suggests or urges that the particular intervention studied be specifically described. Career counseling has been construed as everything from individual counseling and programmatic intervention to placement efforts. It has focused on children, adolescents and adults, males and females, and so on, often without specifying who received treatment, leading to a considerable confusion about what has affected what behaviors in what people. Another way to look at the outcome variables that should be specified by career counseling researchers is a list (Osipow, 1982, in press) which includes improved self-awareness, growth in vocational maturity, the development of a list of practical alternatives, development of skills in implementing these alternatives, career entries, satisfaction and advancement, and the widening of an individual's career options, to mention only a few. To sum up, the criterion, according to Osipow (1982, in press) is the major barrier interfering with adequate research inquiry in career counseling.

It should be noted, however, that career counseling does not score badly in terms of its outcomes when the newly developed Meta Analysis Procedure is applied (Spokane and Oliver, 1983, in press). Using the method described by Smith and Glass (1977) and Smith, Glass, and Miller, (1980), Spokane and Oliver calculate the "effect size," which is defined as the difference between the mean of the treated group and the mean of the control group divided by the standard deviation of the control group on a given outcome measure. Applying this procedure to fifty-five studies Spokane and Oliver found that the outcomes of career counseling interventions were positive. One very startling positive conclusion Spokane and Oliver reached based on the fifty-five studies they examined is that clients receiving almost any kind of career intervention are, on the average, better off than more than 80 percent of untreated control group subjects.

CAREER PROBLEMS

The diagnostic taxonomy of adult career problems (Campbell et al., 1979) represents a major step forward in career counseling and career counseling research. Based on the analysis of six major developmental theorists, Campbell and his associates have developed specific statements that describe the events and activities that individuals must deal with from about age twenty through late adulthood and retirement. The object of this effort was to identify events that can lead to problems in career development, so a specific classification could be made to describe the nature of an individual's career difficulty. In the long run, an effort to develop a taxonomy such as the Psychiatric Diagnostic and Statistical Manual is the goal, although a considerable distance remains from the current effort to the attainment of that goal.

The outline of the taxonomy involves statements of problems involved in career decision making, problems involved in the implementation of career plans, and problems involved in organizational and institutional events involving adaptation to those organizations. Each of these four major problem areas are further categorized into subcategories. The four problem areas in career decision making include getting started; information gathering; generating, evaluating, and selecting alternatives; and formulating plans for implementing decisions. The problems in implementing career plans involve the characteristics of the individual and those external to the individual. The problems involved in institutional-organizational performance involve skill ability and knowledge deficiencies, personal factors, and organizational-institutional environment conditions. Finally, the problems in adaptation to organizations involve those associated with initial entry, changes over time, and interpersonal relations.

The taxonomy becomes further specified within each of the problem subcategory areas. The taxonomy is specific to three digits of classifications. The careful reader can easily see how useful such a taxonomy can be to the researcher who is concerned with evaluating the outcomes of various career counseling interventions, as well as to the career counselor who wishes to devise intervention plans tailored to individual clients. While this taxonomy is still so new as to have no substantial research base with which to evaluate it, it represents one of the most substantial steps forward in categorizing career development problems to date.

Summary

Career development theory and practice have developed in the context of a clinical tradition. This tradition has led to some misleading and unproductive efforts because of its overemphasis on diagnosis of problems at the expense of the development of special techniques and programs to facilitate growth. Rather than emphasize stereotyped occupational information, counselors should focus their efforts on the identification and encouragement of desirable career development patterns and provide experiences to facilitate them. In doing so, there should be a greater emphasis on programmatic approaches to counseling. In addition, more realistic career experiences, perhaps with the use of simulation techniques possible through computer technology, should be developed. The goal of career development counseling should be to make career development a more rational and systematic process, as much under the control of the individual as possible.

Finally, it should be noted that career counseling suffers the same liability as other counseling and psychotherapy approaches, in that it is very difficult to devise satisfactory criteria and the means to assess counseling outcomes. This shortcoming limits the degree to which it is possible to assert that definitive intervention effects occur.

REFERENCES

Apostal, R. A. Two methods of evaluating vocational counseling. *Journal of Counseling Psychology*, 1960, 7, 171–175.

Ashby, J. D., Wall, H. W., and Osipow, S. H. Vocational certainty and indecision in college freshmen. *Personnel and Guidance Journal*, 1966, 44, 1037–1041.

Baird, L. L. The undecided student—how different is he? *Personnel and Guidance Journal*, 1969, 47, 429–434.

Barak, A., Carney, C. G., and Archibald, D. The relationship between vocational information seeking and educational and vocational decidedness. *Journal of Vocational Behavior,* 1975, *7,* 149–159.

Brandt, J. D. Model for the delivery of career development programs by college counseling centers. *Journal of Counseling Psychology,* 1977, *24,* 494–502.

Campbell, R. E., Cellini, J. V., Shaltry, P. E., Long, A. E., Pinkos, D., and Crites, J. *A diagnostic taxonomy of adult career problems.* Columbus, Ohio: The National Center for Research in Vocational Education, 1979.

Campbell, R. E., and Cellini, J. V. A diagnostic taxonomy of adult career development problems. *Journal of Vocational Behavior,* 1981, *19,* 175–190.

Crites, J. O. A model for the measurement of vocational maturity. *Journal of Counseling Psychology,* 1961, *8,* 255–259.

Crites, J. O. Proposals for a new criterion measure and improved research design. In Borow, H. (Ed.), *Man in a world of work.* Boston: Houghton Mifflin, 1964.

Crites, J. O. *Career counseling.* New York: McGraw-Hill, 1981.

Crites, J. O. *Career counseling: models, methods, and materials.* New York: McGraw-Hill, 1981.

Farmer, H. Career counseling implications for the lower social class and women. *Personnel and Guidance Journal,* 1978, *56,* 467–471.

Fitzgerald, L. F., and Crites, J. O. Career counseling for women. *The Counseling Psychologist,* 1979, *8,* 33–34.

Flake, H., Roach, J., Jr., and Stennid, W. F. Effects of short-term counseling on career maturity of tenth grade students. *Journal of Vocational Behavior,* 1975, *6,* 73–80.

Ford, D. H. Group and individual counseling in modifying behavior. *Personnel and Guidance Journal,* 1962, *40,* 770–773.

Fretz, B. R. Evaluating the effectiveness of career interventions. *Journal of Counseling Psychology Monograph,* 1981, *28,* 77–90.

Gonyea, G. G. Appropriateness of vocational choice as a criterion of counseling outcome. *Journal of Counseling Psychology,* 1962, *9,* 213–219.

Gonyea, G. G. Appropriateness of vocational choices of counseled and uncounseled college students. *Journal of Counseling Psychology,* 1963, *10,* 269–275.

Goodstein, L. D. Behavior theoretical views of counseling. In B. Steffbre (Ed.), *Theories of counseling.* New York: McGraw-Hill, 1965.

Greenhaus, J. H., and Simon, W. E. Career salience, work values, and vocational indecision. *Journal of Vocational Behavior,* 1977, *10,* 104–110.

Harren, V. A. Preliminary Manual for Interpretation of the Assessment of Career Decision Making. (Form B). Unpublished manuscript. Southern Illinois University, 1976.

Healy, C. C. *Career counseling for teachers and counselors.* Boston: Houghton Mifflin, 1975.

Healy, C. C. *Career counseling in the community college.* Springfield, Ill.: Charles C. Thomas, 1974.

Healy, C. C. *Career development: counseling through the life stages.* Boston: Allyn and Bacon, 1982, in press.

Hershenson, D. B. Life-stage vocational development system. *Journal of Counseling Psychology,* 1968, *15,* 23–30.

Hershenson, D. B. Techniques for assisting life-stage vocational development. *Personnel and Guidance Journal,* 1969, *47,* 776–780.

Hewer, V. H. Evaluation of a criterion: realism of vocational choice. *Journal of Counseling Psychology*, 1966, *13*, 289–294.

Hill, A. H., and Grieneeks, L. Criteria in the evaluation of educational and vocational counseling in college. *Journal of Counseling Psychology*, 1966, *13*, 189–201.

Holland, J. L., Gottfredson, G. D., and Nafziger, D. H. Testing the validity of some theoretical signs of vocational decision making ability. *Journal of Vocational Psychology*, 1975, *22*, 411–422.

Holland, J. L., and Holland, J. E. Vocational indecision: more evidence and speculation. *Journal of Counseling Psychology*, 1977, *24*, 404–414.

Hollender, J. W. Development of vocational decisions during adolescence. *Journal of Counseling Psychology*, 1971, *18*, 244–248.

Ivey, A. E., and Morrill, W. H. Career process: a new concept for vocational behavior. *Personnel and Guidance Journal*, 1968, *46*, 644–649.

Izard, C. E. Personality characteristics associated with resistance to change. *Journal of Consulting Psychology*, 1960, *24*, 437–440.

Kohen, A. I., and Breinich, S. C. Knowledge of the world of work: a test of occupational information for young men. *Journal of Vocational Behavior*, 1975, *6*, 133–144.

Krivatsy, S. E., and Magoon, T. M. Differential effects of three vocational counseling treatments. *Journal of Counseling Psychology*, 1976, *23*, 112–118.

Krumboltz, J. D., and Schroeder, W. W. Promoting career planning through reinforcement. *Personnel and Guidance Journal*, 1965, *44*, 19–26.

Krumboltz, J. D., and Sheppard, L. E. Vocational problem-solving experience. In Krumboltz, J. D., and Thoresen, C. E. (Eds.), *Behavioral counseling: cases and techniques*. New York: Holt, Rinehart and Winston, 1969.

Lowe, B. The relationship between vocational interest differentiation and career undecideness. *Journal of Vocational Behavior*, 1981, *19*, 346–349.

Lunneborg, P. W. Interest differentiation in high school and vocational indecision in college. *Journal of Vocational Behavior*, 1975, *7*, 297–303.

Lunneborg, P. W. Vocational indecision in college graduates. *Journal of Counseling Psychology*, 1976, *23*, 402–404.

McCabe, S. P. Hazards in the use of clinical techniques in vocational counseling. *Personnel and Guidance Journal*, 1965, *43*, 879–881.

McGowan, A. S. Vocational maturity and anxiety among vocationally undecided and indecisive students—effectiveness of Holland's Self Directed Search. *Journal of Vocational Behavior*, 1977, *10*, 196–204.

Magoon, T. M. Innovations in counseling. *Journal of Counseling Psychology*, 1964, *11*, 342–347.

Magoon, T. M. Developing skills for educational and vocational problems. In Krumboltz, J. D., and Thoresen, C. E. (Eds.), *Behavioral counseling: cases and techniques*. New York: Holt, Rinehart and Winston, 1969.

Marks, E., Ashby, J. D., and Noll, G. A. Recommended curricular change and persistence in college. *Personnel and Guidance Journal*, 1966, *44*, 974–977.

Marks, E., Ashby, J. D., and Zeigler, M. L. Recommended curricular change and scholastic performance. *Journal of Counseling Psychology*, 1965, *12*, 17–22.

Mendonca, J. D., and Siess, T. F. Counseling for indecisiveness: problem solving and anxiety management training. *Journal of Counseling Psychology*, 1976, *23*, 339–347.

Mitchell, T. R., and Beach, L. R. *Expectancy theory, decision theory, and occupational choice*. Technical report 75-75, Department of Psychology, Department of Management and Organization, University of Washington, Seattle, Washington, December, 1975.

Morgan, J. I., and Skovholt, T. M. Using interexperience-fantasy and daydreams in career counseling. *Journal of Counseling Psychology*, 1977, *24*, 391–397.

Morrill, W. H., and Forrest, D. J. Dimensions of counseling for career development. *Personnel and Guidance Journal*, 1970, *49*, 299–305.

Nachmann, B. Some comments on clinical appraisal in vocational counseling. *Personnel and Guidance Journal*, 1965, *43*, 884–885.

Oliver, L. W. Outcome Measures for Career Counseling Research. Technical paper 316, U.S. Army Research Institute for the Social and Behavioral Sciences, August, 1978.

Oliver, L. W. Outcome measurement in career counseling research. *Journal of Counseling Psychology*, 1979, *25*, 217–226.

Osipow, S. H. *Manual for the career decision scale*. Columbus, Ohio: Marathon Consulting and Press, 1980.

Osipow, S. H. Research in career counseling: an analysis of issues and problems. *The Counseling Psychologist*, 1982, in press.

Osipow, S. H., Carney, C. G., Winer, J., Yanico, B., and Koschier, M. *The career decision scale*. Columbus, Ohio: Marathon Consulting and Press, 1976.

Pepinsky, H. B. The selection and use of diagnostic categories in clinical counseling. *Applied Psychological Monograph*, No. 15, 1948.

Phares, J. E. *Locus of control in personality*. Morristown, N.J.: General Learning Press, 1976.

Pritchard, D. H. The occupational exploration process: some operational implications. *Personnel and Guidance Journal*, 1962, *40*, 674–680.

Rose, H. A., and Elton, C. F. Attrition and the vocationally undecided student. *Journal of Vocational Behavior*, 1971, *1*, 99–103.

Salinger, M. D. Adapting a college-level occupations course to meet expressed student needs. *Personnel and Guidance Journal*, 1966, *45*, 272–275.

Seligman, L. *Assessment in developmental career counseling*. Cranston, R. I.: Carroll, 1980.

Smith, M. L., and Glass, G. V. Metz-analysis of psychotherapy outcome studies. *American Psychologist*, 1977, *32*, 752–760.

Smith, M. L., Glass, G. V., and Miller, T. I. *The benefits of psychotherapy*. Baltimore: Johns Hopkins University Press, 1980.

Spokane, A. R., and Oliver, L. W. The outcomes of vocational intervention. In Osipow, S. H., and Walsh, W. B. (Eds.), *Handbook of vocational psychology*. Hillsdale, N.J.: Lawrence Erlbaum, in press.

Super, D. E. The preliminary appraisal in counseling. *Personnel and Guidance Journal*, 1957, *36*, 154–161.

Talbot, D. B., and Birk, J. M. Does the vocational exploration and insight kit equal the sum of its parts?: a comparison study. *Journal of Counseling Psychology*, 1979, *26*, 359–362.

Titley, R. W., Titley, B., and Wolff, W. M. The major changers: continuity or discontinuity in the career decision process. *Journal of Vocational Behavior*, 1976, *8*, 105–111.

Vetter, L. Career counseling for women. In Harmon, L., Birk, J. M., Fitzgerald, L. E., and Tanney, M. F. *Counseling women*. Monterey, Calif.: Brooks/Cole, 1978.

Whiteley, J. M., and Resnikoff, A. (Eds.), *Career counseling*. Monterey, Calif.: Brooks/Cole, 1978.

Yabroff, W. Learning decision making. In Krumboltz, J. D., and Thoresen, C. E. (Eds.), *Behavioral counseling: cases and techniques.* New York: Holt, Rinehart and Winston, 1969.

Yates, C., Johnson, N., and Johnson, J. Effects of the use of the vocational exploration group on career maturity. *Journal of Counseling Psychology,* 1979, *26,* 368–370.

CHAPTER EIGHTEEN
A COMPARISON
OF THE THEORIES

We have now examined in considerable detail major viewpoints concerning the process of vocational decision making and subsequent career behavior. In doing so, the theories have been scrutinized, the relevant research described and its implications for the theories considered, and applications of the theories to the problems of human career behavior discussed. The next objective is to contrast the various theories with regard to their strengths and weaknesses according to a variety of criteria. As a result of such a comparison, it might be possible to reach some conclusions, not about which theory is "best" but rather under what conditions one theory might be more useful than another as a conceptual guide. Furthermore, such a comparison might be a useful stepping stone to the consideration of a synthesis of the theories and directions for future theorizing about career behavior. In this chapter we will compare the theories with regard to two general criteria: the formal adequacy of each theory as a theory and the adequacy of each in contributing to the understanding and facilitation of career development.

FORMAL ADEQUACY

Theories may be assessed according to a number of criteria. In this book, we have chosen to consider theories in terms of their explanatory adequacy; the degree to which they are supported empirically; how general they are, that is, how broadly they are related to other bodies of scientific literature, data, and observation; the simplicity or parsimony of their concepts; how operational they are with respect to translations into both research and practice; and how logically consistent or inconsistent they are.

Explanatory Adequacy

Explanation in science characteristically accounts for phenomena at increasingly detailed levels of observation or introduces hypothetical concepts which relate events and describe the nature of the functional relationship between two sets of observations. The first kind of explanation is commonly called reductionistic, the second type constructive. Examination of the theories reveals that all are constructive in their explanation of the phenomena of career behavior. The theories offer little in the way of reductionistic explanation. Nevertheless, there is some variation among them. For example, Holland's theory (1959; 1973) identifies the function of constructs which underlie vocational behavior, while most of the other theories describe both the *development* and *functioning* of vocationally relevant constructs. The trait-factor approach, similar to Holland's theory in conception, explains little about vocational behavior, relying more on description than explanation. Similarly, the sociological thinking about career development is mostly descriptive in nature and attempts to illustrate the situational parameters that influence vocational behavior. Only the need theories have any substantial degree of reductionism inherent in their explanation of career behavior. Since needs include a physiological component, the needs theory approach to occupational behavior can be viewed as reductionistic to the degree that physiological needs may be reduced through vocational activities such as earning and ingesting food to reduce hunger or sublimating sexual energy through vocational endeavor.

Most of the theories, thus, are clearly constructive, ranging from that of Holland, who identifies constructs which underlie vocational behavior, to that of Super, who postulates hypothetical constructs and processes, such as the self-concept and the interaction with situational events, to account for career behavior. In general, there seems to be little from which to choose among the theories as to explanatory adequacy because of their great similarity in explanatory approach. The theories are generally descriptive rather than explanatory. Only the more recent writings of Super (Super et al., 1963b) seem detailed and explicit enough to provide the basis of an *explanation* of the career development process.

Empirical Support

While the explanatory modes of behavior are very similar among the theories, the range of empirical support is wider and more varied. Some data exist on which to assess all the theories, but variations exist even in the degree to which different theoretical points of view have stimulated research. With a few exceptions, the research on career behavior has not been experimental in nature. Too often, research designs have used convenient samples and have observed the behavior of subjects over a period of time, concentrating on possible differences in vocational behavior as a function of the original sorting into groups. For example, groups sorted on childhood experiences are expected to enter predictably different occupations, or students scoring in certain ways on personality instruments are expected to express vocational preferences of a predictably different kind than other students with somewhat different personality traits. Only rarely have conditions similar to those of an experiment been arranged.

In addition, the research has gradually been shifting from an emphasis on the testing of response-response laws to the examination and production of hypothetical constructs (Borow, 1960). The theories of career development have played a significant role in stimulating this change in research activity, since the theories have provided guides in the development of predictions and hypotheses and in the identification of profitable areas of investigation.

A considerable proportion of research based on Super's theory has resulted in empirical confirmation of the two fundamental aspects of his theory: that career choice is seen by the chooser as a way in which to implement his self-concept and that throughout life one is confronted with a series of career developmental tasks which specify the particular vocational decisions that must be made. Although a wider occupational base than now exists would be desirable, a number of recent research efforts have moved the data base from only those occupations possessing obvious potential for self-concept implementation (for example, nursing) to others of a more dubious nature.

The behavioral style approach to personality and career has strong empirical support, but it has been applied to a very limited range of career situations. As for Holland's theory, the descriptive elements have had some experimental validation, but the results have by no means uniformly indicated that validity of Holland's personality types and their relation to career membership or goals. Thus, Holland's theory needs to reconcile the discrepancies that exist between measured personality style and the model personality required for satisfied functioning in a given occupation. On the positive side, Holland's theory has been well integrated into other major instrumentation and classification systems (for example, the SCII and the *Dictionary of Occupational Titles*).

Psychoanalytic concepts have received mixed empirical support because of the wide variety of specific approaches and variations in their translation into operational terms. Thus, some concepts, like the role of identification with appropriate adult models in career development, have received considerable empirical support, whereas the notion that psychic energy may be sublimated in vocational activity has received little support, because it is difficult, if not impossible, to make the latter problem explicit enough for research.

Needs theory, personal values, and the Ginzberg group approaches all have some empirical support, but the relevant data suffer from serious deficiencies. The needs and values data are too dependent upon paper-and-pencil tests and produce data which are largely of a response-response type. These data are subject to interpretations in addition to those consistent with the theory under discussion. The Ginzberg group produced data relevant to its theory, but the sampling limitations of the study very seriously interfere with the inferences that may be drawn from the study.

The sociological theories set out to be more descriptive in nature than the other approaches, so the application of a criterion of empirical support is not as legitimate for them as for the other approaches. In a similar way, because of its heuristic conception, the trait-factor approach is strictly empirical and, thus, the data obtained in the trait-factor frame of reference can only be supportive, or it would be excluded from the trait-factor frame of reference. Only one theory has consistently failed to be empirically supported. Though the research design is open to some criticisms, the investigations testing Roe's theory have almost uniformly failed to provide validation; exceptions to this failure to support Roe's theory have occurred in one or two recent studies; but the overwhelming weight of the evidence casts doubt on the validity of the theory.

Lofquist and Dawis' theory is satisfactory empirically, but empirical evidence is unusually sparse in quantity considering the age of the theory. Tiedeman's theory has only limited empirical support. Social learning (Mitchell et al., 1979) approaches also have somewhat minimal empirical support, most of which relies on the reinterpretation of old data.

Generality

Several distinctive referents in basic psychological literature have served as anchors for the theories of career development. Virtually all the theories have to some extent roots in personality theory. The range has varied from the one extreme of a mere nod in the direction of personality theory, illustrated by the needs or values approaches, to the other extreme of the development of a miniature personality theory, exemplified by the work of Holland (1959) or Roe (1957).

In addition to personality theory, however, other streams of thought have influenced career development theory. Principal among these has been developmental psychology. The influence of developmental concepts has been strongly felt in the work of Super (1963a), for example, in the concepts of the vocational developmental task, and in that of Roe (1957), in the emphasis she has placed on the role of early family experiences on the development of childhood personality traits.

Psychoanalytic thought has permeated psychology in many ways, and in addition to the explicitly analytic theories of career development, it has influenced the work of Roe, Ginzberg and associates (1951) and the social systems line of thought. Because of its emphasis on the role of childhood in shaping personality, psychoanalytic thinking has injected another aspect of developmental psychology into career development theory. Learning, too, has been superimposed with personality theory in the behavioral style stream of research on personality and career. Motivation and reinforcement are brought into the analysis of career behavior in the consideration of the way in which personality styles develop and are maintained, and in a sense, the personality style line of thought about careers is more closely attuned to psychological concepts in general than the other theories.

Somewhat more divorced from the center of psychological theory are the needs and values approaches to career development and the trait-factor and Holland approaches. The latter two theories share a dependence on the testing movement, to which Holland's theory adds a dash of Spranger's (1928) "types of man" approach. Despite their basis in personality theory, the needs and values approaches applied to career development have taken an empirical form and consequently are distantly related to psychological theorizing in general and instead have become heuristic.

Lofquist and Dawis (1969) and Social Learning theory approaches (Mitchell et al., 1979) are sufficiently general to be of use to theorists and counselors, but Tiedeman's theory (1961; Tiedeman and O'Hara, 1963) is so general as to be somewhat circumscribed in its use as a consequence.

Parsimony

The Ginzberg (1951), Super (1953; 1963b), and personality style models are essentially simple proposals. In the Ginzberg and Super approaches, the principles of developmental psychology play a major role. Neither theorist has significantly embellished those principles. The personality style system actually extends the needs approach since it generates principles to describe the way needs motivate human behavior in a vocational setting. Roe and Holland have also built their theories on only a few major concepts. Personality types, the level hierarchy, and environmental factors form the basis of the Holland theory, while genetic factors and family experiences are fundamental to Roe's theory.

Most of the theories are more than adequate on the criterion of the parsimony of the concepts they introduce to describe and explain vocational behavior. Some of the theories may be even too parsimonious with the concepts they employ. The trait-factor personality approach is almost a nontheory since it is bascially empirical in nature. The viewpoint merely proposes that certain personality traits are more likely to be associated with some occupations than others. The needs and values approaches go one step beyond the trait-factor theory, adding the postulate that the particular values and needs (constructs in themselves) a person has influence his choice of career, his behavior in it, and the degree to which the career satisfies him.

Both the Lofquist and Dawis and the Social Learning theories are straightforward and parsimonious in their approach. The Tiedeman theory, however, is complex and complicated enough to be "docked" points for parsimony.

Operational Adequacy

The question of how operational the theories are must be considered in two parts, that is, the ease with which the theories lead to research applications and their relevance to program development and counseling. Generally, the theories appear to be more adequate when their research applications are stressed than when they are examined for counseling applications. Among the theories easiest to convert into research terms are the personality style, Super, trait-factor, needs, and Holland theories.

The trait-factor, needs, and Holland theories are similar as far as research is concerned. Fundamentally empirical in nature, their hypothetical concepts (if any) are close to the descriptive level of behavior, and hence, translation into research follows rather easily. The occupational preferences, persistence, or satisfaction of a population sorted by needs, personality, or some other variable are observed and related to the theory.

Super and the personality style approaches form another set. They are not as easy to translate into research terms, not because their concepts are more comprehensive but rather because the interrelation between the concepts is complex and requires sophisticated research procedures. The personality style approach lends itself, better than all other views of career decision making and behavior, to the experimental method. Super's theory, on the other hand, seems best suited to longitudinal research concerning patterns of career behavior over long periods of time.

The remaining theories (Ginzberg, psychoanalytic, social systems, Roe, and values) are difficult to implement in research terms. The difficulty lies primarily in the diffuseness of the concepts they employ (cf. psychoanalytic, Ginzberg, values) or in the relative inaccessibility of the important data (cf. Roe, social systems). Only the psychoanalytic theories of career development are contorted and exaggerated. These approaches have typically introduced the complex concepts of psychoanalytic theory in general to describe career development.

Another aspect of operational adequacy to be considered is the instrumentation associated with each of the theories. Holland has consistently paid attention to the development of means to measure personal attributes associated with the constructs in his theory. The Vocational Preference Inventory has been revised numerous times in this effort, and, more recently, the Self-Directed Search has been published, a measure which combines personality assessment with self-reported estimates of competencies. In addition, a number of recent efforts have been made by Holland and others to integrate his system in other systems, with the result that the Strong Campbell Interest Inventory, for example, now has an operational relationship with the theory, as does the *Dictionary of Occupational Titles* classification system.

Lofquist and Dawis (1969), in the development of their adjustment to work approach, have also generated a number of instruments especially tailored to use in connection with their theory. These instruments include the Minnesota Satisfaction Questionnaire, the Minnesota Satisfactoriness Scales, the Minnesota Importance Questionnaire, and the Job Description Questionnaire.

Super himself has directed less energy to the development of instruments to measure constructs associated with his theory than other investigators. He is responsible, however, for the Work Values Inventory, which measures one aspect of personality implementation in career, and is senior author of the Career Development Inventory, a measure of vocational maturity, another construct which grew out of his theory. Others, such as Crites, Gribbons and Lohnes, and Westbrook, have developed instruments designed to measure vocational maturity. Measures of the implementation of the self-concept have been less common, and most scales have been developed in connection with specific research projects. Nevertheless, both the developmental and self-concept aspects of Super's theory lend themselves well to instrumentation, and more can be expected from this quarter in the future.

Roe has not extended much energy in developing instruments, but the Parent Attitude Research Instrument is an example of one attempt to provide instrumentation for her theory, and the Hall Occupational Interest Inventory represents an independent effort to measure interests within the frame of reference described by Roe's theory.

The general personality approaches are relatively well represented in instruments. For example, needs relative to occupations can be measured by the Adjective Check List, the Edwards Personal Preference Schedule, and the Minnesota Importance Questionnaire; occupational values are frequently measured by the Work Values Inventory or the Allport-Vernon-Lindzey Study of Values; and general personality traits are frequently measured for their occupational relevance by means of the Minnesota Multiphasic Personality Inventory, the California Psychological Inventory, the Omnibus Personality Inventory, Cattell's 16 PF, and many other instruments.

Only the psychoanalytic, social systems, and Ginzberg approaches have little instrumentation associated with them, and the reasons for this seem evident. Psychoanalytic theory in general avoids psychometric evaluation, the social systems model tends to be descriptive rather than clinical or experimental in application, and the Ginzberg approach in many significant ways is a precursor (at least with respect to the emphasis on developmental aspects of careers) of the approach described by Super. As such, the Ginzberg approach has had little development since its initial formulation and presentation, and efforts along developmental lines associated with career growth have tended to be investigated in the context of the general ideas proposed by Super.

The operational adequacy of both the Lofquist and Dawis and the Social Learning theory approaches are satisfactory. Tiedeman's approach is very difficult to make operational, with only a few satisfactory attempts to do so extant to date (for example, Harren's *Assessment of Career Decision Making,* 1976).

Logical Consistency

Only two of the theories have serious problems of internal inconsistency. Roe's failure to deal adequately with the effects of changing family environments on personality development poses a problem. Children are not always treated the same by their parents; two parents may have different styles of child rearing; parents may react to children differently at different ages; a parent may die. All of these factors introduce apparently insoluble difficulties for Roe's theory. Explaining adult behavior in terms of childhood environment under these circumstances is nearly impossible. In a similar vein, the Ginzberg theory suffers from some logical difficulties by introducing pseudoconcepts which can easily serve as explanatory loopholes if events do not occur as predicted.

THE PROCESS OF CAREER DEVELOPMENT

Normal Development

The main thrust of several of the theories is in the descriptions of how the career decisions of normally developing people evolve. The theoretical treatment given to normal career development seems to follow one of three general lines of thought. Roe (1957), Super (1953; 1963a), Ginzberg and associates (1951), and psychoanalytic thought all describe career behavior fundamentally in terms of general concepts of human development. Super emphasizes how the self-concept is shaped. According to Super, each phase of life exerts its own particular emphasis on human behavior, including individual vocational behavior. It is thus possible to chart, in general terms, the vocational activities that are to be expected of an individual in Western culture.

The Ginzberg approach, similar to Super's, describes career development as a series of events in a predictable sequence. Each aspect of the sequence presents the individual with a particular set of problems to be solved. Thus, in the vocational realm, the Ginzberg theory attempts to predict the sequence of behaviors relevant to career decision making. Ginzberg's approach does not lead to the prediction of occupation as much as it allows one to anticipate the vocationally relevant behavior an individual will engage in.

The developmental flavor is also prominent in the psychoanalytic approach to career behavior. While the developmental phases of analytic theory are not closely attuned to career behavior, the analytic approach places a heavy emphasis on the idea that personality development is crucially related to the events of early childhood and that the ensuing personality causes the kind of occupational behavior that may be seen later.

Roe's description of the normal career development process is not as explicit as Super's description. She assumes that individuals differ physically and psychologically at birth. Added to these differences are the effects of parental attitudes and behavior styles, which lead the maturing child to favor one of a number of interpersonal styles of behavior. The combination of the genetic features and the familial patterns leads to the prediction of general vocational behavior. Roe's theory is primarily concerned with predicting what kind of occupation a person will choose, but says little about vocational development subsequent to the choice.

Both the Holland and social systems approaches emphasize the view that vocational behavior is situationally bound. In the social systems approach, normal career development must be viewed in the context of its situational determinants such as social class membership, economic opportunities, and the organization of the world of work. For Holland, the important situational determinants seem to lie more in the individual's organization of his perceptions of the vocational world and how he might best interact with it. Thus, the youth, according to Holland, might develop images (or stereotypes) of the activities involved in a variety of kinds of work and then try to integrate these images into his own view of how he fits into the world. The determinants of his view, of course, probably include factors such as social class membership and personality developments as emphasized by the other theorists.

The Social Learning career development theory goes into considerable detail in describing how individuals should develop under normal circumstances. Similarly, Lofquist and Dawis' approach has as one of its strengths a detailed theoretical description of the normally developing individual.

The other personality approaches, trait-factor, personal style, needs, and values, are really weak conceptually in their characterization of normal career development. The only generalized view expressed by any of these approaches is that of the trait-factor group, that people with certain traits in common will be engaged in occupations similar to one another. It fails, however, to describe how these people came to resemble one another. These approaches, rather, are likely to be built upon one of the developmental lines of thought concerning career behavior. They illustrate how personality might influence or be related to career behavior once the personality pattern of the individual has developed.

Our review of the theoretical views of normal career development reveals several significant attitudes. Rarely does a theory attempt to predict a specific occupational choice. More typically, the theories predict entry into general vocational areas, personality requirements of these areas, influences that may shape personality in vocationally relevant ways, and age-level behaviors of importance to career development. In effect, the theories emphasize all the nonability aspects of human behavior that relate to vocational preference, selection, attainment, and satisfaction and pay very little direct attention to the role of aptitudes in career behavior.

Problems in Career Development

Before one can consider how career development can go awry, some clear idea about the meaning of misdirected career development must be developed. For example, it might refer to vocational indecision, conflict, failure, or a choice that is not consistent with information about the individual. In fact, depending upon the theory under consideration, it might be any of these. According to the developmental theorists, career development goes awry when individuals fail to keep pace with the demands of their culture or their age mates. Ginzberg's group specifically points to several behaviors that must develop in order for mature career behavior to occur. The ability to perform the reality-testing task, the development of a mature time perspective, the ability to delay the gratification of desires, the ability to compromise, and the ability to identify with appropriate adult models are all important. If these abilities fail to materialize during the adolescent period, career decisions will be inadequate and the individual will continue to be employed in a career in which he is dissatisfied or will engage in numerous unsatisfying occupational pursuits.

The Ginzberg group also specifically related the ability to make good vocational choices to emotional stability, a relationship that most of the theorists seem to regard as valid but which has only on occasion been made explicit, notably by Super and by psychoanalytic authors writing about careers. In general, it is agreed that if the psychological development of the individual is not adequate, career development will not progress smoothly. Unfortunately, many theories have failed to show how career development can become misdirected in theoretical terms.

Roe and Super are not explicit about how career development can go wrong. It is possible, however, to infer from Super's writings that problems of maturation in general are related to the proper performance of the vocational developmental tasks required at a given age level, much in the way the Ginzberg group suggests. Similarly, in describing the shaping of the self-concept, Super leaves the way open for inferences to be drawn about what factors might create distortions in self-concept and what effects these distortions might have on career behavior. For Roe, the question of misdirected career choice is not appropriate, since she has described how choices are made without seriously trying to evaluate their adequacy.

Holland's theory is very explicit about how poor career choices may be made. Holland discusses this problem in terms of conflict or indecision in career matters. If the modal personality style leads to an occupational decision that is blocked and there is no strong second modal personal orientation, vocational indecision will be observed. Similarly, if two orientations are nearly equal in strength, conflict in vocational decision will occur. In terms of abilities, a poor choice could be made if the individual did not evaluate his talents accurately and thus his level hierarchy was over or underinflated. In that case, the individual would either be observed to aspire to a career which might be consistent with his modal orientation but too difficult for him, or choose one that failed to use his talents sufficiently.

Social Learning theory approaches, as well as Lofquist and Dawis' theory, describe how problems develop in career decision making and development and logically lead to some proposed interventions to deal with these problems. In that regard, the Social Learning theory approaches are stronger in suggesting interventions than are Lofquist and Dawis.

The theories rely on four main factors to account for misdirected career development. Most prominent of the four is the likelihood of a retarded rate of development in general which causes an individual to fail to have the skills necessary to cope with the vocational developmental tasks relevant to his age and position level. The other three factors, inadequate emotional adjustment, inaccurate self-evaluation, and frozen behavior between two attractive behavior sequences, are seen as possible sources of difficulty but do not seem to be viewed as pervasive in causing difficulties in career development.

Facilitation or Modification of Career Behavior

Of all the theorists, only Super has written extensively about how career development might be corrected if it has gone astray or how it might be facilitated in the normally developing individual. Given Super's emphasis on the total life span, it is not surprising that he has devoted attention to the applications of career development theory to practice. The vocational development tasks enumerated by Super point the way to programmatic and individual approaches to correct and facilitate career development. According to Super, specific programs for adolescents should expose them to the necessary information for making the decisions required of them at that stage of development in order to avoid future errors or to correct past decisions. All through the life cycle, programs may be developed to enable people to make these decisions on a sounder basis.

While interviewing represents only one aspect of Super's approach to the facilitation or correction of career behavior, for most of the theorists, interviewing remains a primary procedure. The Ginzberg group generally proposes that if career development is not proceeding as it should in an adolescent, efforts should be directed toward the identification of his present stage of development, and experiences should be provided which accelerate the individual through previous periods of development and bring him to his appropriate level.

Aside from interviews designed to provide more insight into an individual's personal orientation, Holland's theory might lead to the proposal to exert more efforts toward the identification of satisfactions to be obtained in various work environments, as well as instruction for the individual to help him or her exert more control over the life situations open. Picking the "right" school or industrial organization should provide a work atmosphere conducive to vocational satisfaction.

Since psychoanalytically oriented career counselors devote their energies to the identification of how and where an individual's impulses may be expressed vocationally with the greatest adequacy, their main efforts are devoted to interviewing procedures which attempt to lead to greater awareness of impulses and the identification of wholesome ways to express them in general. Roe's theory, too, leads the counselor to help his client in trying to understand the forces that shaped his or her personality and better identify the conditions under which he or she might work with the greatest satisfaction.

Critical Periods and Critical Agents in Career Development

Once again, several distinctive lines of thought about when the most significant experiences for career development occur and what the critical sources of influence are emerge upon examination of the theories. The Ginzberg group and Super fall into one category. These writers agree that among the most critical agents influencing career development are the kind of adult models available during youth and adolescence, and for Super, models continue to be important. According to Super, many important periods of life exist for career development, largely because there are numerous points in the life span when critical decisions affecting careers must be made. The Ginzberg theory emphasizes the age range from about ten to twenty-four years, since it is during this period that educational and vocational decisions are made affecting one's entry job.

Roe and the psychoanalytic writers seem to form a second category of thought about important periods and influences on career behavior. Their views emphasize the role of parents in the shaping of mature personality during early childhood.

According to this approach, later events exert a less significant impact on occupational behavior. Holland, personal values, personality behavior style, and the social systems approach form a third view. Although none of these treat any particular period of development as crucial, they do have something to say about the source of influence on decisions. For Holland, family factors, left unspecified, and social institutions are highly critical in the development of personality types and occupational images as well as opportunities. Similarly, the social systems view places a heavy emphasis on family variables such as social class, education, and income, in combination with economic opportunities and social and industrial organization, as major forces which shape the individual's vocational development. To a less explicit extent, the personal values line of thought sees family and cultural factors as forces which shape values. Finally, the behavioral style approach necessarily assumes the importance of situational variables in determining the behavioral styles an individual learns, as well as providing a basis for eliciting these styles. Although not a category because they say nothing about either critical periods or critical agents, the trait-factor approaches form a final unit. This line of thought has nothing explicit to say about the forces which shape occupational behavior.

The Role of Interests in Career Development

Interests play an intimate role in career development theory, but the particular role is not typically stated in an explicit fashion in the theories of career development. Some theorists, like the Ginzberg group, assign interests a significant role at a particular age period. Others, like Super and Roe, tie interests more directly to occupational behavior. Super's theory views interests as an aspect of the self-concept, whereas in Roe's theory interests derive from psychic energy and lead to one's fundamental orientation toward or away from people. Interests are seen as growing out of individual need hierarchies by the needs theorists; to the trait-factor theorists and Holland, interests are another aspect of the person-occupation equation, something to be assessed but not necessarily analyzed. The social systems and values approaches are likely to view interests as reflections of the forces of society and family.

Social Learning had as an integral aspect of its conception the role of interest development, aptitude development, and the family. These factors are integrated into the approach and are used both in describing how people become the way they are and in suggesting interventions in their behalf. Lofquist and Dawis also devote substantial attention and energy to describing how interest and aptitude both develop and how they interact to shape important key concepts in career development.

The Role of Aptitudes in Career Development

Aptitudes are given varying emphasis by the theories. To the trait-factor theorists, including Holland, aptitudes comprise part of the equation involved in choice. Roe and the social systems approaches view aptitudes as genetically determined, and thus achievement is partly a function of heredity but also the result of culture and environment. Neither Holland, Roe, nor the social systems view emphasizes the role of aptitudes in career development, however. On the other hand, Super sees aptitudes as a factor to be considered in career decision making, an entity to be assessed and tested against reality. The needs and values approaches simply view the role of aptitudes in career development as a factor which interacts with the more critical variables, that is, needs or values. To the behavioral style theorist, aptitudes are part of the situational context, which both contributes to the situation and interacts with it, and within which individuals' career behavior occurs. The work adjustment approach of Lofquist and Dawis fully includes performance and aptitude variables, through the vehicle of job satisfactoriness, one of the independent variables used to predict job tenure. Finally, consistent with the psychoanalytic antecedents of its thought, the Ginzberg group fails to consider aptitudes seriously. Ginzberg and his associates do consider the roles that unusual and highly specific talents play in overdetermining career development, for example, the role of musical talent in the precocious musician's commitment to a musical career.

The Role of the Family in Career Development

The personality approaches, represented by trait-factor thought, needs, values, and behavioral style, fail to discuss the role of family influences on career development in any distinctive manner. Values and needs are seen as being shaped in a vague way by the family context; the family contributes to the situational context as seen by the behavioral style approach and to the traits the individual develops with which the trait-factor theorist is concerned; not much more than passing attention is given to the family by proponents of these views.

The Ginzberg theory, Super, psychoanalytic thought, and social systems views concern themselves with the family in a slightly more explicit way. To Super, the family plays a critical role in the formation of the individual's self-concept and in the provision of a context for its implementation. Psychoanalytic thought sees psychosexual development as significantly influenced by the family structure and interactions of its members. To Ginzberg and the social systems theorists, the family creates a highly significant situation which plays a major role in determining the specifics of the career decisions as individual will make. Factors associated with family membership determine an individual's social class, financial resources, and attitudes toward work. In the view of the Ginzberg theorists, a poor family will accelerate the career development of their offspring, but will not alter in any significant way the sequence through which he or she goes. In addition, the lower-class family is likely to be more passive in its general behavior and attitudes than middle- or upper-class families and thus its members may try to exert less direct influence on their career patterns than upper- or middle-class people. Only Roe rests the hub of a theory on the family. To Roe, the family plays a crucial role in determining, in fairly specific ways, the kinds of interactions with people that the youth will learn to develop.

It seems obvious that familial factors are important to career decisions, both in the determination of the situational variables involved in career development (such as educational, economic, hygienic and medical resources, social support and reinforcement, and the provision of a context for work) and in the intraindividual variables (such as the physical and psychological characteristics that have a strong genetic component). It is striking that so little theorizing has been done to relate explicitly the role of the family to occupational behavior, particularly when extensive data exist showing how the family background influences the kind of initial choice made and the manner in which it is implemented.

SUMMARY

One conclusion to be drawn from this comparison of the theories is that the various theories differ not only because the thinking of their authors about careers is distinctive but also because they are trying to accomplish different objectives in their theorizing. Some theorists are trying to explain why people make the choices they do (for example, Holland); others are emphasizing the development of career choices over time (for example, Super). Further, some theorists seem to be working harder than others at providing practical techniques for facilitating vocational development or attempting to examine the characteristics that differentiate members of occupations from one another. The theorists do, however, share a tendency to imply that their concepts are universally applicable. It is this implication that occasionally gets in the reader's way when he is trying to sift through the data and concepts of the theories to generate applications.

The theories' strength lies in their general explanation of the way career decision making occurs. In terms of formal adequacy as theories, much seems to be lacking. In general, the theories have failed to pay serious attention to the satisfaction of the criteria applied to the scientific evaluation of theory. There is a tendency to describe the career development process in very general terms, probably more general than is useful to researcher and practitioner alike. The major exceptions are Super's and Holland's revised theories, which have taken on an increasingly applied and operational appearance.

Considerable data pertinent to career development and occupational psychology have been accumulated in theoretical terms. If closer ties to basic psychological theory existed, the theories would be strengthened. Some signs of the development of closer ties exist, and these signs augur well for the increasing adequacy and potency of career development theory in years to come.

Generally, the similarities between the theories outweigh the differences; they emphasize the same kinds of critical agents and periods in career development. The differences between the theories lie in their choice of emphasis, the research methods suitable to each, and the degree to which they specify the relations between various events.

As a conceptual model, Super's theory seems to be the most highly developed and advanced. This is reflected in its explicitness, its fairly high degree of empirical

TABLE 18.1. A Summary Comparison of Some Theories and Subtheories of Career Development with Respect to Some Key Aspects

THEORY	EXPLANATORY MODE	EMPIRICAL SUPPORT	GENERALITY	COMPLEXITY	OPERATIONALITY	KEY VARIABLES
Roe	Attempts to be somewhat explanatory; predicts molar career decisions and process	numerous studies; mostly negative results	very broad in design; most applicable to upper-level careers	many complex constructs	somewhat hard to make operational; instruments to assess major variables exist; occupational classification system helpful	family; experiences
Holland	mostly descriptive; predicts molecular decisions	numerous studies; mostly positive results	very broad applicability	relatively simple in conception	easy to make operational; instrumentation available; numerous practical applications	interests; occupational stereotypes; information about self and careers; environment
Super	mostly explanatory; predicts relatively molecular events, but also includes process predictions	numerous studies; mostly positive results	very broadly applicable	moderately complex in conception	potentially operational; instrumentation available; many practical applications	self-concept; developmental stages and tasks
Ginzberg et al.	mostly descriptive; process not product-oriented	few studies; some support for general structure	narrow in applicability	average complexity	not very operational or practical	developmental stages; social variables
Psychoanalytic	mostly explanatory; predicts process, not product	some studies; numerous concepts have been supported	broad in design but narrow in practice	very complex constructs	hard to make operational; could lead to practice but hasn't reached potential	sublimation; ego; identification mastery

Theory	Type	Research support	Scope	Complexity	Operationality/Practicality	Key concepts
Lofquist-Dawis	molecular; deductive	mostly positive support	very broad in scope; work-setting-oriented	numerous complex constructs and relationships	very operational; many instruments available; has some practical applications	needs; traits; satisfaction and satisfactoriness; job tenure
Trait-factor	molecular; empirical	many studies; results highly variable	potentially broad but narrow in execution	essentially empirical and not conceptual in nature	operationality varies with availability of personality-aptitude instruments, practical for selection purposes	personality traits; aptitudes; needs
Needs	explanatory but includes molecular predictions	many studies; results frequently support, but variable	broad in scope	relatively simple in concept	operationality varies with availability of instruments to measure needs; not very practical	needs and their satisfaction; needs hierarchies
Values	explanatory, process-oriented	many studies; results frequently support	broad in scope	relatively simple in concept	operationality varies with availability of instruments to measure values	values
Social systems	descriptive, process-oriented	many studies; results frequently support	very broad in scope	relatively simple concepts at times, empirical in nature rather than conceptual	not easy to make some aspects operational, though other aspects lend themselves to operational methods; not highly applied	social class, family; sex, age, race, culture; economy
Tiedeman	molar; descriptive	sparse	very broad, abstract	very complex	poor	self; developmental stages
Social Learning	molecular; decision process	mostly reinterpretation of old data	adequate	simple in concept	adequate	person; environment; reinforcers

support, and its substantially larger number of applications to human affairs. The personality-style approach, on the other hand, seems to be the most amenable to the experimental and scientific method and the closest to basic psychological concepts, but still lacks a wide base of empirical support.

Table 18.1 summarizes the status of twelve of the theoretical approaches on a number of important dimensions. *Explanatory Mode* is designed to reveal the theory's major style of explanation, that is, is it primarily attempting to predict specific career choices, describe the process of career development, or explain how choices come about? *Empirical Support* refers to the overall nature of the number of studies pertaining to a theory and their general results. *Generality* is a summary of the scope of the theory: does it aim at and succeed in applying itself to workers in a broad array of jobs in various cultures, or is it mainly pointed to high-level workers, college students and their choices, and so on? *Complexity* is a summary statement of the number and abstractness of the concepts used in the theory. *Operationality* refers to the ease with which the concepts of the theory may be translated into research hypotheses, instruments, and practical applications. Finally, *Key Variables* attempts to summarize the most important variables used in the theory to explain or describe career events.

REFERENCES

Borow, H. Research programs in career development. *Journal of Counseling Psychology,* 1960, *7,* 62–70.

Ginzberg, E., Ginsburg, S. W., Axelrod, S., and Herma, J. L. *Occupational choice: an approach to a general theory.* New York: Columbia University Press, 1951.

Harren, V. A. Preliminary Manual for the Interpretation of the Assessment of Career Decision making. (Form B). Unpublished manuscript. Southern Illinois University, 1976.

Holland, J. L. A theory of vocational choice. *Journal of Counseling Psychology,* 1959, *6,* 35–45.

Holland, J. L. *Making vocational choices: a theory of careers.* Englewood Cliffs, N.J.: Prentice-Hall, 1973.

Lofquist, L. H., and Dawis, R. V. *Adjustment to work: a psychological view of man's problems in a work oriented society.* New York: Appleton-Century-Crofts, 1969.

Mitchell, A. M., Jones, G. B., and Krumboltz, J. D. (Eds.). *Social learning theory and career decision making.* Cranston, R. I.: Carroll, 1979.

Roe, A. Early determinants of vocational choice. *Journal of Counseling Psychology,* 1957, *4,* 212–217.

Spranger, E. *Types of men.* New York: Stechert, 1928 (translation).

Super, D. E. A theory of vocational development. *American Psychologist,* 1953, *8,* 185–190.

Super, D. E. Self-concepts in vocational development. In Super, D. E., et al., *Career development: self-concept theory.* New York: CEEB Research Monograph No. 4, 1963. (a)

Super, D. E., Starishevsky, R., Matlin, N., and Jordaan, J. P. *Career development: self-concept theory.* New York: CEEB Research Monograph No. 4, 1963. (b)

Tiedeman, D. V., Decisions and vocational development: a paradigm and its implications. *Personnel and Guidance Journal,* 1961, *40,* 15–21.

Tiedeman, D. V., and O'Hara, R. P. *Career development and adjustment.* New York: College Entrance Examination Board, 1963.

CHAPTER NINETEEN
PERSPECTIVE

On the basis of the previous chapters it is clear that many problems and unresolved issues remain in the theoretical structure of career development. This chapter aims to bring these issues into clearer focus. After examining the theories, as well as the research and applications that derive from them, several issues become prominent. It seems to be generally accepted that career choice is most profitably viewed as developmental in nature and based on principles of developmental psychology as Beilin (1955) has explicated. Beilin has pointed out the tendency for human behavior to move from the general, dependent, self-oriented, and isolated to the specific, independent, social, and integrated. Career development has been construed by many writers as one aspect of this maturing process.

Of course some dissenting voices may be heard. The dissenters are represented by writers such as Calia (1966), who point out the limitations of the developmental approach to careers and emphasize the indisputable fact that in practice, counselors rely heavily on the trait-factor approach despite its heuristic emphasis. A defense of the use of the trait-factor approach to career counseling appears to be especially apt in view of new procedures in automated data processing. Furthermore, Calia has criticized the career view because of the limitations that many unpredictable events impose on anticipating careers. How can one anticipate the sudden illness of a superior which results in a premature advancement, or a technological development which makes an industry obsolete in a decade? Because there have been few attempts to translate career development theory into practice, the trait-factor approach continues to be the foundation of career counseling. Nevertheless, most writers prefer to view the trait-factor thought as one aspect to be considered in the analysis of the role of abilities, personality traits, interests, and family influences in the shaping of eventual career membership and occupational behavior. Most writers have chosen to emphasize the roles of one or two of these variables over those of the others, but nearly all have acknowledged that many factors operate to influence career development.

Whether existing emphases will change in the years to come is debatable, though most theoretically oriented writers seem to assume that important changes will occur. Super (1972) has predicted that four major activities will exemplify career development work over the next twenty years: the development of career models by means of such devices as lattice theory, Markov chains, path analysis, and the career tree; the extension of our knowledge regarding exploratory behavior; the development of better measures of vocational maturity; and the extension of self-concept theory. Holland (1972) and Roe (1972) hope for a greater investment of effort in the study of "important" problems and better interaction between the practitioner and researcher. Roe further sees more interdisciplinary research, more attention paid to vocational development in lower-level occupations, and more longitudinal research. Tiedeman (1972) anticipates a greater impact for technology, such as computer technology, in both research and vocational counseling. Osipow (1969) sees future developments largely in terms of increasing understandings about occupational effectiveness and satisfaction and the predicting of occupational membership by means of improved and novel techniques of measuring and observing vocationally related events. Others, such as Campbell (1969), have also anticipated a more comprehensive study of vocational development through "social systems" approaches, or, like O'Hara (1969), have called for an improved research base to apply to the practice of vocational counseling. Finally, the career education movement is likely to exert an influence in the direction of generating applications of theories of career development to programs and practice.

A growing emphasis has been placed on the impact of social forces in career development. It has become increasingly evident that when the situational determinants of career development are ignored, serious limitations are imposed on theoretical endeavors. In order to avoid limiting the impact of theory to this time and place, situational factors must be systematically built into career development theory. Often our theories seem to assume that career choice is static and thus seem to be designed to describe career development only in the context of mid-twentieth-century America. The question of career development in other cultures is ignored. For example, what are the career patterns that emerge in developing nations? Attention to the problems of emerging nations might help us answer questions concerning the career development of disadvantaged Americans, who in many respects face career problems similar to those of individuals in newly developing countries. How does one quickly acquire modern attitudes to technological skills? Lyon (1965) has warned that current theories of career development will soon be obsolete if they continue to fail to take the social context into account in their formulations. Cultural patterns exert a strong influence on the interaction between personality and occupation. Lyon has pointed out that American culture is rapidly bringing to an end the day of "straight line" career, that is, the career which lasts from youth until death or retirement, and is replacing it with the "serial" career, in which one's occupational life occurs in phases, and one moves from one level and activity to another with increasing maturity and experience. Similarly, class differences in America are leveling, and the differences between class expectations regarding occupational activities are disappearing.

The process of career choice is so deeply imbedded in cultural and economic factors that it is unreasonable to try to develop a theory of vocational development without including those variables. Social and economic conditions have changed drastically in the United State between the 30s and 80s and so has career development. Thus, it is not unreasonable to expect significant changes in the economy and culture in the years ahead, bringing about concomitant changes in career development. Most (if not all) career theorists have recognized the impact of cultural change on career development and have used increasingly abstract concepts in their formulations of career behavior, with individual development given continuity by the notion of the implementation of a self-concept as a guiding factor in career behavior.

It seems to be growing increasingly clear that a theory of career decision making and behavior must be developed which will possess the generality to deal effectively with environmental variables. Mierzwa (1963) has reported data illustrating the usefulness of the concept of multidetermination of career choice. He has proposed the use of a systems analysis for career behavior and counseling about vocations.

Thus, a systems view of career behavior is gradually emerging. The systems view explicitly recognizes that various situational and individual factors operate to influence career behavior in a broad way. With a highly sophisticated systems approach to career development, questions about the role of the biological, social, and situational factors in occupational behavior would become more explicit and hence more open to scrutiny, and, as a consequence, understandings of the interactions between these views would be more likely to emerge.

An Ecological Approach

The ecological approach to career development is most clearly seen in the analysis of decision making. Decisions may be viewed as links in a chain. Each decision can be made only immediately prior to action, yet preparation for the act of deciding and plans for the implementation of the decision itself are necessary. Furthermore, even though decisions have immediate implications, the long-range effects of decisions and estimates of their effects on future decisions are to be considered even though not made final now. Figure 19.1 illustrates the process.

T_1 represents the present, T_0 the past, and T_2 the future. The lowercase letters a, b, c represent small decisions, and the uppercase letters A, B, C represent major decisions. On the basis of a network of decisions made during T_0, the individual arrives at T_1, which may be the time of registration in college. At that time a series of small decisions, a, b, and c, are made, which may be to take math, English, and

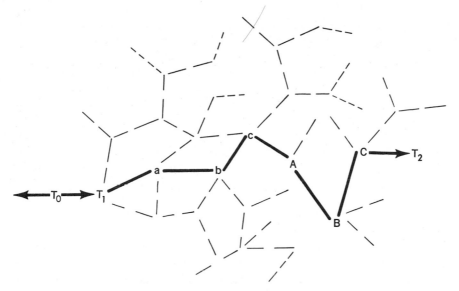

FIGURE 19.1.   Schematic representation of a decision making network.

physics courses. The dotted lines represent potential avenues which for various reasons were not followed. They each have highly intricate potential networks for decision. These decisions lead to experiences which may be interpreted in a variety of ways at T_1 plus and which lead to more significant decisions such as A and B. Eventually, after working through a multitude of such alternatives the student emerges at another major decision point, T_2, possibly college graduation. The previous experiences and decisions created the context in which a number of small decisions and a large decision could be made. In such a manner, then, the individual might go on making the decisions necessary to life. The role of the researcher is to identify the factors involved in influencing decisions at the numerous choice points; the role of the counselor is to help the individual cope with the discontinuities introduced at these junctures.

Approaches to the Study of Decision Making

A variety of somewhat sophisticated attempts to deal with decision making has been made. Hsu (1970) describes a quantitative system based on decision theory and designed to analyze the decision-making process. Included are what Hsu considers to be the essential variables involved in decision making: outcomes, valences of outcomes, expectancies of outcomes, and possible alternatives. Hsu does not, however, present any data to accompany the model and the several formulae he proposes. Marshall (1967) has tried to show how Bayesian decision as opposed to classical decision making can be applied to educational programming. Marshall's work has potential application to individual decision making with regard to educational-vocational choice, but needs further elaboration to make it testable. Katz (1966) has elaborated his views about decision making for careers, views which rest heavily on the role of values in career planning. Miller (1968) has attempted to show how learning theory might be applied to the study of vocational decisions, but his presentation does not really suggest practical applications of learning theory to the educational-vocational decision-making task.

A number of writers, notably Gelatt and Clarke (1967) and Thoresen and Mehrens (1967), have tried to apply the use of the concept of subjective probability estimates of success in vocational decision making. In a review of research on preferences, gambling behavior, and level of aspiration, Gelatt and Clarke (1967) observe that it is possible to construe that what goes on in educational-vocational decision making is a series of estimates of probability of success combined with the personal value of the activities available.

Career decision making may be viewed as a kind of "increasing approximation" method (Gelatt, 1962). When confronted with a set of alternatives for an educational-vocational problem, an individual collects information designed either to lead to a plan to deal with the problem or to identify more information essential to solving the problem. The sequence is thus: collect information, assess the information and predict outcomes of various courses of action in terms of probability and desirability, identify alternatives, evaluate and select, and finally implement the decision. The implementation may either terminate the problem or be a preliminary solution designed to provide more information, in which case the process would be repeated.

Kaldor and Zytowski (1969) have described a system which, in a complex way, appears to be a variant of subjective estimate of probabilities methods. Kaldor and Zytowski seem, in an implicit way, to go beyond the consideration of the utility of the outcome for the chooser as an important variable and, instead, include the effect that the "costs" to the individual interact with his estimates of probabilities of various outcomes. In other words, Kaldor and Zytowski imply that what an individual will choose depends on estimates of the likelihood of various outcomes in combination with the expense in time, effort, and so on in producing each outcome.

Appel and Haak (1968) have presented a good analysis of assumptions underlying thinking about career decision making and supporting data regarding these assumptions. According to Appel and Haak, it is assumed that the best vocational decisions have an informational base, but the data available do not necessarily support such assumptions; in fact, there is some reason to believe that an overload of information can interfere with good decision making. Appel and Haak also suggest that evidence tends to support the notion that vocational decisions are best made when an individual is ready, not at some arbitrarily determined time. Not generally supported is the assumption that vocational choices are the result of a narrowing process; partially supported, in the view of Appel and Haak, is the assumption that occupational attractiveness is a function of anticipated rewards rather than success; some people appear, however, to prefer safe goals to risky ones.

Cognitive Dissonance in Career Decision Making

Hilton (1962) chose to organize his thinking about career decision making along the concept of cognitive dissonance. Cognitive dissonance (Festinger, 1957) is the discord introduced into one's perceptions of the world by the observation of events that are grossly at variance with expectations. For example, a man who views his son as a brilliant student would experience cognitive dissonance were the boy to fail in his studies. According to Festinger, attempts to reduce cognitive dissonance provide a very potent motivating agent behind human behavior. Thus, the father cited in our example would search for causes for the son's failure that did not detract from his son's brilliance as a student in order to reduce the very dissonant event of his failure in school.

Hilton summarizes his view of the process as follows: some event stimulates an individual's attention to the need to make a career decision. This stimulus may be the offer of a different job, the need for more money, the desire to live in a more agreeable climate, and so on. If the dissonance introduced by this stimulus cannot be tolerated, the individual will reexamine and perhaps change long-held beliefs about self and work and, as an outgrowth of the reexamination, may change jobs. To the degree that the changes initiated reduce the dissonance, the individual will continue along the new line or make further revisions.

In this scheme it becomes critical to identify the factors which can increase occupational dissonance. Some of these, such as occupational opportunities, institutional pressures, and interpersonal conflicts, come readily to mind. Nevertheless, the potential variety of factors for introducing dissonance is immense and must be identified specifically for each individual by the counselor. Furthermore, counselors must develop strategies to deal with dissonance. They may even want to consider the introduction of counter-dissonance agents, for example, suggesting to the ill-advised premedical student that physicians work too hard. A counselor might help a person avoid a premature identification with an educational or vocational plan by warning that the need to modify the plan might create excessive dissonance for him or her and prevent an appropriate change later.

Hershenson and Roth (1966) have used cognitive dissonance in another way. They have made explicit the notion that vocational decision making reduces the range of subsequent vocationally related experiences and thus reduces the variety of career alternatives open to an individual. The range is reduced because the individual becomes attracted to a field by virtue of personal experience, fails to know much about other possibilities, is too heavily committed to a course of action to change or recognize the need for a change, and is getting along reasonably well in the situation, uncomfortable as it may be. Thus, the more intent on a vocational objective or direction one becomes, the more one will try to avoid the effects of cognitive dissonance by interpreting both consistent and inconsistent factors as being in accordance with one's current vocational plans and activities.

The above approaches are schematic and thus inadequate to identify the specific content involved in making decisions. Perhaps countering this deficiency is Fletcher's (1966) hypothesis that career decisions are based on the effect associated with the career at the time of decision and thus the adequacy of the decision is a function of the individual's breadth of experience, realism, and ability to resist irrelevant stimuli. These factors can explicitly be taken into account, and a counseling objective may be to increase the experience and realism of clients and strengthen their ability to identify and resist irrelevancies, preceded by an assessment of the clients' development in each of these three areas.

Other Elements in the System

All the literature reviewed in this book suggests that there is an interdependence between personality variables, choice dimensions, and environmental conditions. One person, with a particular set of attributes in a given culture and operating under a special set of economic circumstances, will be confronted by a series of choice points which will lead to an idiosyncratic sequence of decisions. Vigorous, energetic, restless, and intelligent people in nineteenth-century America were attracted to entrepreneurial fields as a result of social and economic press. In twentieth-century America, such individuals may seek technological careers because they represent the same potential for achievement that entrepreneurial activities provided for their nineteenth-century counterparts.

Thus, it can be seen that individual A in culture B under economic conditions C will make a series of decisions x, y, and z. The situational variables B and C are interdependent and determine the specific nature of x, y, and z, which are sequential. What has typically been done in research on personality and career decision has been to examine the effects of individual variables, for example, the need for achievement, as if these variables have a constant value, while ignoring social and economic variables. Thus, one might observe as White (1963) did, that compulsive people tend to become bank tellers, without recognizing the possibility that compulsive people in another social and economic milieu may become mechanics or art critics.

What appears to be necessary is to study occupational behavior by controlling two of the variables and varying the other. For example, if the effect of social forces on occupational membership within given personality types under constant economic conditions were studied, it might be observed that certain personality attributes are advantageous at one social level and troublesome at another.

Moderator Variables

Also intriguing is the possibility that personality might have a different effect on behavior as social and economic factors vary. The functional relations among personality, economy, and society might be more explicit if empirical data were available to describe better the way they covary. The particular nature of the relationship of these variables to one another is very significant and suggests the use of the concept of the moderator variable to describe the role that personality plays in vocational development and decision making.

Holland's theory of career choice (1959; 1973) represents a simplified version of the use of the moderator variable in vocational choice. The personality type provides the major source of impetus toward an occupational environment, but the specific choice is influenced by the level hierarchy. According to theory, it is the level hierarchy which dictates the specific occupation that will be selected within the personality mode appropriate to the major personal orientation to life. The level hierarchy, in turn, is a function of self-evaluation and intelligence. Thus, the eventual occupational choice is *moderated* by intelligence and self-evaluation.

As an example of how these factors operate, let us imagine how conformity might serve to moderate the effect of intelligence on creative behavior. One might suppose that at low levels of intelligence and high levels of conformity little in the way of creative production would occur and that at high levels of intelligence and low levels of conformity creative potential would be at its maximum. However, the relationship between the two variables and creativity is not necessarily linear, and the concept of conformity as a moderating factor in creative behavior could be productive in the study of creativity.

For a vocational example, it seems very reasonable to expect that certain personal styles may lead to one kind of behavioral decision under one set of conditions and another quite different kind of decision under other conditions. Thinking in terms of career patterns, these decisions are likely to be affected by the age of the decision maker. Furthermore, personality style may also be expected to affect an individual's cognitive structure as a function of ability, background, and so on.

Consider a young person, impulsive, lower-middle class socially and economically, aspiring to upward mobility, and confronted with a high risk but high payoff occupational decision. Such a person can be expected to take the risk eagerly. Twenty years later, assuming the risk was taken and successfully managed, this same individual has been affected by the consequences of the decision and should not be expected to behave the same way in risk-taking situations. Impulsive behavior and a tendency to take risks is likely to be reduced when many of the ambitions for upward mobility have been achieved. Obviously, different predictions about vocational behavior in a risk-taking situation will be made now than twenty years earlier. Looking at personality traits alone, one might overlook the changed status and make predictions about occupational behavior similar to those made earlier. The factors of economics and social standing will have altered weights in the behavioral equation of this person.

What do moderator variables mean for career development? They mean more complex research designs, a need for better instruments to assess personality, and a revision of the concept of personality away from static traits (for example, achievement and abasement needs, compulsive traits, and so on) toward a conception of personality style which allows the integration of the disparate traits inherent in the trait-factor approach into a *behavioral* (situational) context. They would also imply the development of instruments to assess personal style, socioeconomic factors that press on the individual, and ways of integrating this material and summarizing it so that it can be useful to the decision maker.

Summary

The systems approach is in a position to take the most useful concepts of each theory of career development and apply them to the understanding of individual behavior. Elements of the social, personal, and economic situation within which individuals operate may be more explicitly analyzed, and the relationship of the larger systems to one another may be more clearly understood than in the traditional approaches to behavior, which tend to emphasize only one major segment of either the individual or the environment. The description of the research concerning career development has revealed a number of shortcomings. Most notable is the lack of experimentation and the heavy reliance on descriptions of career behavior based on observations of convenient samples. Meaningful research has also been seriously hampered by a lack of valid instruments to measure such concepts as personality traits, career satisfaction, needs, values, and family environment.

Thus far, career development research has primarily described the processes relevant to career behavior. What is needed is an "experimental vocational psychology" (Crites, 1965) which will lead to explanations as well as descriptions of vocational development. The goal should be to formulate lawful relationships and hypotheses concerning career behavior, so that research data can be interpreted only in one way and not be subject to the wide variety of interpretations (or none at all), as is frequently the case now.

THE STATUS OF CAREER DEVELOPMENT THEORY

A number of assertions seem possible about the status of career development theory as we move into the middle 1980s. While these assertions might be interpreted by some readers to represent the author's "theory" of career development, they are simply a set of statements with which the author feels comfortable.

1. Career decision is a function of the *range* of possible choices, for example, economic conditions, personal resources, society's technological status in the current environment, and the choices available to the individual. People cannot make choices that exceed the options available to them or that exist outside the boundaries of society's technology.

2. When career options are many, individuals emphasize expectancies regarding satisfaction and interest. When career options are few, personal skills and abilities, along with their implementation, are emphasized by individuals in their

career decisions. This condition describes one of the significant constraints that operates in individual career development. In a shrinking or stable labor market, individuals must find jobs in the face of considerable competition from other people. Under such conditions employers and hiring institutions in general focus on what the employee is likely to be able to do for the employer. In a time of labor shortage, individuals have the upper hand and thus can emphasize qualities typically important to employees, such as satisfying their interests, finding work that they like to do and that is comfortable for them, and personal fulfillment. This principle has not been sufficiently recognized in early career development theorizing, although it is implicitly assumed by some of the theories.

3. Choice activity varies as a function of the time since the last overt choice was made. Individuals increasingly engage in behaviors that reflect "decisional activity" as the time elapses since the last occasion when they made a career decision. This seems to be the result of the decreasing fit of earlier decisions, which in turn is the result of changes in the individual and his or her environment that render decisions made earlier less compatible with the individual's characteristics.

4. Decisional *demand* is a function of the institutions in which the person is involved, the person's age, and the time since his or her last decision. In other words, a press is placed on individuals to decide about careers, which is defined partly by the structure of the institutions with which the person must deal; if an educational system requires a commitment about a training program at age sixteen or in grade nine, a person is confronted with the need to do so and will usually respond appropriately. As noted in statement 3, the length of time that has elapsed since the previous decision is also a factor which influences an individual's level of activity concerning career decision making.

5. Finally, most theories involve *predecisional* behaviors such as represented by Social Learning theory's description of the shaping of preferences and abilities. Thus the following equation may be expressed:

$$Y = A\,(T\alpha_0,\, D\alpha_1,\, E\alpha_2)$$

where Y = decision
$\quad\;A$ = personality
$\quad\;D$ = demographic variables
$\quad\;E$ = environmental variables
$\quad\;T$ = time

and $\alpha_1 = 1 - \alpha_0 - \alpha_2$

Translated (literally), that equation means that decision is a function of technology and population variables; that is, personality times demographic variables times environmental variables. Such an equation is universal across time, culture, and people, but is, unfortunately, so abstract as to have almost no meaning at all.

*The author is indebted to Dr. Howard Tuckman for bringing this equation and its meaning to his attention.

What Do Theorists Predict?

The various theories are somewhat hard to compare because they are not all concerned with the same dependent variables. Even when outcomes are similar they are long range in nature, while the theorists are predicting shorter-range events. So Holland, for example, predicts occupational satisfaction by means of congruence; Super's theory predicts occupational satisfaction by means of self-concept implementation and developmental skills; and Social Learning theory approaches predict occupational choices as a function of skill in making decisions. The point is that too often the theories have been compared along dimensions that are not appropriate because comparisons have been forced that violate some of the tenets of the theory. By some definitions, for example, occupational choice is an abstract work selection, career choice has no real meaning unless it be a life style, and job choice is the implementation of a specific work-related activity. Occupational development describes the increase in scope and function of a particular occupational activity, while career development describes the enhancement of individuals by means of their careers.

Some theories seem to emphasize the choices or decisions themselves. Trait-factor theories such as those of Roe, Holland, the self-concept aspects of Super, and the Social Systems approaches seem to fall into that category. On the other hand, some theories emphasize *how* decisions are made. These include information-oriented theories, economic theories, and the developmental aspects of Super's theory, Tiedeman's theory, career maturity-based theories, and to some degree Social Learning approaches. Some theories emphasize *outcomes* related to the choices themselves, such as job tenure and satisfaction. These theories include those of Lofquist and Dawis and the status attainment approaches described by sociologists. Finally, to further complicate the matter, it is necessary to contend with those writers who describe theories of *interest* development as if they mean the same thing as theories of *career* development.

CONCLUDING SUGGESTIONS

It becomes clear, as the assessment of career development theory is concluded, that several shortcomings exist. Crites (1969) talks about theories of vocational choice and theories of vocational adjustment, as well as of psychological, nonpsychological, and general theories within the adjustment and choice categories. The approach in the present work takes the stance that the theories described are theories of career development, combining both choice and adjustment. While most of the theories seem to emphasize vocational choice, the developmental aspect is implicit, and sometimes explicit, in all of them, and is due for increasing attention.

An aspect of the theories that is open to criticism has to do with technical construction. Carkhuff, Alexik, and Anderson (1967) have taken issue with the theories in terms of their formal adequacy. Crites (1969), in a more detailed analysis of theory construction in the terms proposed by Marx (1963), has elaborated upon the differences between models (designed to fit observations), deductive theories (which go from concepts to data), functional theories (where a continuous interaction between data and concepts occurs), and inductive theories (which go from data to empirical relationships). To some extent, the theories represent all the various approaches to concept development, though few, if any, of the theories conform closely to a systematic way of theory building. In an effort to introduce greater rigor and systematically integrate research and writing in the study of work behavior, Hershenson (1969b) has suggested a series of definitions to be accepted by scientists and practitioners dealing with the science of "ergology."

Overall, while the theories appear to be generally too broad in scope and generally too skimpy in detail, vocational psychology seems to be moving toward a collection of miniature theories, each dealing with circumscribed, explicit segments of vocational behavior, to be woven into a broad theory after the smaller theories have been shaped by empirical findings. A miniature theory describing the decision-making process, a theory explaining job satisfaction, and a theory explaining how career development is related to self-concept implementation, could all be developed independently and, when the details are in order, connected by other theoreticians to a larger conception of how the human personality develops and functions.

Another difficulty in the understanding of career development lies in one of the central assumptions most investigators make, an assumption questioned only by an occasional writer (for example, Ginzberg et al., 1951; Zytowski, 1965). It is generally assumed that everyone wants to work and desires vocational activities. Seldom is any consideration given to the likelihood that a given individual may have negative attitudes toward work. It is entirely possible that the idea of becoming involved in a career could acquire fearful stimulus properties which lead to the avoidance of occupationally related behavior and which could account for some of the difficult-to-understand behavior concerning career decisions that is sometimes observed in reasonably well-endowed individuals.

A third problem lies in the continuing inadequacies of the treatment of female career development by the theories. Few special explanations or concepts have been devised to deal with the special problems of the career development of women, yet all who have observed or counseled women with respect to their career behavior realize that special problems exist for them as opposed to men and that most of the masculine-based tests and theories fail to provide a useful vehicle for the understanding of the career development of women.

The concept of interest has been overemphasized, and in its traditional guise, it is not really very helpful either in understanding career development or in helping people to make sound educational-vocational decisions. It is a static concept as now used, representing the current state of a person's development without the recognition that interests change, that job settings change, and that there is considerably more involved in career satisfaction than finding "interesting" work. The limitations of the concept of interest are implicitly recognized by the failure of any of the theories of career development to use the concept directly; in fact, the theories represent attempts to go beyond the traditional and limiting notion of interest to uncover its ingredients. It would be appropriate to try to salvage the concept by redefining it and by rethinking factors that account for the development of interests (Osipow, 1979). What is the role personality plays in the development of interests? How are interests acquired? Are they, as Strong (1943) has suggested, the reward of effective abilities put to good use?

In redefining interest, care must be taken to differentiate kinds of interest (Super and Crites, 1962). The failure to do this has contributed to the devitalization of the concept. First, there is tested interest, which can be measured by testing knowledge that reflects involvement in an activity. Interest in mechanical matters can be measured by administering a test assessing mechanical knowledge. Inventoried interest is measured by asking individuals to tell, in various ways, what it is they like to do. The Kuder Preference Record and the Strong-Campbell Interest Inventory are examples of such instruments. Finally, there is manifest interest, which may be inferred by observing what a person chooses to do when a relatively free choice exists. Presumably, although all three of these interests are related to one another, they are not identical. Hence, when interests are discussed without specification about what kind of interest is under discussion, some error in communication is likely to result.

Related to the importance of the concept of interest has been its close relationship to the trait-factor approach to careers, that is, predictions about the field of job entry. Interests have been used to make these predictions, and the two concepts have become involved in an unfruitful static attempt to predict a one-shot event, when in fact interests and jobs are really constantly changing. Differentiating between educational and vocational decisions is another but similar problem. The two are not the same, yet are often discussed as if they are and as if educational choices lead irrevocably to specific careers, when the fact is that relatively little connection exists between the two.

It is behavior that needs to be predicted. The particular behaviors that are of concern to career development theory need to be identified. Manifested interests, to be sure, must be one of these behaviors. The behaviors of relevance to career development should be observed and related to environmental conditions, thus minimizing chance effects.

The fruitful career development theory will take shape within the larger context of human development and behavior theory. The role of vocational psychology should be to devise subtheories to deal with special areas of behavior of particular interest to vocational psychologists, these areas to be defined along the lines Borow (1964) has suggested. For example, areas of interest to career psychologists may be developed along the lines of either process variables or agents of behavior. The process variables might focus on, for example, the career development of men by social class, differentiation of abilities, personality, and the interaction of the above. Theory might examine along similar lines the process of occupational satisfaction or of behavior in the job setting. Focusing on the agents involved in career behavior would lead to attention to the effects of familial, social, situational, and age variables on career behavior. Ultimately, the aim would be to relate, at a higher level of abstraction, these separate endeavors to concrete events.

Whatever may occur, it must be kept in mind that in a highly complex society, counseling represents an attempt to individualize group processes. Counselors in educational settings are in a particularly favorable position to take account of the individual differences among people, which are so important to the development and effective application of human resources. Effective concepts must be devised to guide the efforts to help people use their special characteristics well.

REFERENCES

Appel, V. H., and Haak, R. A. Decision-making process: a basis for the reappraisal of vocational counseling. Presented at the APA Convention, San Francisco, 1968.

Beilin, H. The application of general developmental principles to the vocational area. *Journal of Counseling Psychology*, 1955, *2*, 53–57.

Borow, H. An integral view of occupational theory and research. In Borow, H. (Ed.), *Man in a world at work*. Boston: Houghton Mifflin, 1964.

Calia, V. F. Vocational guidance: after the fall. *Personnel and Guidance Journal*, 1966, *45*, 320–327.

Campbell, R. E. Vocational ecology: a perspective for the study of careers. *The Counseling Psychologist*, 1969, *1*, 20–23.

Carkhuff, R. R., Alexik, M., and Anderson, S. Do we have a theory of vocational choice? *Personnel and Guidance Journal*, 1967, *46*, 335–345.

Crites, J. O. The vocational development project at the University of Iowa. *Journal of Counseling Psychology*, 1965, *12*, 81–86.

Crites, J. O. *Vocational psychology*. New York: McGraw-Hill, 1969.

Festinger, L. *A theory of cognitive dissonance*. Stanford, California: Stanford University Press, 1957.

Fletcher, F. M. Concepts, curiosity, and careers. *Journal of Counseling Psychology*, 1966, *13*, 131–138.

Gelatt, H. B. Decision-making: a conceptual frame of reference for counseling. *Journal of Counseling Psychology*, 1962, *9*, 240–245.

Gelatt, H. B., and Clarke, R. B. Role of subjective probabilities in the decision process. *Journal of Counseling Psychology*, 1967, *14*, 332–341.

Ginzberg, E., Ginsburg, S. W., Axelrad, S., and Herma, J. I. *Occupational choice: an approach to theory*. New York: Columbia University Press, 1951.

Hershenson, D. B. Toward a science of ergology. *Journal of Counseling Psychology*, 1969, *16*, 458–459.

Hershenson, D. B., and Roth, R. M. A decisional process model of vocational development. *Journal of Counseling Psychology*, 1966, *13*, 368–370.

Hilton, T. L. Career decision-making. *Journal of Counseling Psychology*, 1962, *9*, 291–298.

Holland, J. L. A theory of vocational choice. *Journal of Counseling Psychology*, 1959, *6*, 35–45.

Holland, J. L. The future of vocational development theory and its practical implications. In

Whiteley, J. M., and Resnikoff, A. (Eds.), *Perspectives on vocational development.* Washington, D.C.: American Personnel and Guidance Association, 1972.

Holland, J. L. *Making vocational choices: a theory of careers.* Englewood Cliffs, N.J.: Prentice-Hall, 1973.

Hsu, C. Y. A conceptual model of vocational decision-making. American Psychological *Experimental Publication System,* October, 1970, *8,* Ms. No. 270-6.

Kaldor, D. B., and Zytowski, D. G. A minimizing model of occupational decision-making. *Personnel and Guidance Journal,* 1969, *47,* 781–788.

Katz, M. R. A model of guidance for career decision-making. *Vocational Guidance Quarterly,* 1966, *15,* 2–10.

Lyon, R. Beyond the conventional career: some speculations. *Journal of Counseling Psychology,* 1965, *12,* 153–158.

Marshall, J. C. Bayesian decision. *Journal of Counseling Psychology,* 1967, *14,* 342–345.

Marx, M. H. (Ed.). *Theories in contemporary psychology.* New York: Macmillan, 1963.

Mierzwa, J. A. Comparison of systems of data for predicting career choice. *Personnel and Guidance Journal,* 1963, *42,* 29–34.

Miller, A. W. Learning theory and vocational decisions. *Personnel and Guidance Journal,* 1968, *47,* 18–23.

O'Hara, R. P. Comment on Super's papers. *The Counseling Psychologist,* 1969, *1,* 29–31.

Osipow, S. H. Some revised questions for vocational psychology. *The Counseling Psychologist,* 1969, *1,* 17–19.

Osipow, S. H. Learning about interests and intervening in their development. In Mitchell, A., Krumboltz, J. D., and Jones, G. B. (Eds.), *Social learning theory of career decision making.* Cranston, R.I.: Carroll Press, 1979.

Roe, A. Prospectus. In Whiteley, J. M., and Resnikoff, A. (Eds.), *Perspectives on vocational development.* Washington, D.C.: American Personnel and Guidance Association, 1972.

Strong, E. K., Jr. *Vocational interests of men and women.* Stanford, Calif.: Stanford University Press, 1943.

Super, D. E. Vocational development in 20 years: how will it come about? In Whiteley, J. M., and Resnikoff, A. (Eds.), *Perspectives on vocational development.* Washington, D.C.: American Personnel and Guidance Association, 1972.

Super, D. E., and Crites, J. O. *Appraising vocational fitness* (Rev. ed.). New York: Harper & Row, 1962.

Thoresen, C. E., and Mehrens, W. A. Decision theory and vocational counseling. *Personnel and Guidance Journal,* 1967, *46,* 165–172.

Tiedeman, D. V. A machine for the epigenesis of self-realization in career development: description, subsequent development, and implications. In Whiteley, J. M., and Resnikoff, A. (Eds.), *Perspectives on vocational development.* Washington, D.C.: American Personnel and Guidance Association, 1972.

White, J. C. Cleanliness and successful bank clerical personnel—a brief. *Journal of Counseling Psychology,* 1963, *10,* 192.

Zytowski, D. G. Avoidance behavior in vocational motivation. *Personnel and Guidance Journal,* 1965, *43,* 746–750.

NAME INDEX

SUBJECT INDEX

Achievement motivation, 130–132, 258–260
Activeness, 120
Adults, career satisfaction of, 220–221
Age, changes of occupational values in with, 221–222
Assessment of career decision-making scale, 286

Behavioral, career development theories of, 11
Biosocial, factors of in careers, 162
"Birds of a feather" hypothesis, 125
Bordin, Nachmann, Segel career theory, 42–43

Career
  barriers to for women, 270, 271
  change of in midlife, 217–220
  critical agents in, 304–305
  critical periods in, 304–305
  cross-cultural studies of, 250–251
  development of, in adults, 211–224
  differences and similarities of in ethnic groups, 239–240; 240–241
  ecological approaches to study of, 314–317
  effects of moderator variables on development of, 318–320
  effects of cognitive style behaviors of, 137–140
  effects of culture on development of, 244–253
  effects of industrial organization on, 240–250

effects on women of aptitudes, interests, and achievements, 264–265
facilitation of behaviors in, 303–304
normal development of, 301–302
parental influences on development of in women, 262–263
perspectives on development of, 312–326
predictions of by theories, 322
problems in development of, 288–289; 302–303
process of development of, 301–307
relationship of to minority group membership, 237–243
role of the family in, 306–307
role of, interest in, 305
satisfaction in, of adults, 220–221
similarities of men and women in, 260–262
similarities of to parents, 230–231
situational effects on development of, 225–237
sociological theory of development of, 245–247
status of theories of, 320–322
theories of, comparisons of, 294–311
  empirical support for, 295–296
  explanatory adequacy of, 295
  formal adequacy of, 294–300
  generality of, 297–298
  logical consistencies in, 300
  operational adequacy of, 298–300
  parsimony of, 298

337